D1647725

PLOUGHSHARES
INTO SWORDS

BRIGADIER GENERAL JOSIAH GORGAS
as Vice-Chancellor of the University of the South

PLOUGHSHARES INTO SWORDS

Josiah Gorgas and Confederate Ordnance

By FRANK E. VANDIVER

Carl A. Rudisill Library
LENOIR RHYNE COLLEGE

AUSTIN: 1952

UNIVERSITY OF TEXAS PRESS

UNIVERSITY OF TEXAS PRESS

Austin 12

THOMAS NELSON AND SONS LTD

Parkside Works Edinburgh 9
3 Henrietta Street London WC2
312 Flinders Street Melbourne C1
5 Parker's Buildings   Burg Street   Cape Town

Thomas Nelson and Sons (Canada) Ltd
91–93 Wellington Street West   Toronto 1

Société Française d'Editions Nelson
25 rue Henri Barbusse Paris V^e

973.7
V28p

27873
Qp'52

Copyright, 1952, by the University of Texas Press.
Printed in Austin by the Printing Division
of The University of Texas.

FOR
EUGENE CAMPBELL BARKER
AND
WALTER PRESCOTT WEBB

Preface

THE DECISION, MADE IN 1942, TO WORK ON A BIOGRAPHY OF GENeral Josiah Gorgas seemed natural to me. His name had appeared again and again in the course of research on the history of the Confederate Commissary Department, and the contrast between his quiet efficiency and the querulous rantings of the Commissary General made Gorgas seem unique. The project, work upon which began in Washington, D.C., started in the most naïve manner, I suppose, for I looked in the Washington telephone directory for the name "Gorgas." The closest thing to it was the Gorgas Memorial Foundation, which, it developed, had no specific information on Josiah, but would be happy to help with data on his son, Dr. William C. Gorgas. Officials of the Foundation were able to give me the name of General Gorgas' granddaughter, Mrs. William D. Wrightson, who lives just outside Washington in Chevy Chase, Maryland.

Mrs. Wrightson was more than helpful; she placed me deeply in her debt by making instantly available what manuscripts were in her possession, including part of a typescript copy of General Gorgas' journal, kept from 1857 to 1877, and by her constant interest in the work. She told me that much more material would be found in the possession of her aunts, living in Tuscaloosa, Alabama. In the course of time, I went to Alabama and spoke to General Gorgas' three surviving daughters— Miss Mary Gayle Gorgas, Miss Maria Bayne Gorgas, and Mrs. Christine Gorgas Palfrey—about my desire to do a biography of their father. These three ladies were most kind and encouraging and promised to see what papers they could find, pending another visit by me.

A year elapsed before I could return to Tuscaloosa, and in that time Miss Mary Gayle Gorgas died. Her two sisters, sharing her interest in the project, permitted me to go through a large trunk, full of General Gorgas' official and private letters. These manuscripts proved invaluable in constructing the story of the Confederate Ordnance Bureau. In this trunk, in addition to the letters, were three manuscript diaries kept by the general at various periods of his life. The large journal previously mentioned was found here *in toto*. Miss Maria Gorgas and Mrs. Palfrey graciously gave me the privilege of printing part of the journal covering the Civil War period.

Mrs. Palfrey's daughter, Mrs. Jessie Leake, was extremely helpful in locating more and more family papers in various places. Through her diligent efforts, Gorgas' letters covering his trip to Europe in 1845–46 came to light, as did many of his letters to his wife. Mrs. Leake also found a highly important file of letters from General Lee to Gorgas.

While the National Archives yielded vast numbers of official letters and orders from Gorgas to his subordinates, and many letters to him from various ordnance installations, the work would have been wholly incomplete without the Gorgas family papers. I am unable adequately to thank Miss Maria Gorgas, Mrs. Palfrey, and Mrs. Leake, but wish to express my affectionate obligation to them, not only for their help but also for their abiding patience.

I am indebted to countless others for aid in the preparation of this book, and a section of acknowledgments is inadequate to the task of thanking them all. Particular mention must be made of my debt to the late Charles W. Ramsdell, for many years Professor of American History at the University of Texas. Professor Ramsdell's interest in the subject of Confederate supplies, particularly ordnance, long antedated my own and did much to steer me to the subject. Mrs. Ramsdell has very generously permitted the use of her husband's note files, an invaluable source of material and references.

I wish to thank Dr. Douglas Southall Freeman, Richmond, Virginia, for his steadfast encouragement and unfailing understanding. He is, in large measure, responsible for making possible the research on this book.

Special thanks are due to Dr. Eugene C. Barker and Dr. Walter P. Webb, of the University of Texas, for their encouragement and indulgence. Dr. Barker and Dr. Webb have extended courtesies and kindnesses which transcend words of gratitude. As a partial expression of thanks I have dedicated this book to them.

There are many more persons to whom I should make acknowledgment. Among them are Colonel Calvin Goddard, Washington, D.C., who gave freely of his infinite knowledge of the history of small arms. Mr. Richard D. Steuart, of the Baltimore *News-Post,* extended many courtesies and gave much valuable information on Confederate weapons. Dr. Otto Eisenschiml, indefatigable chemist-turned-historian, of Chicago, Illinois, unhesitatingly lent me copious notes on Gorgas, which he had taken preparatory to a biography which he regrettably did not complete. He also took much of his time to read the manuscript critically and make extensive suggestions for revision, which I gratefully accepted. Dr. Barnes F. Lathrop, of the University of Texas, is perhaps more responsible for this book than he is willing to admit; he has borne with me through many days of travail and has never permitted irritation to show. He will, of course, be disappointed with the finished product, but without him it would have been even worse.

At Tulane University, New Orleans, Louisiana, I am particularly obliged to Dr. Wendell H. Stephenson, Dr. Fred Cole, Dr. William R. Hogan, and Dr. Gerald M. Capers, who served as my dissertation committee, and who read and reread the manuscript several times, each time offering helpful and constructive suggestions for improvement. This committee served not only as official arbiters but also as friends. The book was not undertaken with the idea of making it into a dissertation; the first draft was complete when I entered the Tulane Graduate School. The History Department kindly permitted me to submit this book as a doctor's thesis.

Miss Fannie E. Ratchford, Rare Books Librarian at the University of Texas, and renowned Brontë scholar, has done more than read the manuscript. She has helped reshape it and has acted as a sort of mother confessor. I should like to make affectionate acknowledgment of her wise counsel.

Dr. E. M. Coulter, of the University of Georgia, has constantly aided and abetted my searchings for material and has contributed many valuable references from his note files on the Confederacy.

Mr. and Mrs. Paul Tracy, of Austin, Texas, are deserving of special mention for their painstaking labors in typing the first rough draft of the manuscript from my handwritten copy—a task that defies appreciation.

Many individuals in various libraries and manuscript collections have been extremely kind. At the University of the South, Sewanee, Tennessee, the late Reverend Alexander Guerry was particularly helpful, and Mrs. Sarah Hodgson Torian made her extensive knowledge of the history of Sewanee available.

At the University of Alabama, Dr. A. B. Moore, Dr. William Stanley Hoole, and Dr. J. B. Sellers were generous in placing material at my disposal. Dr. Hoole, editor of the *Alabama Review*, kindly gave me permission to reprint as Chapter 20 of this book an article which appeared in Volume II of that magazine. I am indebted to him for myriad courtesies.

Dr. Thomas D. Clark, editor of *The Journal of Southern History,* granted permission to reprint as Chapter 2 an article which appeared in Volume XIII of that magazine, for which I thank him.

I should like to express my thanks to the Advisory Board and staff of the University of Texas Press and to Dr. William Peery for their kindness in making publication possible and for helping me to get the manuscript into printable form.

There are many more still who must be mentioned: Dr. Elizabeth Drury, of the National Archives; Mr. R. E. Lewis, Jr., editor of *American Ordnance;* His Excellency Sir William Murphy, Governor of the Bahamas; Mr. Willian E. S. Zuill, of Hamilton, Bermuda; Mrs. Lyon G. Tyler, of Holdcroft, Virginia; Mr. E. G. Swem, of Williamsburg, Virginia; Mr. John M. Gibson, of Montgomery, Alabama; Miss Genevieve M. Burton, of Winchester, Virginia; Mr. Edwin Pugsley, of New Haven, Connecticut; Colonel Martin L. Crimmins, of San Antonio, Texas; Mr. E. W. Winkler, of Austin, Texas; Dr. Matthew F. Kreisle, of Austin, Texas; Mr. James A. Green, of Cincinnati, Ohio; Colonel J. W. Morton, librarian of the United States Military Academy; Mr. Stanley Forman, archivist of the United States Military Academy; Mr. George Stansfield, of the National Archives; Mr. Alvis Fitch, of Ashby, Alabama; Dr. C. C. Crittenden, archivist of the state of North Carolina; Mrs. Earle H. Kennard, of Bethesda, Maryland; Mr. Alfred E. Newman, of St. Petersburg, Florida; Mr. W. L. Andrews, editor of the *Yorkshire Post,* and Mr. J. C. McClagen, both of Leeds, England; Mr. and Mrs. Andrew Goss, of Glasgow, Scotland; Hon. Hereward Watlington, of Hamilton, Bermuda; Dr. William C. Binkley, of Vanderbilt University; Dr. Nels M. Bailkey, of Tulane University; Dr. John R. Betts, of Tulane University; Mr. Edward L. Anderson, of Tulane University; Dr. A. A. Tisdale, of Austin, Texas; Dr. E. P. Schoch, of Austin, Texas; Mr. Howard Southwood, of Gainesville, Florida; Dr. James L. Nichols, Jr., of Stephen F. Austin College, Nacogdoches, Texas; Mr. Thomas R. Hay, of Locust Valley, New York; Dr. John R. Hubbard, of Tulane University; Dr. A. P. Brogan, of the University of Texas; Mrs. John Doole, of Austin, Texas; and Miss Emma Hosmer, of St. Petersburg, Florida.

Miss Susie Smith, of Dallas, Texas, is deserving of special thanks for many and varied attentions during the course of final composition.

Dr. Bell I. Wiley, of Emory University, Atlanta, Georgia, caught me in one serious misinterpretation of evidence and several lesser crimes. I am indebted to him for pointing these errors out and for general criticism.

I would here make grateful acknowledgment to the Rockefeller Foundation for two fellowships which made possible most of the work on this book. The Foundation has been patient in awaiting some form of results, and I cannot adequately express my indebtedness to the Humanities Division for allowing me wide latitude of action.

Finally must come my love and thanks to my mother and father, who have cajoled, financed, persuaded, and listened for nine years.

FRANK E. VANDIVER

Austin, Texas
November, 1951

Key to Footnote Abbreviations

(Bibliographical information for works listed here does not appear in the footnotes. For description and location of manuscript collections here referred to, see Bibliography. Conventional short-titles are not here included.)

AGPF   *Adjutant General's Office, Personal Files.*
Broun   William LeRoy Broun, "The Red Artillery."
Burton *Burton [James H.] Papers.*
CRLR   *Letters Received by the Confederate Secretary of War.*
CROB   *Records of the Confederate Ordnance Bureau.*
GCWD   *Civil War Diary of General Josiah Gorgas.*
GMSD   Gorgas' *Manuscript Diary.*
GMSS   *Gorgas Manuscripts.*
GOC   Josiah Gorgas, "Ordnance of the Confederacy, I, II."
Mallet John W. Mallet, "Work of the Confederate Ordnance Bureau."
OLR   *Ordnance Records, Letters Received by the Chief of Ordnance.*
OLS   *Ordnance Records, Letters Sent to Ordnance Officers.*
ORA   *War of the Rebellion: A Compilation of the Official Records of the Union and Confederate Armies.*
ORN   *Official Records of the Union and Confederate Navies in the War of the Rebellion.*

Contents

PLOUGHSHARES
INTO SWORDS

I

"An Officer and a Gentleman"

ON A JUNE DAY IN 1837 JOSIAH GORGAS, A STOCKY FARM BOY WITH
a soup-bowl haircut, passed his entrance examinations at the United
States Military Academy. Earnestly seeking a college education, he had
no real ambition to be a soldier, but on that day began a military
career which was to contribute more than that of any other man, with
the exception of Robert E. Lee, to the success of the armies of the
Confederacy.

A quarter-century later this Yankee from Running Pumps, Pennsylvania, was to attempt and accomplish the impossible: as Chief of Ordnance of the Confederate Army he was to supply an almost completely
agrarian nation with the arms, ammunition, and industries necessary
to keep its armies in the field against a mighty industrial foe. The soldiers of the South frequently were without adequate food, the winds
knifed through the tattered rags which they called clothing, and their
bare feet left bloody footprints on the rutted Southen roads; but never,
until the end, did they lack for munitions. The world has hardly seen
such a miraculous transformation of ploughshares into swords.

There is little in Gorgas' career before the Civil War to indicate
that he possessed a latent genius for military administration. He was
the type of man whose true ability is apparent only in a position of
responsibility and in a time of crisis.

Family life in the hamlet where Josiah was born apparently had
little that was conducive to the formation of superior qualities. His
father, Joseph Gorgas, moved from job to job—as clockmaker, mechanic, farmer, and innkeeper. He and his wife, Sophia Atkinson, had
been forced to work brutally hard to live and raise their ten children.
As they grew old enough, each child had to help his parents earn the
family's livelihood. But even the aid of the older boys, William,

[3]

Thomas, and Charles, and the older girls, Sarah and Mary, did not make the cotton factory at Running Pumps a profitable venture; and in 1818, not long after Josiah's birth on July 1, the family moved to the valley of Fishing Creek, about five miles above Harrisburg. Prolonged family illness there making it impossible to establish a new home, Joseph Gorgas took his family for a time to a rented farm and at length settled at Myerstown, in Lebanon County.[1]

By this time only four children were still at home, and here Solomon, Elizabeth, Christine, and Josiah, the youngest, passed ten happy years of their childhood. Josiah had been a delicate boy, but despite frequent sickness, he developed into a healthy young man, alert though somewhat untutored in books. Finally his father was able to send him away to school for a few years—long enough to convince him that he wanted more education.

When he was seventeen, Josiah—a reserved young man with dark hair, a prominent and markedly crooked nose (he had tripped over his father's foot at the age of three), and a medium build which was offset by steady and penetrating eyes—went to live with his sister Elizabeth in Lyons, New York. Her husband, Daniel Chapman, became Josiah's acting guardian and found him a job as the youngest apprentice in the printing office of the Lyons *Carrier's Address.*[2] Perhaps as that paper's delivery boy, or possibly through his guardian, Josiah came to the attention of Graham Chapin, Lyons lawyer and representative in Congress.[3] Josiah's earnest desire for learning seems to have made an impression on the Congressman, for soon the young man was reading law in his office. Josiah's aptitude for study so impressed his friend Chapin that he recommended the youth's appointment to

---

[1] The above account of the Gorgas home and family life is taken from the unpublished *Solomon Atkinson Gorgas Diary.* For the locations of all manuscript collections cited herein, see Bibliography. Symbols in roman capitals are explained in the table "Key to Footnote Abbreviations," p. xii.

[2] Christine Gorgas Zerbe to Mary Gayle Gorgas, Cleveland, Ohio, September 25, 1884, GMSS; life of Josiah Gorgas by Amelia Gorgas, *ibid.;* GMSD, January 8, 1874.

[3] Graham Hurd Chapin was born in Salisbury, Conn., February 10, 1799, and moved to Lyons, New York, in 1817. He was graduated from Yale College in 1819, studied law, was admitted to the bar in 1823, and practiced in Lyons. He was surrogate of Wayne County, 1826–33, and district attorney in 1829 and 1830. He moved to Rochester, N. Y., in 1833 and continued the practice of law. He was elected as a Democrat to the Twenty-fourth Congress (March 4, 1835–March 3, 1837). He died in Mount Morris, Livingston County, N. Y., September 8, 1843. *Biographical Directory of the American Congress, 1774–1927* (Washington, 1928), p. 802.

West Point. This was the only way for Gorgas to receive a higher education.

Joel R. Poinsett, then Secretary of War, proved amenable to Chapin's recommendation and appointed Gorgas a cadet in the Military Academy. With the consent of his father[4] and his acting guardian, Josiah, in a consciously firm hand, wrote the Secretary of War: "I have had the honor to receive an appointment as a Cadet, under the date of March 1st, 1837, which I accept." Chapman indorsed this note: "I, Daniel Chapman, the acting Guardian of the above named Josiah Gorgas do hereby agree and consent that the said Josiah may sign articles by which he will bind himself to serve five years, according to the usual terms required of Cadets in the service of the United States, Lyons, April 7, 1837."[5]

Two months later young Gorgas successfully passed his entrance examinations and was officially admitted as a member of the Cadet Corps.[6] He and his fellow plebes were soon introduced to the rigors of military life. On July 14 the authorities decreed that until further orders a dress parade would be staged every morning save Sunday at eight o'clock, followed by a parade-ground inspection.[7] This event was made more irksome by the inconvenience of the strictly prescribed uniform. As today, the coat was gray, trimmed with black braid and heavily decorated with brass buttons. In the cooler months to come, a vest would be issued to go under this high-collared garment. The winter pantaloons, which fastened under the shoes, were of the same heavy fabric as the tunic. The only concession to the year's changes in temperature consisted of summer trousers of white drill. One item of his uniform which the cadet prized above all the rest was his high full-dress hat. It had a tall wool pompon that surmounted an already high-crowned leather cap. Adding to the natty appearance of the full-dress uniform were the white crossbelts, which seemed a bit like the uniform of the British. These crossbelts[8] were intended to serve the practical

---

[4] Gorgas to his mother, Mrs. Sophia Gorgas, Watervliet Arsenal, N. Y., December 17, 1842, GMSS.

[5] Gorgas to Joel R. Poinsett, Lyons, N. Y., April 7, 1837, AGPF, Josiah Gorgas.

[6] Orders Number 76, West Point, June 22, 1837, *United States Military Academy Archives, Post Order Book*, No. 6, 1833–37.

[7] Orders Number 80, West Point, July 3, 1837, *ibid.*, and Order Number 74, *Battalion Order Book*, July 14, 1837.

[8] Joseph B. James, "Life at West Point One Hundred Years Ago," *Mississippi Valley Historical Review*, XXXI (1944–45), 24.

purpose of supporting a bayonet and cartridge box, but they added a dashing touch to the uniform.

In their new barrack quarters, the fourth class, in addition to beginning their actual studies, also gave particular attention to the book of cadet regulations. Slanted toward weeding out unfit men, the book of regulations was part of the Point's system developed by Colonel Sylvanus Thayer, the "Father of the Military Academy." Although bound by these and other iron rules, including prohibition of cards, whiskey and tobacco, the cadet did enjoy such privileges as walks about the grounds and to the "hotel," where friends and relatives might visit him, and later, attendance at the periodic "hops." Then, too, the cadets provided their own fun, regulation and otherwise. During forbidden after-taps gatherings, the frugal fare of the mess hall might be augmented by turkey, hash, chicken, potatoes, roasted over a grate fire.[9]

Supplanting the comparative ease of the summer days, the autumn academic curriculum tightened the yoke on Josiah and his classmates. As the days grew shorter, there was less and less time for any sort of recreation, since from the call to quarters, one hour after sundown, until tattoo the cadets were expected to study.[10]

Most of Gorgas' time came to be monopolized by study and recitation. It was important that the examinations in January, 1838, be passed, for these would determine whether or not he could stay in the Academy. In this connection he was worried, of course, about the effect of demerits upon his standing. Given for any small breach of the regulations, such as "hair too long," "swinging arms while marching," "late at reveille," and similar offenses, they multiplied swiftly. By the end of his first year Gorgas had accumulated thirty-one demerits, but since two hundred per year were permitted, he was doing well.[11]

During his plebe year a good portion of his studies centered around mathematics. He took algebra, trigonometry, geometry, and also a course in French. Fortunately Josiah had natural mathematical ability and passed the January examinations easily enough. As Gorgas and his class entered the new year, they were introduced to more advanced mathematics in the form of analytical geometry and calculus, engineering and drawing. Josiah's two closest friends at the Point, Smith Stansbury and his own roommate, Nathaniel Lyon, were both excellent in mathematics, and the three stayed close together in class standing.

[9] *Ibid.*, pp. 21, 27, 35.   [10] *Ibid.*, pp. 30–31.
[11] *Ibid.*, p. 31; *U. S. M. A. Archives, Disciplinary Record Book*, 1837, p. 171.

Records do not show whether Josiah was numbered among the cadets who frequented the famous Benny Haven's Tavern, but if so, he doubtless enjoyed the fine assortment of wines, liquors, and tobacco that could be had there, and the suppers whose amplitude made up somewhat for regulation issue.

Once during the year 1838 the commandant took particular notice of the cadet mess—at Christmas. Suspending academic routine for that day, a post order instructed the mess purveyor to "provide as good a dinner for the corps as the nature of the case will permit endeavoring to make it acceptable to them."[12] The cadets were, of course, overjoyed at this relaxing of the accustomed discipline and proceeded to celebrate boisterously. Sixty-one pieces of furniture were taken from the mess hall, undoubtedly as a symbol of the cadets' enjoyment of the meal. Major Richard Delafield, the Superintendent, remarked in orders that this furniture belonged to the cadets and would have to be replaced at their expense, thereby imposing some expenditure even upon those who had nothing to do with the disappearance of the furniture. Major Delafield threatened to discontinue Christmas and New Year's as holidays, and assigned a number of cadets (not including Gorgas) to extra tours of guard duty for taking part in the mess-hall sacking.[13]

Two occurrences in April, 1839, served to vary Academy routine for Josiah. On April 12, he was in bed asleep during morning inspection, for which he did one extra tour of guard duty, the only extra tour he had to perform during his whole attendance at the Point. A little over a week later it was announced that, in conformance with the regulations of the Academy, his name had been listed in the *Official Army Register* as one of the five most distinguished in his class.[14]

As Josiah's class entered their third year at the Academy, their curriculum was broadened considerably. It now embraced chemistry and philosophy, though philosophy resembled little the courses now designated by that name. Instead of studying the Stoics and Epicureans, the cadet of 1839 was given theoretical and experimental physics. The course in drawing was succeeded by landscape painting,[15] and the ab-

[12] James, *op. cit.,* pp. 32–33, 36; Orders Number 189, West Point, *Post Order Book,* No. 7, 1838–42.

[13] Orders Number 192, West Point, December 31, 1838, *Post Order Book,* No. 7.

[14] Special Orders Number 37, West Point, April 12; Special Orders Number 44, April 22, 1839, *ibid.*

[15] James, *op. cit.,* p. 33. One of Gorgas' landscapes is still displayed at the Academy.

stract and theoretical nature of most of these subjects became a matter of widespread cadet criticism.[16]

Added to military and academic routine, the cadets were also required to attend chapel each Sunday, the only acceptable excuse being guard duty or illness.[17] From this required worship, Josiah must have learned how to serve as a chaplain, an accomplishment which was to be amusingly useful to him later.

By dint of hard work and an excellent record, Josiah was made cadet sergeant in December, 1839, and discharged the duties of the office without apparent strain, standing fourth in the class after the June, 1840, examinations,[18] with only one demerit for the year.

Granted leave from June 18 until July 7, 1840,[19] he returned to begin his last year at the Point. It was by far his busiest. What with debates of the Dialectic Society (a group in which he was most interested), and the visits of distinguished lecturers, together with a vastly accelerated academic program, Gorgas had little time for personal recreation. For the first time since arriving at the Academy, he studied military tactics—under the fine tutelage of R. Auchmuty Wainwright, who would remain a good friend. Josiah's engineering course now took up fortifications, bridge and road construction, railroads, canals, and rivers and harbors improvements.

He also studied ethics, mineralogy, rhetoric, geology, and political science, which included international and constitutional law, and he received instruction in riding, fencing, and infantry and artillery maneuvers.[20] He was again given extra duties, having been appointed a cadet lieutenant on June 18, 1840.[21]

His daily routine was rigorous in the extreme. From five until seven in the morning the first class did infantry drill and broad or small sword exercises; from nine until ten, artillery drill and riding; from quarter-past ten until half-past twelve, more artillery drill, riding, and laboratory exercises. From half-past two until half-past three in the afternoon there were recitations in artillery, and from half-past three

---

[16] *Ibid.*, p. 34.   [17] *Ibid.*, p. 37.

[18] He had stood fifth in his class the previous year. See *Register of the Officers and Cadets of the U. S. Military Academy, West Point, New York, June, 1839* (West Point, 1839), p. 11; *ibid., 1840* (West Point, 1840), p. 11; Orders Number 89, West Point, December 23, 1839, *Post Order Book*, No. 7.

[19] Orders Number 31, West Point, June 18, 1840, *Post Order Book*, No. 7.

[20] James, *op. cit.*, pp. 33, 34; interview with Mr. Stanley Forman, Archivist of the United States Military Academy, June 30, 1947.

[21] Orders Number 35, West Point, June 22, 1840, *Post Order Book*, No. 7.

until half-past four, more sword exercises. From five until twenty-past six in the evening there was battalion or company drill, as directed by the commandant of cadets.[22]

As the close of his last year approached, Gorgas and his fellow first-classmen faced the problem of buying their officer's uniforms, which had to be paid for by themselves. This probably concerned Josiah more than the final examinations, since it was not easy for him to raise the money for a uniform. Then, too, the matter of the class ring would have to be decided, and the branch of service must be determined. Ranking in the top third of his class, he was free to select whatever service he desired, and he chose the Corps of Ordnance.

On the basis of the June, 1841, examinations, Josiah ranked sixth in his class of fifty-two, and his friend, Smith Stansbury, fourth. Josiah had collected twenty-one demerits during his last year at the Point and a total of seventy-nine for all four years; thus he ranked fifty-fifth of all four classes in conduct.[23]

After much anxiety, Gorgas secured enough money from relatives to buy his uniform, and prepared to attend commencement.[24] Following graduation the new brevet second lieutenants had about three months leave before proceeding to their duty stations all over the country—some to the Indian frontiers, some to permanent forts, some to the Seminole theater, and some to arsenals.

By Ordnance Corps standards Gorgas' first assignment was to a choice post. As a brevet second lieutenant and assistant ordnance officer at Watervliet Arsenal, near Troy, New York,[25] he was close to promising centers of social life; he made frequent trips to Philadelphia and various large cities to patronize theaters and sample other forms of recreation. His brother Solomon, now a successful man of business, occasionally shared these ventures, and these joint meetings became one of Josiah's fondest memories.[26]

A sudden transfer to Detroit Arsenal, planted in a God-forsaken wilderness near the thriving hamlet of Detroit in the Northwest,

[22] Orders Number 43, West Point, July 10, 1840, *ibid.*

[23] *Register of Officers and Cadets, June, 1841* (West Point, 1841), pp. 9, 19.

[24] Gorgas might have received some financial help in this instance from his immediate family, but on May 27, 1841, his father had died, and the family's resources were all but wiped out. *Solomon Gorgas Diary;* Gorgas family Bible, GMSS.

[25] George W. Cullum, *Biographical Register of the Officers and Graduates of the United States Military Academy* (Cambridge, 1891), II, 66.

[26] Gorgas to Solomon Gorgas, Watervliet Arsenal, August 7, 1841, GMSS.

abruptly halted Josiah's endeavors toward cultivation of the genteel arts. Diligent maneuvering achieved his reassignment to Watervliet in January, 1844, but this new situation was to be short lived.

Early in 1845 one of his most intimate friends, John Hillhouse, a former classmate, mentioned his need of a companion on a projected European trip. Much of the importance of Watervliet disappeared from the assistant ordnance officer's mind. He had always shared the American lust for foreign travel, and the possibility of making the "Grand Tour" overshadowed practicality. In most conceivable situations in his youth Josiah was not wasteful of his money, and in the years following graduation from the Military Academy he had saved a small amount.[27] Casting off his usual Dutch frugality, he decided that a trip to Europe would be an excellent investment—professionally, educationally, and socially.

With his trip authorized by the Adjutant General on March 22, 1845,[28] Gorgas, on April 26, wrote from Watervliet Arsenal to Secretary of State James Buchanan, offering to take dispatches to United States ministers abroad and asking for letters of introduction to these officials in St. Petersburg, Paris, Berlin, and Vienna.[29] Buchanan replied on the first of May, saying that no dispatches were in need of transmission and that Josiah's passports were in the hands of the Collector of the Port in New York. No mention was made of letters for Gorgas to American ministers. After considering this apparent slight hastily, Josiah wrote a reply direct to the Secretary. This characteristically candid letter was passed on to the War Department. Here the effect was immediate—the Department ceased to feel quite as friendly as before toward its restive brevet lieutenant of ordnance.[30]

Aware that he was not going to get letters from Buchanan, Gorgas, who had gone to New York in early May, wrote Colonel George Tal-

---

[27] Account of financial transactions with Charles R. Gorgas, Apple Creek Post Office, Wayne County, Ohio, in *Diary of Josiah Gorgas in the Mexican War,* GMSS.

[28] Gorgas to Talcott and Gorgas to General Roger Jones, both Watervliet Arsenal, March 15, 1845, OLR, 1845, File G, Doc. 28; Special Orders Number 22, Adj. Gen.'s Off., Washington, March 22, 1845, copy in GMSS.

[29] This letter is noted in letters to and from the Secretary of State, in *State Department Records;* Gorgas to William L. Marcy, London, July 8, 1845, OLR, 1845, File G, Doc. 75.

[30] A careful examination of the correspondence files of the Secretary of War failed to produce this letter. It has probably been removed from the official files. All discussion of it in the text is based on evidence found in various other letters which were written in consequence of the one to Buchanan.

cott, Chief of Ordnance, that since the Secretary of State "has not deigned to notice" his request, it would be a great help if Talcott would secure a letter to someone in the legation at St. Petersburg. Without such aid, he would have no means of introduction there.[31] Talcott, a sincere friend, wanted to help, but the situation created by the letter to Buchanan tied his hands—he could not request a letter.[32]

Meanwhile, armed with a letter of credit on Baring Brothers in London amounting to $1600,[33] Gorgas, with Hillhouse, sailed early in May on the "Henry Clay,"[34] arriving in Liverpool on June 2, 1845.[35] From there the two went on to tour England, Scotland, and Ireland. On this excursion Josiah sought out as many galleries as possible and indulged his interest in art to the full. At the end of this digression, Gorgas and Hillhouse returned to London on June 29.[36]

Travel had successfully absorbed Gorgas' attention, and had taken his mind from the problem presented by the attitude of the War Department toward his Buchanan letter. A letter from his old friend Major R. S. Baker at Watervliet Arsenal was awaiting his return to London, and this document indicated that Gorgas' startling communique to the Secretary of State had made his chances of an extension of leave poor. Gorgas realized the seriousness of the situation—he knew that Buchanan and Secretary of War William L. Marcy were irritated, although Talcott could be counted on to do all he could to placate them. Some sort of amends would have to be made, for Talcott's sake as well as his own; but after all, he could not apologize. He explained this to Talcott, and pointed out that in writing Buchanan he had only expressed what he felt,

and that as I thot in tolerably temperate language; besides if an offense at all, I have certainly committed no military one, for in no light can the Secy of State be regarded as my superior officer. To the Secy of War I should certainly have hesitated addressing a remonstrance of the kind at which offense is taken, but in the Secy of State I recognized only a high functionary of Government, and not a military superior. . . . I should be

[31] Gorgas to Talcott, New York, May 5, 1845, OLR, 1845, File G, Doc. 51.

[32] Indorsement in Talcott's handwriting: "Write Majr B[aker] to inform him that I could not ask for letter—cause—his very singular letter to the Secy of State."

[33] Prime, Ward, and King to Gorgas, New York, May 3, 1845, GMSS.

[34] Receipt for passage, GMSS.

[35] *Travel Diary of Josiah Gorgas,* June 2, 1845, GMSS. The travel part of this chapter is based almost entirely on this diary, and where no other reference is given, it is my source of information. [36] *Ibid.,* June 29, 1845.

very sorry to be recalled at the end of my present leave, for I cannot see what I have set my heart on seeing. Tomorrow I set out for St. Petersburg, where the Emperor has assembled 150,000 troops for manoeuvers. . . . Perhaps if I cannot have six months I may get 5, or 3 or even two months extension. I should rejoice at even the least—

If, Gorgas calculated, Talcott would let him know at Geneva by the first of September whether his leave could be extended or not, he could regulate his travels accordingly. It would be a simple matter to get back to Liverpool if he were recalled at the end of six months.

In this same letter Gorgas took up professional matters in some detail, perhaps with conscious guile—emphasizing the knowledge of foreign ordnance he was amassing wherever he went. And, with commendable, if unique, caution, he added a postscript to his letter to Talcott: "I enclose a blank sheet with my signature should you deem it advisable to alter the form of my application." This idea was the better part of wisdom, for along with this letter was enclosed not only a formal application for extension of his leave, but also an "explanatory" letter to Secretary Marcy. This letter reads:

Having ascertained through the Chief of the Ord. Dept. that a letter addressed by me to the Hon. James Buchanan, Secy of State, the contents of which have been made known to you, has created impressions to my prejudice, I have the honor to submit the following in explanation to you of my conduct on that occasion.

In the month of April last I obtained from the War Department leave of absence for six months with permission to leave the United States. Wishing to see Military establishments abroad, & this was my chief desire, I was advised to obtain letters of introduction from the Secy of State to our ministers abroad, as the best means of securing access to the arsenals &c. of Foreign Powers. I accordingly addressed to the Hon. the Secy of State a letter, in which I offered to bear any communications the State Dept. might wish to intrust me with & asking letters to St. Petersburg, Paris, Berlin & Vienna. To this the Hon. Secy made answer that no occasion existed for sending dispatches, & closed by saying that my passports had been sent to the Collector of Customs at N. Y. which might be had on application and a description of my person, &c., without deigning to notice the gist of my letter, the application for letters of introduction to Ministers.

Stung with what appeared to me a most unnecessary omission of courtesy on the part of the Secy of State, I replied in terms which I regret to hear have injured me in the estimation of the Secy of War, but which

I shall only learn to regret when I am convinced that they were errone-
ously applied.[37]

Such an explanation might well have been fatal had not Talcott been
a wise and good friend. Talcott understood his unruly subordinate and
possibly admired his independence in the face of the War Department's wrath. The Chief of Ordnance did not send the letter to Marcy;
he filed it with the indorsement: "It was thought that this letter would
not mend the matter—therefore as suggested by Lt. G—in such event,
it was not handed to the Secretary of War." Instead the Chief of
Ordnance somehow calmed the Secretary, and Gorgas' application for
extension was pushed through and approved. Receiving the two
missives from Gorgas on August 5, Talcott got Marcy to grant an extension the next day.[38] But Marcy could hold a grudge.

Having gone to Holland, Germany, Austria, and Italy while fearing
an early recall, Gorgas was in Rome when news of his extension of leave
reached him in mid-September. His plans were changed quickly, and
he began an independent tour of Switzerland, returning to Rome at the
end of October.

According to previous arrangements Gorgas rejoined Hillhouse on
October 30 at St. Peter's Cathedral—"glad enough to meet him"—and
began sight-seeing. On the morning of November 1, Gorgas got a clear
view of the Pope as he entered the Sistine Chapel, and, after this
treat, he went again to St. Peter's to see the devotees kissing the "great
toe," which Gorgas noted as "very much worn." The mosaics in this
church, priceless and exquisitely beautiful, held him in rapt awe, and
he observed that "On the left of the Tribune as you face it is the tomb
of Paul III, with a figure of Justice so beautifully modelled that circumstances occurred which rendered drapery necessary—an amateur
was one morning found behind it, having passed the night with her."

Entertainment for the two Americans was not completely cultural.
Rome's beauties were not all stone and oils: "went to see the woman
in the forum, & adventure thereupon."

In early November the two friends left Rome for a quick tour of
other parts of Italy, and thence to Athens and Constantinople, and
finally Paris—reserved for the last. On the way to Paris they stopped at
Lyon on January 24, 1846. There, a masked ball—to which they cap-

[37] Gorgas to Marcy, London, July 8, 1845, enclosed in Gorgas to Talcott, London, July 8, 1845, OLR, 1845, File G, Doc. 75.   [38] Indorsement, *ibid.*

tured invitations with customary finesse—impressed them greatly: "Oh! what loveliness—what morals."

Paris was reached on January 27, and as might be expected, Gorgas could not long refrain from visiting the Louvre and other galleries. He also found it necessary to try out the opera, and February passed easily with the assistance of these diversions. Then, too, Gorgas was granted permission to visit certain of France's most important military schools and factories. In March he extended his scrutiny of Paris to Versailles, and later to St. Cloud.

Hillhouse could remain longer in Europe, but Gorgas' travels were drawing to a close. He left Paris on April 2, with his objective the port of Dover and passage home. Passing through Belgium, he arrived in Dover on April 9, was in Liverpool by the 10th,[39] and from there he sailed for New York. On May 28 he found himself "willingly" taking charge "of the recruiting at this [Watervliet] Arsenal."

A year's independence was behind him, but this change left its mark. He was slowly shedding his youthful impatience and indecisiveness, and after a few more years would be ready for the responsible role of Chief of Ordnance of a new nation fighting for its life.

---

[39] There is some confusion concerning the date of Gorgas' arrival in Dover, his diary seeming to imply that he reached there April 10. In GMSS there is, however, a certificate of arrival at the Port of Dover, which certifies that Gorgas arrived from Belgium on April 9, 1846. For the sake of clarity, the date of the certificate has been used in the text.

For some delightful, albeit fictionalized, accounts of Gorgas' travels in Europe see Gorgas and John Hillhouse, "Epistolary Gossipings of Travel and its Reminiscences," *Russell's Magazine,* V (1859); VI (1860). For identification of Gorgas and Hillhouse as the authors, see Frank E. Vandiver, "The Authorship of Certain Contributions to *Russell's Magazine," Georgia Historical Quarterly,* XXI (1947), 118–20.

II

War and Pettiness

FIGHTING HAD ALREADY BEGUN ON THE MEXICAN BORDER BY THE time Gorgas boarded ship to return to the United States, and after his arrival at Watervliet he watched the operations along the Texas-Mexican line with much interest. It seemed that he might at last get a chance to test in war what he had so long studied in peace. Circumstances seemed to indicate that his opportunity for action would be with the forces of General Zachary Taylor but he soon heard that his best chances might lie in another quarter. His friend, Brigadier General John E. Wool, was to have command of an expedition which would invade Mexico. This force of regulars and volunteers, infantry and cavalry, was to rendezvous at San Antonio, Texas, and then move south. A conversation with Wool drew the information that he needed extra staff officers and would ask that Gorgas be assigned to his headquarters.[1]

Satisfied by the combined statements of Wool and the Chief of Ordnance that his appointment was assured, Gorgas was rudely surprised when another officer was chosen in his stead. Hurt by what seemed such duplicity on Talcott's part, Gorgas took him to task. "I cannot express to you," he wrote, "my exceeding disappointment that I have not been designated . . . for this duty—a duty to which I have

[1] This conversation cannot be precisely dated, but it must have taken place some time during May or June, 1846. See Gorgas to Talcott, Watervliet Arsenal, June 12, 1846, OLR, 1846, File G, Doc. 55. Gorgas wrote: "Genl Wool intimated to me in conversation the probability that an Ordnance Officer will be required upon his staff at an early day, & also his desire to have me detailed in case one should be designated: I have the honor therefore to request that should the General require an officer of our Corps I may be appointed to the duty." See also Wool to the Adjutant General, Headquarters, June, 1846, *Adjutant General's Office, Letters Received*, 1846.

been looking forward . . . & for which I was encouraged by your verbal assurances to prepare myself."[2] But he did not abandon hope of eventually obtaining the assignment, nor did he seem to suspect that the real explanation of his failure might have been his unfortunate letter to Buchanan in 1845.

In November, 1846, by which time Gorgas might reasonably have given up hope of assignment to an active theater, Captain Benjamin Huger asked that Gorgas be sent to New York to discuss possibilities of service in Mexico. Huger, a South Carolinian and an industrious and able ordnance man, had been selected to accompany General Winfield Scott on the Vera Cruz expedition as chief ordnance officer.[3] Gorgas left Watervliet on November 30 for the New York ordnance depot on Governor's Island, and from there reported by letter to Huger at Fort Monroe.[4] During December plans were formulated for the organization of a "Siege Train" of artillery for Mexican service as part of Scott's army. Huger was to command, with First Lieutenant P. V. Hagner and Second Lieutenants Gorgas and C. P. Stone as his commissioned assistants. Talcott wanted the train to be on its way to Mexico as soon as possible, and Huger, who was to sail with the main division of the army, gave Gorgas the task of whipping it into shape.[5]

On January 16, 1847, Gorgas reported the company ready and issued its table of organization.[6] On that day he also informed Talcott that the ship "Tahmaroo" was lying in the stream, ready for sea, with siege train and equipment complete. The men were embarked that afternoon in expectation of sailing the next morning. This was later than Gorgas originally had hoped to leave, he explained, but a number of annoying delays had retarded departure. Stores due from the Watervliet Arsenal had been held up on the Housatonic Railroad, and Gorgas had also found it necessary to go to Bridgeport to hurry the shipment of a sling cart and a battery wagon.[7] After putting to sea, he

[2] Gorgas to Talcott, Watervliet Arsenal, July 1, 1846, OLR, 1846, File G, Doc. 58.

[3] Benjamin Huger was later to have an important post in the Confederate Army—one that would put him in close contact with Gorgas.

[4] "Orders," Ordnance Office, Washington, December 5, 1846, OLS, Book 71, p. 384; also Maj. R. S. Baker to the Adjutant General, Watervliet Arsenal, December 1, 1846, *Adjutant General's Office, Letters Received*, 1846.

[5] Huger to Gorgas, New York, January 1, 1847, in *Copybook of Lieut. Josiah Gorgas of the Siege Train Sent to Mexico*, pp. 1, 2, GMSS.

[6] "Company Order No. 1," *ibid.*, pp. 6–7.

[7] Gorgas to Talcott, New York, January 16, 1847, OLR, 1847, File G, Doc. 6.

issued orders establishing and regulating the guard on the ship and assumed, in addition to his other duties, those of company chaplain.[8]

The "Tahmaroo" was ordered to the Lobos Islands, which had been selected as the point of assembly of Scott's expedition, and Gorgas was directed to report to Huger at Tampico if convenient.[9] The General was anxious to get under way for Vera Cruz, and after the arrival of most of General William J. Worth's regulars, the expedition set out on March 2.[10]

Scott's attacking fleet of transports, supply ships, and naval supports gathered off Vera Cruz. There, after most of the main units had arrived on March 5, preparations were made for a landing on the 8th, but the false threat of a norther forced a delay of one day. The beachhead was established on the mainland opposite Sacrificios, two miles south of the city, on the 9th. Fears of formidable resistance to the landing were unfounded, and the first brigade dug in safely under the loud but futile objection of the Fortress San Juan de Ulua. So light was the opposition, in fact, that the regular investment of the town progressed almost without interruption. At length, Camp Washington, a seven-mile semicircle of entrenchments and gun positions, was completed and the siege opened.

The time had come for the emplacement of the batteries designed to crush the Mexican artillery. A site selected on March 16, proving too exposed to enemy fire, was abandoned. On the 18th a better location, partially screened from enemy cannon, was found. At this spot were located two mortar batteries intended to throw shells over the city walls, some half mile distant.

Delays of all kinds hampered the final erection of the batteries for opening the barrage. Most of the necessities for siege operations were lacking, and the ammunition requisitioned by Scott in mid-November of 1846 had not yet appeared. But hard work resulted finally in the

[8] Writing from Vera Cruz nearly a year later, Gorgas recalled having acted "the part of Parson." Gorgas to his mother, January 16, 1848, GMSS.

[9] Brevet Brig. Gen. George M. Brooke to the Adjutant General, New Orleans, February 11, 1847, *Adjutant General's Office, Letters Received,* 1847. Brooke stated that Gorgas had "all the mortars, & siege train, with powder, shell, shot, &ct &ct," with him.

[10] For excellent accounts of the preliminary organization of the Vera Cruz force and the opening of the siege, see Charles W. Elliott, *Winfield Scott; the Soldier and the Man* (New York, 1937), pp. 444–56, and Justin H. Smith, *The War With Mexico* (New York, 1919), II, 17–30. For further details of the siege and reduction of Vera Cruz, see John S. Jenkins, *History of the War between the United States and Mexico* (Auburn, Ala., 1851), pp. 247–65.

mounting of seven ten-inch mortars in three batteries by two o'clock in the afternoon of March 22. Gorgas had a major part in all of these preparations. He was the only Army ordnance officer present during the emplacement of the three batteries and the only one on the field when these commenced firing at four-fifteen that afternoon.[11]

Vera Cruz, supported by San Juan de Ulua's powerful ordnance, replied to the American guns with everything at its command. Gorgas estimated that forty Mexican cannon were answering. For three hours "the smoke & whizzing of shot, rockets & shells combined with the deafening discharges of the mortars were rather trying to nerves unaccustomed to that kind of music," but even so, Gorgas thought the whole scene a stirring sight. Toward six o'clock the city's fire slackened materially. By ten it had become so routine that Gorgas lay down on a parapet and dozed off. Writing of the day's happenings to his mother, he said he did not "mind it any more now than the flash of an old fowling piece in my younger days."[12]

Strenuous efforts to increase the volume of fire directed at the city walls resulted in the addition of three guns to the batteries on March 23, but the ultimate outcome of the bombardment with the equipment at hand was doubtful. Mortar fire, while having some effect on morale in consequence of its sound, did little real damage to vital military objectives. Heavy ordnance was not available, and Gorgas could do little more than keep a steady stream of ammunition coming to the guns which were working.

Scott realized that the success of the siege hinged on his ability to bring heavy ordnance to bear on the city and breach its wall. Though he would have preferred to keep all the glory of this operation for the Army, he was forced to ask the Navy for heavy guns. Commodore Matthew C. Perry quickly sent them but insisted that they be served by Navy personnel—a request impossible to refuse. The heavier artillery, plus Santa Anna's failure to bring relief, broke the city's resistance, and Vera Cruz surrendered on March 27.

[11] Gorgas to his mother, Vera Cruz, March 27, 1847, GMSS. Maj. R. S. Baker later wrote the Secretary of War that Gorgas arrived at Vera Cruz "in advance of every other Ordnance Vessel, and furnishing thereby, nearly the Entire Ordnance & Stores for the prosecution of the Siege." Baker to Marcy, Watervliet Arsenal, December 28, 1848, *War Department Records, Letters Received by the U. S. Secretary of War*, 1851, File O, Doc. 7.

[12] Gorgas to his mother, Vera Cruz, March 27, 1847, GMSS. For another account of the opening of the bombardment, see Robert Anderson, *An Artillery Officer in the Mexican War, 1846–1847* (New York, 1911), pp. 90–93.

In the plans which were immediately made for the march on Mexico City, Vera Cruz became the main base of supplies; and ordnance, commissary, and quartermaster depots were established to receive and store supplies as they arrived from the United States and send them on to the troops. The American advance into the interior was begun on April 8, and four days later Scott himself moved forward. On April 17 Gorgas left Vera Cruz with an ordnance unit of "two guns and a train of 20 wagons" which was to join the main army at the delightful town of Jalapa, about seventy-five miles inland. His joy at being allowed to go with the army was not in the least dimmed by the evidence of battle around Cerro Gordo; instead he expressed his disappointment that he had arrived three days too late for the fighting. Later, in describing the scene of the clash to his mother, he wrote that "dead Mexicans lay along the road, & dead horses & mules literally putrified the air—broken carriages and dismounted cannon showed where the fight had been the hottest."[13] Even the fact that a young officer friend of his was wounded did not cool his desire to have a part in a "good field fight where troops are deployed on a plain & fire away, and where squadrons charge."[14]

In perverse answer to his wishes to get into a good fight, orders came through sending him back to Vera Cruz to take charge of the ordnance depot. This was not at all what he wanted. Vera Cruz was widely known as a veritable hell-hole in the summer months because of yellow fever and filth, and the fear that the scourge would strike his army before he could move the bulk of his men inland had been an important factor in Scott's decision to make a quick move for the capital city. It was debatable whether an assignment with the army in the field would be more dangerous than a station at Vera Cruz. Many, and Gorgas was among them, would have vastly preferred participation in the fighting to long residence in the unhealthful coast town.

What was of the utmost importance to Scott was the ordnance already on hand and that which would arrive. It had to be received and in turn prepared for shipment to the army by trained personnel, and the direction of this work was assigned to Gorgas, while Captain Huger and

---

[13] Gorgas to his mother, Vera Cruz, May 10, 1847, GMSS. For an account of Scott's campaign to Mexico City, see especially Smith, *War with Mexico*, II, 37–164. Other accounts of value are Jenkins, *War between the United States and Mexico*, pp. 266–432; E. Kirby Smith, *To Mexico with Scott* (Cambridge, 1917), pp. 133–217; and Roswell S. Ripley, *The War With Mexico* (New York, 1849), II, 53–89.

[14] Gorgas to his mother, Vera Cruz, August 6, 1847, GMSS.

Lieutenants Hagner and Stone, the other officers of the ordnance unit with which he had come to Mexico, were attached to General Scott's staff for the campaign inland.[15] In his efforts to make the best of what he considered an undesirable situation, Gorgas devised a scheme whereby he hoped to escape the fever and to lessen the discomfort of Vera Cruz's notoriously hot nights. He felt that by sleeping on board ship and practicing temperance in eating and drinking, he might avoid both evils. But the departure of all vessels by May 15, 1847, forced a change of lodgings. A building was rented for quarters for himself and a sergeant and for use as an office. He arranged for his own cooking, which another officer shared with him.[16] But his expenses increased. Rent on his quarters, for example, which had started at a monthly rate of forty dollars, rose after October 1 to sixty dollars.[17]

The departure of all shipping left Gorgas holding the embryo ordnance depot alone. He was an indifferent bookkeeper, and Talcott had already found it necessary to chide him occasionally about his accounts. But this was not all that worried the depot commander. He viewed with anxiety the drastic spread of the fever. Stretching the truth a bit, he told Huger that the town was "tolerably healthy," but to his mother admitted his real fear.[18]

A sudden accumulation of work served to direct his thoughts into new channels, and he soon reported to Talcott that, although he had managed to supply all demands reasonably well thus far, there were deficiencies of muskets and accoutrements, rifle and carbine ammunition, and percussion caps.[19] In view of the fact that the Watervliet, Washington, and Baton Rouge Arsenals had pooled their resources to send 2,000 muskets and 1,000 infantry accoutrements, in addition to 809,000 percussion and flint rifle cartridges, 169,000 carbine cartridges, and 25,000 percussion caps, Talcott was amazed that a shortage could be reported. Admitting, however, that his Vera Cruz officer was in a better position to know what was happening, Talcott authorized Gor-

---

[15] See *Memoirs of Lieutenant General Winfield Scott* (New York, 1864), II, 460–63, where these three officers are named as members of his staff but no mention is made of Gorgas.

[16] Gorgas to his mother, Vera Cruz, May 10, August 6, 1847, GMSS.

[17] Gorgas to Talcott, Vera Cruz, October 13, 1847, OLR, 1847, File G, Doc. 131.

[18] Gorgas to Huger, Vera Cruz, May 15, 1847, *Huger Papers;* Gorgas to his mother, Vera Cruz, May 10, 1847, GMSS. Gorgas could hardly have been encouraged over the admonition of his friend, Lt. P. V. Hagner, to "take care of the Vomito [yellow fever]." Hagner to Gorgas, no place, no date, *Huger Papers.*

[19] Gorgas to Talcott, Vera Cruz, May 17, 1847, OLR, 1847, File G, Doc. 69.

gas to draw directly from Baton Rouge Arsenal all equipment which he considered necessary.[20] Fortunately there was an abundance of artillery ammunition—so much, in fact, that in order to economize storage space, seven ships containing cargoes of heavy ordnance and equipment were sent to unload at Baton Rouge Arsenal.

Even more serious was the problem of moving supplies to the interior. Because of the scarcity of transportation facilities, battery replacements had to be deferred until adequate means of moving equipage and ammunition became available. Not only did this delay nullify the advantage gained in capturing at Vera Cruz some Mexican ordnance stores which would fit American guns, but Gorgas found himself surveying a city that was yet in ruins, rapidly filling with ordnance, as well as with quartermaster and subsistence items, which could not be stored for want of space nor shipped for want of transportation.

In June came an unwelcome diversion. Yellow fever at last struck the city with full force, and Gorgas fell a victim. His proved to be a mild case, however, and seems to have run its course in a few days; but it naturally interfered with the conduct of his official business.[21] Many others were not so fortunate, for the toll of this disease was heavy that summer. "A great many deaths have occurred here," he reported, "chiefly among that class of people who neither have the means nor care to take pains about health—such as Qr. Mr's. men & soldiers—they have died by the hundred of yellow fever, dysentery and bad wounds. Occasionally an Officer is stricken down, but altho' all nearly have been sick, few have died, because they have had good attendance & good treatment."[22] He reassured his mother, in writing of his illness, by saying that since it was all over, he had never been in better health.

Even comfortable living quarters, health, and a foreign city, however, offered too little diversion from the humdrum of routine business at the depot. Duty at West Point, which he had frantically avoided in 1843, now definitely appealed to him. The glamor of war had worn off, and he was getting homesick. He wrote Talcott on June 18, asking to be reassigned to West Point for a year or so and "as the *big wars* have I think pretty much come to an end here I ask to be sent there

[20] Capt. William Maynadier to Gorgas, Washington, June 9, 1847, OLS, Book 75, p. 384.
[21] Gorgas to Huger, Vera Cruz, June 4, 1847, *Huger Papers*.
[22] Gorgas to his mother, Vera Cruz, August 6, 1847, GMSS.

without fear of being thought desirous of getting away from the fighting."[23] Nothing came of his request, however, and the business of the depot continued. In August a job of guerrilla hunting was offered to him, and though he was not enthusiastic, he felt that he should accept. Supplied with a horse and a troop of twenty-eight volunteer dragoons, he set out at three-thirty in the afternoon of August 5 for the Antigua River. After riding until eleven that night, the party reached the river and discovered guerrillas on the other side. Gorgas ordered a bivouac, deciding on an attack in the morning. Morning, unfortunately, brought the realization that it was impossible to cross the river and get at the enemy's camp. Disgusted, Gorgas pulled his troops out of bivouac and started back for Vera Cruz, followed by a few wild shots from the irregulars.

This expedition involved a march of forty miles in less than twenty-four hours, with only one meal and no sleep. The prowess of the Mexicans did not impress Gorgas at all, since six miles of his route followed along a narrow path, wide enough for only one rider at a time, through dense chaparral, "where six resolute Americans might have beaten us back, but we were not molested." He confided to his mother that he would not volunteer again for such duty since he knew that he would be stiff for several days as a consequence of the ride. Also, he had no faith in the performance of the volunteers—an opinion shared by the majority of the regular Army men.[24] This affair ended his actual participation in combat.

In the meantime, Scott's instruction to Talcott to provide 2,000,000 small arms cartridges monthly at Vera Cruz had a strange effect on the Chief of Ordnance. He believed that the supplies arriving at Vera Cruz were totally inadequate and was afraid that Scott would run short. He thought that the General-in-Chief expected heavy expenditures and losses in transportation, and he meant to have no deficiencies. On July 13 Talcott advised Gorgas that 1,000 muskets, 1,600 rounds of six-pounder ammunition, 800 rounds of twelve-pounder howitzer ammunition with portfires and slowmatch, and 400,000 flint and percussion cartridges, with 200,000 carbine cartridges, had been sent to him that day.[25] This deluge of material posed another problem

---

[23] Gorgas to Talcott, Vera Cruz, OLR, 1847, File G, Doc. 78. As early as May 10 he had written to his mother that the general feeling was an earnest desire to see the war finished.

[24] Gorgas to his mother, Vera Cruz, August 6, 1847, GMSS.

[25] Talcott to Gorgas, Washington, July 13, 1847, OLS, Book 75, p. 175.

for the hard-pressed commander of the Vera Cruz depot, for he could find no space in which to house it. Besides, in the Castle of Ulua he had 700 pounds of powder, at least 400 of which were surplus and should have been sent back to the United States. In addition, he had 3,500,000 cartridges in boxes, with no idea of how to use or dispose of them.[26] And his problem of storage space was still further complicated by the growing accumulation of damaged and unserviceable arms which kept coming to the depot as Scott's campaign progressed. Having neither the authority to discard them nor the facilities for making repairs at Vera Cruz, he finally solved this problem by obtaining permission late in September to ship them to Baton Rouge Arsenal where there were ample repair facilities.[27]

But Talcott, not knowing just how urgent Scott's needs might be, was not willing to have gunpowder or ammunition returned to the United States. Gorgas was told that he could make issues for current service from the barrels and reserve the boxed cartridges for shipment to the army. The Chief of Ordnance with some reluctance did stop sending more ammunition to Vera Cruz, but he sought to impress on Gorgas the necessity for pushing forward the supplies already on hand. "It would be a most severe reflection upon the Ordnance, if the Army should be ill supplied, when there is such an abundance under your charge," he said; "therefore whenever a train passes up, with a suitable escort—you will push forward, a full supply of ammunition of all kinds."[28] About two weeks later he wrote again to remind Gorgas that there should be at least two hundred rounds of ammunition with each piece in Scott's hands, and that the supply should be replenished at every opportunity.[29]

[26] Talcott to Gorgas, Washington, August 6, 1847, *ibid.,* p. 215. See also Talcott to Gorgas, July 13, *ibid.,* pp. 175–76, advising of shipment of Colt pistols; Gorgas to Maynadier, Vera Cruz, June 26, OLR, 1847, File G, Doc. 86, stating that there was a good supply of all kinds of ordnance at Vera Cruz, and that no more small-arms ammunition need be sent; and Gorgas to Talcott, Vera Cruz, August 14, *ibid.,* Doc. 103, asking permission to send surplus stock back to the United States.

[27] Gorgas to Talcott, Vera Cruz, August 20, 1847, OLR, 1847, File G, Doc. 106; Maynadier to Gorgas, Washington, September 11, OLS, Book 75, p. 259.

[28] Talcott to Gorgas, Washington, August 6, 1847, OLS, Book 75, p. 215. See also letter of August 30, *ibid.,* p. 244.

[29] Talcott to Gorgas, Washington, August 23, 1847, *ibid.,* pp. 237–38. In his reply to this letter, Gorgas stated that the siege train with Scott had two 24-pounder siege guns, two 8-inch siege howitzers, two 10-inch mortars, and two or three Coehorn mortars. He thought that the 24-pounders had 200 rounds each, the 8-inch howitzers 100 each, and the 10-inch mortars 150 rounds each between

Efforts to carry out Talcott's instructions to sustain the army, which by this time was preparing to fight the battles of Contreras and Churubusco, met with difficulties which could not be understood in Washington. Inefficient as Mexican guerrilla warfare might seem, it had a real place in the Mexican plan of defense. A chance for victory for Santa Anna lay in the fact that Vera Cruz was Scott's main depot. The American lines of communication stretched over some of the most treacherous country in the whole of Mexico, and Scott was moving ever farther from his base, leaving these long lines exposed and open to attack at almost any point. The guerrillas were not slow to see their advantage and exploited it to the utmost. On June 4 they attacked and succeeded in stopping a money train escorted by 600 men. Only the timely arrival of 500 reinforcements saved the specie. Even with the addition to its escort, the train lost 24 of its 130 wagons. Six weeks after this train had departed, another left Vera Cruz for the army and met a similar fate. Early in August 1,000 soldiers, under Major F. T. Lally, set out with two six-pounders and 64 wagons. No merchandise was lost, but four brushes with the guerrillas cost 100 men killed, wounded, and missing. A train which followed Lally's with 200 men and some ammunition lost 40 men killed and had to turn back.[30] In mid-August a small train of ten wagons left Vera Cruz, bound for Major Lally's camp at the National Bridge, with an escort of one company of cavalry and two of infantry. Attacked, the escort was routed and nine wagons lost. In this skirmish Gorgas lost 84 rounds of canister and a small supply of slowmatch, portfires, and priming tubes. He noted that the guerrillas were armed with two small field pieces, and this convinced him that in the future he must supply all convoy escorts with artillery.[31] Accordingly, he began to look about for a few mountain howitzers, which he considered well suited for this work because they required few horses. Talcott was advised by Gorgas that it

---

them, plus spare powder and bags. Gorgas to Talcott, Vera Cruz, September 9, 1847, OLR, 1847, File G, Doc. 118.

[30] Smith, *War with Mexico*, II, 76–77, 171, 365, 422, 423. Ironically, on the day that Lally's train left Vera Cruz, Gorgas wrote to his mother of his wish that he might have gone along. Gorgas to his mother, Vera Cruz, August 6, 1847, GMSS.

[31] Gorgas to Talcott, Vera Cruz, August 20, 1847, OLR, 1847, File G, Doc. 106. The system of sending out supplies was really a modification of the convoy plan. Troops and supplies waited until a sufficient force had collected in Vera Cruz to justify a convoy, and then the train set out with troop protection. Smith, *War with Mexico*, II, 365.

would be a good idea to send a few more of them down, and two were duly dispatched to Vera Cruz on October 8.[32]

But Gorgas did more than supply artillery to the guerrilla hunters. In July Colonel John Coffee Hays, commanding a regiment of Texas Rangers, was ordered to take the field against all the skulkers of the hill country. His regiment dressed as outlandishly as possible. All of the men wore beards, and there were no distinguishing marks between men and officers. Their horses were of all sizes and colors, and each man had a rifle, a pair of pistols, and one or two Colt five-shooters,[33] which Gorgas had been called upon to furnish. The supply of Colt's revolvers was so small that it was thought necessary to have him personally see that they reached their destination; but before he was able to accomplish this he had to overcome the opposition of Colonel Henry Wilson, the military governor of Vera Cruz, who attempted to prevent him from leaving the city. The guns were finally delivered, however, and Gorgas had the satisfaction of knowing that they were being used effectively by Hays' men.[34]

Meanwhile, the problem of transportation had grown still more serious. As soon as Gorgas heard of the battles of Contreras and Churubusco, he requisitioned transportation from the quartermaster department for 56,000 rounds of small-arms cartridges, field ammunition, and ordnance stores to go by earliest convoy to headquarters. The overworked quartermasters could furnish no more than eight wagons— enough for only 10,000 pounds—and Gorgas forwarded this small amount on September 19.[35] Within the next few weeks the strain of trying to overcome such difficulties, combined with his desire to get away from Vera Cruz, apparently brought his temper to the breaking point, and toward the end of October he became involved in a violent clash with Major General Robert Patterson over a minor matter. Patterson was going forward to Scott's headquarters with a large convoy, and Gorgas wanted to send some clothing for ordnance men along

[32] Gorgas to Talcott, Vera Cruz, September 9, 1847, OLR, 1847, File G, Doc. 118 (indorsed on back in pencil, "Send Mountain How's"); and Talcott to Gorgas, Washington, October 8, OLS, Book 75, p. 292, saying that two other guns had previously been sent. [33] Smith, *War with Mexico*, II, 423.

[34] See Gorgas to Talcott, Vera Cruz, August 2, 1847, OLR, File G, Doc. 100; and Talcott to Gorgas, Washington, August 8, 1847, OLS, Book 75, pp. 217–18. Two receipts for ordnance and ordnance stores, signed by Col. John C. Hays, October 19, 26, 1847, in *Huger Papers,* acknowledge the delivery of 394 pistols.

[35] This convoy was the train of Gen. Joseph Lane. See Smith, *War with Mexico,* II, 176–78.

with this train. When his request was bluntly refused, he fumed at Patterson and wrote in disgust to Huger that "the d—d old fool" was exceedingly indignant "that any wagons had been appropriated to the department until all his wants had been satisfied." And in the same letter he added: "I hope you think of having me relieved here—I have certainly done here a large share of the most disagreeable duty."[36]

At about this same time Gorgas received word that orders had already been issued in Washington for his transfer from Vera Cruz to an assignment with a rocket and howitzer battery at Scott's headquarters, as soon as Captain J. A. J. Bradford could arrive from North Carolina to take charge of the ordnance depot.[37] His initial joy at this news gradually gave way to mounting disappointment, however, as November passed and Bradford failed to appear; and in desperation he wrote to Talcott: "No news from Capt. Bradford—should he fail for Heaven's sake send some other officer & let me go to the Mtn. Howr. [mountain howitzer]."[38] It was to be two more months, however, before he was free to go to his new assignment, and his depression over this delay was undoubtedly a contributing factor in the development of a quarrel with Huger concerning credit for his work.

With no thought of casting aspersions on his subordinate, Huger had written innocently to Talcott that no supplies had been received from Vera Cruz up to September. This letter naturally caused some consternation in the office of the Chief of Ordnance, and on October 23 he wrote Gorgas, tactfully commending him for having sent supplies to the army and mentioning Huger's statement that not a "single article" had been received from Vera Cruz. "As we do not know of the capture of ammunition," he continued, "I infer that the troops of the several teams kept the whole lot for their own use. This is very surprising and cannot be accounted for—if the troops had not captured quantities of ammunition the troops would have been in a bad fix."[39] Construing this as unfavorable comment, Gorgas was deeply

[36] Gorgas to Huger, Vera Cruz, October 29, 1847, *Huger Papers.*

[37] Talcott to Gorgas, Washington, October 4, 1847, OLS, Book 75, p. 284, announcing Gorgas' relief; Talcott to Capt. J. A. J. Bradford, Washington, October 4, 1847, *ibid.,* p. 285, transferring Bradford from Fayetteville, N. C., to Vera Cruz.

[38] Gorgas to Talcott, Vera Cruz, November 18, 1847, OLR, 1847, File G, Doc. 156.

[39] Quoted from an extract made by Gorgas from Talcott's letter of October 23, 1847, enclosed with Gorgas to Huger, Vera Cruz, November 22, 1847, OLR, 1847, File H, Doc. 82.

hurt by its implications. He felt that his whole unpleasant stay in Vera Cruz would be in vain if all his hard work and honest effort to move supplies to the front was to be callously condemned. In self-defense, therefore, he wrote Talcott that he knew all supplies sent by the convoys of August 6 and 27, excepting three boxes of ammunition, had got through safely. These shipments, including 800,000 rounds of small arms ammunition, represented real effort. Huger had written him, he told Talcott, to the effect that supplies received from Vera Cruz at Puebla had "set them up." He added: "since the army left Puebla *no train* has gone thro' & therefore nothing *could* have reached them, & I presume this is what Capt. H. meant to say."[40]

Not satisfied with explaining matters to Talcott, he composed a bitter letter to Huger, whom he now regarded as having purposely involved him in trouble with the higher-ups. Gorgas had learned with "surprise and regret," he stiffly told Huger, that the Captain had reported to the Department that "not a single article had been received" from the Vera Cruz depot up to September 27. Since Huger, by his own admission, had been "set up" by the stream of supplies arriving at Puebla, and since another officer had seen all of the supplies arrive safely by the last train which could have reached the army, Gorgas was "utterly at a loss how to account for such a statement on your part— a statement so injurious to me." Gorgas explained to Huger that Talcott appeared willing to believe that all efforts had been made to supply the army, "but it is passed his comprehension that they [the supplies] *never* reached their destination." All of Gorgas' experience had gone into the packing of the stores which went forward from Vera Cruz, and Huger was invited to notice that only three boxes of stores had been reported lost. Gorgas closed on this note: "I perceive by the tone of Col. Talcott's letter that this [Huger's] report has produced an exceedingly unfavorable impression and I beg you will do me the slight justice to make the proper correction at your earliest convenience."[41]

Huger not only kept his temper on receipt of this missive, but also saw the justice of Gorgas' position and realized how the misunderstanding had arisen. He divined that Talcott had not meant to cast censure on Gorgas but was merely expressing his perplexity at the apparent huge losses of ammunition and stores from causes unexplained.

[40] Gorgas to Talcott, Vera Cruz, November 18, 1847, OLR, 1847, File G, Doc. 156.
[41] Gorgas to Huger, Vera Cruz, November 22, 1847, OLR, 1847, File H, Doc. 82.

On December 26 he wrote to assure the Chief of Ordnance that he, himself, had meant no reflection on the efforts of Lieutenant Gorgas. The main basis of the misunderstanding, he thought, was the loss to the enemy of two of his letters—one to Gorgas, the other to Talcott— which had acknowledged the receipt of supplies. He now explained that the whole purpose of his letter of September had been to show how completely the army was cut off from Vera Cruz, and that he had intended to say that

nothing *had* been received or *could* have been recd. after we left Puebla,— I regret particularly that my letters to Lieut. G. were captured, for as the Genl in Chief had directed me in May last while in Jalapa, to express to Lt. G. his disappointment at the limited supplies recd. by a train which he had expressly directed should bring a certain amount; I took occasion on the arrival of the supplies by Genl Pillow's train which reached Puebla in July, to assure the Genl in Chief that everything had been recd. that I could expect under the circumstances; and that with his permission I would express to Lt. Go. his satisfaction—That letter was lost it seems— but when I wrote my *note* to you of 27 Sept. from here I was not aware of the fact, as I recd. no communications from Vera Cruz until the 18th of Nov.[42]

Fair as this explanation was, Gorgas was in no humor to be pacified. Early in January, before he could have known of Huger's explanation, he wrote Talcott that he could not understand why, in opposition to the compliments of Huger's subordinates with the army, "so disparag- ing a reference should have been made to my name." And as for Huger, he added: "So keenly do I feel this *slur* so publicly made, that I cannot regard Capt. H. with those kindly feelings which I would wish to maintain towards an officer under whom I am to serve; and I shall immediately on my arrival in the Capitol [Mexico City] frankly tell him so, & shall strenuously object to serving under his orders."[43] He would seek duty on a general's staff.

That Gorgas had not allowed this controversy to interfere with the performance of his duties is indicated by his report of depot operation for the fourth quarter of 1847. During that quarter, he said, 320 six- pounder blank cartridges were fabricated, and 1,000 Mexican prim- ing tubes, four office tables, and a large number of items of equip-

[42] Huger to Talcott, Headquarters, December 26, 1847, OLR, 1847, File H, Doc. 82. Huger enclosed with this letter the one from Gorgas cited in n. 41.
[43] Gorgas to Talcott, Vera Cruz, January 3, 1848, OLR, 1848, File G, Doc. 13.

ment were repaired from an unserviceable state. Among the last were sixteen Mexican carriages within the fortifications of Vera Cruz, four musician's swords, fifty-one cavalry sabres, eleven horse carts, one field battery, and twenty-nine percussion rifles. By far the most important task which he performed was entered modestly: "70 Wagons loaded and despatched to Head Quarters."[44] And it was during that same period that he established his first contact with some of the officers with whom he was later to have many dealings in the Confederate Army. On November 19, for example, he issued ordnance supplies to Lieutenant Mansfield Lovell of the Fourth Artillery, later to be the defender of New Orleans; on the 22nd Lieutenant Richard S. Ewell of the First Dragoons drew supplies from him; and on the 25th Captain William J. Hardee presented a special requisition for ordnance stores.[45]

His drooping spirits were somewhat revived following the receipt, on December 6, of his commission as first lieutenant, dated March 3, 1847,[46] and in his next letter to his mother he even expressed the hope that he might soon receive a brevet captaincy. In this same letter, written on January 16, 1848, he also commented on the beauty of some of the Mexican women and, after jokingly asking what his mother would do if he should bring one of them home as his wife, he stated that as soon as he got back to the United States he would get married, provided he could find someone of whom his mother would approve and who would have him. References to the infrequency of letters from other members of his family suggest that he was homesick, and this feeling was given definite expression in his statement that since he could not hope for early release from Mexican duty, he would plan to remain in service about a year longer and then ask for a few months' leave, which he would spend at home with his mother, brothers, and sisters, "in whose company I enjoy the only real and heartfelt satisfaction that I have yet experienced in the world."[47]

Still stationed at Vera Cruz when this letter was written, he had become convinced that if his desire to get to Mexico City should ever be realized, he would be too late for any fighting; but he now wanted

[44] "Statement of Fabrication and Repairs at the Depot" in Vera Cruz, in the quarter ending December 31, 1847, *Huger Papers.*

[45] Receipts, *ibid.*

[46] Gorgas to Adj. Gen. Roger Jones, Vera Cruz, December 6, 1847, *Adjutant General's Office, Letters Received,* 1847.

[47] Gorgas to his mother, Vera Cruz, January 16, 1848, GMSS.

to see it purely as a tourist. His long-promised relief—this time a
Captain J. Williamson—finally arrived, and he transmitted his property
receipts and returns to Washington on January 18. Another transportation shortage, however, delayed his departure for the interior until
the first week in February. At length a train was ordered to headquarters, and he hastened to join it. His journey to the capital is described in a letter to his mother, written immediately after his arrival:

After a very tedious and disagreeable march of 24 days, I have at
length arrived at this famous city. My face is quite blistered up from the
effect of the Sun on the wide and level plains over which the road passes,
after it leaves Perote. The next time I have to pass them I shall be wise
enough to wear a wide brimmed hat instead of the little uniform Cap
which I have hitherto worn. I am disappointed in the appearance of this
country about which we have made so much ado. Instead of the green
valleys and pleasant farms I had hoped to see, I saw nothing but brown
leafless mountains, barren looking plains and dirty uncultivated wastes,
broken with gullies and strewed for a great part with volcanic stones and
cinders. From Vera Cruz to Jalapa there [is] little but sand & hot sun and
a great deal of very uncomfortable vermin, such as fleas, ticks, and more
dangerous animals. Around Jalapa the country is indeed beautiful, &
very fertile—the climate too is delicious. From Jalapa to Perote you pass
through a hilly country, cultivated to some extent & here the nights
are very cold. We suffered a good deal from cold. About 8 miles from
Perote the road enters on the vast plain which extends, broken by hills
of more or less height to the mountains which separate this plain from
the valley of Mexico. Perote is an exceedingly mean looking town with but
one two story home in it—the celebrated Castle of that name is a strong
square work standing at a short distance from the town in the midst of a
plain. We were much annoyed by the dust here, which darkened the
air—and all over as far as the eye could reach you could see moving
columns of dust—standing up like pillars, & moving slowly along with the
whirlwinds. Puebla is a large and handsome town all built of brick &
stones with wide and paved streets. I stayed here two days. Yesterday I
saw this valley for the first time. The view of the high snow-capped mountains on one side and the long valley dotted with lakes and covered with
cities is certainly fine; but still there seems to me to be an air of barren-
ness over the whole that prevents one from being very much delighted
or pleased.[48]

At a meeting that must have been strained, at least for Gorgas, he
reported for duty to Huger on March 1, and was attached at once to

[48] Gorgas to his mother, Mexico City, March 1, 1848, GMSS.

the rocket and howitzer battery to which he had originally been assigned.[49] Despite Huger's efforts to straighten out their difficulties, Gorgas had not forgiven him. His duties in his new station presented little variety. They consisted of administrative details connected with the battery, the command of which ultimately devolved on him. Drab routine was just as monotonous here as at Vera Cruz but cast in a different mold. The battery was stationed throughout April and May in the small city of Toluca, capital of the state of Mexico, and since hostilities were now ended, most of the period was taken up in conducting tests with the twelve-pounder mountain howitzer and with rockets.[50]

On his arrival at Mexico City, Gorgas discovered that fighting had ceased immediately after the secret signing of the treaty of Guadalupe Hidalgo on February 2, a few days before he had left Vera Cruz, and thus that he was again deprived of his long-sought opportunity to have an active part in the war. This disappointment, added to his feeling that circumstances, and perhaps individuals, had conspired to keep him out of combat service during the whole of Scott's campaign, served to increase his discontent. His dissatisfaction at the lack of activity, coupled with lingering resentment against Huger, under whom he was now serving more directly than at Vera Cruz, apparently led him to act upon his earlier threat to Talcott that if he was forced to serve under Huger he would request duty on the staff of a general officer.

On April 2 he wrote to his old friend, General Wool, who was now in command of the American forces in northeastern Mexico, outlining his situation and expressing his discontent. Wool was immediately sympathetic and expressed his desire to have Gorgas appointed as his aide-de-camp.[51] Realizing, however, that such a transfer from one branch of the service to another would require the consent of Secretary Marcy, he must have recalled the failure of his efforts to obtain a similar appointment for Gorgas two years earlier. But he promised to try again; and when, as before, Gorgas did not receive the desired ap-

[49] Huger to Talcott, Mexico City, March 2, 1848, OLR, 1848, File H, Doc. 95; Special Orders No. 10, Headquarters, Army of Mexico, March 3, 1848, *Copybook of Gorgas*, p. 46. This battery was a part of a regiment of Voltigeurs commanded by Lt. Col. Joseph E. Johnston, and it is probable that this association marked the beginning of the strong friendship which developed between Gorgas and Johnston.

[50] "Statement of Practice with Rocket and Howitzer Battery," Toluca, Mexico, April and May, 1848, OLR, 1848, File G, Doc. 90.

[51] Wool to Gorgas, Headquarters, May 17, 1848, GMSS.

pointment, he was left to wonder if the ghost of his letter to Buchanan had once more risen to haunt him. He remained with the rocket and howitzer battery until the evacuation of Mexico City, and in July, shortly after his thirtieth birthday, he sailed from Vera Cruz with Scott's army to return to the United States and to his duties as an Ordnance officer in the peacetime military establishment.

The Mexican War was important to Gorgas for a variety of reasons. As a young, headstrong, and somewhat willful lieutenant of ordnance, he developed in Mexico a certain sense of discipline. He also became militantly aware of some of his prerogatives. But, above all, he learned his profession thoroughly, for actual participation in war was a far better teacher than any of the textbooks which he had studied at West Point from 1837 to 1841. This thorough training was a fine foundation for the years of routine duty that were about to begin.

III

The Sound of a Voice

A BRIEF STAY IN WASHINGTON AND A VISIT WITH TALCOTT BROUGHT
a temporary station before reassignment to Watervliet Arsenal. Major
Silas Halsey, the commander of Champlain Arsenal, was dead, and
Gorgas was at once ordered to Vergennes, Vermont, to survey the
Major's accounts. Affairs there were in a chaotic condition. Halsey had
left his family destitute, even indebted to the government. Pleading its
case, he wrote the Chief of Ordnance: "Your benevolence will easily
enable you to picture the distress of a family thus suddenly deprived of
comparative ease and comfort thrown upon the world, in the depth
of their affliction, proverty stricken and dependent upon the kindness
of their friends for even the necessaries of life.—Much as I should dislike hibernating in this inhospitable climate I would yet consent to pass
the winter here—or at least a portion of it—to afford Mrs. H. and her
family the use of the quarters here until spring." Further, Gorgas urged
the appointment of a Mr. Woodbridge as Military Storekeeper of the
Arsenal, since it was apparent that his selection for the post would be
helpful to the Halsey family.[1]

Staff duties would not allow the young lieutenant to remain long in
Vermont. He returned to Watervliet by mid-December and thought
he had finally succeeded in closing the troublesome property accounts
of the Mexican War Rocket and Howitzer Battery.[2] But all contact
with Mexico was not yet severed. The War Department adopted the
policy of brevetting officers who had served with distinction in the late
war. In fact, brevets were given to almost all of the officers who had
been in action. But Gorgas got nothing. The reason undoubtedly was

[1] Gorgas to Talcott, Champlain Arsenal, November 20, 1848, OLR, 1848,
File G, Doc. 188.
[2] Gorgas to Talcott, Watervliet Arsenal, N. Y., December 19, 1848, OLR,
1848, File G, Doc. 197.

Marcy's long-harbored grudge against him, since all other ordnance officers who had seen duty in Mexico were given full consideration.

Requested by the President to submit the names of officers of the Ordnance Corps whom he considered worthy of a brevet, Talcott included Gorgas in his list. In setting forth Gorgas' qualifications, Talcott said: "This officer served with the Siege Train at the capture of Vera Cruz and Castle of St. Juan d'ulloa, and there rendered valuable and gallant service." Talcott stated that when Gorgas was assigned to command the Vera Cruz Depot, he was put in a position with as much hard work and responsibility and of perhaps more danger "than to have accompanied the army in its onward march. It was duty very distasteful to him, but which he has continued to discharge with fidelity and zeal, until lately relieved therefrom."[3] But this recommendation proved of no avail, and Gorgas' friends decided to assist. Franklin Townsend of Albany, New York, wrote his cousin, Representative Henry Nicoll, that Gorgas deserved a brevet. Obviously unaware of the Marcy-Gorgas impasse, Nicoll requested Marcy to confer this honor. Many others endorsed the petition, but nothing happened.[4]

Gradually his old urge for active service came over Gorgas again. Routine was palling, and the turbulent situation in California caught his fancy. He was feeling the "canker of a long peace," and was anxious to join the gold rush, which had begun the year before. Talcott had no pressing need for an ordnance officer in California, but he would keep Gorgas' wish in mind.[5]

[3] "Details of the Service of Ordnance Officers from Official Reports," Talcott, February 24, 1849, *War Department Records, Letters Received by the U. S. Secretary of War,* 1851, File O, Doc. 7.

[4] Nicoll to Marcy, Washington, January 15, 1848 [1849], *War Department Records, Letters Received by the U. S. Secretary of War;* Huger to Marcy, Washington, December 28, 1848, *ibid.;* Baker to Marcy, Washington, December 28, *ibid.;* Talcott to Marcy, Washington, December 28, *ibid.;* Wool to Marcy, Troy, N. Y., February 3, 1849, *ibid.* In writing of Gorgas, Wool said: "Altogether I know of no young officer more deserving or who has exhibited greater zeal, activity and industry, at the same time manifested greater anxiety to promote the honor and interest of the country than he has, and yet he is the only ordnance officer who was *in action in* Mexico who has not received a brevet. Allow me to request your attention to his case with the hope that he will receive the reward which has been so liberally extended to most others who have served in Mexico."

[5] Gorgas to Talcott, Watervliet, March 15, 1850, OLR, 1850, File G, Doc. 25; Talcott to Gorgas, Washington, March 21, 1850, OLS, Book 82, p. 280. Gorgas' attitude had changed considerably in a year. He had written his mother from Watervliet on April 25, 1849, that he was not anxious to go to California. He observed that California fever had not seriously affected him as yet. He even went so far as to say that "I have roved sufficiently for a good while to come." GMSS.

Lack of activity gave Gorgas time to brood over his failure to secure a brevet. It was rumored that the Senate, in January of 1851, was on the point of considering applications for this honor from some officers who had, up to that time, been neglected. Gorgas immediately presented his case again. In forwarding the application to Charles M. Conrad, the Secretary of War, Talcott wrote that if Gorgas was rightly informed about the reconsideration of brevet claims, he had some additional officers to recommend. In his reply to the President's inquiry concerning eligible promotions, in February, 1849, Talcott had named two officers who had likewise been overlooked, "why I have never understood."[6]

In the meantime, Gorgas had secured a transfer to New York Arsenal on Governor's Island, but found it too small.[7] A little maneuvering brought assignment to Pittsburgh Arsenal,[8] which remained attractive for a scant three months. In July, 1851, Gorgas asked Colonel H. K. Craig, the new Chief of Ordnance, if he might obtain the command of Charleston Arsenal in case Major Hagner was transferred.[9]

Transfer to Charleston, however, did not materialize. Instead, Craig wrote Gorgas in mid-November that when relieved of duty at Pittsburgh Arsenal, he should proceed to Fort Monroe Arsenal for duty.[10] There his association with the Tredegar Iron Works in Richmond began. There, too, he was able to indulge his interest in inventions and to conduct some tests of gun-barrel iron.[11]

While involved in these experiments during April, 1853, Gorgas heard a rumor that he might be ordered to Mount Vernon Arsenal in Alabama. He wished the transfer might be delayed at least until October, and so expressed himself to the Chief of Ordnance, saying: "My reasons for his request will suggest themselves to the Head of the Dept.

[6] Talcott to C. M. Conrad, Washington, January 31, 1851, *War Department Records, Letters Received by the U. S. Secretary of War,* 1851, File O, Doc. 7.

[7] It is regretted that the date he took command cannot be given. The first notice of his being at New York Arsenal is a letter, Gorgas to Talcott, New York Arsenal, January 28, 1851, OLR, 1851, File G, Doc. 7.

[8] Gorgas to Talcott, New York Arsenal, March 6, 1851, OLR, 1851, File G, Doc. 30, expressing his wish to be stationed at Pittsburgh; indorsement by Conrad, March 29, 1851, approving a proposal to send Gorgas to Allegheny (Pittsburgh) Arsenal, in *War Department Records,* Secretary of War's "Orders and Indorsements," II, 1851, 161.

[9] Gorgas to Craig, Allegheny Arsenal, July 16, 1851, OLR, 1851, File G, Doc. 78.

[10] Craig to Gorgas, Washington, November 11, 1851, OLS, Book 86, p. 365.

[11] Gorgas to Craig, Fort Monroe Arsenal, January 14, April 4, 1852, OLR, 1852, 1853, File G, Docs. 8, 41.

. . . on account of the duty still unfinished here. I should dislike to spend the hot months in a climate to which I am unused."[12] But a few weeks later he was jumping at a whiplash from Craig. He assured the Chief of Ordnance that he would hasten to obey orders, and after his arrival at Mount Vernon would go on to inspect the ordnance at Forts Pickens and Morgan at Pensacola and Mobile. Still, he was anxious to get Charleston as a permanent station. Explaining that Mount Vernon might "prove a sufficiently solitary place for a bachelor," he said that as long as there was work to do in and around Mobile, he would not be dissatisfied.[13] Gorgas arrived at his new post on June 14, 1853,[14] and left the next day for Pensacola to inspect the harbor defenses. He returned to Mobile in a little over a week and wrote his findings to Craig, who approved his recommendations for repairs.[15]

June passed slowly in boiling heat. By the end of that month Gorgas was ready for any assignment that would take him north. When the telegraph brought news of the death of Pikesville Arsenal's command-ing officer, Gorgas at once wrote Craig, expressing the hope that this news was false but at the same time pointing out that, should it be true, he would appreciate a transfer to that Arsenal. He added that he would "not be reconciled to a long residence at the South, and I beg you therefore to take this opportunity to give me a post at the North." He followed this request with another letter pleading his case. He was aware that "the Department is not supposed to know in their assignments to duty, whether an officer be married or single; but I take the liberty respectfully to suggest that the command of this Post, should if possible be alloted to the former class. The absence of all society neutralizes to a bachelor the advantages which make it a pleasant resi-dence to a family." He further argued that his assistant was willing to return to Mobile for permanent station after his marriage, and was thoroughly able to command Mount Vernon. Furthermore, Gorgas hoped that command of Pikesville would be in some way connected with duty at the Richmond foundry, which he much desired.[16]

[12] Gorgas to Craig, Old Point Comfort, April 14, 1853, OLR, 1853, File G, Doc. 50.
[13] Gorgas to Craig, Old Point Comfort, May 26, 1853, *ibid.*, Doc. 64. Gorgas said that he would already have been on his way south but was anxious to finish his report on the last firing at Old Point.
[14] Gorgas to Craig, Mount Vernon Arsenal, June 14, 1853, *ibid.*, Doc. 73.
[15] Craig to Gorgas, Washington, July 8, 1853, OLS, Book 4, p. 41.
[16] Gorgas to Craig, Mount Vernon Arsenal, June 30, July 9, 1853, OLR, 1853, File G, Docs. 82, 88.

He was right in assuming some connection between Pikesville and the Richmond foundry, for Craig informed him that command of Pikesville was reserved for the officer charged with superintending foundry work,[17] and this officer was not Gorgas.

Craig probably did not know the underlying reason for another, and stranger, request of Mount Vernon's commander. On December 1, 1853, Gorgas asked permission to cultivate fifty or seventy-five acres of the arsenal grounds. He indicated the purpose was to reduce the cost of some of the food consumed at the post and wanted authority to employ a farmer to do the work.[18] Possibly this interest in a truck garden arose from personal rather than official considerations—perhaps he wanted to vary the humdrum diet of the arsenal for a young lady visitor, whose recent arrival there had changed things a great deal for Gorgas.

Miss Amelia Gayle, sister of Dr. Matthew Gayle, post surgeon, was staying at the arsenal to take care of her sister's children. She had brought them to Mount Vernon to escape the terrible siege of yellow fever in Mobile. The arsenal, for some mysterious reason,[19] was free from the dread disease.

Miss Gayle soon developed the habit of spending the afternoons on the veranda of her brother's quarters, entertaining the children by reading to them for several hours at a time. Since Dr. Gayle's quarters adjoined those of the post commander, Gorgas could hardly avoid hearing some of these reading sessions. He was immediately struck by the enchanting young voice and determined to meet the owner. Not entirely certain about the relationship of the children to the young lady, he, of course, contrived business with the post surgeon. Gorgas was fortunate; the young lady was Miss Gayle, and, happily, the children's aunt. The tempo of life at Mount Vernon quickened for Josiah. No longer did his plaints for transfer go in every mail; he had a reason for wanting to stay where he was.

Before long Josiah had developed an over-all strategic plan. He would conduct a whirlwind campaign with matrimony as the objective. There is, to be sure, some indication that Amelia met this strategy with token resistance. Josiah really had no choice in the matter; he had fallen victim to Amelia's charm and forceful personality. Amelia's trim, graceful figure, lovely dark hair, and striking features fascinated the

[17] Craig to Gorgas, Washington, July 16, 1853, OLS, Book 4, pp. 48–49.
[18] Gorgas to Craig, Mount Vernon Arsenal, OLR, 1853, File G, Doc. 154.
[19] Mount Vernon was on high, dry ground.

young lieutenant. She was not beautiful, perhaps, but her bright, kind eyes and warm smile put everyone at ease with her. It seemed impossible to Josiah that anyone could fail to love her as he did.

Amelia's father, Judge John Gayle, was a former governor of Alabama, once a representative in Congress, and confidant of many of the country's great. In the days of his attendance in Congress, Amelia had been head of his house, since her mother had died some years before. While in Washington, Amelia had become close friends with many of the nation's most able statesmen. She and her father had shared a house with John C. Calhoun. She had even collected a kiss from Henry Clay, who excused his liberty as a result of poor eyesight (he thought Amelia was somebody else). Reveling in the gay social life of the capital, Amelia had become almost a cosmopolite.[20]

Josiah's devoted attention to his strategy produced results in a reasonably short time; on December 26, 1853, Amelia and he were married. The years immediately to follow were to be the happiest of Josiah's life.[21] Mount Vernon, no longer a God-forsaken wilderness, seemed ideal for a honeymoon and for starting married life. There began the quiet domestic serenity which always characterized the Gorgas household. It was doubtless at Mount Vernon, also, that the perennial family habit of reading aloud in the evening was established. This diversion was one of Josiah's greatest pleasures, and he delighted in translating foreign books for his own and Amelia's benefit.[22] In a sense marriage completed Gorgas' pattern of happiness. A man who could be lonesome, he now had a loving and constant companion.

The months at Mount Vernon passed happily, and on October 3, 1854, Amelia presented her husband with their first child—William Crawford Gorgas—named after Josiah's brother-in-law, Dr. William Crawford. If the family did not then guess that Willie would do great things, his father, at least, was determined that he should have the educational and moral equipment necessary to do them. His concern

---

[20] This is based partly on family tradition as related to the writer by Miss Maria Bayne Gorgas, Mrs. George Palfrey, and Mrs. William D. Wrightson, and partly on accounts in Marie Doughty Gorgas and Burton J. Hendrick, *William Crawford Gorgas* (Garden City, 1924), pp. 24–31, and Hugh C. Haynsworth, *Haynsworth-Furman and Allied Families* (Sumter, S. C., 1942), pp. 79–82.

[21] Gorgas himself said that the years following his marriage were his happiest. See GMSD, January 8, 1874.

[22] Several manuscripts, the results of Gorgas' translations, are preserved in the GMSS at Tuscaloosa. In a letter to the writer, February 29, 1944, Miss Mary Gayle Gorgas wrote that her father "read French and German fluently."

for his children was always a prime consideration and became intensified with the birth of his first daughter, Jessie, on March 27, 1856.[23]

In early March of 1854 Gorgas thought it wise to take up the matter of repairs to the forts at Pensacola—work having been delayed because of yellow fever in the fall. Craig wholeheartedly agreed and told Gorgas to get to Pensacola and to begin the work as soon as he could.[24] The repairs had to be handled carefully. Funds for the Ordnance Department were running low, and economy was the watchword. Craig was adamant: spending had to be cut down—appropriations must not be overdrawn. But Gorgas did not at first hear of these conditions. He had to admit to the Chief of Ordnance that he had exceeded the funds allocated for "Arsenals," being under the impression that there was more cash on hand. In addition, his inspection of Pensacola's bastions had led him to believe that he should spend some money on them. He had four carpenters and two laborers at work on Fort Pickens, repairing carriages. He intended to make a minute investigation of Fort McRae after Pickens was in shape, and repair it also. The armament of Fort Morgan impressed Gorgas as being in "very good condition."[25]

Taking seriously his general responsibilities for middle Gulf-Coast fortifications, Gorgas made a new and careful investigation of Fort McRae in June. His inspection the previous June had revealed that the fort was in such a confused state of affairs that it was impossible to tell exactly what was needed there. He now discovered that all but three barbette carriages had been dismounted and that all the others would have to be remounted or lowered to the terreplein and stowed in casemates. He determined to make the necessary repairs at once and received official approval.[26]

The Ordnance Office could hardly have realized the ultimate wisdom of this decision at the time. But because it backed Lieutenant Gorgas' plan for repairing Fort Pickens, it secured that work for the Union during the Civil War. If the condition of this fort had not been improved prior to 1861, the Confederate Army might well have taken possession of it at the outbreak of the war. Gorgas, however, did his job so well that even he could not undo it seven years later.

---

[23] GMSS.

[24] Gorgas to Craig, Mount Vernon, March 7, 1854, OLR, 1854, File G, Doc. 38; Craig to Gorgas, Washington, March 16, 1854, OLS, Book 4, p. 291.

[25] Gorgas to Craig, Mount Vernon, May 13, 1854, OLR, 1854, File G, Doc. 69.

[26] Gorgas to Craig, Mount Vernon, June 14, 1854, *ibid.,* Doc. 82; Capt. Maynadier to Gorgas, Washington, June 22, 1854, OLS, Book 4, p. 380.

While its commander had been busy attending the wants of other places, Mount Vernon had come out second best in a prolonged engagement with the weather. On Gorgas' return home he found that certain unoccupied quarters at the arsenal were decaying at an alarming rate. Rain had beaten through the north wall, and the plaster was falling. The woodwork on the rear piazza was so badly decayed that there was danger of momentary collapse. Gorgas wrote Craig: "It is painful to me to see decay without an effort to arrest it." The wharf, in a ruined state, was useless. Gorgas was using neighbors' landings, through their kindness. He was moved to further expression: "There is no arsenal which more absolutely needs a small appropriation than this one. I sincerely hope it will not be over-looked next year in the apportionment of the appropriation for 'Arsenals.' "[27] Lieutenant Gorgas was working hard to enlarge the importance of Mount Vernon.

He gave special attention to personnel relations. By recommending promotions and demotions on a strictly fair basis, he was able to maintain the good morale of his military command.[28] Civilian workers at Pensacola, however, had gone on strike despite his efforts. The strike was not his fault; the workers heard that $1.50 a day was the wage at the Navy Yard—so they demanded a raise. Gorgas told the Chief of Ordnance that he had met the Navy Yard's figure but would decrease the rate to $1.30 a day after the 1st of October because of the shorter day.[29] In later years Josiah was to hear many similar complaints.

His usual success in dealing with enlisted personnel may be traced to his just views on discipline, which he stated to Craig in a letter: "Where a command is governed as at this Post without resort to the personal violence so much deprecated by the Commander-in-Chief, it is sometimes indispensable to make the men aware of the tribunals to which they are amenable under the Rules and Articles of War."[30]

Trouble proverbially comes in large doses, and it certainly did to Mount Vernon's harrassed lieutenant. The Navy's Commander David G. Farragut, who would later be concerned with the fortifications of

[27] Gorgas to Craig, Mount Vernon, September 6, 1854, OLR, 1854, File G, Doc. 132. On September 13, Craig informed Gorgas of the allocation of $600 to Mount Vernon for use on the unoccupied quarters. Craig to Gorgas, Washington, OLS, Book 4, p. 463.

[28] For example see Gorgas to Craig, Mount Vernon, July 26, 1854, OLR, 1854, File G, Doc. 109, recommending the promotion of an armorer because of his ability as a mechanic and because he had erected a small drill press for use in altering flint muskets.

[29] Gorgas to Craig, Mount Vernon, September 14, 1854, *ibid.*, Doc. 136.

[30] Gorgas to Craig, Mount Vernon, July 24, 1855, *ibid.*, 1855, Doc. 110.

Mobile, sent Gorgas a copy of his report of experiments relating to the strength of naval guns made by him at Fort Monroe in 1852–1853. The communication reopened an old wound:

I am thus painfully reminded of the apparently entire neglect with which the similar report prepared by me under the orders of Major Ramsey, in May, 1853, has been received. I believe that due attention was paid to the subject, & that the facts set forth in that report were as fully entitled to attention as those recorded in the Report of Commander F. . . . I can scarcely be deemed obtrusive in venturing to express the mortification the reflection gives me that an entire year of zealous labor should be so consigned to oblivion and be productive of no practical conclusions. . . .[31]

This communique brought results, and at length Gorgas received information that his report of experiments at Fort Monroe might be published. Pointing out to Craig that he would like to have his name appear below that of Major Ramsey as having been associated with his superior officer in the experiments, he explained that he was not pleased with the fact that his name was appearing only incidentally as the affair then stood. He was sure that the Major would have no objections "and exact truth & justice to me requires it."[32] Craig appears to have overlooked this letter officially since there is no record of a reply. But this, and several other letters of like tenor already mentioned,[33] may have made a bad impression. They were distinctly remindful of certain letters from Mexico.

One particular job occupied Gorgas from January of 1855 and would continue to occupy him until late July—the repair of Fort Barrancas. He was most interested in refurbishing the armament and carriages. By July 9 he was writing Craig from that place, using his new rank of captain in the signature, that he intended to conduct some tests by firing the guns in barbette and in casemate to determine the value of the repaired carriages and also to see if all casemate ordnance was fit for action.[34]

The rest of the summer and fall passed without incident, but in December Gorgas developed a new idea for an iron suspension carriage, which he described in detail and of which he sent a sketch to Craig. The Chief of Ordnance did not hesitate to give his views that the

[31] Gorgas to Craig, Mount Vernon, September 17, 1854, OLR, 1854, File G, Doc. 138.
[32] Gorgas to Craig, Mount Vernon, December 3, 1854, *ibid.*, Doc. 180.
[33] See those relating to Gorgas' transfer to Mount Vernon Arsenal.
[34] Gorgas to Craig, Fort Barrancas, Fla., OLR, 1855, File G, Doc. 105.

carriage would fail, but seems to have been pleased that Captain Gorgas was thinking about improvements. This may or may not have been a factor in the move he was about to make, but at any rate he wrote Gorgas in December: "In consequence of the detail of Captain Callander for service in the Pacific Department, Kennebec Arsenal has been left under the temporary command (for this winter) of 2nd Lieut. Howard. It is my intention to assign you to that command next spring."[35] This was welcome news in the Gorgas household and doubtless made the next three months less tiresome. But by late March impatience had again set in. Craig received a request to send orders to Kennebec as soon as possible, since the Gorgas family wanted to avoid the June heat at Mount Vernon.

Having argued his case for early departure from Alabama, Gorgas turned once again to repairing the armament at Fort Pickens. This duty occupied him until late May, when Special Orders Number 49, dated May 8, 1856, reached him and he was at last relieved of duty at Mount Vernon.[36] But by the middle of June Gorgas' relief had not arrived, nor had a word been heard from him. Gorgas hoped that Craig would send someone else to relieve him as soon as possible.[37] The delay was prolonged for another week, and on June 26 Josiah wrote Craig a letter stating his reasons for earnestly begging to be sent north. They were concise but may have sounded too personal:

The Department will appreciate my anxiety to escape passing another summer, when it recollects that of the *ten* summers ending with this one, I have spent *seven* at the South, & five of those in a climate wholly foreign to my constitution. I have never recovered, wholly, from the effects of over a year's residence at Vera Cruz. I am fully conscious of the baleful effects on me of the long summer heats. I hoped to have been permitted to leave this in time to avoid exposing myself to a *fourth* summer here; but I again find myself in the midst of its potent heats, and can only ask the Department to relieve me with as little delay as possible.

I am aware that the War Department adopts the rule of a four year's tour of duty and I would not be importunate, did I think my action were any embarrassment to the Dept.

But it having been determined to change my Post, it can scarcely be otherwise than that I should be solicitous to escape the extreme heat of

---

[35] Craig to Gorgas, Washington, December 21, 1855, OLS, Book 11, pp. 6–7.
[36] Craig to Gorgas, Washington, May 27, 1856, *ibid.*, p. 205; Gorgas to Craig, Mount Vernon, May 31, 1856, OLR, 1856, File G, Doc. 93.
[37] Gorgas to Craig, Mount Vernon, June 19, 1856, OLR, 1856, File G, Doc. 103.

THE SOUND OF A VOICE

the summer here & to avoid a too sudden exposure to the cold of the North.[38]

Gorgas' replacement put in a belated appearance on the 1st of July, and the Gorgas family left for Maine on the 7th, with Josiah assuming command of Kennebec Arsenal on the 18th.[39]

[38] Gorgas to Craig, Mount Vernon, *ibid.*, Doc. 107.
[39] Gorgas to Craig, OLR, index book 26, 1856, G-119, giving synopsis of letter (missing from file) stating that Gorgas was to leave Mount Vernon on July 7; Gorgas to Craig, Kennebec Arsenal, Augusta, Me., July 18, 1856, OLR, 1856, File G, Doc. 121, announcing his assumption of command of that post.

IV

Last Years in the Old Army

KENNEBEC ARSENAL WAS BADLY IN NEED OF REPAIRS. AND, OF COURSE, all the Ordnance Office need do if it desired a report on the physical condition of an installation was to send Captain Gorgas to the place in question. He had frequently demonstrated his interest in the appearance of his posts, and his observations were always concise and to the point. So it was with Kennebec.[1] The river-retaining walls had been a considerable worry for some time—a worry which Gorgas inherited. Loath as Craig was to part with funds, he was at length convinced by the urgency of Gorgas' appeals for some repairs at Augusta. Switching his stand, Craig became interested in fixing the wall and, characteristically, turned into an exacting taskmaster until the job was underway.[2] But Gorgas, used to the crusty Chief of Ordnance by this time, proceeded in his own way whenever he felt he had to.

Sometimes, however, these arrangements irked Craig. In January, 1858, Gorgas, on his own responsibility, spent money which Craig thought wasted. The latter did not hesitate to tell his subordinate that he was not pleased with needless expenditures for repairs and improvements and wrote letters in rigid style:

However desirable you may have considered the execution of the objects stated, they do not appear on their face to be of that character which the public wants of the Arsenal demanded; nor such as might not have been delayed until you could have reported your views and recommendations concerning them to this office, and received instructions thereon.[8]

[1] Gorgas to Craig, Kennebec, July 25, 1856, OLR, 1856, File G, Doc. 124.
[2] Gorgas to Craig, Kennebec, October 2, 1856, *ibid.*, Doc. 167; Craig to Gorgas, Washington, October 6, OLS, Book 11, p. 360; Gorgas to Craig, Kennebec, October 10, OLR, 1856, File G, Doc. 174.
[8] Craig to Gorgas, Washington, January 28, 1858, OLS, Book 15, p. 426.

[44]

The political condition of the country added to Gorgas' worry over this attitude on the part of Craig. He felt that northern political schemers would exploit the slavery question to the limit, although as late as January, 1857, he did not envision an early disruption of the Union—though he felt that "an eventual separation appears but too inevitable."[4]

All these combined uncertainties no doubt increased the family's growing homesickness for the South. The "frankness of southern manners" and the balmy climate of Alabama (they had temporarily forgotten the blistering heat) were looming large in their thoughts. His family's increasing desire to go South was clearly a deciding factor in Gorgas' declining an instructorship at West Point. If the Military Academy had been south of the Mason-Dixon Line, he thought, "I might incline to go there; as it is I have no special desire to go there to turn teacher." And then, too, he was motivated by another consideration, his intense personal hatred for "Black Republicans."[5]

Summer and early winter passed with the usual arsenal duties to occupy Gorgas' time. October, however, brought joy to the family circle, for on the twenty-eighth of that month Mary Gayle Gorgas was born, and was christened with Jessie in the Episcopal church.[6]

At this juncture a rumor reached Kennebec that Gorgas might be sent to command the Charleston Arsenal. Josiah knew what a disappointment it would be to Amelia if this transfer did not come through. Many things, other than homesickness, had shaped her hunger to return South. The servant problem was one,[7] and the more pressing was the easier living conditions in a more hospitable climate. The family had been shocked at the penury of some of the arsenal employees. One newly married young man particularly evoked their sympathy. Though earning only $4.50 a week, he had to pay $4.00 for board. This was the basis for a request, in February, 1858, that Craig assign to Kennebec an additional $150 on account of ordnance and ordnance stores. Gorgas explained that he had given employment, "at low wages, to a few poor people, pressed by the want which winter always develops here—for whom there is work enough in the [arsenal] laboratory."[8] Craig indorsed the request: "remit . . . early in March."

News of the Charleston transfer was long delayed, and Gorgas' resolution wavered. Did he want to go to Charleston after all? The

---

[4] GMSD, January 12, 1857. [5] GMSD, January 12, February 11, 1857.
[6] GMSD, December 13, 1857. [7] *Ibid.*
[8] Gorgas to Craig, Kennebec, February 11, 1858, OLR, 1858, File G, Doc. 37; GMSD, February 12, 1858.

family had settled into its usual pattern of night reading;[9] Willie had reached an interesting age, and it seemed a shame to pull up the family's roots so abruptly.[10] But Amelia was still anxious to go. At last she got her wish. On May 3 Gorgas received orders to report at Charleston. But the trip was held up, as usual. Willie had become desperately ill with typhoid fever. A doctor advised Gorgas that, assuming the boy lived, he should not be moved for three or four weeks. With a heavy heart Gorgas had to write Craig that his departure would necessarily be delayed. He gamely said that should the Chief of Ordnance think it best to make other arrangements under the altered circumstances, he would be content to remain at Kennebec through the working season.[11] Craig, in a rare mood of sympathy, replied at once, putting Gorgas at ease by saying that the chief reason for an immediate move to Charleston was so that Gorgas might get there before the hottest part of the summer. No other arrangements would be made, and Charleston Arsenal was still his. Gorgas should write the commanding officer there and tell him when he thought he could arrive. Craig added that the new arrangement was "entirely justifiable."[12] A much relieved Gorgas stayed at Kennebec for two additional weeks. Meanwhile, he devised a new plan. He would go on to Charleston alone, take command, and pave the way for the rest of the family. Then about two months later, he would return and collect the clan. He finally left Kennebec, wife, and children on May 24, and assumed command of Charleston Arsenal on June 1.[13]

For some time after his arrival Gorgas, as was his custom, concentrated on beautifying the premises. Buildings at the post had obviously not been painted for years, and he hoped Craig would approve a new coat of paint.[14] But no amount of work could dispel his loneliness. Amelia and the children were uppermost in his thoughts. He lived from mail to mail for word from those whom he affectionately called his brood. Nothing ever worried him more than his family. "Suppose that they were all lost to me . . . what would become of the remainder of my life? It is a thought which, like that of annihilation, the mind refuses

---

9 GMSD, February 12, 26, March 15, 1858.

10 GMSD, March 17, 1858.

11 GMSD, May 9, 1858; Gorgas to Craig, Kennebec, May 5, 1858, OLR, 1858, File G, Doc. 100.

12 Craig to Gorgas, Washington, May 8, 1858, OLS, Book 20, p. 93.

13 GMSD, May 19, June 1, 1858.

14 Gorgas to Craig, Charleston, June 19, 1858, OLR, 1858, File G, Doc. 131; GMSD, June 16, 1858.

to contemplate." In the depths of this loneliness learning of Amelia's fears about her father's health, he poured out his own feelings in writing her:

I do not think you need be alarmed as yet about your father—We can go so as to be there during Christmas. . . . It is strange what an attraction he exercises toward even me—a stranger to his blood—But I owe him "Heaven's last best gift"—my darling wife—and he is associated with all the happiest periods of my life—our courtship—our wedding—& the birth of two of our babies—What events! Talk of battle, politics, travels! A man has no experiences worth mentioning until he loves the woman he weds, & has children born to him by her—These are the things that sink into the memory. . . .[15]

After a time Gorgas heard that Kennebec Arsenal was to get an appropriation for the repairs on the retaining wall which he had so strongly recommended. He thought he might get a sixty-day leave during which he could collect his family and possibly secure an assignment for temporary duty at Kennebec to help with work on the wall. He knew that he had a better understanding of the problems involved than the officer in interim command, and consequently sent Craig a request for leave and assignment to special duty.[16]

And therewith began Captain Gorgas' decline from favor. He was the only officer at Charleston Arsenal, and no others were available for short assignment. The Chief of Ordnance, therefore, disapproved the application, apparently convinced that Gorgas was one who would not stay put. Then, too, the request may have sounded selfish, since Gorgas also wanted to bring his family slowly south, stopping for a while at Old Point Comfort. Craig's refusal hurt, though Gorgas had expected objections. He remarked that if he had been in the habit of asking for leave, he would not be so disappointed; "but I have had no leaves of absence for six years." If he could not have sixty days, he was willing to take what he could get—"forty, thirty, or even twenty days."[17] He

[15] GMSD, June 27, 1858; Gorgas to Amelia, Wednesday [probably July, 1858], GMSS.

[16] Gorgas to Craig, Charleston, July 1, 1858, OLR, 1858, File G, Doc. 137. This is his application for leave. See Gorgas to Craig, July 4, 1858, *ibid.*, Doc. 140, for his hope of assignment to special duty.

[17] Gorgas to Craig, Charleston, July 9, 1858, *ibid.*, Doc. 149; Craig to Gorgas, Washington, July 7, 1858, OLS, Book 20, p. 171; Gorgas to Amelia, Wednesday [probably July, 1858], GMSS. It is interesting to note the speed achieved by the mail service between Washington and Charleston. Craig wrote on the 7th, and Gorgas answered on the 9th.

reminded Craig of a conversation they had had in Washington: that he would have to have leave to bring his family south—and that the Colonel had agreed and approved without question the length of the leave. Gorgas pulled no punches in this dressing down. Craig had been unusually harsh, and he was so informed. Gorgas considered the whole matter carefully and was still nettled[18]—so was the Chief of Ordnance. This situation presented an opportunity to attack Captain Gorgas—a thing Craig relished. Gorgas' remarks in explaining his reasons for requesting a leave, Craig wrote,

had not induced the Department to change the decision made . . . the 7th inst. . . . Your reminiscence of the conversation between us, in which you intimated your desire to return for your family when it would be safe and proper to take them to Charleston, was entirely unnecessary. When an Officer asks an indulgence of time to do a certain act, the inference is fair that no more than was sufficient for the accomplishment of the avowed purpose would be consumed.

In waiving objection to your errand I certainly could not anticipate that your absence was to include a visit to a Watering place, though no reference was made to its duration.[19]

A truce, of sorts, was worked out. Gorgas was granted ten day's leave, to take effect on the arrival of an ordnance sergeant from Fort Myers, Florida. "Heaven knows when that will be. This is 'asking for bread and receiving a stone' with a vengeance." In writing Amelia of this exchange, Josiah gave vent to his feelings toward Craig, who, he thought, was growing "imbecile & obstinate, (I hope we may soon add, obsolete)—"[20]

Yellow fever, a curious force in the Gorgas story, now did its bit to aid the young Captain. When he left Charleston on August 7 (his relief had arrived on the fourth), there was no yellow fever in the city nor the faintest whispering of it. By August 25 it had assumed epidemic proportions. Gorgas arrived at Augusta on August 11, and after an unpleasant ocean trip found everyone well and Amelia looking much

[18] Gorgas to Craig, Charleston, July 10, 1858, OLR, 1858, File G, Doc. 152; GMSD, July 14, 1858. In the latter reference Gorgas says that he was "much annoyed and very indignant" at the way he was treated and adds: "I am mortified at such want of consideration. I have not yet expressed it to the Colonel, but shall probably do so after a fuller digesting of the matter, and some others I have in mind."

[19] Craig to Gorgas, Washington, July 13, OLS, Book 20, p. 182.

[20] GMSD, July 25, 1858; Craig to Gorgas, Washington, July 19, 1858, OLS, Book 20, pp. 189–90; Gorgas to Amelia, Friday [probably July, 1858], GMSS.

better. News of yellow fever in Charleston reached the family at this time, and when they arrived in Philadelphia, on their way south, it so alarmed Gorgas that he wrote Craig he would appreciate an extension of his leave, which would expire on the twenty-ninth. He planned to await the outcome of this application at Old Point Comfort.

The matter of extension was unceremoniously taken from Craig's hands by an unexpected bit of luck. On the day the Gorgases were traveling from Philadelphia to Baltimore, John B. Floyd, Secretary of War, happened to be riding in the same car. Upon hearing of the condition of things in Charleston, Floyd granted Gorgas a verbal extension and then put him on temporary duty at Fort Monroe.[21] Floyd undoubtedly knew Judge Gayle. Craig probably growled in his lair but had to abide by Floyd's decision.

While stationed at Fort Monroe Gorgas learned of the death of one of Charleston Arsenal's blacksmiths—dead because of "yellow jack." He was the only white member of the arsenal's population who had yet contracted the scourge, though one Negro boy was reported sick.[22]

Living at Fort Monroe was far from luxurious, but Amelia enjoyed it, despite "bare floors and scanty larder," because of the society it afforded. When they first arrived at Old Point Comfort, the family took rooms in a hotel, but after several weeks of waiting finally obtained quarters in the fort itself. Probably the most interesting aspect of the leave for Gorgas was the life at the hotel. There he dined at the same table with Secretary of War Floyd, Captain William Maynadier of the Ordnance Office, and most important, with General Winfield Scott and his staff.[23] Willie and Jessie had the time of their lives on the beach, and nurse Anne Kavanagh liked Old Point so much she would have been glad to remain permanently.

In the meantime, the situation at Charleston had greatly improved, and on October 29 Craig was asked to send orders directing Gorgas'

[21] For the whole involved question of leave and extension, see, in addition to sources already cited, Gorgas to Craig, Charleston, August 3, 1858, OLR, 1858, File G, Doc. 182; Craig to Gorgas, Washington, August 7, 1858, OLS, Book 20, p. 221; Gorgas to Craig, Philadelphia, August 25, 1858, OLR, 1858, File G, Doc. 202; GMSD, January 19, 1859. This last entry includes a description of Gorgas' trip north. He went by steamer to New York and reaffirmed his determination never to go by sea when he could go by land. He thought Dr. Johnson right in saying that being at sea was "living in a prison with the privilege of being drowned."

[22] Gorgas to Craig, Old Point Comfort, October 6, 1858, OLR, 1858, File G, Doc. 226; Gorgas to Craig, Old Point Comfort, October 11, 1858, *ibid.*, Doc. 230. [23] GMSD, January 19, 1859.

return to the arsenal. The illness of the ordnance sergeant in temporary charge of the post made Gorgas anxious to get back, and he thought that it would be safe to return about November 10. Craig seemed glad to comply with this request. About the tenth of November the family packed their trunks, stuffed their carpetbags, and, with "babies, baggage and a vigorous lunch, said good-bye to . . . Old Point friends, not a few of whom accompanied us to the wharf."[24]

Gorgas no doubt was glad to be returning to his fortnightly billiard games with Dr. Dawson, and Amelia to the South. Christmas and New Year's passed, and January went by uneventfully. But the Captain was not long away from his favorite pastime, puttering around in the garden. In February he was trying to devise a way to build a small aquarium in the arsenal's yard. Even so, he was not completely lost in his landscaping. Amelia managed to get him to go to the races in February, 1859, and he enjoyed them, recalling that he had not seen a horse race in thirty years.[25]

Life moved lazily in Charleston, and leisure gave Gorgas a chance to indulge his interest in writing. In May, Paul Hamilton Hayne, distinguished southern poet and editor of Charleston's *Russell's Magazine*, began the publication of some letters on travel written by Gorgas and his travelling companion, John Hillhouse. Gorgas was not impressed by the literary merit of the series, but "what is writ is writ," so he consented to publish them.[26]

Other things contributed to making life at Charleston rich and full. On June 4, 1859, the family was increased to six when Christine Amelia—more often called "Minnie"—was born. Her father described her as "a wee, blackheaded, plump thing," and wished her a long and happy life. The next month, however, the family was greatly saddened by the death of Amelia's father, Judge Gayle, on July 21 at Mobile. When Amelia heard of it, she "was overcome with grief and wept as if her heart would break." A meeting of the Mobile bar did ample justice to Gayle's professional memory, and Gorgas was pleased to recall the many offices held by him. He had successively been representative in the Alabama legislature, judge of the Circuit Court, governor of Alabama for two terms (1833 to 1837), member of Congress in 1847 and 1848, and, at the time of his death, United States District Judge.[27]

---

[24] Gorgas to Craig, Fort Monroe, October 29, 1858, OLR, 1858, File G, Doc. 244; Craig to Gorgas, Washington, November 1, 1858, OLS, Book 20, p. 346; GMSD, January 19, 1859.   [25] GMSD, July 25, 1858; February 13, 1859.
[26] GMSD, May 24, 1859.   [27] GMSD, June 4, October 28, 1859.

By the summer of 1859 the political sky was clouding in earnest. The Republicans appeared certain to win the election of the following year, and the South seethed with the slavery question. For some weeks in November, 1859, Gorgas wrote, "the country has rung with the name of John Brown."[28] The situation began to trouble the War Department and the Ordnance Department as early as the middle of May, 1860. At this time the state of South Carolina wanted to purchase some ordnance stores in the depot at the Charleston Arsenal for the use of the state militia. This request Gorgas forwarded to the Chief of Ordnance, who replied that the "propriety" of selling stores to state militias had been submitted to the Secretary of War, and that until such time as he rendered an opinion, Gorgas should not act. If this looked serious to Gorgas, he had little time to worry over it; for on June 8, 1860, he was ordered to Frankford Arsenal at Philadelphia.[29]

He was pleased indeed to receive the command of such an important arsenal but confessed that he found "this constant breaking of fresh ties more and more disagreeable." He did not want Willie to take a commission in the Army for this very reason. This desire was to remain with him until Willie's own determination decided the issue years later. Still regretting the necessity of pulling up roots and going north, he mused: "I continually fancy how happy I could be with a spot of earth which I could call my own, which I could plant and improve; where the same things would constantly be about me; where I could live and die, and where some of my children might live and die after me."[30]

But underneath the fact of his transfer to Frankford was a story then unknown to Gorgas. Senator David L. Yulee of Florida had requested a better post than Apalachicola Depot for a friend—Storekeeper Frederick C. Humphries. This request gave Craig the opportunity for which he had been waiting, and he seized upon it, stating that a captain was wanted at Fort Leavenworth, Kansas Territory, and that the shift of Humphries would coincide with sending Gorgas to Kansas. Craig was sure that at last he could put the Captain where he could do no harm; but the singular good luck which never seemed to fail Gorgas in a moment of crisis once again intervened in his behalf. The Secretary of War himself, knowing Gorgas, made a change in the orders and sent the popular Major Hagner to Kansas and gave Gorgas his post, Frankford. Gorgas became finally aware of all this, and was

[28] GMSD, December 5, 1859.
[29] Craig to Gorgas, Washington, May 17 and June 4, 1860, OLS, Book 27, pp. 48, 78; GMSD, June 3, 1860.   [30] GMSD, June 3, 1860.

duly grateful to Floyd. Captain Maynadier quaintly described the result of Craig's attempted *coup d'etat* by telling Gorgas: "Our Colonel aimed at a Crow, and shot his neighbor's sow."[31]

The Gorgases left Charleston July 9 and, stopping for a day's visit with the Aiken in-laws at Winnsboro, South Carolina, reached Frankford Arsenal on July 13, 1860.[32] Most of his time there Gorgas spent in experimenting with tin and brass cartridge cases. This experience was to prove of considerable use later.[33] His knowledge of and interest in ordnance and its improvements had now aroused the attention of his superiors. On October 6, 1860, he was appointed to the Ordnance Board. This was no small honor. The Board had charge of considering and recommending all new inventions and improvements for the Ordnance service, and from the manner in which Craig announced Gorgas' appointment to him, it seems that Floyd must personally have made the assignment.[34]

Not all of Gorgas' time was consumed on his post. Some of it he used to make inspection tours to investigate the powder made by the Hazard Powder Company, at Hazardville, Connecticut, and by the E. I. Dupont de Nemours Company of Wilmington, Delaware. He made a few such trips in February of 1861.[35]

At this point fate again took a hand in the affairs of Captain Gorgas, when Colonel Craig made one of the biggest mistakes of his career as Chief of Ordnance. In February, during the initial organization of the Provisional Government of the Confederate States of America, Gorgas, at the behest of General P. G. T. Beauregard, had been offered a majority in the Confederacy's corps of artillery, to be detailed to ordnance duty. He declined, giving as his reason a desire to stay at Frankford through the summer because of Amelia's

[31] GMSD, June 14, 1860.   [32] GMSD, August 7, 1860.

[33] Craig to Gorgas, Washington, September 24, 1860, OLS, Book 27, p. 240.

[34] Gorgas was in excellent company on the Board. Appointed with him were Maj. T. T. S. Laidley, Capt. A. B. Dyer, and Capt. T. J. Rodman. Rodman was an inventor of the first rank. His process for determining the gravimetric densities and hydometric properties of niter was to aid the Confederacy considerably, though Rodman himself remained with the Union. See Cullum, *Officers and Graduates of the U. S. M. A.*, II, 67–71. Craig's letter informing Gorgas of his appointment reads: "By direction from the War Department, of this date, you are appointed a Member of the Ordnance Board." Craig to Gorgas, Washington, October 6, 1860, OLS, Book 27, p. 253.

[35] Craig to Gorgas, February 2, 9, 1861, OLS, Book 27, pp. 386, 397; Gorgas to Craig, Frankford Arsenal, February 22, 1861, OLR, 1861, File G, Doc. 73. See Gorgas' Inspection Report, dated March 4, 1861, OLR, Book 31, March 5, 1861, Doc. 80.

health. But, of course, such a move involved serious and soul-searching consideration. Craig became the instrument of Providence and on March 20, 1861, ordered Gorgas to foundry duty. He was to turn over command of Frankford to Captain Maynadier, whom Craig had at last succeeded in getting out of Washington, and report to the Inspector of Ordnance, Colonel Benjamin Huger.[36] This was an assignment which made Gorgas rage, and he felt that he "might as well make one move of it and go where I should ultimately have to go, I doubt not."[37] Craig's obvious revenge, plus the advent of Simon Cameron as Secretary of War and the urgings of his Southern friends, encouraged Gorgas to resign, March 21, 1861, effective April 3.[38] It was a heart-rending decision for him, and he made it alone, for Amelia had remained a silent onlooker. She knew that all of Josiah's ties—except his politics—were with the Union and that all his relatives were good Yankees. She knew also that he must decide for himself—must weigh states' rights and "Black Republicanism" against each other, and think of the spectre of the Marcy-Buchanan controversy, which had never been totally forgotten. Then, too, there was Craig's animosity. Southern though she was by birth and tradition, Amelia was content with any course her husband could take.

The decision to resign had been made easier in one sense by the fact that the Confederacy offered a place to go. Although knowing Gorgas only slightly, General Beauregard had continued to recommend him to President Davis as the man for the post of Chief of Ordnance. Beauregard had been in correspondence with Gorgas about the possibility of a commission in the Confederate service; and as conditions got worse under Craig's heavy hand, Gorgas began to give more serious consideration to these proposals. On a trip to Watervliet in March he had received another letter from Beauregard, and on the 10th he replied:

Before definitively [sic] accepting a position in the Confederate States, I must know the nature of the place I am to fill. I hope you will have written to me before this reaches you. All my sympathies are with you. Yet as affairs look more peaceful now than ever perhaps, I hesitate to act, unless I am wanted, or unless I am tempted greatly to my advantage.

[36] Craig to Gorgas, Washington, March 21, 1861, OLS, Book 27, p. 439.
[37] GMSD, March 31, 1861.
[38] Gorgas to Craig, Frankford, March 27, 1861, OLR, 1861, File G, Doc. 99; GMSD, March 31, 1861. It seems clear that Cameron's appearance in the War Department coincided with the deterioration of Gorgas' Army status. Just why is not clear, but the circumstance should not be overlooked.

Being in command it would be impossible for me to throw up my duties until relieved. If you have not written please write what my place is to be. With renewed prospects of a peaceful separation, I hope there will be the less necessity for haste. . . .[39]

The news of his choice as Chief of Ordnance made his final decision almost a foregone conclusion, apart from political or family considerations.

The choice of Gorgas for the important office of Chief of Ordnance of the Confederacy was largely one of necessity. His record in the Army was not particularly distinguished, but he was the only professional ordnance man apparently available. Neither Beauregard nor Davis deserves credit for prescience in this appointment—only for practicality.

Gorgas' letter of resignation to President Lincoln was sent to the Ordnance Office, thence to Simon Cameron, Secretary of War, and was accepted on April 2. As he thought of it some years later, Gorgas felt that Washington officials had accepted his resignation with alacrity and that he obviously had not been a favorite with the hierarchy at that time.[40]

With mixed emotions he transferred the arsenal to Maynadier on April 2, and the family left next day for Charleston, from where Gorgas proceeded alone to Montgomery to report to the newly elected President of the Confederacy, Jefferson Davis, whom Gorgas knew slightly, and to the Secretary of War, Leroy P. Walker.[41] He accepted the commission as major of Artillery on Ordnance duty, and his course for the next years lay clearly before him.

---

[39] Abstract of Gorgas to Beauregard, Watervliet Arsenal, March 10, 1861, printed in Catalogue 1148, "The Beauregard Papers," auctioned by Stan V. Henkels, Philadelphia, October 25, 1915, p. 68, No. 327.

[40] Gorgas to Amelia, Winnsboro, S. C., May 4, 1865, GMSS.

[41] GMSD, March 31, 1861.

V

The Confederate States of America

WHEN MAJOR GORGAS REPORTED FOR DUTY, LEROY POPE WALKER and his Department of War presented a picture of chaos. War seemed imminent; Lincoln had called for volunteers to enforce the laws of the Union, and the South grappled with the problem of infusing some sort of order and discipline into the swarming humanity which constituted her armies. Obviously no one quite knew what was going on or where troops should go. Perhaps location made it expedient to send troops collecting in the Confederate capital of Montgomery to General Braxton Bragg, who had been charged with the task of maintaining Confederate control of the harbor of Pensacola, where the Federal garrison of Fort Pickens refused to surrender. Despite various efforts to dislodge them, the Federals were able to hang tenaciously to their little spot of ground. This fact may have somewhat perturbed Gorgas, since it was probably because of his repairs to the fort several years before that the Union troops were able to hold out.

As Gorgas surveyed the job he suddenly found thrust upon him, on every hand were all kinds of good intentions, but they were misdirected and dissociated. Many of the Southern states, acting on the spur of the moment and in the first flush of restored "sovereignty," had made loose, haphazard efforts to prepare for some sort of conflict, though they apparently thought fighting would be on a Lilliputian scale.

Acting far ahead of the rest in self-protection as it had in secession, South Carolina early had established a Board of Ordnance to take charge of the state's needs in the matter of arms, and the people's convention as well as the legislature showed immense interest in making

[55]

appropriations for public defense.[1] The chief ordnance officer, Colonel Edward Manigault, soon engaged in strenuous efforts to collect and prepare arms and ammunition for the state forces. Though the Confederate government ultimately would take over the task, Manigault and the South Carolina board continued to function as a state agency.[2]

No sooner had other Southern states accepted responsibility for their own defense than they, too, engaged in plans and efforts to provide means of protection. Tennessee, for example, put its limited powder-making facilities in Nashville to work, and Texas, never to be outdone, established the Texas State Military Board to handle its military affairs.[3] North Carolina also went into the matter of military preparation with accustomed verve. Soon the legislature began active subsidy of one war industry. The firm of Waterhouse and Bowes, located on a little creek near Raleigh, started powder manufacture, which would attract the favorable notice of the Confederate Ordnance Bureau.[4] The Tar Heel state also developed a zealously guarded monopoly on Confederate supplies of milled cloth.[5]

Prior to the organization of the Confederate government in Montgomery in February, 1861, certain seceding states had, on their own initiative, undertaken a rather nebulous form of military co-operation. South Carolina and Georgia, the latter state militantly led by vociferous Governor Joseph E. Brown, decided to aid Florida and Alabama as much as possible. This act of generosity undoubtedly had its foundation as much in a desire to have other partners in secession as in pure altruism. At any rate, Governors Brown and Francis Pickens exchanged telegraphic messages concerning the number of guns their respective states could send to their neighbors, with South Carolina deciding that

[1] Proceedings of the South Carolina House of Representatives, quoted in the Charleston *Daily Courier,* December 5, 1860; *Pickens and Bonham Papers* (microfilm in The University of Texas Archives Collection); *Miscellaneous Military Papers Concerning South Carolina; Acts of the General Assembly of the State of South Carolina, passed in November and December, 1860, and January, 1861* (Columbia, 1861).

[2] Vandiver, "The South Carolina Ordnance Board, 1860–1861," *Proceedings of the South Carolina Historical Association,* 1945, pp. 14–22.

[3] For an excellent discussion of the duties and activities of this board, see Charles W. Ramsdell, "The Texas State Military Board, 1862–1865," *Southwestern Historical Quarterly,* XXVII (1923–24), 253–75.

[4] See the Raleigh *State Journal,* January 15, 1862.

[5] Charles W. Ramsdell, "The Control of Manufacturing by the Confederate Government," *Mississippi Valley Historical Review,* VIII (1921–22), 231–49.

four thousand United States muskets could be spared Florida without detriment to herself.[6]

Since no state entered the Confederacy without having made some individual move toward self-preservation, Gorgas, on his assignment to the Ordnance Bureau, would have to take into careful, tactful consideration all of the men and plans the states had developed. Tact would be a prime necessity because of the intense jealousy displayed by some of the states for their rights and prerogatives.

By the time Special Orders Number 17, Confederate Adjutant General's Office, officially assigning Major Gorgas as Chief of Ordnance, was issued on April 8, 1861, the Confederate Provisional Congress had already made some provision for the creation of an ordnance bureau. On February 20, 1861, it had passed "An Act to provide Munitions of War, and for other purposes," authorizing the President or the Secretary of War to contract for the purchase and manufacture of heavy ordnance and of small arms; for machinery to manufacture or alter small arms and ammunition, and to employ the necessary agents and artisans to accomplish these objectives. The act also provided for the establishment of powder mills and for the manufacture of powder.[7] The powder provision undoubtedly was included because of Jefferson Davis' personal conviction of its necessity. Eight days after this act was passed, another, entitled "An Act to raise Provisional Forces for the Confederate States of America, and for other purposes" found approval, authorizing the President to receive all the arms and munitions which the several states had captured from the United States, and such other equipment as the states might wish to give to the Confederacy.[8] On March 6, 1861, Congress passed the law which most affected Gorgas. "An Act for the establishment and organization of the Army of the Confederate States of America" provided for the formation of a Corps of Artillery, charged with ordnance duty, and set up a table of authorized personnel. This allowed one colonel, two lieutenant colonels, and ten majors. Gorgas, following Confederate practice, was appointed

[6] Brown to Pickens, Milledgeville, Ga., January 8, 1860 [1861], *Miscellaneous Military Papers Concerning South Carolina;* James Jones to Pickens, Charleston, January 19, 1861, *Pickens and Bonham Papers; Appleton's Annual Cyclopaedia,* 1861, p. 656.

[7] James M. Matthews (ed.), *Statutes at Large of the Provisional Congress of the Confederate States of America* (Richmond, 1864), Stat. I, Chap. IV. For the order assigning Gorgas as Chief of Ordnance, see ORA, Ser. IV, Vol. I, 211.

[8] *Statutes of the Provisional Congress,* Stat. I, Chap. XXII.

to the Army with the rank of major, one grade above that which he had held in the United States Army.[9] This same law authorized the President to enlist as many master-armorers, master-carriage makers, master-blacksmiths, armorers, carriage makers, blacksmiths, artificers, and laborers as might be required, so long as the number appointed did not exceed one hundred. Following up this initial move toward mobilizing an orderly ordnance service, the Provisional Congress, on March 16, appropriated $110,000 for "the purchase of ordnance and ordnance stores."[10]

These official moves had been supplemented by certain efforts made by Davis himself. Not convinced that the South would be allowed to escape the drain of a long, desperate struggle, the President early became an advocate of careful preparation. Acting on this impulse he selected a trusted officer, Raphael Semmes, formerly of the United States Navy, to undertake a purchasing mission to the North. To a man of Semmes's temperament, such a mission could have been nothing short of exhilarating. With much battle experience in the Mexican War behind him, he was serving on the sedentary Lighthouse Board in Washington when the war began. At once he cast his lot with his native Alabama, proceeded to Montgomery, and accepted the President's secret commission. Under these orders he visited Washington, New York, and various New England cities to buy munitions. He met with more success than probably either he or Davis had anticipated, and by the time he returned to the Confederacy had shipped or had arranged the shipment of a considerable quantity of supplies.[11]

So it came about that on all hands Gorgas encountered abounding enthusiasm to do what was best but abysmal ignorance of the correct course to pursue. From the outset he understood the peculiarities of the problems facing Confederate supply bureaus. First, of course, they had nothing to work with—no supplies to issue. This brought up the question of accumulation. Second, they had limited funds with which to do their purchasing. This brought up the perennial question of money. Third, they commanded outright only limited transportation, and that mostly in the form of wagons. This brought up the question

[9] *Ibid.*, Chap. XXIX.

[10] "Ae [An] Act making additional appropriations for the support of the Army, for the year ending the first of March, eighteen hundred and sixty-two," *ibid.*, Chap. LXV.

[11] Jefferson Davis to Raphael Semmes, Montgomery, February 21, 1861, ORA, Ser. IV, Vol. I, 106–107; W. Adolphe Roberts, *Semmes of the Alabama* (Indianapolis, 1938), p. 38.

of relations with privately owned railroads. Fourth—and this seemed particularly an ordnance problem—few modern weapons were available in arsenals or depots in the South. This raised the problem which pressed the hardest: where could the Confederacy get an ample supply of guns and munitions?

On the credit side of the ledger, Gorgas saw, of course, that the South had a certain tactical advantage which could, if utilized wisely, mitigate some of the adverse factors which it was facing. The Confederate States could wage war at all points on an inner line of communications. This held true on the coast line or along the western frontier. Confederate logisticians had to capitalize on this advantage since it was about the only one they possessed. But this logistical situation posed a problem in itself. The Confederacy's efforts to obtain, store, and issue quartermaster, commissary, medical, engineer, and ordnance supplies were the basis for an idea which Gorgas conceived and would long cherish—the need for the establishment of a central testing and manufacturing laboratory and a national armory.

Though overburdened by his duties as Chief of Ordnance, Gorgas, undoubtedly because of his known qualifications along military mechanical lines, on April 8, 1861, was given the additional assignment of Acting Chief of the Engineer Bureau, a position which alone imposed more administrative and clerical work than one man could handle.[12]

Taking careful stock of what resources he had with which to begin the seemingly impossible job of putting guns and bullets into eager hands of infantry and cavalry organizations, and cannon and ammunition into the hands of the Confederacy's field and fort artillery, Gorgas first tallied the amount of arms and munitions transferred by the various Confederate states to the general government. He knew that existing facilities for manufacturing ordnance stores in the South were meager and crude and that he would have to rely on Virginia's large Tredegar Iron Works, in Richmond, for almost all of the heavy ordnance and heavy machinery, and on the Richmond and Fayetteville arsenals for the production of small arms. The production of ammunition would have to be farmed out to all the arsenals and armories in the southern states, and to any other shop or laboratory which could possibly be persuaded to undertake the job.[13]

[12] ORA, Ser. IV, Vol. I, 1176.

[13] See Broun, p. 366; Mallet, *passim;* and [Thomas L. Bayne], "Sketch of the Life of Josiah Gorgas," *Southern Historical Society Papers,* XIII (1885), 216–228.

He had to watch, too, for the best way to further the interests of the Engineer Department as well as his own bureau. He wrote, apparently for the information of the War Department, several elaborate papers on the proper lines of Confederate defenses, taking the somewhat radical view that it was unnecessary to place heavy armament or concentrate troops at Pensacola, but that these should, instead, go to such outer lines in the North and West as the Confederacy proposed to hold.[14]

While the newly appointed Chief of Ordnance had to be concerned with the purely administrative task of forging the crudest sort of initial organization for his bureau, he had also to take care of the wants of the various Confederate military forces crying for arms and ammunition. The loudest pleas came from General Albert Sidney Johnston, commanding the Confederate forces charged with holding the frontiers of Tennessee and with the defense of the Mississippi River. Ammunition had to go to Charleston and Pensacola, to the jittery troops along North Carolina's coast, and, on the secession of the Old Dominion, to the troops holding the Confederacy's northern border along the Potomac. The whole task of this initial supply Gorgas had to accomplish virtually alone. The complete organization of his bureau, with its comparatively well-experienced personnel, would not materialize until well along in 1862, and until then Major Gorgas was the mainspring of Confederate ordnance. He was not slow to conduct a complete survey of the number of small arms in the South and of all the ordnance supplies of various kinds that he could draw upon.

To the chairman of the congressional Committee on Military Affairs, F. S. Bartow, Gorgas confided the figures on the Confederacy's ordnance resources in a report on May 7, 1861. Bartow was told the cold, hard fact that the South had found in all its arsenals the appallingly small total of 159,010 small arms of all kinds. Baton Rouge Arsenal contained United States rifle muskets, caliber .69 rifle muskets, new and altered percussion muskets, flint muskets, Harpers Ferry rifles, Colt rifles, Hall rifles, various types of carbines, Colt and percussion pistols— in all some 47,372 arms. Mount Vernon Arsenal held 19,455; Charleston, 22,469; Augusta, 27,714; Little Rock, 10,000; Fayetteville, 37,000. Gorgas estimated that there were about 3,200,000 cartridges for small arms in all the southern arsenals, along with 168,000 pounds of musket and rifle powder, which could be made into some 1,500,000 more cartridges. Almost all the Confederacy's available cannon powder

[14] Bayne, *op. cit.,* pp. 217–18.

was located at the various permanent fortifications, only a limited amount being held in a general reserve. Baton Rouge Arsenal gladdened the heart of the Chief of Ordnance by having on hand enough fixed ammunition "to supply ten batteries of six guns each." The supply of percussion caps, one of the most vital needs of the Ordnance Bureau, exceeded two million in Montgomery, with "a good many at the arsenals and bundled with the cartridges." It was Gorgas' understanding that "Georgia has 150 tons of saltpeter, with a proportionate quantity of sulphur; this will make quite 200 tons of powder."[15] The question was: could Governor Brown be persuaded to part with these items?

Fully understanding the magnitude of his task, Gorgas began to organize for provisional operations. One of his first moves was to recommend the dispatch of an agent to Europe to purchase arms and munitions for the Ordnance Bureau. The man selected for this important mission, Major Caleb Huse, had a solid military background and enjoyed Gorgas' complete confidence. He undertook the job armed only with letters of credit on the English import-export banking firm of Fraser, Trenholm & Company, amounting to the pitifully small sum of £10,000. But the wisdom of sending Huse to Europe and of the choice of the man would be amply demonstrated as the war progressed.[16]

The Chief of Ordnance moved, also, to develop and expand the South's existing resources, industrial, mechanical, and mineral. After inspection, the various arsenals in the Confederacy were overhauled and enlarged. For example, the workshops at Charleston—Gorgas' old post—were expanded and steam power was installed; shops were maintained at Montgomery for the repair of small arms and for the manufacture of leather goods; small ordnance establishments were started at Knoxville, Tennessee, Jackson, Mississippi, and Dublin, Lynchburg, and Danville, Virginia. The ordnance shops at Nashville were among the most important for the maintenance of supplies for Johnston's army in Tennessee. Columbus, Georgia, obviously because of its central location and transportation facilities, became one of the prize establishments of Gorgas' department, he himself referring to it as "the nucleus of our Ordnance establishment."[17] The Confederacy's sources of niter were restricted to what was captured and to what could be secured from caves and artificial niter beds. Iron could be obtained in fair quantity in Alabama, but only with great effort.

[15] ORA, Ser. IV, Vol. I, 292.   [16] *Ibid.*, p. 220.   [17] GOC, p. 284.

Of the three sources of arms, blockade-running, home manufacture, and capture on the battlefield, only the last held any prospect of immediate return on investment. Blockade-running would certainly prove of vast importance, but only in time. Home manufacture showed little chance of yielding appreciable results for a considerable period, and then only after heartbreaking work on the part of the Ordnance Bureau. The main stumbling block in this connection was the amazing dearth of skilled mechanics. But the battlefields were a solvent account. Fort Sumter had been taken in April, and the Army was shifting to take up the line of the northern frontier, with its position apparently centering along Bull Run Creek near the town of Manassas, Virginia. But as yet there had been no serious military contact. Even so, this seemed to be the most immediate source of relief for the Ordnance Bureau, always providing, of course, that the Confederate Army won the battles.

Major Gorgas, however, could not sit by and count on the might of untried Confederate arms to solve his dilemma. He had already begun to act and now went into the question with even more vigor. By April 21 news had reached the people that Harpers Ferry, with its famed United States Arsenal, had been abandoned by Federal forces and burned, with the Confederates capturing some five thousand Minié muskets.[18] This was a valuable addition to Gorgas' stores, and he made plans to utilize, also, whatever machinery had not been made useless by the flames.[19]

Gorgas' efforts were not confined to the acquisition of the Harpers Ferry machinery. He began, perforce, a practice which under more stable circumstances he would probably have avoided. Realizing the inadequacy of governmental manufacturing facilities, he cast about for companies with whom he could contract for equipment. One of the most promising of these firms proved to be the Etowah Foundry in Georgia. It was of sufficient size to justify the hope that, with adequate government coddling, it might produce artillery. Many reasons could be found to dictate caution in making a contract with any company for government supplies; the subsidy might tempt the contractor to slow down production to obtain further financial aid, or, worse yet, the

[18] Montgomery *Weekly Post,* April 24, 1861.

[19] Gorgas to L. P. Walker, Montgomery, April 25, 1861, *Confederate States War Department Reports* (Montgomery, 1861). Gorgas was not certain that the state of Virginia would permit the transfer of the Harpers Ferry machinery to the Confederacy, but he was sure enough to recommend to Walker the appropriation of extra funds.

whole project might fizzle out after considerable waste of time and money. But Gorgas was in a situation which demanded action, cost what it might. Besides, he felt that the Etowah Works possessed the advantage of excellent sources of iron ore. He placed an order "for a number of eight and ten inch Columbiads, with iron carriages for them together with ordnance of small calibre, mortars and beds, shot and shell."[20]

Concerned, of course, with the strength of the Confederate sea fortifications, Gorgas ordered twenty fifteen-inch Columbiads from the Tredegar Iron Works and, relying also on the guns ordered from the Etowah Foundry, felt reasonably well satisfied about coastal forts. He had reported to the Secretary of War a scant eight days after the bombardment of Fort Sumter that Forts Moultrie, Sumter, and Castle Pinckney, in Charleston Harbor, held 375 guns, and that other fortifications and various arsenals contained enough heavy artillery to bring the total number of guns to 429.[21] He also told the Secretary that "iron clad steamers are of no avail against eight, ten and fifteen inch Columbiads, and when the armament contemplated shall be in position, our seaboard may be regarded as secure against attack by sea."[22] This prediction was somewhat premature.

At the same time that he was endeavoring to make the coastline impregnable, Gorgas submitted to Secretary Walker the quarterly estimate of funds required by the Ordnance Bureau. Previous appropriations, which when made seemed so large, now were dwarfed by the estimated cost of myriad duties imposed on the service. The Secretary read that for the quarter ending June 30, 1861, Gorgas would need, to cover outstanding orders and future purchases of ordnance, $1,066,252.47, minus $666,252.27 which he was in the process of spending. The Chief of Ordnance estimated the need for the quarter ending September 30, 1861, at $1,880,000. At the same time, in his capacity as Acting Chief of Engineers, Gorgas estimated the needs of that service as $100,000 for the quarter ending June 30, and $250,000 for the quarter ending September 30.[23]

[20] *Confederate War Department Reports.*

[21] Exhibit of ordnance on hand, signed by Gorgas, Montgomery, April 20, 1861, ORA, Ser. IV, Vol. I, pp. 227–28. When this exhibit was made up, Gorgas had stated his estimate of small arms on hand as 106,165 (as compared to 159,010 estimated in May). He admitted that the returns for the various forts and arsenals were incomplete and that he could not, as a consequence, give an accurate account.

[22] Gorgas to Walker, Montgomery, April 25, 1861, *Confederate War Department Reports.*

[23] Estimate of funds, signed by Gorgas, April 25, 1861, AGPF, Gorgas.

Gorgas' views on other matters pertaining to the ordnance service had not gone unheeded by the Secretary of War. In a report to the President dated April 27, Walker urged the necessity of providing some domestic source of powder since the Northern avenues opened up by the President's early efforts had now been closed. The Secretary earnestly recommended the establishment of powder mills in the Confederacy and relied on the President's judgment of the seriousness of the problem. At the same time he added with satisfaction that all of the separate states had completed the cession of their military sites and equipment to the Confederate government.[24] The Secretary was optimistic.

The Chief of Ordnance still counted on the states for considerable assistance in the problem of mobilizing the various local units for Confederate service. He suggested to Walker that the governors be notified that arms and ammunition would be supplied to troops at points where they were to rendezvous for active duty.

Let the troops be notified beforehand by the State authorities to equip themselves with such temporary knap sacks, haversacks, and canteens as each individual can prepare for himself. The central Government will supply these of good quality at the place of rendezvous as fast as they can be made. This will in a great measure prevent the perplexing and mischievous requisitions of Governors of States on the arsenals.[25]

Gorgas did not allow himself to become enmeshed in useless trivia. He saw this plan as a way to avoid unnecessary confusion and did not hesitate to adopt it. His fearless determination to shun the tentacles of detail was one of the cardinal factors in his gift for organization.

Meanwhile, during the time he had been directing all of his attention to purely military measures for the public defense, certain private citizens of the Confederacy had also been concerning themselves with the same problem, but from a different standpoint. A group of neocapitalists in Alabama, anxious to attach themselves to the Confederate bandwagon and ride for all the subsidy was worth, urged on their representatives in Congress the wisdom of buying the Selma Manufacturing Company for ordnance purposes.[26] Two members of this group,

[24] Walker to Davis, Montgomery, April 27, 1861, ORA, Ser. IV, Vol. I, 249.
[25] Gorgas to Walker, Montgomery, May 4, 1861, ibid., p. 280.
[26] Edward T. Watts, R. N. Philpot, and J. M. Lapsley to Robert H. Smith and Colin J. McRae, Selma, Ala., February 22, 1861, ibid., pp. 107–108. The argument for an armory in Selma was supported by the Montgomery Weekly Post, May 8, 11, 1861. See also GOC, p. 284.

Colin J. McRae and J. M. Lapsley were to have a long and profitable connection with the Ordnance Bureau, but the problem posed by groups such as these men represented, each pressing its own pet industrial project, each insistent on attention and exorbitant remuneration, would give the Chief of Ordnance many worried days.

By the time the Confederate government packed up its various offices and moved to Richmond in late May, 1861, Gorgas could look with justifiable pride on his accomplishments during the short time he had been in charge. He had convinced a somewhat skeptical Congress that the Ordnance Department would have to have money and lots of it—had convinced Congress so well, in fact, that on May 21, the last day it met in Montgomery, it appropriated $4,440,000 for the ordnance service.[27] Among many other things, this money was to purchase heavy ordnance, shot, and shell; sixteen field batteries of six pieces each; and 50,000 small arms along with 5,000 pistols and holsters. Some would be used, too, for arsenal bullet and cap machinery.

Gorgas had so persevered in improving the condition of Confederate arsenals that Augusta Arsenal had been put to work preparing ammunition and knapsacks; Charleston Arsenal and Savannah Depot had been directed to attend the wants of the harbor defenses in those ports; Baton Rouge Arsenal rapidly moved toward production as did Gorgas' old Mount Vernon, though "none of these had had facilities for the work usually done at an Arsenal." Fayetteville Arsenal, in North Carolina, still in state hands, was occupied in repairing some arms and making a limited amount of small arms ammunition. Richmond Arsenal contributed most of the supply of artillery ammunition.[28]

As to actual issues to troops, Gorgas had managed to supply the army in observation at Harpers Ferry and at Manassas with old batteries of six-pounders, twelve-pounder howitzers, and a few Parrott guns. Johnny Reb carried a unique assortment of many-calibered weapons, ranging from 1812 flintlocks to Enfield rifles.[29] Having thus scratched together ragtag equipment for a tatterdemalion army, Gorgas picked up his office furnishings and departed with the other War Department bureaus for Richmond in late May of the war's first year.[30]

[27] Gorgas to Walker, Montgomery, April 25, 1861, *Confederate War Department Reports; Statutes of the Provisional Congress,* Stat. II, Chap. XXXV.
[28] GOC, p. 213.　　[29] *Ibid.*
[30] Montgomery *Weekly Post,* June 5, 1861.

VI

State Rights and Hurried Organization

GORGAS ARRIVED IN RICHMOND ON SUNDAY, JUNE 2, 1861. THAT evening he walked around the city by moonlight, pondering his problem. Darkness brought some relief from the oppressive heat of the day[1] and made walking the wide, uneven streets more comfortable. From the rows of houses down by the armory, to the rows of tobacco warehouses along the river, Richmond was now an armed camp. Major General Robert E. Lee of the Virginia state forces had achieved amazing success in putting the Virginia army in fighting trim, and Richmond with its industrial resources supplied most of the state's munitions. Now Gorgas must take over for the entire Confederacy. Though his job no doubt worried him, he must at the same time have been encouraged to see the glow of the furnaces at the Tredegar Iron Works reflected against the night sky. These works, which had been making munitions since 1840, were built up to such a high production level by able ironmaster Joseph R. Anderson, that they became the most important in the southern states. Now that Virginia had joined the Confederacy, Gorgas looked with confidence to the Tredegar for heavy equipment of all kinds.

As Gorgas continued his reflective walk, his eye picked out buildings and his mind made notes. By the time he had returned to the Spotswood House,[2] his temporary headquarters, he had evolved a *modus operandi*. The old Virginia Armory itself would serve as the main ordnance office; with its proximity to the Tredegar Works, it would provide a fine point of command for the Chief of Ordnance. Gorgas knew that there were many other small iron foundries in Richmond, which would have to be relied on for desperately needed material.

[1] *Daily Richmond Examiner*, June 4, 1861.   [2] *Ibid.*, June 3, 1861.

There had to be an arsenal, and a number of tobacco factories at the end of Seventh Street, between the James and Cary Street, seemed to present the most suitable place to establish one.[3] Gorgas was not slow to put his plans into effect. By evening of the next day, the third, he had obtained possession of such buildings as he thought indispensable to the Ordnance Bureau and set up his office.[4] It could not have been long after Gorgas got it running that he found out the extent of the trouble brewing with the Virginia State Ordnance Department, commanded by acid Colonel Charles Dimmock.

It could not have been long, because Dimmock was not the silent sort. Besides, he harbored the smoldering idea that Gorgas would in time take over his job. Consequently he jealously guarded the rights of Virginia in all of the machine shops, iron factories, and other plants around Richmond. Still more important and irksome, he steadfastly maintained the title of the state to the rifle and musket machinery taken from the United States Armory at Harpers Ferry. It will be recalled that Gorgas had wanted these machines, for they were particularly adapted to the making of rifles and rifle muskets. But Dimmock stood his obstructionist ground and waited. Soon he learned the result of his policy. Secretary Walker received a letter from the Chief of Ordnance, which candidly pointed out the serious consequences arising from Virginia's stand on sovereign rights. "It is impossible," wrote Gorgas, "to attend satisfactorily to the wants of the troops in the field without having control of the supplies prepared here. The ammunition and other Ordnance Stores are at present issued only on the order of Colonel Dimmock. . . . This should be remedied at once by placing all operations of the State Ordnance Department under the control of the Bureau of Ordnance of the Confederate States. I earnestly ask your attention to this subject."[5] Still Dimmock waited for orders from John Letcher, Governor of Virginia.

By the time Gorgas outlined to the Secretary of War a plan for supplying regiments by sending stores to the ordnance officer of the largest unit under which the regiment operated, for issue locally,[6] his trouble with the Virginia authorities had again flared. Having found that the Texas Arsenal had 4,200 arms on hand, Baton Rouge, none,

[3] Broun, p. 367.

[4] Amelia Gorgas to Thomas L. Bayne, Tuscaloosa, August 9, 1883, GMSS.

[5] Gorgas to Walker, Richmond, June 5, 1861, CRLR, 1861, Doc. 1245. Microfilm copies of all letters cited from this collection are in the writer's possession.

[6] Gorgas to Walker, Richmond, June 23, 1861, ibid., Doc. 1674.

Mount Vernon, 1,200, Augusta, none, Charleston, 500, Lynchburg, 1,100, Montgomery, 3,000, and Richmond 5,000—in all 15,000[7]— Gorgas pushed harder for the final transfer of the Harpers Ferry machinery to his jurisdiction. On July 3 he issued an order directing that all the "shafting, vises, tools, &c., now at the Central depot, from Harpers Ferry, belonging to the rifle factory, will be transferred to W. S. Downer for shipment to Fayetteville as rapidly as possible." A general inventory was to be made of the machinery in Richmond, and a detailed inventory at Fayetteville, and anything belonging to the musket factory was to be returned to Richmond—by order of the Secretary of War.[8] It mattered not who directed or issued these instructions, since the Chief of Virginia Ordnance did not feel at all constrained to obey any directive concerning his precious machinery. It was a situation calling for abounding tact on everybody's part, and Dimmock, possessed of little, refused to obey orders. James H. Burton, Dimmock's subordinate, wrote him on July 8 that during the morning Major Gorgas (whose disparity in rank did nothing to raise Confederate prestige in this matter) had sent him instructions to supply certain essential equipment for the repair of arms. Virginia's master-armorer had received orders, also from Gorgas, said Burton, to turn over three turning lathes and driving gears. Burton had become cautious, possibly as a result of association, and added: "I have as yet received no authority to comply with such requisitions, and I therefore respectfully request that you will favor me with your instructions as to how I shall act in the premises." Dimmock's directions were curt: "Until the order of the Governor is received this department cannot be governed by orders from elsewhere."[9] Apparently undismayed by Dimmock's disobedience, Gorgas on the eleventh directed the master-armorer to deliver to Downer the lead which had recently been received from Harpers Ferry. This order, too, was issued under the direction of the Secretary of War, but Dimmock again instructed the master-armorer to await orders from the Governor. He argued, somewhat obtusely, that the lead from Harpers Ferry was not machinery but material, apparently conceding some rights to the Confederacy. In disgust Gorgas forwarded this reply to the

[7] "Statement of Arms in the hands of the Confederate States with their location, not in the hands of Troops," signed by Gorgas, Richmond, June 29, 1861, *Dreer Manuscripts Collection.*

[8] Order, signed by Gorgas, Richmond, July 3, 1861, ORA, Ser. IV, Vol. I, 471.

[9] Burton to Dimmock, and indorsement, Richmond, July 8, 1861, *ibid.,* p. 472.

Secretary without comment.[10] But he did give vent to his feelings in a letter to Dimmock. Dimmock's indorsement, wrote Gorgas, had been referred to the Secretary of War. "You will excuse me for calling your attention to the fact that your action may involve serious embarrassment to the troops in the field."[11]

Finally deciding that some sort of understanding would have to be reached if the Confederacy hoped to accomplish anything with the Virginia machinery, Gorgas, on the twelfth, wrote Dimmock: "Will you do me the favor to see me at your leisure in reference to the tools required. . . . By retaining the tools necessary to our operations in the laboratory the State does great injury to the common defense." Dimmock, however, sagely avoided an interview with the piercing Gorgas. "The tools," he argued, "never were in the laboratory, and never formed any part of that establishment, but belong to the musket machinery."[12] He had wandered considerably from the point in his eagerness to avoid contact with the Chief of Ordnance. Gorgas had not maintained that the tools in question ever had been a part of the laboratory—the point was that Virginia insisted on retaining the tools for state use. Dimmock stood on exceedingly weak ground and he knew it. Backing up his Chief of Ordnance with creditable promptness, Walker wrote to Governor Letcher the same day inquiring whether, in view of an enclosed letter from Gorgas with Dimmock's indorsement, "the government of Virginia designs to keep up a separate and distinct ordnance department?" The point had to be understood, and soon. Walker added:

The precise point to which I would now call the attention of Your Excellency is whether the lead taken from Harper's Ferry on Tuesday last is to be subject to the orders of this Department, or only to the orders of the Virginia authorities. In deciding this point I beg Your Excellency will recollect that the lead aforesaid has been removed since the transfer to the Confederate States of the machinery, &c., which had been seized at Harper's Ferry.[13]

This missive brought prompt results. The next day George W. Munford, Secretary of the Commonwealth, replied for the Governor that in accordance with established policy Dimmock had been ordered to com-

[10] Gorgas to S. Adams, and indorsement, Richmond, CRLR, 1861, Doc. 2022.
[11] Gorgas to Dimmock, Richmond, July 11, 1861, ORA, Ser. IV, Vol. I, 470.
[12] Gorgas to Dimmock, and indorsement, Richmond, *ibid.*, p. 472.
[13] Walker to Letcher, Richmond, *ibid.*, p. 473.

ply with Gorgas' requisition. Under a tacit agreement between the Governor and the President as to a division of work between the Confederate and Virginia ordnance services, Munford explained, the Governor had directed that everything pertaining to the manufacture of ammunition should be handled by Confederate Ordnance, while the manufacture of gun carriages, caissons, and accouterments belonging to artillery and the issue of artillery and arms should be handled by the Virginia department. "In conformity to this supposed understanding, Major Gorgas has superintended the construction of ammunition in the building established therefor and with the laborers employed by the State, and Colonel Dimmock . . . has continued the manufacture of gun carriages at the expense of the State." Then, adopting the argument of Walker, Munford continued:

It is proper to know if it is desired that this arrangement and distribution of duties should continue or all these duties be performed by the Ordnance Department of the Confederate States. Some arrangement ought to be made for the completion of these orders. With every disposition to act in the utmost harmony with the Government of the Confederate States in all its departments, and in no manner to throw obstacles in their way, we are yet compelled to conform to the positive requirements of our laws.[14]

Whether the central government would take over the armory to operate the Harpers Ferry machinery was a question to which the War Department could not categorically answer yes or no. The fortunes of war could abruptly change any decision then made. While "a full confidence in the safety of . . . Richmond" was held, prudence dictated caution. Walker could say, however, that "it is the present intention of this Department to continue the operation of this machinery in the armory at Richmond, and under all circumstances, so long as possible, to continue the use of the armory for the objects to which it has been devoted in the service of the Confederate States."[15] There could be little room now for misunderstanding.

Under a resolution of the Virginia convention, an inventory of the Harpers Ferry material was made mandatory, and Gorgas was selected to represent the Confederacy in the proceedings.[16] At last it seemed that the end of this unreasonably troublesome matter was at hand, but James

[14] Munford to Walker, Richmond, July 13, 1861, *ibid.*, p. 476.
[15] Walker to Letcher, Richmond, July 21, 1861, *ibid.*, p. 492.
[16] Munford to Walker, Richmond, July 18, 1861, *ibid.*, p. 488.

Burton now did his best to get Gorgas to retain the machinery in Richmond. He urged the point, arguing that the plant, already partially completed, would produce 15,000 arms annually, and the removal of any part of it would seriously cripple the plant's capacity.[17] Munford indicated, however, that if the inventory could be completed, a written agreement could be signed which would preserve Virginia's right to title in the equipment but would relinquish possession to the Confederacy. Munford knew that it was "indispensable to the vigorous prosecution of the public work that the authorities of the Confederate States should have exclusive control over all the public buildings appertaining to the armory," but the Governor was as yet unaware that any Confederate agent had been appointed to co-operate in the transfer. The matter of arms on hand in the armory would have to be worked out too. Munford understood that the Confederate government wanted these arms, and would repair them at government expense; issues would be made to Virginia troops equally with others. This arrangement did not suit the state of Virginia. The commonwealth had liberally given of her limited stock, said Munford, and now wanted to keep what was was left for any emergency. The state hoped that the Confederacy would continue the efforts already under way to repair and modernize these arms and reserve them for state use.

Munford expressed some confusion over Walker's statement that it would be highly desirable to push the erection of gun carriages and caissons, to abolish the office of colonel of ordnance, and to remove the public guard. The Secretary, Munford understood, had previously expressed[18] the wish that these construction operations be completed by the officers who had begun them. Munford argued that when the construction and other work of fabrication was completed, there would be no further need for the Virginia officers, particularly the colonel of ordnance, and this point was one that should be settled by written agreement. Again the commonwealth's Secretary pleaded the state's desire to do nothing to obstruct the Confederate cause, but added that in such a large undertaking as the transfer of the armory, in which the state would retain the right of property, the regulations imposed by the legislature would have to be met.[19]

Gorgas knew the job of conducting the inventory would be fraught with petty disagreements and bickering. Not intending to do it all alone,

[17] Burton to Gorgas, Richmond, July 20, 1861, *ibid.*, pp. 509–10.
[18] See Walker to Letcher, Richmond, July 21, 1861, *ibid.*, p. 492.
[19] Munford to Gorgas, Richmond, July 31, 1861, *ibid.*, pp. 511–12.

he requested the Secretary of War to put Professor A. T. Bledsoe, of the Bureau of War, on the commission with him.[20] Bledsoe was a scholarly, shambling sort of man, unobtrusively competent. The Governor, for his part, appointed Dimmock and H. R. Tucker to confer with Bledsoe and Gorgas with a view to settling all the questions arising from the transfer of property.[21]

In December Gorgas informed Judah P. Benjamin, the new Secretary of War, that there was still a considerable amount of machinery at Harpers Ferry which the Confederacy could put to good use. Some force, equipped with artillery, would be required there for a few days to remove all of the useful equipment, Gorgas believed, and suggested that Benjamin call General Thomas J. Jackson's attention to the matter.[22] The whole question of the armory was again brought to the attention of Letcher, who vented his spleen on Gorgas. In reply to an earlier letter from Benjamin, Letcher ranted:

This furnishes another instance of the inclination of your Ordnance officer to control the disposition of the property of Virginia without consulting her authorities. The conduct of this officer has been characterized by a disregard of the rights and authorities of the State of Virginia that cannot longer be submitted, and I must respectfully request you as his superior officer to put an end to it. . . . It is due . . . to the State authorities that Col. Gorgas shall consult with them before he gives orders respecting its [Harpers Ferry machinery] disposition. . . . I am prepared at all times to respond promptly to any call that may be made upon me to promote the cause, the success of which is indispensable to our safety. I must insist, therefore, that Lt. Col. Gorgas shall not be permitted to ignore the State of Virginia, and her constituted authorities.[23]

The action of two of the Confederate states just now presented interesting studies in differing concepts. Perhaps farsightedly Gorgas complained to Benjamin on December 15 that it appeared Virginia's Ordnance Department had induced a workman at the Confederate Armory to leave and go into state service for higher wages.[24] Gorgas

[20] Gorgas to Walker, Richmond, August 1, 1861, CRLR, 1861. For Gorgas' appointment to the inventory commission, see Walker to Gorgas, Richmond, July 29, 1861, ORA, Ser. IV, Vol. I, 506.
[21] Munford to Walker, Richmond, August 6, 1861, ORA, Ser. IV, Vol. I, 534.
[22] Gorgas to Benjamin, Richmond, December 5, 1861, CRLR, 1861, Doc. 8224.
[23] Letcher to Benjamin, Richmond, December 3, 1861, *ibid.,* Doc. 8234.
[24] The comparison between this action and that of the various agencies of the United States government in World Wars I and II is interesting.

remarked that "the different branches of the same service should not interfere." He, himself, had established a set policy on this question. No one would be employed by the Ordnance Bureau, he directed, without a recommendation and release from his last employer, and it seemed only fair to expect other agencies to adopt this policy.[25] Time would, unfortunately, illustrate the naïveté of this hope.

On the other side of the picture stood the fine example set by Alabama's new Chief Executive, John Gill Shorter. In a letter to General Braxton Bragg, Shorter stated his earnest desire to do all that seemed best for the cause. During the first week in December, he told Bragg, Governor A. B. Moore, his predecessor, had heard from Albert Sidney Johnston of the need for state-equipped, twelve-months troops "for the defense of the Vallies [sic] of the Tennessee, Mississippi and Cumberland rivers." Shorter wanted to know how his office could help.[26] The Confederacy possessed too few men with such views and, as the war dragged on, would possess fewer.

With all of these problems Gorgas had more than enough trouble. In desperation he wrote the Secretary of War in June, 1861, that the vast multitude of reports and returns coming into his office from various engineer officers posed a clerical problem with which he alone could not cope. "No attention can be paid to them by me. It is no longer possible. You will see the absolute necessity for ordering an Engineer officer in charge here. [Edward P.] Alexander of the Engineers is here, I understand. Let him take temporary charge."[27] Finally, on August 3 special orders were issued relieving Gorgas and giving the duty of Chief of Engineers to Major Danville Ledbetter.[28]

It was only natural that the various branches of the War Department should have myriad differences among themselves. Realizing that competition between departments or bureaus for claims upon the treasury would produce detrimental results, President Davis solved the problem to the entire satisfaction of the Chief of Ordnance and ended speculation on the subject. "The President," wrote Gorgas much later, "whose practical sagacity was rarely at fault, early reduced these interests to logical sequences. He said 'For the infantry, men must first be fed,

[25] Gorgas to Benjamin, Richmond, December 15, 1861, CRLR, 1861, Doc. 8605.
[26] Shorter to Bragg, Montgomery, December 6, 1861, *Shorter Letter Book* (Answers to Letters), 1862.
[27] Gorgas to Walker, Richmond, June 29, 1861, CRLR, 1861, Doc. 1822.
[28] ORA, Ser. IV, Vol. I, 531.

next armed, and even clothing must follow these; for if they are fed and have arms and ammunition they can fight.' Thus the Subsistence Department had in a general way a preference for the requisitions on the Treasury." Ordnance came next, followed by the Quartermaster Department. The Medical Service had a general precedence, since it was necessary "first of all to keep the hospitals empty and the ranks full."[29]

Following the Battle of Bull Run, July 21, 1861, Gorgas had an opportunity to appraise the ability of his bureau to stand the shock of combat, and found that some of the fears which had plagued Confederate military commanders before Manassas were unfounded. He had been unable to put more than fifty to seventy rounds of small arms ammunition in the cartridge boxes of the men who fought Irvin Mc-Dowell, and some officers had expressed deep concern because the full issue of two hundred rounds called for by the *Ordnance Manual* was not met. "In examining the returns of Ordnance Officers . . ." Gorgas answered, "I found that the reduction of ammunition amounted to from about 19 to 26 rounds per man." He voiced the opinion that "there need be no scarcity with 60 rounds on hand, or even fifty."[30]

Even with the ammunition collected from the field of Manassas, some Confederate military units were still woefully short of ordnance stores. General Lee, in a letter written on July 24, informed the Chief of Ordnance that General Henry A. Wise, former Governor of Virginia, commanding in the Kanawha Valley, was almost without ammunition. Could the Chief of Ordnance send a full supply by rail to Lewisburg? The needs of troops west of the Mississippi were no less pressing. General Ben McCulloch, the intrepid Texas Ranger, now a Confederate Brigadier, badly needed arms and ammunition, which Baton Rouge Arsenal was directed to supply.[31]

In taking stock, once again, of the department's resources, Gorgas wrote tactfully to Colonel Edward Manigault of South Carolina's Ordnance Department, asking for an estimate of the amount of powder on hand. He explained to Manigault that "you may well imagine that I feel anxious to ascertain how long we can *hold out* before being thrown on our own resources, which are daily developing."[32] Gorgas had next to turn his attention to the especial development of one of

---

[29] GOC, p. 216.   [30] GOC, p. 287.

[31] Lee to Gorgas, Richmond, July 24, 1861, ORA, Ser. I, Vol. II, 995; Gorgas to the Secretary of War, Richmond, July 27, 1861, CRLR, 1861, Doc. 2485.

[32] Gorgas to Manigault, Richmond, July 21, 1861, *Heartmann Collection*.

these resources—powder. When the war began, the supply of gunpowder in the whole Confederacy could not be counted on to last more than a month. While the United States, and foreign powers, had long-established sites for the manufacture of gunpowder, the Confederacy entered the conflict with no powder mills of consequence—two in Tennessee and two in South Carolina being little more than local suppliers.[33]

Davis and Gorgas together selected George Washington Rains for the job of expediting Confederate powder manufacture, giving him *carte blanche*. They could have chosen no better man. An enthusiastic scientist, Rains left Richmond on July 10, 1861, to start his task. He knew that the comparatively small amount of powder captured at Norfolk Navy Yard, as well as the small amount obtained from other sources, had long since been distributed to troops, and that the army of General Albert Sidney Johnston had hardly a pound on hand. To Johnston's army Rains turned his first attention. Under the stimulus of its energetic Governor, Isham G. Harris, and the Military Committee, Tennessee had made efforts soon after secession to supply Johnston with powder by making contracts for saltpeter with the Sycamore Powder Mill, near Nashville, which was to be enlarged. When Rains reached Nashville, the state turned these contracts over to the Confederate government and offered to co-operate in every way possible. Rains found that even after the Sycamore Mill got into operation, its facilities for preparing saltpeter were so limited that its over-all product would be small until considerable refitting was done. It proved to be the latter part of September, after the installation of new stampers and other parts, before a daily capacity of five hundred pounds was reached. Even so, there remained the crying need for a special refinery of saltpeter. A plant designed to fit this need was almost completed at Nashville by October 9, 1861, and on that day 1,500 pounds were refined. This product was increased until a daily capacity of 3,000 pounds was reached.[34]

No one knew better than Rains the desperate need of the Confederacy for niter. He was immensely relieved that Governor Brown had managed to secure a cargo of saltpeter from Philadelphia before the port of Savannah was blockaded. "This store," he said, "although comparatively small, was of extraordinary value, as from it mainly the gunpowder for General A. S. Johns[t]on's army was supplied, as

[33] GOC, pp. 213–14; George W. Rains, *History of the Confederate Powder Works* (Newburgh, N. Y., 1882), p. 3.
[34] Rains, *Confederate Powder Works*, pp. 4–5.

well as the Batteries at Fort Pillow, Island Number 10, and Memphis, on the Mississippi river."[35] But Rains and Gorgas could not hope for Fortune to knock again in such timely fashion. Either the Confederacy would have to produce saltpeter, or it would have to give up—and the idea of giving up crossed no one's mind. Instead, Rains bent his efforts towards extracting from Confederate caves what amounts of niter he could find. Limestone caves in Tennessee, Alabama, Georgia and in states west of the Mississippi had earth rich in nitrate of lime. This could be turned into saltpeter by lixiviation and saturating with lye from wood ashes. Some of these caves Rains himself visited, and to others he sent agents.

Rains's unceasing efforts on behalf of powder manufacture met with success. He estimated that before the fall of Nashville in February, 1862, 100,000 pounds of powder had gone to Johnston, in addition to a considerable amount sent to New Orleans and other places. After arranging powder-making facilities in New Orleans, he turned his full attention to the erection of the government powder works, which he decided to locate at Augusta, Georgia. He had more than his share of luck in getting the Augusta Powder Works going. By pure chance he obtained a copy of a pamphlet written by the Superintendent of the Waltham Abbey Powder Works in England, describing the processes and machinery used at that factory—then the best anywhere. The pamphlet had one limitation, however; it said nothing about working plans, details of buildings or apparatus. For these Rains had to rely on his own ingenuity. On July 20, 1861, he visited the Augusta Canal and viewed other resources of this town on the Savannah. Later he selected the site of the old United States magazine, half a mile from the western city limits. Land surrounding it was purchased, and also a two mile stretch between the canal and the river, "so that the different buildings required, might be separated by intervals of at least one thousand feet for safety in case any one of them should have an explosion." The spot had all the essential points to be considered in the erection of such works: central location, transportation facilities, water power, proximity to a fairly large city with a labor supply, building materials, temperate climate, earth free from lime and salts, cheap wood for charcoal, and sufficient distance from a town or city to avoid damage in case of explosion.[36] Rains could later record that "the total cost

[35] *Ibid.*, p. 5.
[36] *Ibid.*, pp. 8, 9, 10. See *ibid.*, p. 10, for Rains's excellent presentation of essential considerations in erecting the plant.

of the entire works did not exceed three hundred and eighty-five thousand dollars"—a truly remarkable achievement. Economy was a prime consideration with Gorgas, who viewed with alarm the fact that the dangers involved in importing gunpowder had increased its per-pound price through the blockade to $3.00. According to Rains, 1,000,000 pounds of powder made by the works during the first year of the war cost the government, including the materials, $1,080,000, a saving of $1,920,000.[37] But the day of such economy was rapidly passing.

On April 10, 1862, official operation of the Augusta Powder Works began. No other undertaking would be of such importance; no other long-range building project would succeed so well. Gorgas knew that he could not have selected a more capable man than George Rains, who forged the first dramatic achievement of Confederate Ordnance.

In the meantime, the Chief of Ordnance had been making other efforts to supply powder. The Secretary of War had been able to tell an inquisitive Congress[38] that contracts for the manufacture of powder had been let by the War Department, and that the Confederacy possessed enough powder to make 20,000,000 cartridges for small arms, "more than sufficient, according to the ordinary estimate, to supply an army of 400,000 men for twelve months." Large contracts had been let in Europe by Ordnance agents. Secretary Walker had to admit that no deliveries on contracts had yet been made, but he had faith in all the contractors. Congress was told of large-scale domestic arrangements for the manufacture of powder, and that the government had obtained considerable supplies of sulphur and niter. Walker announced to Congress, optimistically,

it is hoped that it will not be long before the Confederate States will be independent of foreign supplies in this important munition of war. The arrangements made in Europe for the purchase of powder are believed to be complete and satisfactory. A large quantity has been already purchased, which will be ready for early shipment, and arrangements have

[37] *Ibid.*, pp. 10–11, 11.
[38] On July 27, 1861, Congress passed a resolution "requesting the Secretary of War to inform Congress whether his Department has made contracts for the manufacture of powder of the different grades and varieties required in the military service . . . whether the persons with whom such contracts have been made have yet fulfilled their contracts in whole or in part, and whether they are actually engaged in the execution of their contracts, and whether they possess requisite material and means for the energetic and prompt execution thereof." *Journal of the Provisional Congress of the Confederate States of America* (Washington, 1904), p. 288.

been made for its importation which it is confidently hoped will elude the utmost vigilance of the blockade.[39]

Gorgas saw, of course, the advantage of diversified sources of powder. In this connection he had had some correspondence with North Carolina's Governor Henry T. Clark, who wrote him in October, 1861, that the state had concluded a contract with Messrs. Waterhouse and Bowes to establish a powder mill near Raleigh. The powder would be delivered at a cost of 15 cents per pound above the cost of pure niter. Operations could begin soon, but Clark confessed that there were no raw materials at hand. He offered Gorgas a deal. If the Ordnance Bureau would furnish the niter and sulphur, the state would furnish the finished powder on these terms, reserving such amounts as were deemed essential to the defense of the state—and the Governor thought that this amount would be relatively small. The price paid by the Confederate government for the niter and sulphur would naturally be subtracted from the price of the powder sold to the Ordnance Bureau.[40] Gorgas did not hesitate to accept a proposition so profitable in appearance. Four months after the initial correspondence with Clark, Gorgas received a report from two of the officers sent to examine the first samples of Waterhouse and Bowes' powder. The product was almost as good, they said, as Dupont's celebrated powder; at any rate it was entirely satisfactory.[41]

Despite the obvious importance of its job, Gorgas knew that his bureau had not as yet graduated to the status of a major industry. True, the Ordnance Bureau, as such, did not exist; it merely functioned *de facto* under the Artillery Corps, but its *de facto* existence was nonetheless real. Its need of funds, also, was real. Under the general "Public Defense" appropriation act of August 21, 1861, Congress earmarked $57,000,000 for army pay, quartermaster supplies, transportation, commissary stores, for ordnance in all its branches, for engineering supplies, and for the medical service. Secretary Walker, acting under authority granted in the law, allotted $39,500,000 to the Quartermaster Department, $12,000,000 to the Commissary Department, $1,000,000

---

[39] Walker to Howell Cobb, President of Congress, Richmond, July 31, 1861, ORA, Ser. IV, Vol. I, 510–11. Gorgas remarked that small quantities of powder came in during this period from Wilmington to Galveston, "some of it of very inferior quality." GOC, pp. 213–14.

[40] Clark to Gorgas, Raleigh, October 2, 1861, in Governor Clark's Letter Book, p. 136, cited from *Ramsdell Note Files.*

[41] Raleigh *State Journal,* January 15, 1862.

each to the Medical and Engineer Departments, and $3,400,000 to the Ordnance Bureau.[42] Two days after Walker had informed Secretary of the Treasury Christopher Memminger of his division of the funds, Gorgas sent a memorandum to the War Office announcing that he had monetary requisitions from abroad amounting to $907,055.54, which would go to Caleb Huse.[43] With such large foreign commitments, the recent congressional appropriation seemed so small as hardly to be worth-while.

But Congress did help in other ways. On August 21 it passed "An Act to increase the corps of artillery, and for other purposes," which allowed the President to appoint one or more superintendents of armories "for the fabrication of small arms,"[44] and on September 3, Congress consented, conditionally,[45] to the appointment of Gorgas as a lieutenant colonel in the artillery.

Acting rapidly on the authority granted in the stopgap legislation, Walker had promoted Gorgas to lieutenant colonel on September 2, and on the same day appointed the former lieutenant colonel of Virginia ordnance, James H. Burton, superintendent of armories in the Confederacy at a salary of $2,500 per year in addition to the quarters and fuel allowance of a major in the army.[46] Burton accepted and was ordered to report to Gorgas.

[42] Walker to C. G. Memminger, Richmond, September 4, 1861, ORA, Ser. IV, Vol. I, 599.
[43] Gorgas to Walker, Richmond, September 7, 1861, CRLR, 1861, Doc. 4062.
[44] *Statutes of the Provisional Congress,* Stat. III, Chap. XXXIV.
[45] The condition was not directed at Gorgas or at anyone else mentioned in the long list of nominations sent by Davis to Congress on August 27. It was brought about by the failure of Congress expressly to approve the nominations by the time it adjourned, so that it made necessary the passage of a bill "To authorize the President to continue the appointments made by him in the Military and Naval Service, during the recess of Congress, or the last or present session, and to submit them to Congress at the next session." A unique thing happened to this bill. It was engrossed and passed on August 31, the last day of the third session of the Provisional Congress. But something occurred in the transmission of the act to the President—he never received it, and it consequently failed to become law. This placed the government in an embarrassing position, and Davis issued a Proclamation calling a special session of Congress, on September 3, 1861. He sent Congress a message explaining his predicament and requesting that something be done. Accordingly, Congress engrossed and passed another act of the same kind that day. See *Journal of the Provisional Congress of the Confederate States,* pp. 423, 460, 466; *Statutes of the Provisional Congress,* Stat. IV (Called Session), Chap. I; for Davis' proclamation calling the extra session, see *ibid.,* appendix, and Richmond *Enquirer,* September 3, 1861.
[46] Pay Voucher No. 523, September 30, 1861, AGPF, Gorgas; Walker to Burton, Richmond, September 2, 1861, Burton; *Statutes of the Provisional Congress,* Stat. III, Chap. XXXIV.

The Chief of Ordnance wasted no time in tightening his organization. He issued a circular on September 10, to officers commanding arsenals and ordnance depots, saying that they were expected to exert themselves on their own behalf to furnish supplies without waiting for special instructions from the Ordnance Office. In further decentralizing command functions, Gorgas directed that these officers should contract for arms, swords, sabers, pistols, artillery, and cavalry equipments in anticipation of the calls which would be made on their installations, reporting their activities from time to time.[47] This was in line with a concept which had long been popular with him. Thomas L. Bayne, a subordinate, close relative, and personal friend, said of him long after the war that

in nothing was he more wonderful than in what appeared as a gift of prescience, which enabled him to provide for the wants of every battlefield. The movement of arms and munitions in his department was often the very first indication of an approaching battle. He carefully studied the dispositions of opposing commanding officers, and followed the movements of every body of troops in order to meet all sudden exigencies. He was constantly in receipt of letters from officers recognizing that he had anticipated their movements and provided their wants.[48]

Secretary of War Judah P. Benjamin had ideas on war that to some extent coincided with Gorgas' own. Perhaps the most able member of the cabinet—suave, versatile, personable, facile in judgment, and always smiling—Benjamin engendered some jealousy among the lesser lights. He had been born, of Jewish parentage, on the island of St. Thomas, British West Indies, in 1811. Reared in Charleston, he was admitted later to the New Orleans bar. From there he had gone to the United States Senate and now to the Confederate cabinet.[49] Unlike his predecessor, Benjamin recognized the full military potential of the North. Walker, thought Benjamin, had kept his monetary estimates lower than necessary because of his natural optimism. The enemy had succeeded in putting more than 500,000 men in the field, and there were thousands more to come. As a result of this realization Benjamin estimated on the basis of at least 400,000 men in Confederate ranks. He thought that the War Department would need, for December, 1861,

[47] Ordnance Circular, Richmond, September 10, 1861, CROB, CXL, 5.
[48] Bayne, *Southern Historical Society Papers*, XIII, 222.
[49] See the fine sketch in Robert S. Henry, *The Story of the Confederacy* (Indianapolis, 1931), pp. 89–90; also Robert D. Meade, *Judah P. Benjamin: Confederate Statesman* (New York, 1943).

and January, February, and March, 1862, more than $90,000,000. He also thought it would be unreasonable to expect the expenditures of the War Department to be less than $24,000,000 per month until the restoration of foreign commerce or until the achievement of peace. For the coming quarter the Secretary put the Quartermaster and Commissary departments ahead of Ordnance in funds, the Quartermaster getting $72,323,701, Commissary, $13,650,807, and Ordnance, $4,-000,000. Other bureaus fared much worse, almost to the point of absurdity.[50]

On assuming the War portfolio, Benjamin, naturally wanting to know what he had to work with, queried his bureau heads. Gorgas, obviously pleased at this display of efficient energy, replied to his inquiry of September 22 by submitting a long, detailed report, based on figures of the quarter which had ended June 30, 1861. Ammunition subject to ordnance requisitions amounted to 1,252,615 rounds for small arms; 24,175 rounds of artillery shot and shell; 133,803 pounds of cannon powder; 15,175 pounds of musket powder; 34,804 pounds of rifle powder; 81,825 pounds of mixed powder; 2,000 pounds of unserviceable powder; and 1,050 pounds of blasting powder. On the last of June Gorgas could have drawn from various depots 2,992 muskets; 351 rifled muskets; 627 rifles; 58 percussion carbines; 456 Colt pistols; 164 percussion pistols; 6 noncommissioned officer's swords; 66 horse artillery sabers; 84 cavalry sabers; and 9 musicians's swords. He would have been alarmed had these figures represented the total supplies on hand, but he explained that they included only those in depot and that the headquarters of the field commanders had not reported their arms issued to troops. The artillery came to 358 guns of all types and varieties from forty-two pounder iron guns to navy carronades. Under contract, and he hoped in some stage of completion, Gorgas could boast of 240 eight-inch Columbiads, 180 ten-inch Columbiads, 15 fifteen-inch Columbiads, 131 three-inch rifled guns, 81 twelve-pounder iron howitzers, 40 twenty-four pounder iron howitzers, and 6 brass six-pounders, as well as carriages, portable forges, sabers, and revolvers. Gorgas was optimistic over contracts for small arms: 20,000 rifled muskets, 16,000 rifles, 5,000 breach-loading carbines, and 1,000 lances. Arsenal production had been climbing, and the Richmond ordnance laboratory could now make from 50,000 to 100,000 rounds of small arms ammunition daily, plus 900

[50] Benjamin to Davis, Richmond, November [?], 1861, ORA, Ser. IV, Vol. I, 764–65. The Medical service received only $370,000; the Engineers, $200,000.

rounds of field artillery ammunition. The Richmond Armory could make, after September 15, 1,000 small arms per month; and the armory at Fayetteville, after March 1, 1862, could probably produce 500 arms per month, providing, of course, that skilled workers were available. Augusta Arsenal, under Rains's sharp eye, could make 20,000 to 30,000 rounds of small arms ammunition per day and was ready to make field ammunition. Charleston Arsenal, under command of Captain F. L. Childs, could make 15,000 to 20,000 rounds of small arms cartridges per day and it, too, was ready to make field ammunition. So was Gorgas' old Mount Vernon Arsenal, which could produce 10,000 to 15,000 cartridges daily. Baton Rouge Arsenal could make 30,000 to 40,000 rounds per day and was about ready to make field ammunition and one field carriage per week. Virginia Military Institute at Lexington, and the ordnance shop at Norfolk, made 5,000 and 10,000 small arms cartridges per day.[51]

The Ordnance Bureau, notwithstanding the good report of its Chief, had its share of bad luck. On December 23, 1861, Lieutenant M. H. Wright, faithful ordnance officer at Nashville, informed the Chief of Ordnance that the Nashville Ordnance Depot had been completely destroyed by fire that morning, together with all its stores. How or where the fire started Wright was unable to say. Everything in the depot had been carefully kept dry, and Wright maintained that no oil or any other inflammable material had been kept in the part of the building where the fire gained its first foothold. He thought that the incident could be traced to incendiaries. The loss of equipment was painful. From 400 to 600 sets of artillery harness, 300 cavalry saddles, 8,000 to 15,000 sets of infantry equipments and accouterments, 2,000,000 percussion caps, 5,000 friction primers, 2 dozen rockets, 300 reams of cartridge paper; and all books except the cash book and cash vouchers, were destroyed. With proper military caution, Wright had requested a board of survey, appointed by General Johnston, to protect him from possible blame.[52]

This unfortunate occurrence added to the pressing need for money and made the allocation by Benjamin of $2,340,000 in additional funds for the month of December imperative.[53] The calls for funds were com-

[51] Gorgas to Benjamin, Richmond, September 26, 1861, *ibid.*, pp. 618–22.

[52] Wright to Gorgas, Nashville, December 23, 1861, ORA, Ser. I, Vol. LII, Pt. II, 242.

[53] Gorgas had asked for only $1,750,000 for December. Gorgas to Benjamin, Richmond, December 4, 1861, ORA, Ser. IV, Vol. I, 766. Benjamin arranged for the transfer of funds apparently through a special act of Congress passed on

ing from all parts of the Confederacy, and Gorgas wrote the Secretary on December 13 that since he had received an additional $500,000 for his bureau under the appropriation act of August 21, further requisitions amounting to $230,850, had come to his office, and the estimates of ordnance officers in the field for current expenses during December totalled over $1,000,000, some of which were urgent. Captain William Richardson Hunt, in Memphis, had to have $100,000 and Lieutenant Wright, Hunt's co-worker in Nashville, urgently needed $230,000 to help repair the damage caused by the Nashville depot fire. These were "must" requisitions. Others less pressing included $200,000 for Captain Smith Stansbury in Richmond; $167,000 for Captain J. L. White at Mount Vernon; $150,000 for Captain W. G. Gill at Augusta; $29,150 for Captain Childs at Charleston; $75,000 for Captain Briscoe G. Baldwin at Richmond; $20,000 for Captain Richard M. Cuyler at Savannah; and $7,500 for Captain John C. Booth at Fayetteville. The West and Indian Territory was represented by a requisition for $50,000 from General Albert Pike.[54] Then, of course, Huse and the blockade agents always needed money. They would continue to need money for some time.

December 18, providing for the transfer of unexpended sums in various acts approved earlier in the year to the appropriation act of August 21. This, of course, gave him authority to apportion such sums in any way he desired. See *Statutes of the Provisional Congress*, Stat. IV, Chap. XII; also Jennings C. Wise, *The Long Arm of Lee* (Lynchburg, 1915), I, 37.

[54] Gorgas to Benjamin, Richmond, December 13, 1861, CRLR, 1861, Doc. 8469.

VII

Blockade-Running

THE WINTER OF 1861–1862 HAD PRODUCED FEW STARTLING EVENTS, excepting, of course, the removal of Confederate Commissioners Mason and Slidell from the Royal Mail Steamer "Trent" in November. This incident alone, however, would have been enough to mark that winter in red letters on Josiah Gorgas' calendar. This, and the foreign trade policy toward the Bahamas practiced by Salmon Chase, Lincoln's Secretary of the Treasury, would contribute a great deal to solidifying Southern sympathy in the Bahamas and in Bermuda.[1] This sympathy, combined with their geographical location, had made it a matter of course that the two islands would be used as bases for blockade-runners. By now Gorgas and others interested in foreign importations, speculators included, had discovered that the Federal blockade imposed certain problems which could be solved only by the use of swift, light-draft blockade-runners specially constructed to sit low in the water and supplied with strong boilers fired with quick-burning Welsh coal. To reach the Confederate coast, above all else one needed speed, for the large and necessarily slow tramp steamers bringing supplies from England simply could not elude the fast Federal pursuit craft.

To meet this challenge, Confederate authorities and businessmen displayed an ingenuity which is one of the distinguishing achievements of the Confederacy. Owing to the reluctance of the administration to acknowledge openly the existence of the blockade, Gorgas decided to take over this clandestine trade for the Ordnance Bureau and to direct

---

[1] In April, 1862, Salmon P. Chase issued regulations prohibiting trade in certain types of contraband, and aimed them at commerce from Nassau and the West Indies. These orders angered many Bahamians. See Collector of Customs Hiram Barney to Chase, New York, June 12, 1862, copy in *Governor of the Bahamas Letters Received from the Colonial Office File;* and Chase to William H. Seward, Washington, June 14, 1862, *ibid.*

[84]

it in person. Taking every factor into account, he developed a master plan which would, in time, greatly relieve his procurement difficulties. He hoped to arrange it so that ultimately Bermuda and the Bahamas would become regular centers of transshipment of Confederate war cargoes. At those points the cargoes of the large merchantmen from England and the continent would be unloaded and reshipped aboard blockade-runners for the final dash to Confederate ports.

There were, of course, precedents for blockade evasion in the history of warfare. One striking parallel to the Southern problem occurred in 425 B.C., during the Peloponnesian War. The Athenians had succeeded in trapping a portion of the Spartan land forces on the island of Sphacteria, off the coast of Pylos, and thus, by maintaining a blockade, learned what the Federal navy and government would in time come to understand: a blockade immobilized, perhaps, some of the enemy's forces, restricted his strategy, and imposed attrition, but it did not of itself bring him to capitulation. Thucydides records that much time was consumed in the blockade of the island because the Spartans had not stood idly by while the cream of their land forces was being starved to death. "The fact was," he wrote, "that the Lacedaemonians had made advertisement for volunteers to carry into the island ground corn, wine, cheese, and any other food useful in a siege; high prices being offered, and freedom promised to any of the Helots who should succeed in doing so. . . . In short, both sides tried every possible contrivance, the one to throw in provisions, and the other to prevent their introduction."[2]

Thucydides reasoned well in considering the material inducement offered the Helots to undertake running the blockade. Those men of the Confederacy who were interested in bringing in supplies from abroad, and who were not involved in the trade officially, had rich material benefits in mind. Although some Confederate officials also succumbed to this temptation, Gorgas stood as an exception to this situation. No one in the whole Confederacy knew better than he the weak links in the chain of supply, and no one tried harder to strengthen them.

He had been instrumental, it will be recalled, in having Caleb Huse sent abroad to purchase supplies of arms and ordnance in anticipation of a long fight. Always liberal in his estimates of funds, recognizing the basic need of large financial credit for profitable competitive purchas-

[2] Thucydides, *Peloponnesian War,* iv. 26–27.

ing, Gorgas constantly pushed the War and Treasury departments to supply Huse with more money. The wisdom of this policy was confirmed by the first shipment of arms to the Confederacy which arrived aboard the "Fingal" on September 28, 1861, and by the fact that from that month to February, 1862, some 15,000 arms reached the South. Huse continued his operations, and between April 27 and August 16, 1862, sent 48,510 stands of arms safely to Charleston, Wilmington, and Savannah.[3] Gorgas had been particularly concerned in all measures taken to promote order and organization in the attempts to evade Federal warships. In this interest he was enthusiastically joined by Secretary Benjamin, who held no insular views on governmental blockade policies. Though unable officially to admit that the Confederacy was participating in blockade-running, he proved more than willing to foster the growth of such activities. In many cases, while apparently sending a Confederate commissioner to a foreign port, Benjamin was actually stationing blockade agents for duty. These men were important. Since it had become necessary to transship supplies at Bermuda, Nassau, and even Cuba, some Confederate officer had to be on duty at these places to handle and oversee the physical transfer.

Late in 1861 Louis Heyliger, Confederate agent at Nassau, reported that apparently through diplomacy, and undoubtedly aided by public sentiment and the consequent good offices of the governor, he had secured "a very important modification of the existing laws, viz., the privilege of breaking bulk and transshipment. This . . . was not previously accorded."[4] John Tory Bourne, commission merchant at St. George's, Bermuda, early in the war had sought to identify himself with blockade-running enterprises and proved willing to provide coal for Southern war vessels.[5] Obviously sympathetic with the cause of the Confederacy, and persistent, Bourne finally became an official representative of the Confederate States in Bermuda, albeit under the eye of army officers stationed there. Still, Bourne is an example of the sort of commissioners Benjamin stationed in advantageous ports.[6] Through the hands of these agents Gorgas sent the consignments of

---

[3] Gorgas memorandum, August 16, 1862, ORA, Ser. IV, Vol. II, 52; also Vandiver (ed.), *Confederate Blockade Running through Bermuda, 1861–1865; Letters and Cargo Manifests* (Austin, 1947), p. xviii.
[4] Louis Heyliger to Benjamin, Nassau, December 27, 1861, ORA, Ser. IV, Vol. I, 816; *Blockade Running,* p. xviii.   [5] *Blockade Running,* pp. 5, 8.
[6] For an example of Bourne's efforts in diplomacy, see Bourne to A. I. M. Gilbert, St. George's, January 4, 1862, and Gilbert to Bourne, January 6, 1862, *Blockade Running,* p. 8.

cotton designed to pay for the purchases made by Huse. From these transshippers the cotton went to England, generally to the firm of Fraser, Trenholm and Company in Liverpool, who acted as the South's main credit bankers abroad.

Gorgas' faith in Huse was matched only by his desire to keep funds going to Europe. Shortage of money was the single factor retarding Huse's work—and a more effective retarder there could not have been. Even though a considerable number of arms and a quantity of accessory supplies came through the blockade from England in mid-1862, Huse could have done immeasurably better had he been as well financed as his Northern competitors for European war material. Although Huse, together with Major Edward C. Anderson (a temporary spy on Huse), had purchased some $2,225,000 worth of equipment during the first year of the war, it represented largely contracts under way and not actual "ready-to-use" supplies.[7] In this connection, Huse placed the business of the Confederacy's long-term contracts almost entirely in the hands of Saul Isaac, Campbell and Company, an English commission house outspoken in its desire to aid the South. This firm so pleased Huse, Gorgas, and Benjamin, that by March 17, 1862, the Secretary of War wrote them that he wanted to acknowledge the obligation felt by the Confederate government "for the kind and generous confidence which you have exhibited toward us at a moment when all others in foreign countries seem to be doubtful, timorous, and wavering."[8]

At last the Chief of Ordnance could look with hope and some confidence toward foreign countries as a source of munitions. He had been so concerned with arranging the blockade-running business that it probably came as a surprise when he realized that from now on regular requisitions could go over to Huse, with good expectation of fulfillment.

But Gorgas had to keep working for money. On January 28, 1862, recognizing the impossibility of obtaining further direct congressional appropriations, he requested Benjamin to transfer at least $500,000 from Quartermaster and $50,000 from Medical Department funds to help defray expenses of Huse, who now announced that he had spent most of his available money for shoes, blankets, cloth, and medicines.[9] Benjamin lost no time in devising a way to make

[7] *Ibid.*, pp. xii, xiii, xiv.
[8] ORA, Ser. IV, Vol. I, 1007–1008; *Blockade Running*, p. xix.
[9] Gorgas to Benjamin, Richmond, January 28, 1862, CRLR, 1862, Doc. 102; Benjamin to Huse, Richmond, March 12, 1862, ORA, Ser. IV, Vol. I, 985; Gorgas to Seddon, Richmond, December 5, 1862, *ibid.*, II, 227–28; *Blockade Running*, pp. xix, xxi.

up the deficiency in ordnance funds. He hastily shoved a bill into the hands of the congressional committee on finance, whose chairman, Robert W. Barnwell, recommended its passage on January 29. This bill, which was passed on January 30, directed the transfer of $3,000,000 in Quartermaster funds to Gorgas' jurisdiction.[10] Such maneuvers, however, did not end Gorgas' worries. On March 18 he urgently told Benjamin that the appropriation for the Ordnance Bureau was "entirely exhausted, and that it will require at least $700,000 to carry us to 1st April exclusive of funds which may be needed abroad." Benjamin again lost no time in trying to supply sufficient credit for foreign purchases. Secretary Walker had told Huse after the battle of Manassas that this victory should only lead the South to increase its efforts, and the obvious magnitude of the war made it a matter of necessity to "depart . . . from the terms of . . . original instructions." By August, 1861, Huse knew that Walker desired him to "operate with a free and sure hand to meet our passing needs, and ship safely, and consider your credit extended to the full of this demand."[11] In addition, Huse was relieved from interference by Confederate diplomatic commissioners.[12]

Despite the broad authority delegated to Huse and the material results he had achieved, Benjamin, as a result of Gorgas' insistence and the woeful inadequacy of Confederate resources, determined to push the acquisition of foreign supplies by all means available. The War Department at the apparent behest of Gorgas, set up a priority system to be followed closely. Small arms and powder had become all important by March of 1862, and Huse was instructed to obtain these to the neglect of everything else. The South found it so difficult to send bills abroad, wrote Benjamin, that the Treasury Department would make regular remittances of cotton—the Confederacy's white gold—to Fraser, Trenholm and Company, who would use it as the basis of credit. No other system tried suited Huse as well as this one, and during its continuance he did his best work.[13]

[10] *Journal of the Provisional Congress of the Confederate States,* pp. 727–728; *Statutes of the Provisional Congress,* Stat. V, Chap. LX.

[11] Walker to Huse and Anderson, Richmond, August 30, 1861, ORA, Ser. IV, Vol. I, 594.

[12] Walker to Huse and Anderson, August 17, 1861, *ibid.,* pp. 564–65; *Blockade Running,* pp. xiii, xiv.

[13] Benjamin to Huse, Richmond, March 22, 1862, ORA, Ser. IV, Vol. I, 1018; Caleb Huse, *The Supplies for the Confederate Army, How they were Obtained in Europe and how Paid for. Personal Reminiscences and Unpublished History* (Boston, 1904), p. 28; *Blockade Running,* p. xix.

Although Benjamin, under Gorgas' guidance, worked out the barter arrangement of the cotton-buying system, he did not succeed in securing the $700,000 which the Chief of Ordnance had declared essential. No sooner did George W. Randolph succeed Benjamin in the War portfolio, in March, 1862, than Gorgas told him of the pressing need for funds, stressing the point: "An immediate appropriation, or transfer of funds for the Ordnance Service is earnestly requested." The new secretary, a personal friend of Gorgas',[14] immediately indorsed the memorandum: "Ask Committee of Ways and Means to authorize transfer from Quarter Master Dept., or to make an appropriation."[15] When Huse's successful operations had overreached the Ordnance Bureau's capacity to pay, Gorgas personally undertook the job of partially financing his agent. Norman Walker, the man whose house in Richmond Gorgas hoped to secure, was dispatched to Europe with $2,-000,000 in Confederate bonds. Gorgas hoped this sum would help relieve Huse's embarrassment. Huse had extended his purchasing expedition as far as Vienna, where he bought 45,000 rifles and arranged the delivery of 30,000 more at Nassau. In all these dealings he had the financial encouragement of Saul Isaac, Campbell and Company of London. By the end of 1862 he had run the Ordnance Bureau into that firm's debt to the extent of $5,000,000, of which $2,000,000 remained unpaid at the time of Walker's departure. Huse's exertions, expensive as they were, had produced more than successful results. Summing up his bureau's operations to James A. Seddon, Secretary of War, on December 5, 1862, Gorgas said that Huse had purchased 157,000 arms, large quantities of powder, some artillery, infantry equipments, harness, swords, percussion caps, saltpeter, lead, and miscellaneous items. "In addition to ordnance stores," said Gorgas, "using rare forecast he has purchased and shipped large supplies of clothing, blankets, cloth, and shoes for the Quartermaster's Department without special orders to do so."[16] To meet the necessary payments on these supplies Huse had been furnished with $3,095,139, but he still owed £444,850, or $5,925,402 in Confederate currency.[17] Feeling that "capacity for running in debt is the best evidence of the ability of Major Huse," Gorgas also knew that "the debt is a matter that calls for immediate attention."[18]

[14] GCWD, pp. 32, 126.
[15] Gorgas to Randolph, Richmond, March 25, 1862, and indorsement, CRLR, 1862, Doc. GWD 113.
[16] Gorgas to Seddon, Richmond, December, 5, 1862, ORA, Ser. IV, Vol. II, 227; *Blockade Running*, p. xxi.   [17] *Blockade Running*, p. xxi.
[18] Gorgas to Seddon, Richmond, December 5, 1862, ORA, Ser. IV, Vol. II, 227.

Gorgas' faith in Huse came to the fore when, in early January, 1863, Major B. F. Ficklen, recently returned from abroad, informed Seddon that he believed Huse was *"robbing* the Confederate Government in a most shameful manner."* Gorgas defended his agent against these charges by saying that the situation, he was certain, had been so thoroughly misrepresented that no action would be taken by him, unless ordered by the Secretary of War. Seddon acceded to the suggestion and did not press the matter.

Foreign purchasing by now was a most promising enterprise. Bermuda seemed to be shaping up as the most logical place to maintain a full-scale intermediate depot for Confederate supplies—even more important than Nassau. As a consequence of Bermuda's obvious importance, Gorgas decided to have Norman Walker proceed there from England and to co-operate with an agent whom Huse had already sent to manage Confederate cargo transshipments at St. George's. Both these missions tended to overlook John Tory Bourne, the avid Southern sympathizer there. Walker, however, understood the wisdom of having someone familiar with the Bermudian markets and one who knew firms working with official representatives of the Confederate States. He regarded Bourne's services as invaluable.[19]

In connection with his new plans for Bermuda, Gorgas, who still had actual charge of all the government's openly avowed blockade-runners,[20] conceived the policy which would make the Confederacy forever famous in maritime annals. To Seddon, who probably lacked any ideas on the subject, Gorgas stated that it seemed the logical duty of the navy to aid in bringing stores through the blockade, but, if this task was to be left to the War Department, "it is highly important that light-draft steamers should be purchased and used solely for the transportation of cargoes from Bermuda."[21] Speed, as has been pointed out, was the essential for any ship hoping to run the blockade safely. Most blockade captains took pride in the swiftness of their vessels, and it was a matter of general news interest in New Providence when the steamer "Antonica" made the trip from Charleston to Nassau in the astoundingly quick time of 53 hours.[22] The growing number of speedy vessels continually drew the attention of United States Consul Charles

[19] *Blockade Running*, pp. xxi, xxii; Bourne to Messrs. Keith and McLean, St. George's, November 30, 1861, and to James M. Mason, St. George's, January 22, 1862, *ibid.*, pp. 8, 9.   [20] *Ibid.*, p. xxxii.

[21] Gorgas to Seddon, Richmond, December 5, 1862, ORA, Ser. IV, Vol. II, 227.   [22] *Bahama Herald*, December 31, 1862.

Maxwell Allen in Bermuda. He duly recorded for William H. Seward's information the arrival and departure of blockade-runners and paid particular attention to the arrival of the "Cornubia" at St. George's. He recorded that she was very fast, and that her "color has been changed . . . to lead since arrival."[23]

As the first step toward setting up a permanent base at Bermuda, following Walker's assignment to that place, Gorgas sent Major Smith Stansbury (his West Point classmate) to St. George's to command the Confederate Ordnance Depot to be located there.[24] Establishment of such an installation seemed necessary since yellow fever played such havoc in the West Indies during the summer months that it precluded the use of ports in that area.[25]

In outlining Stansbury's duties to him, Gorgas estimated the needs of the bureau on the basis of long-run plans. In mid-July, 1863, unaware of the disasters at Gettysburg and Vicksburg, Stansbury would still send orders to Huse based on Gorgas' original estimates. He told Huse on July 14 that every effort should be made to send saltpeter to Bermuda. The Augusta Powder Works badly needed this commodity,[26] and Gorgas considered the need for saltpeter and lead so urgent that Stansbury wanted to ship "at least forty Tons of lead, and sixty Tons of Saltpetre per month" into the Confederacy. He stressed the need for a reserve of 1,000 tons of lead and 800 tons of saltpeter as well as the immediate shipment of four or five million percussion caps.[27] The total amount of lead on hand in Bermuda, available for shipment in July, amounted to 1,500 pigs, weighing 100 pounds each, and no saltpeter could be found.[28]

Efforts of the Chief of Ordnance to make up the deficit in arms occasioned by Gettysburg and Vicksburg naturally affected Stansbury's operations in Bermuda. Gorgas decided that the loss of the Mississippi River made it imperative to supply the Trans-Mississippi Department

---

[23] *United States Consul's Records of Confederate States Ships at Bermuda*, p. 7. The "Cornubia" is described as having been an "iron side-wheel steamer of 588 92/95 tons, 190 feet long, breadth 24.7 feet, and depth 12.7 feet, and is represented as being very fast. She carries a Confederate States register, according to which James A. Seddon, of Richmond, Va., is her sole owner." See ORN, Ser. I, Vol. IX, 274.

[24] GCWD, June 3, 8, 18, 1863, pp. 42, 43, 45.

[25] Bourne to Messrs. Lane, Hankey & Co., St. George's, May 13, 1864, *Blockade Running*, p. 64; see also p. xvii.

[26] Stansbury to Huse, St. George's, *ibid.*, pp. 72–73.

[27] Stansbury to Gorgas, St. George's, July 20, 1863, *ibid.*, pp. 74, 80.

[28] Stansbury to I. M. St. John, St. George's, July 20, 1863, *ibid.*, p. 75.

by direct shipment to Texas,[29] and this bit of policy filtered down through the command chain to become a basic part of ordnance logistics. Naturally the ones most affected by the policy were those charged with seeing that the ordnance and ordnance stores reached the Western Confederacy safely. Walker and Stansbury were directed to see that all sorts of ordnance supplies went to Texas, but the Bermuda agents were unable to send all the things Gorgas listed—they did not have them. For instance, Stansbury confessed to Huse in August, 1863, that he had no "Cavalry Arms (say Carbines), Revolvers, Officer's Swords, Cavalry Swords, English Saddles, Percussion Caps."[30]

The attempt to supply Texas illustrates clearly the extent to which Gorgas' operations were to depend on the fortunes of war, the vagaries of chance, and the blunderings of personalities. On September 9, 1863, the blockade-runner "Ella and Annie" departed from Bermuda for Texas, a week later than Stansbury thought she could have left. Clear of Hamilton harbor she encountered a Yankee cruiser and hastily put into St. George's, at the other end of the islands. Again she tried to leave, this time on September 11. But in the face of a strong gale she returned to St. George's on the morning of the fourteenth "with paddle boxes carried away, and otherwise damaged." Worst of all, her cargo of 12,000 Austrian arms and 484,000 rounds of ammunition, plus sundry other supplies, was badly damaged.

On the surface, this unfortunate accident was called an act of God; but Stansbury thought differently. To Major Walker he wrote on the fourteenth a "Private and Unofficial" note giving his suspicions about what had really been the cause for the protracted delay in the ship's departure. Had she left a week before the 9th, as he maintained would have been possible, the storm would have been avoided and she would have escaped damage. He reported that he and his "faithful and efficient clerk . . . toiled to get the 'Ella and Annie' off with her precious cargo." But that vessel's captain had exhibited a noticeable lack of co-operation. According to Stansbury, he refused to land his steamer at the Confederate warehouse wharf in St. George's, instead insisting on

[29] T. L. Bayne to J. M. Seixas, Richmond, July 7, 1863, AGPF, Bayne.
[30] Stansbury to Huse, St. George's, August 18, 1863, *Blockade Running*, pp. 85–86. In a postscript Stansbury remarked that "another steamer leaving for Wilmington will probably clear us out of all stores here, and we shall only have the cargo of the 'Coral Isle' which is daily expected."

withdrawing his ship into the harbor. Consequently the "Ella and Annie" had to be loaded by a small schooner. While the loading was under way, asserted Stansbury, the captain had amused himself in Hamilton, twelve miles away. "He says that he was sick," remarked the major, "but if common report is to be credited, a woman who came over with him was the magnet, which distracted him from duty."[31]

While the "Ella and Annie" had been getting ready for sea, Stansbury had been busy arranging for supplies to go to Wilmington. The most encouraging news he had for Gorgas came at the time it could do the most good. He had reported earlier[32] that a shipment of 50,000 Austrian rifles, in storage at Bermuda when he arrived, amounted to nothing—they were a "lot of trash, in horrible condition." A month later, though, he changed his mind, after having broken open a box of the rifles and had a close look at them. On August 18 he wrote Gorgas that they "turned out much better than the samples I inspected led me to suppose. With careful cleaning by the soldiers, most of them will, I hope, turn out effective weapons."[33]

Although the Ordnance Bureau had lost a total of 70,000 arms at Gettysburg and Vicksburg,[34] Gorgas could take a little comfort from the information that General Grant thought the arms he captured at Vicksburg far superior to those in the hands of his troops—so much better, in fact, that he traded the United States arms for Confederate. In his *Personal Memoirs* he recorded that "the enemy had generally new arms which had run the blockade and were of uniform caliber. After the surrender I authorized all colonels whose regiments were armed with inferior muskets, to place them in the stack of captured arms and replace them with the latter."[35] Grant's views were an exaggeration, but not too large a one at that. He was wrong in broadly assuming that all Confederate arms were superior and that all were imported (he would have been right had he estimated that two-thirds of the Confederacy's stock of arms had come from abroad). So efficient was the Ordnance Bureau's blockade-running system that during the period from September 30, 1862, to September 30, 1863,

[31] Stansbury to Gorgas, St. George's, September 14, 1863 (official); Stansbury to Maj. N. S. Walker, [St. George's, September 14, 1863?] (unofficial), *ibid.*, pp. 95, 96. For another version of this episode, see *ibid.*, p. 53.
[32] On July 25, 1863. See Stansbury to Gorgas, St. George's, *ibid.*, p. 76.
[33] Stansbury to Gorgas, St. George's, August 18, 1863, *ibid.*, pp. 87, 89.
[34] GCWD, July 28, 1863, p. 55.
[35] Ulysses S. Grant, *Personal Memoirs* (New York, 1885), I, 672.

113,504 small arms were shipped into the Confederacy, plus "large quantities of saltpeter, lead, cartridges, percussion caps, flannel and paper for cartridges, leather, hardware, &C."[36]

But in the meantime, Confederate finances abroad had been going from bad to worse. In February, 1863, the Confederacy still owed £572,883 on purchased ordnance supplies, despite the fact that Fraser, Trenholm and Company had received £613,599 credit on outstanding Confederate bills. The only bright spot on the financial scene was the fact that cotton was selling in England for a high of twenty-two pence a pound.[37] True, Confederate diplomacy had succeeded in making some major strides in Europe, the most important of which had been the floating of the vital Erlanger Loan. Negotiations for this loan had been in progress for some time, and finally the bond issue opened in all the influential financial cities of Europe on March 19, 1863. Theoretically, the loan amounted to $15,000,000, but various factors combined to reduce considerably the amount of cash which the Confederacy received. Estimates vary, but a conservative figure puts the actual cash realized at not more than $3,000,000, though $6,800,000 worth of credit may have been extended.[38]

As early as April, 1863, Gorgas had received authority to "control and manage the sea transportation for the Government,"[39] and had begun to take the business into his own hands. He started by curtly telling James R. Crenshaw, with whom the government had concluded a blockade-running agreement, that no matter what Crenshaw might think about who would manage the business transacted between the Confederacy and Crenshaw and Company of Richmond, the person whose word would thereafter be law in blockade-running affairs was J. M. Seixas, War Department agent for Wilmington, North Carolina, and Charleston. Seixas, who usually made Wilmington his headquar-

[36] Gorgas to Seddon, Richmond, November 15, 1863, ORA, Ser. IV, Vol. II, 956; *Blockade Running*, p. xxvii. Gorgas also tried exporting tobacco as well as cotton through the blockade. Tobacco commanded good barter rates in foreign ports and could be had in quantity. See W. S. Downer to Seixas, Richmond, June 16, 1863, CROB, XC, 409.

[37] *Blockade Running*, pp. xxiv, xxv.

[38] The amount of cash actually received by the Confederacy has been estimated at between $2,599,000 and $3,000,000. See Samuel B. Thompson, *Confederate Purchasing Operations Abroad* (Chapel Hill, 1935), pp. 64, 71; also Frank L. Owsley, *King Cotton Diplomacy* (Chicago, 1931), p. 404.

[39] William G. Crenshaw to Huse, London, April 27, 1863, ORA, Ser. IV, Vol. II, 540.

ters, had general charge of "all importations made for the War Department on its own account."[40]

Gorgas took a hostile attitude toward the numerous "wildcat" blockade-running enterprises which flourished partially under government sanction. Many of them he knew nothing about, and he felt that encouraging these ventures was bad policy since it made for much duplication of effort.[41] In fact, demoralizing effects were produced by the government's fluid attitude toward these concerns. Some struck official fancy, and were subsidized by the War Department without consulting Gorgas. Others, in which he might have taken interest, were coldly disregarded. And yet, he supposedly had general supervision of the government's blockade-running business. Though he would have been justified in allowing his disgust to dim his enthusiasm, he never permitted his or his subordinates' efforts to lag in getting cotton out and munitions in. In the face of such problems, however, he found all kinds of deterrents. For instance, he had to get officers for the blockade-runners by the inconvenient method of having navy men detailed to him and then assigned to blockade-runners—the Secretary of the Navy would not assign them directly.[42]

The harrassed Chief of Ordnance found he could not escape the baleful effects of peculiar personnel problems. Originally suggesting the dispatch of Huse to Europe, Gorgas had retained an implicit faith in his capacity and integrity. After Major B. F. Ficklen had made his vicious attack against Huse, he confessed his inability to prove this allegation. He then went on to say that the loyal Confederates abroad had been shocked at Huse's conduct and recognized that he had not only no sentiments in harmony with the cause, but "the unblushing impudence to express himself in such manner as to disgust all and lead to the inquiry why the Government should be thus imposed upon." These wild ejaculations brought Gorgas quickly to Huse's defense. He stated flatly that he was convinced Ficklen had misrepresented the whole situation and refused to take action about it until ordered to do so by the Secretary of War.[43] Seddon, who could not overlook the growing suc-

---

[40] James R. Crenshaw to Seddon, Richmond, April 20, 1863, *ibid.*, pp. 497–98.

[41] William G. Crenshaw to Huse, London, April 27, 1863, *ibid.*, p. 240.

[42] For examples of this practice, see Gorgas' indorsement on Stephen R. Mallory to Seddon, Richmond, April 29, 1863, CRLR, 1863, Doc. MWD 376; Gorgas to Richard H. Gayle, Richmond, May 8, 14, 1863, ORN, Ser. I, Vol. IX, 280.

[43] Ficklen to Seddon, Richmond, January 3, 1863, CRLR, 1863, Doc. FWD 9; Ficklen to Seddon, January 10, 1863, *ibid.*, and indorsement by Gorgas, January 17.

cess of Gorgas' blockade organization, did not act. But new complaints from a source as authoritative as the Quartermaster General could not go unheeded.

Quartermaster General Abraham C. Myers had been incensed by a letter from Major J. B. Ferguson, quartermaster officer in London. This letter, dated April 18, 1863, stated that Huse had admitted to Ferguson taking a commission on some purchases, out of which he intended to pay his travel expenses and to purchase a military library, which he wanted to give to the Ordnance Bureau. Ferguson declared that, after seeing samples of what Huse was buying for the Quartermaster Department, he had become convinced that the prices paid were exorbitant. From that time on, he said, he determined to keep all quartermaster purchasing in his own hands. Myers, after hearing this, felt it his "duty to express my unwillingness that Major Huse should continue to be an agent of this department." Seddon could not ignore these charges and in sending Myers' letters on to Gorgas, wrote: "This matter seems of serious nature. The taking of a commission is altogether inconsistent with the purpose and duty of a trusted agent of the Department. The matter should be fully investigated."[44]

Gorgas also thought so, but for different reasons. He felt an inquiry ought to be made to clear Huse of the imputation made against him. Gorgas hastened to inform Seddon of his belief, based on information received from an officer who had just returned from London, that Huse would satisfactorily explain his taking of a commission on his purchases. Huse was, after all, an army officer of fifteen years' experience, and fully aware of the seriousness of such an act. Gorgas thought the best proof of his good intentions was Huse's awareness that taking compensation for government purchases "would dismiss him from the service with disgrace; yet he makes confession of this flagrant crime to a stranger in his very first interview with him. It is unnecessary to suggest the propriety of at least hearing Major H's statement." Concerning the charge that Huse was paying exorbitant prices for what he bought, Gorgas said:

I am free to admit that if Major H. had applied to me for instructions as to whether he should procure supplies at such rates, authority to that effect would have been given to him without a moment's hesitation. Purchases made at those rates have saved my department and that of the

[44] A. C. Myers to Seddon, Richmond, May 16, 1863, and indorsements, ORA, Ser. IV, Vol. II, 555–56.

Quartermaster-General millions of dollars if compared with the charges made by Confederate houses at Confederate ports. . . . The matter of Major Huse's unfitness for making purchases is assumed by the Quartermaster-General probably on the testimony of Major Ferguson. I think it proper to say that I am perfectly satisfied with his business capacities, and so far as that is concerned desire no change.[45]

In his rush to come to Huse's support, Gorgas could not know that he was doing exactly what Seddon expected of him—expected with some irritation. The Secretary, whose interest in the import-export ventures of William G. and James R. Crenshaw seemed somewhat more enthusiastic than usual, told one of the two partners that he had been annoyed by the disagreement which had arisen in England between Major Huse, Major Ferguson, and the Crenshaws. He feared these difficulties might seriously embarrass importation activities. "I trust," wrote Seddon, "there will be no hesitation on his part in taking any and all Government freight which it is desirable to the Government to have imported, and submit all matters of controversy afterward to my arbitrament. As a public officer, I can have no private interest to swerve me, and do not doubt my ability to render justice to all concerned."[46]

Not content with letting this affair slide for the second time, Seddon instituted a methodical inquiry into Huse's operations, an investigation which lasted for almost a year. It was conducted by the Confederacy's financial agent in Europe, Colin J. McRae, who arrived there in May, 1863, to consolidate financial policy and to supervise the Erlanger Loan. The final outcome of the investigation, not completed until October, 1864, acquitted Huse of "any charge of intentional error and of any malfeasance of any kind," and recommended a raise in his pay.[47]

Subsequent events indicated that Saul Isaac, Campbell and Company, had been keeping a double set of books on Confederate accounts, showing actual costs and also prices charged the Southern government. This did not surprise Seddon. He maintained his dissatisfaction with

[45] Gorgas to Seddon, Richmond, May 22, 1863, *ibid.*, p. 564.

[46] Seddon to James R. Crenshaw, Richmond, May 23, 1863, *ibid.*, p. 567. Some of the background of the quarrel between Huse and William G. Crenshaw is in Huse to Crenshaw, London, April 14, 1863, *ibid.*, pp. 537–39; also Seddon to Crenshaw, Richmond, June 21, 1863, *ibid.*, p. 600, saying he had directed Colin J. McRae to examine and settle Huse's accounts. See also Thompson, *Confederate Purchasing Operations Abroad*, pp. 25, 26.

[47] J. A. Campbell to Seddon, [Richmond,] April 20, 1864, ORA, Ser. IV. Vol. III, 704; McRae and M. H. Bloodgood to Seddon, Paris, October 1, 1864, *ibid.*, p. 703.

Huse and felt that overconfidence, or some other motive, had led him to overlook the best interests of the government in his dealings with that concern. Seddon alleged that he had continuously admonished Gorgas about Huse, and had urged him to "bring all dealings with that firm to as early a close and settlement as possible." He admittedly wanted to recall Huse, but either respect for, or fear of, Gorgas had so far restrained him. To be sure, he had ascribed his reluctance to his desire not to injure a faithful officer by endorsing all the charges against him.[48] There seems little doubt, however, that Gorgas' strong friendship with the President had much to do with the truce existing between the Ordnance Office and the War Department. Certainly no love was lost between Seddon and Gorgas.[49] On the other hand, Huse had earned Gorgas' support. The importation of 185,000 arms between January 1, 1862, and July 1, 1863, stood as the supreme evidence of Huse's competence and devotion to the Confederacy.[50]

Out of the Huse controversy did come at least one thoroughly beneficial result. The episode convinced McRae that the plethora of all types of Confederate agents buying supplies for different commands and departments[51] seriously hampered his own work, and the competition sharply raised the prices of available supplies. The fact that Fraser, Trenholm and Company were in charge of the financial disbursements for the Ordnance Bureau was a step in the right direction, but McRae complained to Gorgas on September 4, 1863, that the government stood to lose out completely by not taking blockade-running entirely into its own hands. Not a bale of cotton should be allowed to go out of the country, nor a pound of merchandise go in "except on government account."[52] The War and Treasury heads wanted to know what Gorgas thought of the idea, and he explained that it was in line

[48] Seddon to McRae, Richmond, December 29, 1863, ORA, Ser. IV, Vol. II, 1067.

[49] GCWD, January 15, 1865, p. 165: "Benjamin, Mallory and Seddon are obnoxious, especially the latter."   [50] GOC, pp. 285–86.

[51] General E. Kirby Smith, for example, sent an agent to Europe to contract directly for supplies to be sent to the Trans-Mississippi Department. This drew a mild rebuke from Gorgas, who said that "experience has shown that special agencies are not desirable." Smith to Jefferson Davis, Shreveport, La., November 21, 1863, and indorsement, CRLR, 1863, Doc. SWD 750. For material on cotton exportation from Texas, see Charles W. Ramsdell, "Texas from the Fall of the Confederacy to the Beginning of Reconstruction," *Southwestern Historical Quarterly,* XI (1907–8), 200.

[52] McRae to Gorgas, Paris, September 4, 1863, ORA, Ser. IV, Vol. II, 889–90.

with what he had long advocated, but at this time he would not go quite so far. He urged the purchase of more vessels and enlarged shipments of cotton, but he did not think private shippers should be excluded completely from the trade. "If the Government's supply of ships were larger the question might then be considered."[53]

All this agitation pointed to the inherent cause of the weakness in existing blockade-running arrangements: lack of proper instructions from a single responsible authority. Whenever the Secretary of War decided to take a hand in issuing orders on the subject (which he often did) without consulting Thomas Bayne in the Ordnance Office, his orders might well supersede those of the Bureau and thus leave Gorgas stranded in important operations.[54] So McRae had planted a seed that in time would bear fruit.

Gorgas, of course, had done all he could to make the blockade-running business efficient. Realizing that he was devoting too much time to that branch of his task, as he had done with the Engineer Bureau, he again divested himself of the excess burden. He sought official permission to reorganize his bureau further so as to shunt the management of government shipping into other hands. For some time he had delegated this job to his brother-in-law Tom Bayne, but now that the task had assumed full-time proportions with the "Collie" ships of the Collie, Crenshaw Company added to those owned by the Ordnance Bureau, Gorgas wanted official sanction for Bayne's orders and decisions. Still displaying a disinclination to meddle in Gorgas' blockade-running arrangements, Seddon gave consent, and on July 23, 1863, Bayne was announced in Special Orders as the "immediate representative of the War Dept. in all that pertains to the running & management of Steamers under the 'Collie Contract.' . . . He will also be charged with the general management of the Govt. Steamers under the directions of the Chief of Ordnance as heretofore."[55]

Under Bayne's capable eye, blockade-running activities took on the organization and efficiency of the Ordnance Bureau itself. On March 20, 1863, Alexander Collie (Collie, Crenshaw) and Company of Liverpool, had entered into a contract with the Confederate government

[53] Memminger to Seddon, Richmond, November 24, 1863, *ibid.*, p. 979.
[54] Gen. P. G. T. Beauregard and Seddon were prime offenders. See, for instance, Bayne to Beauregard, Richmond, November 7, 1863, AGPF, Bayne.
[55] Special Orders Number 174, Adj. and Insp. Gen.'s Off., Richmond, par. VIII, quoted from copy in AGPF, Bayne.

which provided for the purchase of five steamers, to be owned by the corporation, for the importation of certain amounts of government freight. These five vessels in no way affected the operations of the Ordnance and Medical departments, since these two bureaus transported their own cotton and supplies in the ships owned by the Ordnance Bureau. But Bayne had general supervision of both government and private ships handling Confederate cargoes. His ideas on how to make importation of government supplies more efficient were embodied in a series of proposals offered to owners of private blockade-runners. One plan was to require each ship to take out freight equal to one-third the total cargo capacity of the vessel each trip, for which service the owners would be paid a bale of cotton for each bale so transported at the point of origin. Another plan offered five pence sterling per pound of Confederate cotton carried to any owners who would devote one-half their cargo space to government cargoes. Compensation would be secured, under this plan, from Major Norman Walker at Bermuda or Louis Heyliger at Nassau, who would give a draft on the English consignee of the cotton. The third scheme probably commanded the greatest interest on the part of private shipowners. The government would furnish the whole cargo of a vessel whose capacity might be, say 600 bales, and undertake to pay at the rate of bale for bale, not contingent on delivery—the requirement in the first two proposals. Of the total freight of 600 bales, 300 would be made over to the owners of the vessel, who would then contract to deliver the government's 300 bales in the islands without any further charge.[56]

By late October, 1863, Bayne's plans for making Wilmington the main point of departure for government freight had borne fruit. There he had stationed energetic J. M. Seixas as War Department agent in charge of cargoes, and there, as well, he had established a large government cotton press, capable of compressing five hundred bales a day. Negro labor was used to operate the press and move up the cotton. Huge platforms had been erected, along with several spacious cotton sheds. Bagging and rope had been brought in from abroad, and Bayne's confidence in the success of his enterprise emboldened him to declare to the Quartermaster General in October, 1863, that he thought "five thousand bales of cotton will be sent out this month for War, Navy and Treasury[;] 15,000 bales of cotton per month will be needed

[56] Memorandum of proposals drawn up by Bayne and approved by the Secretaries of War and Navy, no place, no date, *ibid.*

at Wilmington, since freight on the cotton out is, in many cases, to be paid in cotton."[57]

Despite the fact that "our most serious difficulty now is the want of sufficient rail road transportation to Wilmington," Bayne had done remarkably well in making blockade-running a good investment. The three steamers owned by Gorgas' bureau, the "Lee," "Cornubia," and "Eugenie," each had a capacity of 350 bales and exclusively served the Ordnance and Medical bureaus. Three of the Collie and Crenshaw Company steamers (out of a proposed total of five) appeared in Confederate ports by October, 1863, although two of them, the "Venus" and "Hebe" were captured. The company had hopes of getting the fourth vessel into the trade in a relatively short time and advised that, per terms of the contract, the management of these ships would be placed completely in the hands of Messrs. Crenshaw Brothers at Wilmington. Plans called for a time schedule of one trip every twenty days for each ship. And, as a matter of fact, something approximating this schedule was achieved by the vessels based at Wilmington. In a memorandum for the information of Bayne's Bureau of Foreign Supplies, Seixas listed seven vessels, with tonnage capacities ranging from 360 to 975, as privately engaged in running the blockade. According to Bayne's estimate, they departed from Wilmington at least once each month, and Seixas shipped government cotton on every private ship clearing that port.[58]

The Collie and Crenshaw ships served the Quartermaster and Commissary departments exclusively. The total tonnage in government freight accruing from Bayne's three blockade-running plans was divided equally between the War and Navy departments, and that portion of it remaining to the War Department was again divided between the different bureaus, excluding the Ordnance and Medical services. Outbound cargoes of Collie vessels were made up indiscriminately of cotton belonging to either the Quartermaster or Commissary departments, since it was understood that arrangements had been made to borrow abroad funds of one bureau to meet the needs of another. With regard

[57] Bayne to Lawton, Richmond, October 27, 1863, *ibid*. The Wilmington cotton press got into production in late September. Bayne's thorough indoctrination in the need for economy caused him to order the conservation of all the rope cuttings, bagging ends, and damaged cotton for use in making cartridge paper. Bayne to John W. Mallet, Richmond, October 1, 1863, CROB, XXXVIII, 392.

[58] Seixas' memorandum, attached to Bayne to Lawton, Richmond, October 26, 1863, AGPF, Bayne.

Carl A. Rudisill Library
LENOIR RHYNE COLLEGE

to incoming cargoes on private vessels, the government had as yet taken no measures to regulate specifically the amount or portion of the carrying space to be devoted to Confederate goods. "Owners have generally liberally met the wishes of the Govmt. agts. at Nassau or Bermuda at the rate of £30 per ton, payable sometimes in cotton @ 60 per lb., but most frequently by sterling bill."

With this steadily improving organization, Bayne looked forward to expansion and told the Quartermaster General, who had questioned him about methods of exportation and importation, that Colin McRae had been authorized by the Secretary of War to purchase all the ships that his financial situation would permit. Seddon himself had advocated the acquisition of more ships and had written McRae on September 26, 1863: "Strs. are much needed, and as funds allow, many more ought to be acquired. I commend this especially to yr. consideration. If I had at command twenty, of a proper class, I would probably render the Depmt. independent of all foreign loans."[59]

The Federal navy, of course, stood as an ever-present obstacle to unrestricted expansion of blockade-running. Not only were two of the Collie and Crenshaw ships captured, but the "Phantom," one of the Ordnance Bureau's own vessels, passed into Federal hands in October, and in November Gorgas noted with alarm that the "Cornubia" (commanded by Josiah's brother-in-law Dick Gayle), "R. E. Lee," and "Ella and Annie," all loaded with government stores, had been taken. These events shook Gorgas badly, and he bitterly observed that "it is a great reflection on our commanders that they allow their vessels to fall unhurt into the hands of the enemy. . . . People abroad will distrust a nation that conducts its affairs with so little skill."[60]

As the war continued, Bayne's task grew in importance and in volume of work. The value of his bureau became so obvious that on March 17, 1864—to look for the moment a little ahead—Bayne would be relieved from duty with the Chief of Ordnance and assigned to special

[59] Quoted in Bayne to Lawton, Richmond, October 26, 1863, *ibid*.
[60] GCWD, October 22, November 21, 1863, pp. 67, 70. The ill-fated voyage of the "Cornubia" began from Bermuda on November 4, 1863. Her cargo included food, rifles, lead, saltpeter, and brandy. When captured, Gayle is reputed to have remarked to the executive officer of the "James Adger" (the vessel which made the prize) that "though the Cornubia is a small vessel, the Confederate Government could better have afforded to lose almost any other vessel," a statement which the capturing captain took to mean "that her cargo is valuable, or that important dispatches were destroyed." Dispatches, however, were not successfully jettisoned, and were sent to the United States District Judge in Boston. ORN, Ser. I, Vol. IX, 274–76; *Blockade Running*, p. 121.

service under the Secretary of War as director of the Bureau of Foreign Supplies.[61] He would have charge of everything pertaining to cotton exportation, while at the same time new regulations, based on McRae's ideas on blockade-running, would be formulated and put into effect. New laws would be needed to enforce them. The first of the blockade statutes, "An Act to prohibit the importation of luxuries, or of articles not necessaries or of common use," levied heavy penalties. The second, designed to "impose regulations upon the foreign commerce of the Confederate States to provide for the public defense,"[62] also carried heavy penalties and placed the shipment of cotton and tobacco entirely in the hands of the Confederate and state governments. Regulations issued as a consequence of the laws provided that one-half of the outbound and inbound cargo space on all vessels must be devoted to Confederate freight at fixed prices.[63] These rules, which were heartily resented by blockade speculators, for a time were to diminish the volume of private trade.

Designed to streamline blockade organization, these plans should have been adopted as early as 1862. Later, when they did go into effect, it was too late to accomplish any lasting good from them. McRae was sure that the method would succeed; and had the Confederate armies kept the field, he may well have been right. But by August, 1864, he was to find the supply of arms almost exhausted, and Gorgas would report that arsenal production within the Confederacy was drastically curtailed. Gorgas then wanted Huse to purchase 50,000 arms without delay. He estimated that only 30,000 small arms had been imported east of the Mississippi following the loss of the Ordnance steamers, and home production accounted for only 20,000, instead of the 50,000 or 60,000 which he was naïvely anticipating in 1862 and 1863.[64]

While in the early years the most significant fact about the blockade was the ease with which it could be evaded, by 1864 the significant fact became the growing efficiency of the Union guard squadrons. The ratio of safe arrivals to captures during 1861 had been nine to one.

[61] Special Orders Number 64, Adj. & Insp. Gen.'s Off., Richmond, March 17, 1864, copy in AGPF, Bayne.

[62] Statutes at Large (Confederate), 1 Cong., Stat. IV, Chap. XXIII, approved February 6, 1864; ibid., Stat. IV, Chap. XXIV, approved the same day.

[63] ORA, Ser. IV, Vol. III, 187–89; Owsley, King Cotton Diplomacy, pp. 412–13.

[64] Gorgas to Seddon, Richmond, October 5, 1864, CRLR, 1864, Doc. GWD 235; report, Gorgas to Seddon, Richmond, October 13, 1864, ORA, Ser. IV, Vol. III, 733–34.

In 1862 it was seven to one; in 1863 about four to one. In 1864 it would be three to one, and by 1865, only one to one.[65] This is an average for the war of six to one.

Gorgas could not know—to return to Josiah in 1862—what the future of Ordnance Bureau blockade-running might be. He knew only that this operation was then profitable and well-nigh indispensable.[66] Could he have known that during the course of the war his bureau would successfully import not less than 330,000 stand of arms, mostly Enfield rifles, and that state and private ventures would bring in at least 270,000 more[67]—plus 1,933,000 pounds of saltpeter and 1,507,-000 pounds of lead in 1863–1864—he might have intensified his efforts to buy ships.[68] In 1862, however, all he could count on was a gradually increasing stream from abroad—under the most favorable conditions. And events in the Confederacy would constantly remind him of the desperate need for Huse's success.

[65] Owsley, *King Cotton Diplomacy*, p. 285.
[66] Report, Gorgas to Seddon, Richmond, October 13, 1864, ORA, Ser. IV, Vol. III, 733–34; *Blockade Running*, p. xxxviii.
[67] Owsley, *King Cotton Diplomacy*, p. 290.
[68] Seddon to the President, Richmond, December 10, 1864, ORA, Ser. IV, Vol. III, 930.

VIII

"Treachery in the Ordnance Department"

COLONEL GORGAS HAD NOT BEEN ABLE TO DEVOTE ALL OF HIS TIME TO production problems and to blockade-running techniques. While giving much attention to these activities, he had, of course, been compelled to deal with the herculean problem of finding arms for the Confederate troops until production and imports should get into operation. In the meantime, he had issued strict orders to his field ordnance officers to purchase all the private arms they could find and to put as many revolvers in the hands of soldiers as possible—the cavalry having priority. He added, in 1862, that "public arms in the possession of anyone will of course be seized."[1]

No one could have doubted the need for such orders. In Georgia, for instance, Governor Brown, unable to discover the exact number of arms in state militia companies, early in 1862 ordered the manufacture of 10,000 pikes for state issue. In addition, he directed that several thousand large hanger knives be made. Patterns of the pikes were on the way to Gorgas.[2] General Thomas J. ("Stonewall") Jackson, as well as judicious General Lee, favored the use of pikes. Jackson suggested the organization of companies armed with this weapon, and Lee, endorsing the scheme, requested Gorgas to send on 1,000 of them.[3]

At the same time a kind of pike fever seems to have swept the Confederacy, possibly engendered by Gorgas' warning of an arms deficiency. At any rate, Congress, obviously having caught the excitement, authorized the President to organize bodies of troops armed with

---

[1] Ordnance Circular, Richmond, March 13, 1862, CROB, CXL, 81.

[2] Bedney F. McDonald to Benjamin, Camp McDonald, Big Shanty P. O., Ga., March 17, 1862, CRLR, 1862, Doc. MWD 213.

[3] Lee to Gorgas, Richmond, April 9, 1862, ORA, Ser. I, Vol. XII, Pt. III, 844–45; Bell I. Wiley, *The Life of Johnny Reb: The Common Soldier of the Confederacy* (Indianapolis, 1943), p. 295.

pikes in case firearms were not available.[4] Gorgas had an inherent lack of confidence in the practicality of these old-fashioned weapons. Years later he reflected that "no excess of enthusiasm could induce our people to rush to the field armed with *pikes*."[5]

Probably because of dire necessity, patriotism, and possibly a little War Department pressure, some Southern editors undertook to extoll the merits of the pike—a difficult task indeed. The Richmond *Tri-Weekly Enquirer* on April 22 declared cautiously that pikes or lances in the hands of brave men were "not to be despised." Companies of pikemen were being formed, and their appearance was greeted with approval. The general attitude was warmly favorable to the use of such makeshift armament.[6]

Meanwhile, Gorgas had been working on the expansion of his bureau. From the crew of a small chemical adjunct to handle mineralogical experiments Gorgas wanted a separate corps of officers created, charged with "the extraction of niter from the caves, and the construction and supervision of niter beds."[7] The Ordnance Bureau was unable to handle all the work in connection with procuring ores and minerals, and Gorgas had Major Isaac M. St. John in mind as the officer to take charge of such a corps should it be authorized. He wanted a military organization connected with the Ordnance Bureau, thinking that it would be more economical than "agents employed on salaries and not responsible to a court martial."[8] On April 11, 1862, Congress passed "An Act for the organization of a corps of officers for the working of niter caves and establishing niter beds," embodying almost exactly the sort of organization Gorgas had envisioned.[9] Under St. John's guidance,

the whole nitre-bearing area of the country was laid off into districts; each district in charge of an officer. . . . These officers got details of workmen generally from those subject to militia duty in the mountains

---

[4] In "An Act to provide for keeping all fire-arms in the armies of the Confederate States in the hands of effective men," *Statutes at Large (Confederate)*, 1 Cong., Stat. I, Chap. XXII.   [5] GOC, p. 214.

[6] Such concern about pikes made it standard procedure to husband jealously the small supply of Enfield rifles coming into the South. Robert E. Lee thought it advisable that these rifles be given "to the flanking companies at least of . . . old regiments, and that the new troops be armed with muskets. The fine rifles will be more efficient in the hands of tried troops, and, moreover, such a distribution would appear equitable." Lee to Gen. E. Kirby Smith, Richmond, March 27, 1862, ORA, Ser. I, Vol. X, Pt. II, 368–69.

[7] Gorgas to Davis, Richmond, November 20, 1861, CRLR, 1861, Doc. 7934.

[8] Gorgas to Benjamin, Richmond, March 12, 1862, ORA, Ser. IV, Vol. I, 990.

[9] *Statutes at Large (Confederate)*, 1 Cong., Stat. I, Chap. XXVI.

beyond where disaffection existed, and carried on extended works in their several districts. In this way we brought up the nitre production, in the course of a year to something like half our total consumption. . . . It was a rude, wild sort of service, and the officers in charge of these districts, especially in East Tennessee, North Carolina and North Alabama, had to show much firmness in their dealings with the turbulent people among whom, and by whose aid they worked.[10]

Some artificial niter beds had been started in Richmond before St. John's corps came into being; and he set about expanding these, establishing others at Columbia, Charleston, Savannah, Augusta, Mobile, Selma, and other places.[11] The niter business in Selma contributed a bit of doggerel to literature. Human urine, one of the components of niter, was advertised for by Jonathan Haralson, niter agent at Selma. In a local newspaper he reputedly requested the ladies of Selma to preserve their "chamber-lye" for the use of his organization. This furnished too great a temptation to a self-styled wit, allegedly named Wetmore, who composed several stanzas of naughty verse, which are still in circulation here and there.[12]

Holding general authority over the Niter Corps, Gorgas charged it, in addition to the duty of procuring powder, with supervision of the production of iron, lead, copper—in fact "all the minerals which needed development, including the making of sulphuric and nitric acids; which latter we had to manufacture to insure a supply of fulminate of mercury for our percussion caps."[13]

Gorgas had not been so fortunate, however, in his efforts to reorganize his bureau proper. He had wanted to separate it from the Artillery Corps and make it autonomous, but Davis and the Secretary of War had not seen fit to adopt this idea. At length, however, both appeared to realize the need for some change in the relationship of Ordnance with Artillery. On April 16, 1862, General Orders Number 24 were promulgated as a compromise measure. Under them all officers assigned to ordnance duty in the field were to report to Gorgas, and every general commanding an army corps was to assign an officer to duty as his chief of ordnance. There were to be division and brigade ordnance officers, selected on the basis of their fitness for ordnance

[10] GOC, p. 215.   [11] Ibid.
[12] See Wiley, Life of Johnny Reb, pp. 304–305, for a humorous account of this verse, the first two lines of which (according to the writer's copy) read:
John Haralson, John Haralson, you are a funny creature,
You have given to this war, a new and curious feature.
[13] GOC, p. 215.

duties and regarded as attached to the Ordnance Bureau. They would not be changed or reassigned without permission of the Chief of Ordnance. Every regiment commander was to select from the noncommissioned officers of his regiment one best qualified to be ordnance sergeant and to designate an acting sergeant, reporting the appointment to Gorgas. The duties of the ordnance sergeants were among the most exacting in the army. They had charge of regimental surplus ordnance, on which they had to make returns to Gorgas' headquarters. They were responsible, also, for the arms and accouterments of the sick and disabled, which had to be turned over to and accounted for by them. They had, too, general supervision over the arms and ammunition in the hands of the troops, and it was their responsibility to report any waste or damage to the division ordnance officer. The orders also stipulated that no ordnance officer on any general's staff could enter into contracts for, or purchase, ordnance supplies unless especially ordered to do so by the general; otherwise Gorgas would not pay for the material.[14] These orders, coupled with the practical monopoly of manpower given the government by the Conscription Act of April 16, 1862,[15] seemed to grant Gorgas as much authority as he could

[14] General Orders Number 24, Adj. & Insp. Gen.'s Off., Richmond, April 16, 1862, ORA, Ser. IV, Vol. I, 1065–66; also "An Act to increase the Military establishment of the Confederate States, and to amend the 'Act for the establishment and organization of the Army of the Confederate States of America,'" approved April 19, 1862, *Statutes at Large (Confederate)*, 1 Cong., Stat. I, Chap. XLIII.

[15] The Conscription Act of April 16 made all white men, residents of the Confederate States, between the ages of eighteen and thirty-five, subject to military service. The fact that throughout the bill there was no mention of exemptions probably frightened bureau heads. But some exemptions had to be made; everyone realized that. The *Daily Richmond Examiner*, April 18, 1862, commented that the draft bill "provides for no case of exemption, the whole subject being reserved for a distinct and separate act. If such a separate act should not be passed by Congress, we suppose exemptions are to be determined by State laws." An exemption act passed on April 21 provided a system of class exemption. For the two laws, see *Statutes at Large (Confederate)*, 1 Cong. Stat. I, Chap. XXXI ("An Act to further provide for the public defence"); *ibid.*, Stat. I, Chap. LXXIV ("An Act to exempt certain persons from enrollment for service in the Armies of the Confederate States").

Without some provision for a labor supply in government installations, the unbridled conscript and exemption laws would strip every plant of its skilled and unskilled workers. To meet this need the Secretary of War determined to use a policy in effect since the early months of the war; he would detail needed men from the army. When, in 1861, Richmond iron concerns faced a mass migration of their workers into the Army, they had gotten the War Department to detail mechanics back to their plants for duty. This would continue as departmental policy. See Kathleen Bruce, *Virginia Iron Manufacture in the Slave Era* (New York, 1931), p. 358.

want to conduct the affairs of his bureau; but there still were difficulties to overcome.

Some efforts to improve his bureau were to meet with unexpected congressional opposition. On April 19 William P. Miles of South Carolina, a member of the House Committee on Military Affairs, reported a bill to create the office of general superintendent of armories. This prompted Alexander R. Boteler of Virginia to enquire, "if there was not a superintendent to each armory, and if the Chief of Ordnance was not general superintendent of Armories?" Miles admitted this was true. Boteler then thought there was no need for the office. Miles countered by stating that Gorgas had recommended the position, and read a letter from him suggesting James H. Burton as the man to fill the office. Joseph B. Heiskell, of Tennessee, who had heard whisperings concerning Burton, moved to postpone the bill until the first day of the next session. Miles decided not to press the bill, and the motion to postpone its consideration was unanimously carried.[16]

Burton had his pride and so did Gorgas. On April twenty-first Burton sent Gorgas his resignation, as a result of the congressional attack, which he regarded as unjust.[17] Gorgas, obviously angered that Congress would so jeopardize his efforts at organization, immediately jumped to Burton's defense. To Heiskell he said that Burton had been authorized to give his spare time to the pistol-making firm of Spiller & Burr, a decision that had made Heiskell suspicious. This had been done to insure the erection of a productive factory. "I do not hesitate to pronounce him the most competent and valuable officer we have connected with the Bureau, and you will find on inquiry, that my high opinion of him is fully endorsed by the officer at the head of the Bureau of Ordnance of the Navy." He added that he would make "every effort" to have Burton's resignation refused.[18] The bureau did not lose Burton, but he found himself in an unenviable position. He possessed the only set of drawings in the Confederacy of tools and machinery needed to make the Enfield rifle. This fact put his services much in demand by would-be private gunmakers. He became involved in an arrangement with Thomas E. McNeill, an Ordnance Bureau contractor who was to make 20,000 carbines and needed help. Burton probably had little

[16] *Daily Richmond Examiner,* April 21, 1862.
[17] James H. Burton to Gorgas, Richmond, Burton.
[18] Gorgas to Heiskell, Richmond, April 21, 1862, *ibid.* On April 29 Randolph refused Burton's resignation, saying, "your qualifications and services are too well known, and too highly appreciated by this Department to permit its acceptance." *Ibid.*

faith in McNeill's intentions, but had charge of small arms manufacture and wanted to do everything he could to push new firms. Secretary Randolph gave him permission to help McNeill and to receive commensurate compensation.

Unfortunately, circumstances caught Burton in what appeared to be a shady transaction. An inventor of dubious attainment, C. W. Alexander had been working on a breech-loading carbine, hoping to perfect a serviceable military weapon. In it he solicited the assistance of Burton, having heard that on occasion the latter farmed out his experience. Possibly because Gorgas had previously approved such an arrangement, and because he thought it necessary, Burton agreed to superintend the construction of Alexander's carbines, and "to use his influence with the Chief of Ordnance . . . to establish introduction [of the carbines] into the military service of the C. States." In return, Burton would have a half-interest in the concern if a patent was obtained.[19]

On March 13, 1862, Gorgas, who had been away from Richmond, took up the matter of the Burton-Alexander agreement. He was not pleased with the appearance of the arrangement. After some deliberation he wrote Burton. His absence from the capital, he said, had postponed notice of Burton's proposed partnership. He went on to write a firm and for him highly diplomatic letter:

It is by no means proper that you should make your influence with me enter into the Stipulations of a contract: A knowledge of this would destroy the confidence which I have in you.

The reservation that you are to devote only such portions of your time and attention as is compatible with your duties relieves you from any imputation of taking advantage of your position in that respect.

You have in one instance, at my suggestion, been permitted to assist with your well known experience a party who had a contract with the Bureau; this indulgence to you was given because [it was] likely to prove of much advantage to the Dept. in the end; the indulgence was an exception and must not be permitted to pass into a rule.[20]

So much for Alexander.

[19] Burton to McNeill, Richmond, April 25, 1862; McNeill to Burton, May 5; Burton to Gorgas, Richmond, May 6; Burton, *Diary,* May 6, all in Burton. For the statement that both he and the government had been "humbugged" in this arrangement, as McNeill was never ready to fulfill his contract, see Burton to Gorgas, December 4, 1862, *ibid.* Articles of Agreement between Burton and C. W. Alexander, *ibid.*   [20] Gorgas to Burton, Richmond, Burton.

Worry about his friend Burton was not all that troubled the Chief of Ordnance. At Yorktown, General Daniel H. Hill had begun to feel resentful toward the Ordnance Bureau—a feeling he readily passed on to his superiors and the War Department in his dispatches. To General Joseph E. Johnston he observed on April 25 that he had little doubt that the Federals would attack Yorktown in force, since water facilities would allow them to place siege guns close to the Confederate works. A siege of Yorktown would require that Hill have rifles and guns from Norfolk, as the guns sent from Richmond were no good: "I have long believed that there was treachery in the Ordnance Dept."[21] With this letter Hill forwarded one from a Lieutenant Pierson, commanding Randolph's battery at Yorktown, complaining of ordnance received. His complaint, in clear, outspoken language, together with Hill's serious charge, forced Johnston to forward both letters to the Secretary of War.

George Randolph was, in many instances, a timid man. This was such an instance. He and Gorgas were friends, and he knew how Gorgas would react to Hill's allegation—knew and did not relish the prospect. But duty was duty; Hill had charged treachery, and this could hardly be ignored, especially since that officer alleged proof of his point. Randolph sent Hill's letter on to Gorgas, with the indorsement that since the charge had been brought by a trustworthy officer, it had to be considered. The Secretary wanted Gorgas to be president of a board empaneled to see if any change in the manufacture of ordnance and ammunition needed to be made. He obviously hoped by this expedient to cool Gorgas down, but the idea was plainly absurd. How could Gorgas be expected to preside over an inquiry as to whether or not he himself knew what he was doing?

Gorgas delayed his reply about a week. He needed a few days to muster his facts before delivering his broadside. That the answer would be effective Randolph doubtless knew. That it would embarrass someone was equally free of doubt. The situation could be warmly uncomfortable, and it is even probable that Randolph personally discussed the matter with Gorgas. He disliked controversy so close to home—it did not help either that one of the major contestants was an old and punctilious friend. On the first day of May Gorgas wrote Randolph that Hill's charge of treachery was ill-founded, and he categorically disposed of each of Lieutenant Pierson's charges.

[21] D. H. Hill to Johnston, Yorktown, Va., CRLR, 1862, Doc. GWD 231.

An opinion delivered without knowledge of the people thus stigmatized may well be left to the consideration due to it; but I deem it due to myself to state to you that early means were taken to secure loyal workmen in the various workshops by making the workmen take the oath of allegiance. Such as did not take the oath were discharged. This was done in the Laboratory early last summer, at the instance of the Chief Laboratorian Mil[itar]y Storekeeper W. A. [N.] Smith. . . .

It is high time that the imputation of "treachery" which I have now heard several times against the Bureau, should be discontinued. There is I fully believe no foundation for it. The imputation is the offspring of ignorance and thoughtlessness.

That there is ample reason for criticism in the products of our laboratories and foundries is fully admitted. But it must be remembered that the Bureau has had but little assistance in experienced officers. . . .

If an experienced ordnance officer could have supervised the laboratory here; and an officer acquainted with foundry duty had attended to the construction of guns at the Tredeger Works, bad ammunition and worse guns could not now be complained of.

But it is useless to suggest what we might have done—The work must be done with such means as we have. Yet a just and manly criticism will take the means necessarily into consideration.

As to the worthlessness of many of the Tredegar guns I full[y] agree with Genl Hill. That establishment has not sustained its old reputation. Yet I shall ever be slow to attach bad motives to those who carry it on; or attribute to "treachery" what is in great measure due to our failing resources. It will take but little charity to weave for them, and for others engaged with us, a mantle which will perhaps cover "a multitude of sins" but not the plague spot of treason.

I return herewith the letter of Genl Hill. . . .[22]

Randolph must have been surprised at the restraint and forceful logic of this reply. The letter marked a clear change in the pattern of Gorgas' correspondence. He had passed the stage of petulant composition. The responsibilities of command had done much to mature his attitude and to temper his relations with his superiors.

In his search for someone with the necessary experience to handle Confederate laboratory operations, Gorgas suddenly received welcome and unexpected assistance. On the staff of Brigadier General Robert Rodes served First Lieutenant John W. Mallet, a chemist of some renown. His assignment afforded Mallet excellent opportunities to become acquainted with various Confederate leaders—among them

[22] Gorgas to Randolph, Richmond, May 1, 1862, *ibid.*

Gorgas, who, Mallet discovered, "was in need of some one to take general charge of the production of ammunition, both for small arms and artillery, there being much complaint of confusion and irregularity in the supplies for the heterogeneous lot of calibers then alone obtainable."[23]

The Ordnance Bureau needed Mallet badly. Gorgas had been trying for some time to secure for the bureau the services of a scientist, but had hardly expected to get so distinguished a chemist as Mallet. A British subject, he had been born in Dublin on October 10, 1832, and received his education partly in Dublin's Trinity College and partly at Göttingen. He had come to the United States in 1853 and, in 1857, had married Mary E. Ormond, a daughter of Judge Ormond of the Alabama Supreme Court. He was a member of the Royal Society of England, and had served as chemist to the Geological Survey of Alabama before volunteering for Rodes's staff. His arrival in the Confederate Ordnance service seemed providential. He himself recorded the almost accidental way in which it came about:

I was in the summer of 1862 serving most pleasantly as aide-de-camp on the staff of General Rodes, whom I had known well before the war. Another friend of his was Colonel Briscoe Baldwin, chief ordnance officer on the staff of General Lee, and who had been for a while in charge of Richmond Arsenal. Colonel Baldwin visited our camp below Richmond at the time of Seven Pines, talked with me about the state of the Ordnance service, and asked me to go with him to the office in Richmond of Colonel Gorgas, who had expressed a wish to see me. The result of several interviews with him was that I was, though with a good deal of reluctance, transferred to the ordnance corps with a commission as Captain of Artillery, and ordered to at once endeavor to bring order out of the confusion. . . .[24]

Gorgas again did not wait long for a decision; he forced one. He wrote Randolph on May 21 asking a captain's commission for Mallet, who was to be put in charge of Confederate laboratories. "Dr. M. is an eminent practical chemist, and the appointment is of the first importance and necessity." Randolph approved, and Mallet entered on duty, although the Senate did not confirm his captaincy until October 4, 1862.[25]

[23] William H. Echols, "John W. Mallet; Scholar, Teacher, Gentleman," *Alumni Bulletin of the University of Virginia,* January, 1913, p. 13.

[24] Mallet, p. 8.

[25] Gorgas to Randolph, Richmond, May 21, 1862, AGPF, Mallet; *Journal of the Congress of the Confederate States of America, 1861–1865,* II, 422.

The job which Mallet began was not easy for a mild-mannered, scholarly man. He was directed to make a close inspection of the ammunition and chemical laboratories of the Confederacy and to work for uniformity in their products; supervise preparation of buckshot cartridges for Enfield rifles; investigate the packing of ammunition for transportation, with caps packed in each bundle; direct the manufacture of explosive shells; make a "rigid inspection of shot and shell and the getting up of instruments for it"; oversee the manufacture of fuses and rifle gun ammunition; consider the spherical case for rifle gun ammunition and whether the "segment shell" ought to be made; manage the waterproofing of ammunition chests; and check the composition and packing of friction tubes, small arms cartridges, and rockets. The Chief of Ordnance wanted Mallet to promulgate a general rule governing accident prevention to be adopted at all laboratories and to concern himself with increasing the Confederacy's leather supply. Mallet's practical experience with the Alabama Geological Survey particularly qualified him to examine the possibility of extracting sulphur from iron pyrites in Alabama, and, of course, he was expected to handle the entire subject of producing sulphuric and nitric acids, chlorate of potash, sulphur of antimony, and all other chemicals for military use.

The views expressed in Mallet's report of his initial inspection tour strengthened Gorgas' conviction that centralization was badly needed. The Superintendent of Laboratories recommended that a central laboratory be started at once and suggested Macon, Georgia, as the most desirable spot to place permanent works.[26] This recommendation was supported by the fact that James H. Burton, who had gone to Atlanta to establish an armory, shifted his attention to Macon and went there on June 5, 1862, to inspect a site proposed for the armory. The site appeared more favorable, even though Gorgas, too, had been looking at Atlanta as the main point of centralization. Macon already had a Confederate arsenal and a carbine contractor, Thomas E. McNeill.[27] Everything pointed to a rapidly industrialized Macon.

Establishing a new industrial center there would, of course, have its advantages, but only if the Confederate transportation system could stand the strain. This question stood as a problematical one. Rolling stock on Confederate railroads had become so scanty by the beginning of 1862 that even at that early date "railroad men were predicting the utter breakdown of the roads within a short time."[28] Individual

---

[26] Echols, op. cit., p. 13.   [27] Burton, Diary, June 3, 5, 6, 1862.
[28] Charles W. Ramsdell, "The Confederate Government and the Railroads," American Historical Review, XXII (1916–17), 799.

railroad companies, dependent on the government for supplies of iron, were unable to repair track, rolling stock, and other equipment without governmental assistance. They looked, of course, to the Quartermaster Department for aid, but were really dependent on Gorgas and St. John. The Ordnance Bureau had a monopoly on the Confederacy's iron output, and only under the dole of the subsidiary Nitre and Mining Bureau could this commodity be had. An instance of railroad reliance on the Ordnance Bureau is furnished by a letter from W. S. Knox, Secretary and Treasurer of the Alabama and Mississippi Railroad Company, to Randolph, dated June 6, 1862. The company desperately needed spikes, chains, and bolts to complete an unfinished section of the road, and the only establishment the company officials knew was able to furnish these items was the Shelby County Iron Manufacturing Company, at Columbiana, Alabama. The iron firm was willing to supply what was needed, but only if allowed to do so by the government, since the full capacity of the works for twelve months was under contract to the Ordnance Bureau.[29] Other requests appear to have taken precedence over that of the railroad.

Considered from another point of view, the frail condition of the railroads posed a significant tactical problem. If, as would eventually be the case, the rail lines became incapable of sustained long-distance hauls,[30] Ordnance as well as other supply departments would find that large centers of fabrication, while convenient in other ways, could not be maintained. The gradual weakening and slow collapse of Confederate transportation, hastened by the ever-present economic weakness, failing currency, proved one of the most potent factors in Confederate supply shortages. From Gorgas' standpoint this increasing weakness meant that he would have to diversify his centers of supply.

There was a glimmer of light on this otherwise dark horizon. On June 9, 1862, Gorgas issued a circular, in keeping with his policy of standardization, which provided that in the future the standard Confederate cartridge was to be caliber .577, that of the Enfield rifle.[31]

[29] Knox to G. W. Randolph, Selma, Ala., ORA, Ser. IV, Vol. I, 1145–46. For some of the operational problems faced by this firm, see Vandiver, "The Shelby Iron Company in the Civil War: A Study of a Confederate Industry," *Alabama Review,* I (1948), 13–26, 111–27, 203–17.

[30] Ramsdell, *American Historical Review,* XXII, 809.

[31] Ordnance Circular, Richmond, *General Orders from the Confederate Adjutant and Inspector-General's Office,* Ser. of 1863 (Columbia, 1864), p. 234. In conjunction with standardization of caliber and conservation of ammunition, Gorgas on June 24 issued a circular requiring each package of cartridges manufactured to be labelled, stating "kind and calibre of ammunition, and number

If this circular sounded optimistic, it also heralded better things for Gorgas' bureau. Without some assurance that soon most arms issued to troops would be either Enfield rifles or rifles of the same caliber, Gorgas would not have dared to publish these orders.[32]

A great deal of his time now had to be devoted to little things. Since General Johnston had fought the battle of Seven Pines on May 31–June 1, McClellan's advance up the peninsula had become the talk of Richmond, and the people were uncertain of General Robert E. Lee, Johnston's successor. Though Seven Pines had been a Confederate victory, McClellan and his massive aggregation in blue still lay close to Richmond's defense perimeter. If Richmond was to be held, Gorgas would be able to pursue one course; if not, then the policy—even the geography—of the Bureau would sustain a major revision. But Gorgas was not expecting the evacuation of Richmond.[33]

Holding the position he did in the War Department, Gorgas heard some of the inside strategy—indeed, it was not only natural but imperative that he should hear it. So it was that as early as June 22 he had definite information that Jackson would reinforce Lee for the assault on McClellan.[34]

A measure of Gorgas' perceptive capacity may be taken from an examination of his prediction of the date that the Seven Days Battles would begin. On Tuesday, June 24, he noted that there was little firing along the lines and thought that the battle would start on the 25th or 26th, probably Thursday the 26th. "A train leaves tomorrow

---

of rounds in the package," *ibid.* The circular of June 9, having overlooked the caliber of ammunition issued by various states, on July 5 Gorgas wrote Governor John Milton at Tallahassee, Florida, of the advisability of informing the states that the Confederacy was now making arms of caliber .577 exclusively, and, for obvious reasons, he hoped the states would follow suit. Gorgas to Milton, Richmond, July 5, 1862, *Milton Letter Book,* p. 394.

[32] The arrival of 112,000 pounds of powder and four tons of lead aboard the blockade-runner "Memphis," on June 23, gave much better prospects to the cartridge makers. See John C. Pemberton to Randolph, Charleston, June 23, 1862, ORA, Ser. I, Vol. LIII, 254.

[33] Gorgas continued his plans for permanent national ordnance works throughout this period. See Gorgas to Mallet, Richmond, June 28, 1862, CROB, V, 2.

[34] GCWD, p. 7: "Preparations are evidently being made for a general action. Jackson with, I hope, 20,000 men is coming here from Gordonsmith [Gordonsville] to fall on McClellan's right, I presume, while another attack is being made in front by our forces here." Contrast this definite prediction with the statement of J. B. Jones in his *Rebel War Clerk's Diary,* ed. by Swiggett (New York, 1935), I, June 24: "There are some vague rumors about the approach of Stonewall Jackson's army; but no one knows anything about it, and but few believe it."

morning for Hanover, where Gen. Jackson *may* be. It will carry ammunition which he needs, and therefore, he will not be ready tomorrow morning."[35]

When the Seven Days started on Thursday, as he had predicted, Gorgas had done about all he could to prepare Lee and Jackson. On June 29, as the Confederate attack centered at Savage Station, an iron-plated railroad battery went into action against some of the Federal positions. Gorgas, the man many felt might have Federal sympathies because of his Yankee background, had constructed this mobile battery at the suggestion of General Lee. He had heard from the General about it on June 5, and had it completed and ready for service by June 21.[36]

Lee defeated McClellan, and Richmond no longer stood besieged. The Ordnance Bureau had undergone considerable changes in organization; now it seemed to be on the road to a successful mission. Prospects for a good supply of arms and ammunition were much brighter than they had been a year before, and it looked as though the Ordnance Bureau could deliver the goods.

Treachery in the Ordnance Department?

[35] GCWD, p. 7.
[36] Lee to Mallory, Headquarters, Dobb's House, June 21, 1862, ORA, Ser. I, Vol. XI, Pt. III, 610; Lt. Col. Leroy Hodges, "Guns of the American Civil War," pp. 10, 11, 12. For press reaction to the use of the railroad battery, referred to as the "Dry Land Merrimac," see *Daily Richmond Examiner,* July 8, 9, 1862.

IX

"This Inevitable Business"

RICHMOND, LIKE ITS LATE BESIEGERS, LAY QUIETLY AND LICKED ITS wounds. Yankee and Confederate wounded alike jammed the emergency hospitals of the city.[1] After the shock of fighting and victory had begun to wear off in early July, 1862, the city slowly returned to normal. The press again was its usual self. After having worried for some time about the precarious status of the capital, the *Daily Richmond Examiner* could now take time to carp at the results of the battle—it maintained that the enemy had been allowed to get away, to escape complete ruin. Gorgas had no patience with this argument, observing that "the papers (one of them at least), grumble that McClellan has 'slipped thro' our fingers.' We should have gladly compromised for such a 'situation' two weeks ago."[2]

With the temporary relaxation of strain, Gorgas could devote more time to his personal affairs. Separation from Amelia and the children, who were in South Carolina, was "wearisome" to him, and he hoped "it will never recur." The general atmosphere did not contribute to the lifting of his spirits. The weather followed the usual pattern of a Richmond July, and this added to a short period of rather severe illness which Gorgas suffered through the early part of the month. Though he felt so sick that he knew he should take some time off to recuperate, his sense of duty forbade it; to Amelia he wrote that, after all, "I feel so well that I dare not ask for what is not absolutely necessary, at such an hour—Everyone must be at his post."[3] For his own comfort he

---

[1] See the description of the pathetic condition of the wounded in Alfred H. Bill, *The Beleaguered City* (New York, 1946), p. 135.

[2] *Daily Richmond Examiner,* June 30, July 5, 8, 1862. It was of the July 8 issue of the *Examiner* that Gorgas was speaking, GCWD, pp. 9–10.

[3] Gorgas to Amelia [Richmond, July 7, 1862], GMSS.

"practiced abstinence," and felt he would "soon get right again."[4]
Even though he was separated from his family and was unwell, Gorgas
realized he was much better off than he might have been.

He was not immune, however, to the many rumors which spread,
miasma-like, over the Confederacy's capital. Victory had given the
Southern people just the respite they needed to replenish their waning
stock of self-confidence. This spirit now blossomed forth in optimistic
rumor. Gorgas heard that Lincoln and the venerable Winfield Scott had
both visited McClellan's camp. The supposed presence of his old commander gave Gorgas opportunity to observe that "Scott will now be
bro't back to supervise & direct—the old Scoundrel could by his coun-
sels go far to close this war, if his benighted old brain could but be
penetrated with the truth."[5]

Apart from such retrospection Gorgas maintained a keen interest in
Richmond's and the soldiers' recovery. He noted with surprise that
many of the latter were only slightly wounded, and was cheered at the
thought that fatalities would be less than might reasonably have been
expected—though he had been told that about 100 men died every
day. The Quartermaster Department had to find new interment
ground, Oakwood and the other cemeteries having been filled to
capacity.

Officially, of course, Gorgas had much to concern him following
the major actions on the Peninsula. There had been an unpleasant
affair involving Major Briscoe G. Baldwin, commander of Richmond
Arsenal, who had absented himself from that post to go to the field as a
lieutenant colonel of a regiment in action. For this act, Gorgas, on
June 30, had removed him from his position. Baldwin rejoined with the
contention that an officer commanding a post had a right to give himself seven days leave, which he had done, leaving six commissioned
officers on duty at the arsenal. The brigade which he joined needed him
badly—most of its officers had been shot. He returned to see if all was
well at his post and found a note from Gorgas, forbidding him to return
to the front. Baldwin begged Gorgas to rescind this injunction, and

---

[4] GCWD, July 8, 1862, p. 10. For Willie's guidance, Gorgas wrote at some
length on the value of diet. "I impress this important fact on Willie that with
his constitution a few days 'fasting' is worth all the medicine in the world.
Whenever I feel ill I diet, and have thus avoided the use of medicine almost entirely. I have found a half grain of 'blue mass' without anything else, a very good
corrective in warm weather. Sluggishness of the liver seems inherent in my organization; at least I cannot endure warm climates with impunity." *Ibid.*
[5] Gorgas to Amelia [Richmond, July ?, 1862], GMSS.

Gorgas replied by endorsement: "Return as soon as you can. The officers left there are either sick or absent. I found but *one* fit for duty." The words "return as soon as you can" looked to Baldwin as though Gorgas sanctioned his return to battle, and he went. Brought back to Richmond wounded, he was startled to learn that he had been relieved of his post and wanted a court of inquiry to look into all the circumstances. As a matter of fact, his brother, John B. Baldwin, a Virginia Representative in the Confederate House, also wanted an explanation, and so told Randolph.[6]

The Secretary passed Baldwin's letter on to Gorgas for reply. On July 10 Gorgas wrote unofficially to Randolph, setting forth his side of the case. From all indications, the Chief of Ordnance was angry at Baldwin. In a letter indicating a continuing restraint in correspondence, Gorgas said:

I see no good that a court of Inquiry could do. The facts are too apparent. Besides suppose a construction was put upon the endorsement as sanctioning Major B's absence, how would it help him? I claim the right to designate the duties of the officers assigned to me in any event. The opinion of the Court, however favorable would not restore him to his command. And his services are still perfectly acceptable to me in any other position. It needs no court of inquiry to declare his fitness for my purposes. I trust you will assign him to the most important duty. Were I in power I am quite sincere in saying I should make him a Brigadier, despite his *disobedience* to me. If in my order relieving Major B. I expressed a shade of disapprobation, it was only a shade. I could scarcely say less.[7]

If, as John Baldwin had asserted, there existed no basis for, or expectation of, unfriendliness between his brother and Gorgas, the reason for the action of the Chief of Ordnance might, in Baldwin's eyes, lie in another quarter. Gorgas undoubtedly suffered a measure of pique as a result of Baldwin's apparent desertion of the arsenal—but possibly that could have been overlooked, since the Major went to a considerably more dangerous zone. It was unthinkable, however, that the Chief of Ordnance could condone the desertion of a post by one of his subordinates. He could hardly have been more liberal in dealing with

[6] Baldwin to Randolph, Staunton, Va., July 7, 1862, CRLR, 1862, Doc. GWD 423.
[7] Gorgas to Randolph ("Unofficial"), Richmond, *ibid.* On July 26, Gorgas told Randolph in a memorandum (*ibid.*, Doc. 462) that his note to Baldwin allowing him to return to the field was intended to give him time to arrange for someone else to command his regiment.

the wayward Major than to suspend him and assign another, William Leroy Broun, in his stead.[8] In the end the problem was resolved peacefully. The Secretary took Gorgas at his word and made Baldwin Lee's chief ordnance officer.

Gorgas' absence from his own office for a time in July, apparently recuperating from his illness, occasioned a backlog of work when he returned. Powder was arriving in fair quantity at Charleston—the blockade-runners were succeeding reasonably well; on the other hand affairs in Texas, so far as they concerned ordnance, were alarming; Burton and Mallet had more than they could legitimately be expected to handle, and military commanders again resumed their calls for materiel.[9] Had the Secretary of War been asked to report to Congress on the condition of the War Department, he could have said that there was no other bureau of army supply which had received more careful, meticulous administration than ordnance. Fearing to be absent from his duties because "my office got sadly behindhand during my week's absence," Gorgas tended closely to his work. On August 5, he called Mallet's attention to the need for manufacturing chlorate of potash on a small scale—about 3,000 pounds a year, he thought, would be enough for the needed friction primers—though he would hardly frown on production of thrice that amount. The other necessary chemical for primers, sulphur of antimony, would also be prepared in small quantities.[10]

And from Bragg's army came worrisome news. Colonel Hypolite Oladowski, chief ordnance officer of the Army of Tennessee, reported

[8] This remains a matter of opinion. While it is a fact that Gorgas stood ready at all times to defend his official and personal prerogatives, the Baldwin incident might turn not so much on personal reaction as on some underlying cause, and it is barely possible that Gorgas wanted to make room for Broun. In his personal correspondence with Amelia, Gorgas gave no hint at any ill-feeling toward Baldwin. See his letter to her, Richmond, July [?], 1862, GMSS, in which he says that Baldwin was wounded and probably would not resume command of the arsenal.

[9] For the arrival of powder at Charleston, see ORA, Ser. I, Vol. LIII, 256–67; for affairs in Texas see Gen. P. O. Hébert to Lee, Houston, June 18, 1862, *ibid.*, IX, 719, stating that "the great difficulty, almost an impossibility, is in getting arms; men we can command." See also the San Antonio *Weekly Herald,* July 12 and August 2, 1862, for information on the need of artillerists and on living conditions there. For the concern of some military officers about ordnance for their commands, see Gen. T. J. Jackson to Maj. Gen. Richard S. Ewell, Headquarters, Valley District, July 12, *Crutchfield Papers;* H. Oladowski to Gorgas, Chattanooga, July 31, ORA, Ser. I, Vol. XVI, Pt. II, 740–41. For more of Burton's operations, see his *Diary,* July 16, 25.

[10] Gorgas to Mallet, Richmond, August 5, 1862, CROB, V, 7.

that Bragg had ordered the establishment of a depot at Dalton, Georgia, "where supplies should be deposited for 60,000 infantry, 5,000 cavalry and 100 pieces of field artillery." On his own initiative Oladowski had ordered 1,340,000 small arms cartridges and 50 rounds of ammunition for each field piece sent from Tupelo. He believed that supplies accumulated in the various arsenals and depots in his department were limited, "considering demands of armies at Mobile, Vicksburg, etc., . . . and the deficiency of lead does not permit more rapid fabrication of cartridges. Of 34,000 pounds of lead recently purchased at Mobile I was ordered to send 5,000 pounds to General [Theophilus H.] Holmes, 16,000 to Captain Wright, Atlanta Arsenal," and to divide the balance. He wanted Gorgas to send 4,000 muskets to Chattanooga as replacements for unserviceable arms—he declared it impossible to repair arms as quickly as they were damaged. His assertion that replacement of some gun carriages, implements, and harness would be necessary in a few months, and that, should the campaign be prolonged until spring, all the accouterments in the hands of troops would be worn out, proved to be the most painful part of his letter.[11]

Supplying the Army of Tennessee would develop into a major and pressing chore. A depot at Dalton, convenient though it might be, would involve the use of the Western and Atlantic Railroad—and this belonged to Georgia. Although the transportation of Bragg's army from Tupelo to Chattanooga had been accomplished in record time (July 21 to 29), this was no assurance that there would always be equally swift and reliable transportation for supplies.[12] The relatively isolated position occupied by the Army of Tennessee did seem to argue the need for some definite supply point for that force. This was to be one of the significant factors in the general move toward diversification and decentralization attempted by Gorgas somewhat later.

Not all the news received by Gorgas upon his return to Richmond was bad. In a report to the Secretary of War, which Gorgas undoubtedly saw, Major I. M. St. John recounted fine progress in the efforts of the Nitre and Mining Bureau. His report, covering the period from April to July, reminded the Secretary that prior to the organization of his bureau, niter works had been started, under the Ordnance Bu-

---

[11] Oladowski to Gorgas, Chattanooga, July 31, 1862, ORA, Ser. I, Vol. XVI, Pt. II, 740–41.

[12] Robert C. Black, III, "The Railroads of Georgia in the Confederate War Effort," *Journal of Southern History,* XIII (1947), 522. For an example of Bragg's irritation in March, 1863, over the refusal of the Western and Atlantic to carry ordnance, see also p. 523.

reau, in Arkansas, Alabama, Georgia, eastern Tennessee, and western Virginia—but all except one of the important caves had been lost in the military reverses of the last spring. On the first of May, St. John asserted, the entire home production of niter from all domestic sources had not reached a daily average of 500 pounds. As a result of tremendous exertion and skillful management, the receipts of niter from April 15 to June 1 were about 24,000 pounds. From June 1 to July 1 some 24,398 pounds were supplied. The yield during August, St. John estimated, would be about 1,600 to 2,000 pounds a day, though it should be 2,500 pounds. The production would be retarded by anxiety to save crops, scarcity of labor, "and the lamentable condition of the public transportation."

St. John's men had concentrated attention on well-established mines for the achievement of quick results, and by changing a contract had doubled the output of the Wythe Lead Mines in Virginia. Soon they would produce three tons per day. The Silver Hill Mines in North Carolina could be made to produce fair amounts of lead, by neglecting temporarily the silver percentage—although the Petersburg smelting works were in fine condition to desilverize the ore.[13] St. John said that the "present yield from our mines average between three and four tons per working day. This is not equal to the army demand. The residue has thus far been more than met by importation and the collection of scrap lead in which the Bureau Agents have been quite active." Diligent gleaning of the battlefields had secured 60 to 80 tons of lead, and 34,000 pounds had recently reached Mobile, while 90,000 pounds from Texas had arrived at Woodville, Mississippi, on the east side of the river. Bragg had ordered the Mobile lead divided between Atlanta, Columbus, and Selma. Gorgas had earmarked half of the Texas supply for Atlanta—now a major point of fabrication.[14]

Supplies of copper were in better shape: the Ducktown, Tennessee, mines yielded enough for the time being, and St. John said that if need be, mines in Carroll and Grayson counties, Virginia, could be re-

---

[13] GCWD, July 27, 1862, p. 10.

[14] The fact that lead reached the Cis-Mississippi area from Texas in mid-1862 (see Gorgas to Mallet, Richmond, August 5, 1862, CROB, V, 7) is interesting indeed. Gen. Hébert, at headquarters of the Department of Texas in San Antonio, wrote Gen. H. H. Sibley on August 8 that "every effort has been made to procure some arms and munitions both here and from abroad, but with little or no success." Even granting permission to cart cotton to Mexico brought no returns, and Hébert declared it to be impossible to procure arms in Mexico or at any of the Gulf ports. He had begun efforts to purchase from Europe with Trans-Mississippi cotton. ORA, Ser. I, Vol. IX, 730.

opened. He had little worry about the store of sulphur, having made arrangements to start sulphur works if and when necessary.[15]

In the summer of 1862 the general military picture, so far as Gorgas could see, appeared improved. Braxton Bragg had succeeded Beauregard in command of Confederate forces in Mississippi, and had started on the northward movement which Gorgas felt might "drive Buell back and perhaps redeem Tennessee, if not Kentucky." Stonewall Jackson was receiving reinforcements for his opposition to John Pope's Federals. Of the four commanders—Bragg, Buell, Jackson, and Pope—Gorgas had definite opinions which he recorded in his diary: "Pope is morally worthless—Jackson is a just and upright man, and in earnest. Providence will help the righteous man who puts his shoulder to the wheel. Between Bragg and Buell there is little to choose on the score of morality."[16]

Then, too, McClellan appeared to have absented himself from the vicinity of Malvern Hill, and, while breakfasting one August Sunday morning with the Randolphs, Gorgas speculated on the possibilities this presented. "It is now quite certain," he observed, "that McClellan has disappeared from the James River, both banks being clear." He hoped that conditions might return to the status of Manassas, with few troops in Richmond. He thought Lee ought to have about 10,000 more men to undertake a forward movement. "However he has about 50,000 men and that is as much as any body can well handle."[17]

Through the heat of middle August (the ninth and tenth Gorgas thought the hottest he had ever felt in Richmond) Lee gathered his forces for the push against Pope's Army of the Potomac, calling for

[15] St. John to Randolph, Richmond, July 31, 1862, ORA, Ser. IV, Vol. II, 26–30. In this interesting report St. John gave his plan for starting the accumulation of niter resources. "1st. To explore rapidly, but with system, for new nitre caves and deposits. 2nd. To stimulate private enterprise by circular and newspaper publications, personal appeal and instruction, and by affording facilities for work in prompt payment and a liberal supply of tools and utensils. Third. When advisable, to start work on Government account. This plan of exploration embraced all the Confederate States subdivided into districts. . . . As rapidly as competent agents could be found a commencement was made in each district; and during May the survey was in full progress. Known localities were first examined and afterwards new ground; the caves were explored, earth tested, and when practicable measured, and the results communicated to the Richmond office to be mapped and registered."

[16] GCWD, July 27 and August 3, 1862, p. 11.

[17] Gorgas to Amelia [Richmond], Sunday [August 24?], 1862, GMSS. The date is conjectured from the fact that definite news of McClellan's absence was released to the Daily Richmond Examiner on Tuesday, August 19.

R. H. Anderson's division from Drewry's Bluff on the fifteenth, and announcing his intention to go forward beyond the Rapidan. Jackson punished Banks on the ninth at Cedar Mountain, and, at this apogee in Confederate affairs, Congress met and seemed "inclined to vigorous measures." Gorgas thought, considering that the Confederate States had maintained between 300,000 and 400,000 men in the field for a year, Congress and the country should believe it "wonderful" that the expenses of the war had not exceeded $350,000,000.[18] He had a right to be pleased about economy. One of his most constant endeavors was to prevent waste of material and money in the Ordnance Bureau. On August 1, for instance, he told Randolph that he had no reason to think that the funds requested by the officers of the Ordnance Bureau "are more than absolutely necessary for the current expenditures. Every effort, however, will be made to diminish the rate of expenditure."[19]

Such economy in an organization the size of the Ordnance Bureau was surprising indeed. Ordnance needs were more universal than a layman could have known. Mallet, whose foresight and professional proficiency were being daily attested, had launched a new campaign to secure sulphur. In North Carolina he had obtained the facilities of the Rudisell Gold Mine Company in locating deposits of iron pyrites and recovering sulphur from this ore.[20] Though there existed yet no real shortage of this vital product, Mallet was looking ahead like St. John. Gorgas, also looking to the future, expressed the wish that Mallet could induce some capitalists to embark on iron mining operations—the mines in Georgia and Alabama, together with those in other parts of the Confederacy, were inadequate for the over-all task.

The artillery had its needs too. Without harness and other equipment such as knapsacks, gun-slings, and halters, the army's "Long Arm" would be immobilized. For the Ordnance Bureau to fabricate these items required leather in large quantities. To undertake the task of supplying the requirements Gorgas wanted the right man. He began the job of procuring leather in his usual way and searched for the proper officer to do the work. In this case his choice fell on Military Storekeeper W. S. Downer, possibly because of his demonstrated frugality. In response to a query from Gorgas, Downer signified his willing-

---

[18] GCWD, August 11 and 20, 1862, pp. 13, 14.

[19] Gorgas to Randolph, Richmond, CRLR, 1862, Doc. GWD 495.

[20] Samuel Grose, agent for Rudisell Gold Mine Co., to Mallet, Charlotte, August 11, 1862, CROB, V, 10. Evidence that the company was supplied with food by the government is contained in a list of expenses incurred, which accompanies this letter. The list includes an item of 517 pounds of bacon.

ness to "assume the giving out of contracts and undertaking the supplying leather work generally . . . and think it would be [to] the advantage of the service to have it so, as I have been conversant with the prices of Material and Labor." He told Gorgas that with the assistance of one hundred additional hands he could maintain a full supply of harness, cavalry equipments, and the other needs. For the Ordnance Bureau to undertake the manufacture of its own leather goods, he explained, would be prudent saving. "The economy may be very readily shown as in the case of Halters, for which contracts have been made at $6.50 each, the outside cost of which, to us would be $2.50." And to carry out Ordnance policy, he announced his intention to do more work than usual to husband resources, time, and money.[21]

As August drew toward its close and Lee's army began the Second Manassas campaign, Gorgas was making strong attempts to maintain a surplus of ordnance and material above immediate wants. Some of his most important and energetic projects, excluding the permanent laboratory building he had authorized Mallet to erect,[22] had been outlined in recommendations for congressional action. He had asked Randolph on the twelfth to seek an increase in the number of artillery officers on ordnance duty, even though Congress, at its last session, had authorized 80 such officers. Gorgas wanted this corps increased to 150. In the meantime, he could be proud of the stockpile of small arms on hand. Largely because of successful blockade-running policy, as well as diligent combing of the battlefields, Randolph could report to the President on August 12 that "our small-arms alone have increased from these sources not less than 80,000." The ammunition situation was greatly improved, owing to the good results obtained in manufacturing, as well as in blockade-running. Davis was told that soon the country could expect the "active and methodical operations of the Nitre Corps will supply our demand and make us independent of foreign importation."[23]

[21] W. S. Downer to Gorgas, Ordnance Depot [Clarksville, Va.], August 25, 1862, CRLR, 1862, Doc. GWD 559.
[22] On August 26 Gorgas directed Mallet to "select a suitable location at Macon, Ga. for a permanent laboratory establishment (to include the manufacture of percussion caps, friction primers etc.) and [you] will procure a piece of ground for the same, prepare plans and drawings for the necessary buildings, and make contracts for the carrying [of] the design into execution." Randolph approved. Gorgas to Mallet, Richmond, AGPF, Mallet.
[23] Randolph to Davis, Richmond, ORA, Ser. IV, Vol. II, 47, 48.

Amid the pressure of all the myriad necessities and personalities[24] of his bureau, Gorgas became virtually a prisoner at his desk—trapped by the flood of business. "I find myself very closely confined, because the times are very critical, & every resource must be bro't into requisition to equip & supply the troops—We are literally overwhelmed with requisitions of all sorts, & the directing hand must keep wide awake."[25]

As August faded into September, Lee handed Pope a crushing defeat on the field of Second Manassas and prepared to move northward. In the western theater, Bragg marched from Chattanooga on the twenty-eighth, undertaking the first stage of his Kentucky campaign. The next day General E. K. Smith won the action at Richmond, Kentucky.

With Confederate forces either victorious or on the offensive along almost all fronts, and with everything pointing to vigorous fighting, it appeared that the Chief of Ordnance knew whereof he spoke when he told Amelia on August 3 that "this inevitable business will keep me here steadily."[26]

[24] The Seven Days had contributed one more personality to ordnance activities—Maj. Gen. Benjamin Huger was appointed Inspector of Ordnance and Artillery on August 26, 1862. The duties of his office sounded impressive—it must not appear as a demotion for the general—but beyond remaining respectfully civil to him, Gorgas paid little attention to Huger's new designation. See General Orders Number 62, Adj. & Insp. Gen.'s Off., Richmond, August 26, 1862, AGPF, Huger. This order gave wide authority to examine all ordnance and contract plants, as well as all forts and batteries. Huger was to give orders tending to increase the efficiency of these installations. His instruction, however, would be issued through the Office of the Chief of Ordnance. Huger was just the man to fill this office, considering his experience along the same lines while in the United States service, and Gorgas had anticipated his assignment. See Gorgas to Amelia [Richmond], Sunday [July 6?] 1862, GMSS.

[25] Gorgas to Amelia [Richmond] Sunday [August ?], 1862, GMSS.

[26] Gorgas to Amelia [Richmond], GMSS.

X

Personal Concerns

To a man of Gorgas' temperament family affairs were almost as important as official business. In the midst of his duties as Chief of Ordnance, he had cheerfully concerned himself with his personal problems. From the first day he had arrived in Richmond, one of the most pressing problems was where to live. The Gorgases had taken up temporary quarters in four rooms, for which Gorgas drew commutation.[1] But he was far from satisfied. Richmond did offer enlarged social opportunities, but living costs were high and danger was always close at hand.

Amelia looked after the Gorgases' social standing in the capital and hoped to stabilize it by more closely allying herself with the church. A religious person herself, she had long hoped to prevail on her husband to appear frequently at St. Paul's, and she saw to it that the children's religious interests were guided by the popular Episcopal minister, Rev. Charles Minnegerode. On the morning of May 6, 1862 (a fateful day for Norfolk) Minnegerode wrote "Mrs. Col. Gorgas," expressing his regret at not finding her at home the day before, and saying that by a singular providence the rite of Confirmation would be administered again that day at St. Paul's. "President Davis, who would have been confirmed Sunday last, if he had had Baptism will be today. The desire of his wife, who will leave town in a day or two, to be present and witness—is the reason why I applied to Bishop Johns, to hold this special Confirmation. I shall baptize Mr. Davis privately at $9\frac{1}{2}$ at his house. Although it is not my intention to spread the news of it beforehand—I feel it my duty to let you know, in the hope that you—and (ah how I wish it) your husband may embrace the same opportunity."

---

[1] Abstract voucher of commutation, March 28, 1862, AGPF, Gorgas.

He would, said the Reverend Doctor, be able to baptize the Gorgases at home or at church between 10 and 12. If Mrs. Gorgas could reply by 9 o'clock, Minnegerode would appreciate it. He sent the note early, hoping to catch Gorgas before he went to work.[2]

Ordinarily Gorgas might have refused, not being devout, but this time he lacked adequate reasons to avoid the ceremony, and, in company with Amelia and the President, was confirmed by Bishop Johns that day. And he later admitted that subsequently his mind "turned oftener towards religious tho'ts"; and he began more regular church attendance, hoping to "benefit by thus linking myself to the visible church."[3]

Meanwhile, the apparent approach of action in the vicinity of the capital made Gorgas apprehensive for the safety of the family. Mrs. Davis left Richmond for safer climes, and Gorgas saw good reasons for such a move on the part of his own family. Not only would it be safer for them, but living conditions would be better. Life would be lonely for him, but he doubtless expected to be so busy that solitude would be bearable. Amelia approved of the idea, thinking also of the children's welfare. It would be healthier for them away from the city. So it was decided, and "Mama" took the children to Greensboro, North Carolina, where she found refuge in a Methodist college building in company with forty or fifty other refugees. In "refugeeing" to the south, "Mama" and the children were initiated into one of the Confederacy's most honorable orders. People of all classes had been forced to flee homes near the battle lines, and many roamed the safer areas looking for a place to stay. Frequently these people were offered hospitality in other homes, but their life was not pleasant. The irrepressible Confederate humorist, Bill Arp, saw the humor that lay beneath the tragedy of these nomads, and observed that Job had suffered much, but "from careful examination of his sacred record, I do not find that he was ever a refugee."[4] Willie was sent down to Winnsboro, South Carolina, to stay with the Aikens. Gorgas, left to himself, roomed frugally, with little real comfort, but was much too busy to bother unduly about his own mode of living.

As the Seven Days Battles were about to begin, the lonesome Gorgas did take comfort in knowing that his family was at safe distance from

[2] Minnegerode to Amelia [Richmond], GMSS.
[3] GCWD, July 27, 1862, p. 11.
[4] *Ibid.*, p. 10. Arp is quoted in E. M. Coulter, *The Confederate States of America, 1861–1865* (Baton Rouge, 1950), p. 428.

the conflict. In Greensboro, Amelia recorded that "baby Ria" had the measles, but otherwise all was well.[5] During his own illness, which began shortly after the Seven Days, Gorgas longed more than ever to be with his family. In July his malaise, perhaps aggravated by overwork and heat, got the best of him; and on July 15 he wrote the Secretary of War: "I am compelled to ask permission to be absent for *five* or *six* days. I find myself, from indisposition, unfit for duty." In a postscript he added: "I will visit and inspect the laboratory at Petersburgh and the Depot at Greensboro, N. C. I shall go to Petersburgh this afternoon."[6] But rail lines to the south were so jammed with wounded and friends of the wounded that Gorgas could not get a seat. As far as Petersburg he rode in the conductor's car, sitting on a trunk with Senator James L. Orr of South Carolina. Gorgas was not impressed with the administration of the road; "badly conducted, and it is impossible to get along with any degree of comfort. Baggage is no longer taken care of, and travelers must do the best they can. This great struggle in which we are engaged disorganizes everything which is not energetically supervised." From Petersburg, where he approved of the lead smelting works, he went on to Greensboro and the family. As refugees, he discovered, they were not faring badly. They were living in "a fine large building. . . . The surroundings are very attractive, and the air very salubrious. It stands on the outskirts of the little town which has about 1500 inhabitants." The only thing to mar his joy was that Ria "was very ailing, and her poor little face looked pinched and had a fixed expression of suffering."[7]

Gorgas' visit lasted only a week, but he kept in close touch with Amelia after returning to Richmond, and in August heard with relief that Ria was improving; he ascribed her recovery to "Mrs. Stansbury's sedulous attentions." Mrs. Stansbury, wife of Josiah's West Point classmate Smith Stansbury, had been a warm family friend, and Gorgas jokingly said to Amelia: "Suppose we give Ria to her? Dear little puss—she could not be shared." He wanted Willie to join the rest of the family at Greensboro but was afraid of the cramped condition of their living quarters, especially in view of Ria's illness. Speaking of the college building in which his children resided, he told Amelia to "let me know, & if old Methodist does not treat you all well, I will certainly use my endeavors to convert the affair into an hospital." He fondly

[5] GCWD, June 22, 1862, p. 7.
[6] Gorgas to the Secretary of War, Richmond, July 15, 1862, CRLR, 1862, Doc. GWD 442.   [7] GCWD, July 27, 1862, p. 10.

hoped that things would soon be settled enough for him to go south, gather up the clan, and get them all to Richmond. He wished Amelia could move them all to Winnsboro by September 1. Once they were there, he might have a better chance to give himself a legitimate reason to leave Richmond. The reason had to be good now, and he admonished Amelia: "Don't rely on anything which involves my absence from here. . . . You need not however be surprised to see me riding up to your door some of these fine days if I can hear of a riding horse at Danville." Living the life of a bachelor had lost most of whatever charm it may have had at the beginning. Alone, he found that he did very few of the things he might have done otherwise. He did not go to church, breakfast with Mrs. Randolph, or visit the Masons, who just then were giving a series of "very *chatty*" parties. He wanted, he said, to do all this, but just didn't seem to get around to it.[8]

In September, cheered by the presence of brothers-in-law Tom Bayne and Hugh Aiken, who were staying with him, Gorgas learned that Amelia soon planned to move to Winnsboro. An earlier move had been impossible because of Ria's health, but now she was "getting as fat as a little pig again, after her summer of illness."[9] Glad that Amelia was again to see Willie, Josiah had some worries about the family's finances, then hit upon the scheme of having a personal messenger bring Amelia $100. "A month or six weeks at Morganton and then to Winsboro and after that back to Richmond I hope and trust not to be so separated again. Next summer our arrangement must be different."[10]

Not long after, however, he was exhorting Amelia: "Don't hurry your visit for it may be sometime before you will be so much made of again." His sudden caution about the family's return was the result of having found no place to put them. He had decided, after several fruitless tries to find a boardinghouse, that the best solution to the problem was to take up quarters in the armory. "I don't know which I dread most—housekeeping or boarding," he wrote Amelia, "but we must do one or the other, and I decide in favor of the Armory until something better turns up." He had considered various schemes for obtaining a house, enlisted the aid of friends in his search, and considered half seriously a way to obtain the house occupied by the Norman Walkers. Walker wanted a commission in the Ordnance Depart-

[8] Gorgas to Amelia [Richmond], Friday [August 1], August 3, 1862, GMSS.
[9] GCWD, September 7, 1862, p. 15.
[10] Gorgas to Amelia [Richmond], Saturday [August ?], 1862, GMSS. About the middle of September, Gorgas sent Amelia $135.00 by Tom Bayne. Gorgas to Amelia [Richmond], Saturday [September 13 or 14?], 1862, GMSS.

ment, and Gorgas thought that "if he gets his captaincy in the Artillery for Ordn duty for which he has to pass an examination—I can send him to Miss. where his plantation is and then we could get the house—I wish I had known his wants earlier—but he now has to pass an examination."[11] Walker finally passed his tests, but too late to solve Gorgas' housing problem.

The failure of all these efforts forced Josiah to concentrate on the armory as the best available choice, and accordingly he recounted to Amelia his attempts at putting it in livable shape. In these domestic enterprises he was aided by Jack, the family general handy man, who was put to work making the armory kitchen inhabitable. Gorgas, in considering all aspects of the quarters, told Amelia that he thought they could be comfortable there, his only objection being the approach to the place, which took a route through the least desirable streets of Richmond. A week before Amelia and the children were to leave for the capital, Gorgas was writing that although he could obtain the second story of a private residence at $175 per month, and Amelia would probably prefer this place, the ample grounds and fine lookout of the armory made it "very attractive to me."[12]

Another consideration made it convenient to be so close to his duty: the notorious inefficiency of the Richmond transportation system. "Those who use the Street Cars say they are a nuisance and that no reliance can be placed on them." He had deliberated for some time about taking quarters in the armory because taking them he could not draw his "commutation for quarters—so that those 4 rooms would cost me $900 per annum which is more than I am willing to pay." But the armory had a servant's room over the kitchen for the cook whom a friend was supposedly to let the family have. It would have been much better if they could have used the furniture which they had had at Frankford Arsenal, just before secession, and which Gorgas hoped was still safe somewhere. In its place he told Amelia that he had ordered "bedsteads, centre table(!) dining table—2 corner chairs —1 lounge—1 etagere—a sideboard all of which will I hope be done by the time you arrive." He was holding on to "my beautiful Brussels

[11] Gorgas to Amelia [Richmond], Monday [September ?], and [October ?], 1862, GMSS. Gorgas was disgusted at the prices asked by some boarding houses in Richmond. A Mrs. Johnson asked $300.00 a month "for two rooms, and we use our furniture and bed linen!" He declared himself ready to pay as much as $200.00 but no more. Gorgas to Amelia [August ?], 1862, ibid.

[12] Gorgas to Amelia [Richmond], Sunday and Tuesday [September?], 1862, GMSS.

[carpet] until you come—it is perfectly saleable at an advance—I make Cousin Sam (Conf. States) pay for all my fine furniture, etc. as he charges me so high for my quarters." The family raiment also concerned the Chief of Ordnance. He had managed to obtain (probably through the kindness of a blockade-running friend) about eight yards of steel gray cloth, which he thought would make Amelia a fine cloak. If there was not enough material for that, it would be enough for a suit for himself.[13]

His own health did not hold up well. In late September he confided to Amelia that "my teeth and right side of the face ache now regularly every night, beginning about this time in the eveg—I cannot expose myself to the night air at all."[14]

Captain Tom Bayne, now assigned to duty with Gorgas, drew as one of his first jobs the pleasant task of going to Greensboro and escorting Amelia with the children to Winnsboro. Bayne left on September 12, and Gorgas was happy to think that "in three weeks now I shall be a joyful man on seeing them all back around me."[15]

Later in September news of heavy fighting around Sharpsburg, Maryland, produced a brief hope of peace, but this soon gave way to fear of an attack on Richmond. Lincoln's preliminary Emancipation Proclamation moved Gorgas to observe that "it is a document only to be noticed as showing the drift of opinion in the northern Government." And he also heard at this time that a most important bill had passed both houses, making the Chief of Ordnance a brigadier general. He received this news[16] with the feeling that he would "hail the day which returns me to my grade of Lt. Colonel—and peace." But the Senate rejected the bill,[17] and he voiced no bitterness.

The news filtering down from Lee's retreating columns gave Gorgas grave forebodings. "I fear my dear," he wrote Amelia, "that events are

[13] Gorgas to Amelia [Richmond], Saturday [July ?], Monday [October 13?], and Monday [September ?], 1862, GMSS.

[14] Gorgas to Amelia [Richmond], Wednesday [September ?], 1862, GMSS.

[15] GCWD, September 14, 1862, p. 15.   [16] GCWD, October 4, 1862, p. 17.

[17] This measure, "A bill (S. 118) to define the rank of the Quartermaster-General and the Chief of Ordnance in the Provisional Army," was rejected by the Senate on October 6, 1862. See *Journal of the Congress of the Confederate States of America*, II, 427–28; GCWD, October 4, 1862, pp. 16–17. Gorgas expected strong support from Davis in the move for promotion and obviously believed no other supply chief would get a brigadier generalship. He wrote Amelia shortly before the promotion bill came up in Congress: "A vote has been given to make the Chief of Ord[n] Brig. Gen.—The President will I think give it to neither Myers nor anyone in this way, of which I am glad." Letter about mid-October, 1862, GMSS.

crowding upon us again and that the enemy will come with them—I am casting a glance at my stores & shall look to their safety—I have little doubt there will be a second siege of Richmond, & that right soon—I hope Jackson or Longstreet [there had been a rumor that these two were killed] will be marching down this way before long, to give us a little accession of men—We are pretty weak now." He felt it to be impossible to maintain Lee's army as far north as its reported position, unless it was on the offensive. "I fear it is to be a winter of suffering to a portion of our Army, unless new Combinations are made which will enable Lee to resume the offensive where he is."[18]

Though he thus had fears for the Army, Gorgas derived pleasure from the prospect of seeing his family by the first of October. He cautioned Amelia not to leave any of the children, except for a short time. "I long to have them altogether." The threat of diphtheria, which existed in Richmond, frightened him a little, but he hoped the family could come on nevertheless. In his concern he had not neglected one of the dearest of the group—Anne Kavanagh, the children's Nanny. He told Amelia in September that he had bought Anne $300 worth of Confederate bonds, which would settle her account up to October 1. She would draw $24 per year interest on the bonds, and he thought it would be a good investment—"at least I will make it so."[19]

After all these preparations and vain hopes, Amelia and the children did not get back to Richmond until almost the end of the year, and by then the armory was more than ready to receive them. They returned at the height of the Richmond social season, which, despite the war, was marked by its usual gaiety and brilliance.[20] Even though the women's dresses were muslin, the men's coats coarse Confederate gray, and although dinner at a good hotel cost $25.00, the spirit of the city was unbroken. The Richmond Theater had reopened following a fire, and silver and damask could still be seen on dinner tables. Officers returning to the city from the front were invited to a dizzy round of dinners, charades, dances, and benefits.

The Gorgases were not ones to miss the periodic entertainments about the city (though Gorgas would have liked to miss some of them),

[18] GCWD, September 21, 1862, p. 16; Gorgas to Amelia [Richmond], Thursday and Sunday, [both September ?], GMSS.
[19] Gorgas to Amelia [Richmond], Sunday and Tuesday [both September ?] 1862, GMSS.
[20] GCWD, October 17, 1862, and May 23, 1863, pp. 22 and 40. For a good summary of the gaiety in Richmond during the winter of 1862–63, see Bill, *Beleaguered City*, pp. 155–56.

particularly those given by the First Lady. On occasion they would also go to the White House during the evening for some pleasant conversation, and, for the President and his Chief of Ordnance, some serious talk. The coming departure of Major Smith Stansbury to his new post at Bermuda in June, 1863, gave opportunity for more partying; and Mrs. Mary Jones, one of Amelia's best friends, gave Mrs. Stansbury "a little party" on the evening of June 3. The Stansburys and Colonel Wyatt Aiken (one of the in-laws) helped distract Gorgas' mind from his vexing duties by descending on the family as house guests. Amelia, of course, enjoyed entertaining for them.[21]

Entertainment in Richmond was not, withal, inexpensive, and consequently was usually restricted in scope. Living on Josiah's continuously depreciating pay, the Gorgases keenly felt the bite of inflation when they were hosts to General and Mrs. Gustavus W. Smith and Colonel Eugene E. McLean on the evening of June 11, celebrating the occasion with a dinner consisting partially of a piece of lamb which cost $13.00.[22]

By August of 1863 Amelia, who had been in delicate health for some time, once more needed a change of scene and relief from the heat. Gorgas, too, needed a rest. His work had increased almost beyond one man's endurance, and he could use a short vacation in some spot where the word ordnance had no meaning. Hence, he and Amelia decided to go to the country for a week or ten days. The family had a good lawyer friend, J. P. Holcombe, whose rural place beyond Lynchburg always stood at their disposal. On August 14 the Gorgases went there for a week's sojourn. The children, who had seemed likely to make a mockery of their parents' hope of a quiet time, enjoyed the country immensely and seemed charmed with how little the war had affected the interior areas. The efforts to have a restful vacation were a success, and Gorgas was more than satisfied with the trip, observing that "it proved to be a very pleasant quiet one, tho' the going and returning in the present condition of roads and of travel was wearisome."[23]

Family life throughout the remainder of the war continued without undue excitement, except for the birth of Richard Gorgas on November 3, 1864. Upon this happy event Gorgas commented that "two boys and four girls in a family will do very well. May heaven bless and protect them all and bring them safely to years of maturity."[24]

[21] GCWD, May 21, June 8, 1863, pp. 40, 43.
[22] GCWD, June 11, 1863, p. 43.   [23] GCWD, August 13, 24, 1863, p. 59.
[24] GCWD, November 3, 1864, pp. 148–49.

XI

The Top Command Emerges

CONFEDERATE MILITARY FORTUNES WERE DEFINITELY ON THE UP-
swing again in September, 1862, or at least so thought the Chief of
Ordnance before reports of Lee's desperate action at Sharpsburg had
reached him.[1] News of that fight brought shock to Richmond and made
September 21 gloomy indeed. For several days people refused to believe
the news, and the whole implication of events did not register.[2] By
October 4 Gorgas' own reaction was crystallizing. He noted that Lee's
army was not far from Winchester and that it had fallen back across
the Potomac with "nearly all the wounded and all of its baggage and
stores." Considering the battle from this special point of view, he observed that "Longstreet's division [had] lost an ammunition train before the battle, which was the chief loss of material sustained. Four
pieces of artillery were lost . . . from the Corps of Artillery."[3] These
losses were much lighter than he had anticipated, but he did not relax
his efforts.

For some time Gorgas had functioned virtually as industrial czar,
concerning himself with all phases of his bureau's operations and with
subsidiary matters as well. On August 28 he had asked Secretary
Randolph to seek congressional permission to purchase land in Petersburg, Virginia, for the erection of a lead smelting works. He wanted
permission, also, to purchase not more than 500 acres in the vicinity
of Augusta Arsenal for a powder mill site, at a maximum of $25,000.

---

[1] See GCWD, September 14, 1862, p. 15, for an example of Gorgas' hope for
victory as a result of Lee's Maryland campaign. Much of his correspondence
with Amelia at this time reflected this same optimism.

[2] Bill, *Beleaguered City,* p. 149. See the fluctuating reaction of the *Daily
Richmond Examiner,* September 24–30, 1862.

[3] GCWD, October 4, 1862, p. 16.

Authority to purchase a magazine near Savannah was also sought, as was permission to buy a site for a temporary armory at Macon and one for necessary laboratory buildings there. Gorgas wanted Congress to permit the purchase of land for a temporary workshop and laboratory at Atlanta, at a cost not exceeding $3,000. He also asked for land adjacent to Fayetteville Arsenal for more magazines, workshops, a foundry, and rail connection with main lines. Furthermore, it was desirable to have permission to buy lead, copper, or other mineral mines as might be needed for government work. Showing his usual foresight, he confided to Randolph that the first three sites listed had already been purchased under pressure of necessity, and that the smelting works and powder mills were in operation and the magazine built—they were indispensable.[4]

Despite the greatly improved organization of the bureau, ordnance affairs throughout the Confederacy remained uncertain. Bragg's army stood well advanced, and Gorgas faced the same problem with that force as with Lee's; while these armies might live off the country, they had to draw their ordnance supplies from southern bases, and Gorgas had to look to his business to keep the bases stocked. He had undoubtedly been considering this problem when he ordered Captain John W. Mallet, early in September, to visit arsenals and other installations and report their condition.[5] Accurate information on arsenal and laboratory productive capacities was imperative in order to make plans for future supplies. The need for this information is well illustrated by a dispatch from General Samuel Jones, at Chattanooga, Bragg's advanced base. On September 7 he telegraphed Gorgas that he wanted "fire-arms (not pistols) for cavalry. Cannot say how many, as calls are made on me for them daily. Would like from 500 to 1,000. General Bragg directs General [J. C.] Breckenridge . . . to take with him to Kentucky all the arms I can collect here. If arms cannot be sent me from any nearer point than Columbus, Miss., I understand there are many thousands there, but have no control over them. Can you supply the arms?"[6]

Three days later, September 10, Jones wrote Gorgas, saying that he had received requisitions during the past week for more than 2,000

[4] Gorgas to Randolph, Richmond, August 28, 1862, CRLR, 1862, Doc. GWD 663.   [5] Gorgas to Mallet, Richmond, September 1, 1862, AGPF, Mallet.
[6] Jones to Gorgas, Chattanooga, September 7, 1862, ORA, Ser. I, Vol. XVI, Pt. II, 801–2.

cavalry arms, and added that since sending his telegram he had been
informed that there were 15,000 varied firearms at Columbus. He had
no reply to his telegram; just what was the prospect of getting them?
The reason for the desperate need, though obvious to Gorgas, Jones
decided to reiterate: "If the people of Kentucky and Tennessee rally to
our standard . . . as I am assured they will, it is very desirable to have
arms put in their hands immediately. It will discourage those who are
really desirous of joining us and furnish a ready excuse to those who are
wavering if applications for arms for organized bodies of troops are refused on the ground that we have not the arms to give."[7]

Bragg had given assiduous attention to his armament, as his designation of Dalton as an ordnance base had indicated.[8] Gorgas wanted
to do all he could to help Bragg, but the most urgent business had been
attended to already.

At this critical time the Ordnance Bureau had to bestir itself still
further to aid the distant Trans-Mississippi Department. Trying to do
what he could to help that remote area without serious damage to other
places, Gorgas ordered 18,000 stands of arms, 20 pieces of artillery, and
a proportionate amount of ammunition to the western Confederacy.
War Department officials estimated on September 2 that 10,000 of
the small arms must then be crossing the Mississippi. In addition to the
arms, $18,000,000 went to Texas and $14,000,000 to Arkansas for

---

[7] Jones to Gorgas, Chattanooga, *ibid.*, p. 809. On September 16 Jones wrote
Gorgas that Braxton Bragg wanted all available arms sent to Kentucky immediately. "Middle Tennessee reported joining us in great numbers and most of
them without arms. If there are arms at Columbus, Miss., or Gainesville, Ala.,
can I get them by sending for them?" Jones to Gorgas, Chattanooga, *ibid.*, pp.
835–36. Gorgas replied promptly, and on the 20th Jones wrote Bragg that "the
Chief of Ordnance informs me that the arms at Gainesville, Ala., and Columbus, Miss., have been ordered to me for transportation to Kentucky." *Ibid.*, p.
857. Promising the arms was one thing; getting them delivered was another. On
October 11, Jones, who had moved his headquarters to Knoxville, wrote Gorgas
that according to a telegram dated September 16, "you say the arms from
Gainesville, Ala., had been ordered to me some days previously; that those from
Columbus would follow, and that General Price would direct every arm in
hand to Knoxville. Have you given any counter orders in regard to them? If not,
please ascertain why they have not been sent to me, and order them here without delay. There is great demand for arms in this department to arm exchanged
prisoners and convalescents returning to their regiments in Kentucky." *Ibid.*, p.
934.

[8] See W. H. McMain to Gorgas, Dalton, Ga., September 6, 1862, CROB,
XXV, 49.

urgent supplies.[9] Not much, but this was the best Gorgas could do, and it did indicate that he had not forgotten the West.[10]

Every military supply venture in wartime is contingent on two highly variable things: resources and the action of the enemy. In a measure Gorgas could control Confederate resources (or allow for deficiencies), but he had to trust to luck and the Confederate Army for the control of enemy action. In supplying the Trans-Mississippi Department, moreover, he was combating not only the enemy but also distance and a tenuous line of communication. That the Ordnance Bureau lost some supplies on the way to Texas was regrettable and expensive but hardly surprising.

Congressional representatives from the distant western areas took a serious view of their responsibility to urge the importance of the West. Texas and her neighbors now assumed their places as a Confederate frontier—a turbulent Indian-Yankee-Jayhawker frontier. Senator Edward Sparrow of Louisiana, who, as chairman of the Senate Committee on Military Affairs, was in a better position than most to know the situation's gravity, expressed his concern to Randolph on September 13, 1862. The Trans-Mississippi Department, he asserted, had men but no arms, and the people were justly alarmed. He urged as a vital consideration the proportion of slaves to whites, thinking of possible servile insurrections. He understood that Randolph proposed to send 18,000 arms to the West, but learned from Gorgas that 1,500 to 2,000 less were to go. He emphasized the West's importance to the Confederacy and pointed out that road conditions just then were ideal.[11] The Senator's plea apparently struck a responsive chord in the War Department. By November 8, 1862, General Martin L. Smith, at Vicksburg, reported that 18,140 arms had crossed the river there, en route to Little Rock. But, he added, 5,000 had been captured sometime before when the steamer "Fair Play" was taken by the enemy.[12]

[9] J. S. Whitney to Gen. J. E. McCullock, Richmond, September 2, 1862, ORA, Ser. I, Vol. IX, 734.

[10] Affairs in Texas were little short of chaotic. The military commander of Velasco pleaded for the issue of even one gun larger than an eighteen-pounder smooth-bore, "of those lying in the streets of Houston." He wanted, in addition, two six-pounders and a hundred muskets with bayonets to defend his important post. Col. J. Bates to Capt. C. M. Mason, Velasco, September 4, 1862, ibid., pp. 734–35.

[11] Sparrow to Randolph, Senate Chamber, ibid., LIII, 826.

[12] Gorgas to Secretary of War, Richmond, November 8, 1862, CRLR, 1862, Doc. GWD 765.

Though Senator Robert W. Johnson of Arkansas joined Sparrow in anger about the lack of Ordnance support to the West and complained bitterly to the President, Gorgas in a letter to Davis calmly defended his organization. He argued that "the measures taken have secured the transit of the arms, and . . . there is little ground for the reckless charges . . . made against this bureau by Senator Johnson . . . in the letter which Your Excellency showed me." Gorgas did more than reply to the charges; he sent an agent to follow along the route taken by the shipments to the West, for the purpose of seeing if any arms were "loitering" on the way.[13] On September 18 Randolph, under fire from the western congressional representatives, submitted to Senator C. B. Mitchell of Arkansas "and others" a detailed statement of Ordnance and War Department supply efforts in the Trans-Mississippi. He carefully explained that since adjournment of Congress in April, the stock of arms had increased from importation, capture, and manufacture, by about 90,000. The captured arms were mostly damaged and had to be repaired before being issued to troops. "No arms fit for use are retained." He said that 16,000 arms had been sent to the Trans-Mississippi of which 5,000 had been captured, 2,000 were certainly across the river, 4,000 were sent to Macon for repairs, 2,400 to Chattanooga for the same purpose, 1,000 had been repaired and sent out, but probably had not yet reached the Mississippi. "It is the intention of the Department," declared Randolph, "to send 5,000 of the arms captured in the recent battle at Manassas when they are received." One-fourth of those taken in the battle near Richmond were sent to the West, and 20 pieces of artillery had gone since April. Considering the troublesome loss of the 5,000 arms, Randolph hastened to assure Senator Mitchell that an inquiry "into the circumstances of the loss" was already underway. The Secretary could not speak with certainty about "what number of arms can be supplied in future, as the means of the Government depend upon the contingencies of running the blockade and winning battles."[14]

The western military department was not without its own plans and endeavors. San Antonio Arsenal, steadily engaged in fabricating ordnance material, offered job opportunities to numbers of people. There were, in addition, numerous other arms-making establishments of more or less importance throughout Texas.[15]

[13] Gorgas to Davis, Richmond, November 8, 1862, ORA, Ser. I, Vol. XIII, 912.   [14] Randolph to Mitchell, and others, Richmond, *ibid.,* pp. 881–82.
[15] See, for instance, the San Antonio *Herald,* September 13, 27, October 11, and November 1, 15, 1862.

A prime concern during this period of routine was the old personnel problem. The Chief of Ordnance was greatly bothered about the appointment of bureau officers and had to do something about methods of selection, since so many already commissioned were technically incapable. On September 10 he suggested to Randolph that, since some applicants for Ordnance commissions had experience and were willing to stand examination, a board be selected to test them.[16] In evident agreement with Gorgas' point of view, Randolph had the Adjutant and Inspector General issue a general order concerning ordnance examinations. This order convened a board of examiners and set the subjects to be passed for an ordnance commission as "an ordinary English education . . . A knowledge of arithmetic, including fractions . . . A knowledge of the Field Manual prepared under the directions of the Ordnance Bureau." But this general order, like many such documents, soon underwent revision. On September 23 General Orders Number 70 stipulated that applicants for the rank of captain in the ordnance service would be required to pass, in addition to the subjects mentioned in the previous order, "the elements of algebra, plane trigonometry, mechanics, and chemistry as applicable to projectiles and ordnance."[17] And, in accordance with Gorgas' wishes, the Adjutant and Inspector General, on the twenty-sixth, put an end to the trouble arising out of political applications for commissions—applications from people hopelessly unqualified to render service in ordnance—by declaring: "All officers on duty in the Ordnance Corps will hereafter be examined before promotion."[18] This long overdue departmental policy would relieve the Chief of Ordnance of much embarrassment, and, coupled with the

[16] Gorgas to the Secretary of War, Richmond, CRLR, 1862, Doc. GWD 603. In describing the initiation of these examinations, Broun remarked that "what we are now familiar with as civil-service examinations, were introduced by the Confederate War Department in 1862, in the appointment of ordnance officers." Broun, p. 336.

[17] General Orders Numbers 68 and 70, Adj. & Insp. Gen.'s Off., Richmond, September 17 and 23, 1862, ORA, Ser. IV, Vol. II, 85 and 92.

[18] General Orders Number 71, Adj. & Insp. Gen.'s Off., Richmond, September 26, 1862, ibid., pp. 96–97. Broun later recalled that these examinations discouraged many of the applicants. He said that so many candidates recommended by the Board sitting in Richmond were from Virginia that Davis refused to appoint them until opportunity was given to young men from other states. "Hence, I was directed to report to and conduct examinations in the armies of Generals Lee and Jackson in Virginia, General Bragg in Tennessee, and General Pemberton in Mississippi. Under other officers the examinations were conducted in Alabama and Florida. The result of this sifting process was that the army was supplied with capable and efficient ordnance officers." Broun, p. 366.

ban placed on applications for examination "except from officers and privates now in service, or from officers and privates out of service by reason of wounds received in battle,"[19] would reduce the office work load. Randolph fully approved of this plan,[20] and his successor, James A. Seddon, followed suit. In his January, 1863, report to Davis, Seddon said that examining boards had been sent to the field so that equal opportunities would prevail for personnel in remote areas.

Three weeks after Seddon had mentioned this subject to the President, Gorgas put his plans for field examinations into practice. Through the Adjutant and Inspector General he had issued on January 28 a general order directing that candidates for artillery-ordnance commissions who passed the required examinations at the headquarters of any army, corps, or department could be placed on duty as acting ordnance officers. Regular commissions were to be issued when the examinations were completed in all armies.[21] Since his officers had to possess a great

[19] Special Orders Number 234, Adj. & Insp. Gen.'s Off., Richmond, October 7, 1862, ORA, Ser. IV, Vol. II, 110.
[20] Randolph to Davis, Richmond, October 9, 1862, *ibid.*, p. 113.
[21] General Orders Number 12, Adj. & Insp. Gen.'s Off., Richmond, January 28, 1863, *ibid.*, p. 377. This order provided that the number of acting appointments should not exceed one half the whole number of men who passed the examination at any one place, and should be made from the head of the eligible list.

The examinations were designed to be both objective and practical. Specific rules for taking them were promulgated, with each candidate required to sign a pledge that he had received no aid. He was not permitted to copy the questions. The examinations for lieutenants and captains differed considerably. Candidates for commissions as lieutenants were asked rather more practical questions, the following being fair examples.

Arithmetic: "Of 2,031 Enfield rifles, 91 were unserviceable. What per cent was unserviceable? Express 700 *troy* grains in ounces and decimals of an ounce avoirdupois. (7000 *troy* grains = 1 lb. *avoirdupois*)."

English: "Write, in English, twenty lines on *the war.*"

Ordnance: "How is slow match prepared? Describe Hale's rocket. How are cartridges made by hand? Mention injuries caused by service to bronze cannons. Describe the Whitworth gun. What are the materials of gunpowder, and the proportions used?"

Candidates for commissions as captains had to have a good working knowledge of higher mathematics, as the following questions illustrate.

Algebra: "Find the value of y in the following equation:

$$9 - 10y + \frac{1/3\, y^2 - 4 + y - y^2 + 10}{3} = 0.$$

"Find the value of x and y in the following equations:

$$(x + y)^{\frac{1}{2}} - x + 10 = 0.$$
$$x - 3 + (x - y)^{\frac{1}{2}} = 0."$$

Plane Trigonometry: "In a right angled triangle the hypotenuse is *h* and the

deal of highly technical knowledge, Gorgas was determined to guard against the possibility of having them placed on any duty which might waste their talents. In a Bureau Circular, issued on February 18, Gorgas directed that his officers should not be used "on duties not connected with their profession, except when the public interest is subserved, and then only occasionally."[22]

For some time discontent had been growing over the policy followed by the Conscript Bureau in drafting skilled and unskilled workers at government or contract installations. The insecurity felt by the workmen fostered migration through the lines[23] and hampered Gorgas throughout the war. He continually fought for the detail and retention of skilled laborers in ordnance shops. Through General Orders Number 66, September 12, 1862, he made a strong attempt to stabilize conscript policy regarding his labor supply. This order expressly prohibited enrolling officers from interfering with conscripts employed in government or ordnance workshops. All proceedings concerning such employees would be handled through the commanding officers of the plants. The same order, after granting authority to the Nitre and Mining Bureau to impress caves or mines, directed enrolling officers "not to remove or interfere with workmen or employees at the niter, lead, or copper works, or mines worked by Government officers, or by contractors for the Ordnance Department, without first apprising and obtaining the consent of the superintendent or officer in charge, who will be held strictly responsible for any abuse or invasion of the law."[24]

The War Department, on the next day, issued another general order, which seemed to undo all Gorgas had tried to do about securing the

---

angle at the base 30°. What is the value of the base and perpendicular? Express the log. of each in terms of the logs. of the known quantities."

Mechanics: "When the wind is blowing at right angles to the direction in which the vessel is moving, show by a diagram how the force representing the wind may be so resolved as to obtain a component in the direction of the motion of the vessel."

Chemistry: "Give some of the properties of oxygen, nitrogen, carbon, and sulphur. What is gun cotton? How does malleable iron differ from cast iron? How is steel made? Give the process and effect of annealing. Process of case hardening."

For the rules and questions, see Records of the War Department, Office of the Adjutant General, Records and Pensions Office, File Number 568231.

[22] Ordnance Circular, Richmond, February 18, 1863, *General Orders, Confederate States Army*, Series of 1863, p. 236.

[23] Bruce, *Virginia Iron Manufacture*, pp. 387–88.

[24] General Orders Number 66, Adj. & Insp. Gen.'s Off., Richmond, September 12, 1862, ORA, Ser. IV, Vol. II, 83.

permanent assignment of men to ordnance plants. The Surgeon General, Commissary General, and Chief of Ordnance were ordered to report the number of men who could be supplanted in their bureaus by less able-bodied workers.[25] Gorgas fought this policy with grim determination. On September 17 he asked Randolph to issue an order calling the attention of enrolling officers to the provision of the "Act to exempt certain persons from enrollment," passed during the last congressional session, which prescribed the exemption of all "engaged in working iron mines, furnaces and foundries."[26]

As time went on, however, department policy engendered a gradual change of views on labor supply. Colonel George W. Rains at Augusta wondered if skilled workers could not be found in hospitals or on furlough who were unable to stand field service. These might be detailed to government plants as a means of avoiding the cutthroat wage bargaining then going on because of the serious shortage of skilled labor. This strong appeal from an able officer was a salient point of argument. Gorgas, who probably now had decided that any measure which had the least appearance of giving some permanence to the labor supply demanded attention, indorsed Rains's letter to Randolph, requesting that "*disabled* men be substituted for those who are able to perform duty in the field."[27]

There could have been no better evidence of Gorgas' personal efficiency than the continued progress made at the various ordnance establishments. Shouldering the top-level worries, he thus permitted his subordinates at different points around the Confederacy to concentrate on their immediate problems. This policy allowed, also, some latitude for experimentation by the bureau because the main necessities—money, labor, and transportation—were miraculously procured by the Chief of Ordnance, and because his delegation of authority was judi-

[25] General Orders Number 67, Adj. & Insp. Gen.'s Off., Richmond, September 13, 1862, *ibid.*, p. 84. Limited service men were accepted for duty in hospitals and in staff departments. See General Orders Number 58, August 14, *ibid.*, p. 51.

[26] Gorgas to Randolph, Richmond, CRLR, 1862, Doc. GWD 720.

[27] Rains to Gorgas, and indorsement, Augusta Arsenal, October 24, 1862, *ibid.*, Doc. RWD 617. A note was attached to this letter, which is apparently a draft of Gorgas' reply to Rains, saying that Gorgas doubted the practicality of fixing a uniform wage scale since detailed men would resent working beside hired men at a lower wage. This is a reply to an idea Rains broached in the letter. Rains's rank was lieutenant colonel, in keeping with Gorgas' policy of having commanders of all the "greater Ordnance establishments" on a par with chief ordnance officers of armies in the field. See GOC, p. 287.

cious. It is doubtful if more than a select few Confederate Ordnance officers ever came thoroughly to appreciate or understand the miracles performed by Gorgas in managing to provide for the supreme necessities of his bureau. In considering his success, one observes an apparent tendency to assume that Gorgas himself produced the arms and munitions which carried on the war. In a sense, of course, this is true—yet his was a less spectacular task. He supplied the materials that were made into, or the ways and means to import, those arms and munitions. His achievement cannot be evaluated until it is seen that he was the man upon whom everything about ordnance depended. From the outset it was Gorgas who drew together the personnel and built up an organization capable of making ordnance and munitions in an agrarian economy. This organization was so efficient—so reliable—that its chief needed to be concerned only with the top command. In discharging this duty his quiet ability found its most eloquent outlet.

All of the subordinates whom Gorgas selected to command the more important ordnance plants were men who could, and did, exercise wide discretion. James H. Burton had marked ability to get vast amounts of work done. He was tenacious—perhaps stubborn and not a little impractical—but he got Macon Armory built and pushed through the morass of red tape to obtain a clear Confederate title to the lands. In his capacity as superintendent of small-arms production, Burton was, of course, ideal. His experience was an invaluable asset to the Ordnance Bureau. Another point in Burton's favor was his concern for his armory —obvious, unaffected concern. On October 29, 1862, he wrote Gorgas that rumors of intended enemy activity up the Georgia rivers made it seem prudent to obstruct the Ocmulgee River at some defensible spot. This would lessen, if not entirely remove, all threat to Macon.[28]

So it was that in almost all action-level matters, the subordinates formulated the plans while the Chief decided whether the bureau's resources and necessities would permit their execution. Gorgas acted as a faithful watchdog for his subordinates, and the arrangement paid rich dividends in bullets, guns, and bayonets.

In the realm of bureau experimentation, Gorgas had a galaxy of men able to work out new and improved implements. He, himself, had always shown great interest in new inventions, and his service on the United States Ordnance Board had enhanced his natural interest. Captain Mallet had been given a post which called for constant research, a

[28] Burton to Gorgas, Macon, October 29, 1862, CROB, XX, 220–21.

type of work in which he was most at home. Gorgas appreciated and supported his efforts to stimulate better laboratory production. In some of the lesser men, such as William Leroy Broun, Gorgas had able technicians, who were just the men to carry into practical application many of the schemes originating in Mallet's and Rains's laboratories.

The Chief of Ordnance overlooked few possible sources of improvement for his service. Civilian inventors—men with more time to theorize and try—often proved valuable, and their ideas were rarely slighted. For instance, on September 5, 1862, in a bureau order, Gorgas assigned Colonel T. S. Rhett, Captain Mallet, and Broun to the duty of examining and reporting "upon the plans of Mr. D. Morgan McEndre, for the application of steam as a motor for field Art[iller]y."[29] The need for continuing research in ordnance establishments was obvious. The Bormann fuse, issued widely by the bureau as an efficient detonating agent, had come in for the bitterest criticism by Major Edward P. Alexander, chief of artillery for Longstreet's corps. Colonel Rains, who considered the problem, felt that this fuse had distinct possibilities, but in the hands of inexperienced artillerists was unreliable. His recommendation to return to the old paper fuses[30] was adopted. Other important research carried on by the bureau was the constant testing of Confederate powder. Under Rains's able guidance, Augusta powder was uniformly good and getting better—but powder from other sources was constantly tested.[31]

In October, Julius A. de Lagnel, commanding Fayetteville Arsenal, complained that his supply of steel was almost gone and advocated the

[29] Ordnance Circular, Richmond, September 5, 1862, CROB, V, 15.

[30] Rains to Gorgas, Augusta, September 13, 1862, *ibid.*, p. 19. Edward P. Alexander, in his *Military Memoirs of a Confederate* (New York, 1907), p. 54, remarked that Confederate fuses for field artillery were unreliable, and asserted that Southern arsenals "lacked the copper and brass, and the mechanical skill necessary to turn out first class ammunition." He said that Confederate artillerists were "handicapped by our ammunition until the close of the war." Gorgas, who learned after the war of Alexander's allegations, retorted that if Confederate ammunition had been as bad as he painted it, the Rebel artillery would never have dared face the enemy—and this never seemed to be the case. See GOC, p. 288. Gorgas thought Alexander meant spherical case shells prepared with the Bormann fuse and agreed that those shells deserved condemnation. See also Gorgas' indorsement on Gen. J. S. Jones to Gen. R. H. Chilton, New Market, Va., January 6, 1863, ORA, Ser. I, Vol. XXI, 745.

[31] Gorgas to Mallet, Richmond, October 25, 1862, CROB, V, 53. For the discontinuance of the Bormann fuse generally, see Ordnance Circular, Richmond, December 24, 1862, *General Orders, Confederate States Army,* Series of 1863, p. 235; also GOC, p. 288.

use of rolled-iron gun barrels. The idea was basically sound, but the most serious tactical problem facing Gorgas at this time was the shortage of iron. On November 26 he told Seddon that this claimed his most imperative attention. "Our contractors are many of them at a dead stand for lack of Iron, and it will be impossible to supply projectiles for the new guns now in the *field,* unless it can be had." In this dangerous predicament Gorgas thought the Nitre and Mining Bureau ought to be permitted to impress *"one half* the stock of Iron at the furnaces at this time."[32]

Faced with all these varied problems Gorgas continued to hammer at the War Department and the other supply bureaus to get what he needed. He had been pushed by dint of circumstances into the position of advocating the impressment of supplies, a practice which under other conditions he never would have considered. And as the situation now developed, he would have to continue advocating that sort of policy since he had to procure raw materials somehow.

[32] Gorgas to Seddon, Richmond, November 26, 1862, CRLR, 1862, Doc. GWD 810.

XII

Deficiencies and Substitutes

THERE WAS LITTLE TO CHEER THE CHIEF OF ORDNANCE DURING THE
last months of 1862. The drastic shortage of lead forced him to curtail
and place rigid controls on daily ammunition production at the various
arsenals. He assigned to them a given amount of lead for each month
and informed ordnance officers that the stipulated amount was all that
could be counted on "from the Nitre & Mining Bureau. The deficiency
must be obtained as heretofore."[1]

Atlanta Arsenal now occupied a peculiarly vulnerable position. Instead of receiving support from Augusta, Macon, and Columbus Arsenals in supplying the wants of the Army of Tennessee, Atlanta now had
to sustain that force virtually singlehanded.[2] This heavy strain on
Georgia made the location of other lead sources imperative. Major
Richard M. Cuyler at Macon, whose eye had lost none of its wonted
perception, telegraphed Gorgas on November 6 that Commodore

[1] Ordnance Memorandum, Richmond, November [?], 1862, AGPF, Mallet. In
this memorandum Gorgas set the following daily rate of ammunition production:

Station	Rounds of Small Arms Ammunition	Rounds of Field Ammunition		Pounds of Lead Monthly
Richmond Arsenal	60,000	300 to	500	60,000
Charleston Arsenal	10,000	100 to	125	9,000
Augusta Arsenal	30,000	125 to	150	30,000
Macon Arsenal	10,000	100 to	125	8,000
Columbus, Ga., Arsenal	10,000	75 to	100	10,000
Atlanta Arsenal	25,000	125 to	150	20,000
Selma Arsenal	10,000	50 to	75	8,000
Columbus, Miss., Arsenal	15,000	125 to	150	10,000
	170,000	1,000 to	1,375	155,000

[2] McMain to Gorgas, Dalton, November 1, 1862, CROB, XXV, 88; also p.
101.

[148]

Duncan N. Ingraham, at Charleston, had a supply of lead which could be transferred if permission were obtained from the Secretary of the Navy. Cuyler telegraphed Gorgas in desperation that he was absolutely out of lead and could get no help from the Nitre and Mining Bureau.[3]

And from James H. Burton, Superintendent of Armories, came most disheartening information. Replying to a request from Gorgas to prepare during November 2,000 gunstocks for repaired arms, Burton said that "it will be impossible to prepare so large a number in so limited a period, the capacity of the set of stock machines being equal to the production of about 1500 Stocks per month only." He added some words which throw light on the pitiful condition of public carriers:

I will however make every exertion by running extra hours to turn out the greatest number possible and will forward them as fast as it will be possible to prepare a number sufficiently large to justify me sending them in charge of a special messenger, which is absolutely necessary to be done —otherwise they will not go through promptly or safely.[4]

On November 15, 1862, Burton instructed his Acting Master Armorer to have one of the rough turning machines set up "and report to me as soon as possible whether or not it can be completed so as to rough turn gun stocks Model 1842." The immediate need for at least 1,000 stocks in Richmond made Burton's efforts important, and he directed that stocks should be packed for shipment as fast as they were made.[5] On the same day, in replying to a telegram from Gorgas of the day before, Burton said that he was doing everything he could to increase the production of stocks. "That department," he wrote, "is now working from sunrise until 10 o'clock P.M. inclusive of Sundays and if it be possible to accomplish it I will arrange to work all night. Most of the workmen employed on this machinery are new and inexperienced, but will be enabled to turn out more stocks than heretofore."[6]

One of Burton's own pet projects now began to show some return to the government's investment. The Spiller and Burr pistol firm at last sent him the first pistol they had made, which he thought "very

---

[3] Cuyler to Gorgas, Macon, November 6, 1862, CROB, CI, 64.
[4] Burton to Gorgas, Macon, November 5, 1862, CROB, XX, 234.
[5] Burton to J. Fuss, Macon, AGPF, Burton.
[6] Burton to Gorgas, Macon, CROB, XX, 255–56. The stocks were needed at Richmond for repairing arms sent in from the field. Burton, on November 22, telegraphed Gorgas that 800 stocks had been sent to Richmond that day. *Ibid.,* p. 268.

satisfactory."[7] But Burton's most important enterprise was coming along, too. The buildings for the Macon Armory were taking form, and on December 18, 1862, Burton entered in his diary: "Hoisted Flag on Armory Workshops."

Troubles, however, continued to pile up. On November 7 Gorgas, obviously alarmed, ordered Mallet to Jackson, Mississippi, to investigate the cause of an explosion in the laboratory connected with the Ordnance Depot there. He thought that the arrangement of the buildings must have been faulty or the casualties would not have been so numerous. He confided to his loyal associate that accidents could not be prevented entirely but could be guarded against and made less fatal.[8] Gorgas impressed this view on Mallet and urged him to devise safety measures for publication and distribution to laboratories. On November 19 Mallet issued a circular, approved by Gorgas, directing that in all Confederate laboratories one building would be set aside exclusively as a magazine for finished ammunition, all of which would be taken to this magazine, situated at least fifty yards from any other structure. Mallet emphatically directed that in no case would more than the equivalent of one barrel of powder ever be allowed to remain in a workshop.[9] In the meantime, Gorgas asked him to push his efforts to make chemicals, "employ competent persons, submit estimates &c as suggested."[10]

Carrying out Gorgas' directions was not easy. In Georgia, to which the Superintendent of Laboratories looked for a supply of alcohol, competition by the Subsistence and Medical departments reduced to nil the opportunities of obtaining any alcohol for ordnance purposes. Mallet complained to Gorgas that it did not seem right to him that the Subsistence Department, except in cases of dire emergency, should thus monopolize the whole amount of alcohol allotted by Georgia for Confederate use. Up until the time of writing, all types of remonstrances had failed; and Mallet thought some sort of equitable division

---

[7] Burton, *Diary,* December 4, 15, 1862. Burton wanted to raise the prices paid for Spiller and Burr pistols but was afraid Gorgas would think he was trying to get a large cut for himself, since he had an interest in the plant. On December 29 Gorgas agreed to pay more money to Spiller and Burr, and said that "notwithstanding the interest you were permitted to take in their business, by the Secretary of War, I feel sure your interest in the Government, and your professional pride may at any time be cited as sufficient guarantee for the reliability of any recommendation you may make." Gorgas to Burton, Richmond, December 29, 1862, Burton.   [8] Gorgas to Mallet, Richmond, CROB, V, 66.
[9] Ordnance Circular, Macon, *ibid.,* p. 96.
[10] Gorgas to Mallet, Richmond, November 26, 1862, *ibid.,* p. 98.

should be worked out with the Commissary General.[11] Negotiation with the notoriously incompetent Colonel Lucius B. Northrop, Commissary General, produced, unbelievably enough, some favorable results. He seemed willing to allow a limited amount of alcohol for the ordnance service, though he was characteristically imperious in the arrangements.[12]

In Mallet's attempts to push work on the Central Laboratory he encountered numerous annoying shortages. On December 9 Gorgas had to tell him that nails, shovels, and spades would have to be procured in the open market since the Quartermaster Department could not supply them. The one encouragement he met was that Gorgas had managed to get Northrop's agreement to supply Ordnance laborers with commissary stores.[13] The Ordnance Office, on the other hand, contributed its share to Mallet's worries. Before giving final authorization for the purchase of land and a good number of draught animals, Captain Edward B. Smith, one of Gorgas' assistants, told the Superintendent that the bureau wanted to know the need for two brickyards in Macon. Would not James Burton's yard suffice for both the armory and the laboratory?

Although affairs in Macon looked highly promising to Gorgas, affairs in other parts of the Deep South were less favorable. Major J. J. Pope, Chief of Ordnance, Department of South Carolina and Georgia, wrote Brigadier General Thomas Jordan on November 10 that he had been feverishly seeking ordnance supplies all around the Confederacy and had encountered frequent delays in the shipment of stores, due in some measure to haphazard rail freight transportation and in greater measure to the fact "that the arsenals are overworked and cannot furnish what I require." He admitted that "the commanders of arsenals exhibit every disposition to do what they can, and are under engagements to supply some of my requisitions." Paying unconscious lip-service to Gorgas' own plaints, Pope added: "No one who is not in a position to see it from day to day can appreciate the difficulties in securing supplies seemingly most common and abundant and of procuring artisans capable for ordnance work. This must justly be considered in the delays at the different arsenals in supplying stores that we require."[14]

[11] Mallet to Gorgas, Macon, December 19, 1862, CROB, XXVIII, 102–103. Mallet estimated the annual alcohol needs of the bureau at 300,000 gallons.

[12] Bayne to Mallet, Richmond, December 27, 1862, CROB, V, 146. Northrop seems to have misread the amount of alcohol needed by Mallet; he was willing to leave 30,000 gallons for ordnance use.

[13] Gorgas to Mallet, Richmond, December 9, 1862, *ibid.*, p. 119.

[14] Pope to Jordan, Charleston, ORA, Ser. I, Vol. XIV, 675.

More than a month later, Colonel A. J. Gonzales, chief of artillery and ordnance at Charleston, was writing Gorgas that supplies for his city had not improved. He complained that he had no Enfield cartridges, that Colonel Rains had no lead with which to make more than were constantly consumed, and that he had requisitions from Florida which he could not meet. In the matter of projectiles for large and small rifled guns, he reported himself in still worse condition. Thirty-eight projectiles per day were all that the Charleston ordnance works could turn out; in Augusta none could be made for lack of material; in Macon none for heavy guns could be made because the officials had no drawings to follow. This critical situation left Forts Sumter and Moultrie with an average of less than fifty rounds per rifled gun, and with not a single round for the twelve-pounder rifled guns in position on the water. Gonzales explained that the whole state was dependent for its ordnance on the co-operation of Charleston Arsenal and requested that Gorgas instruct Major F. L. Childs to supply that department without delay.[15]

And closer to home Gorgas heard that Lee also wanted certain ordnance items, his cavalry sorely needing carbines. He asked for 500 or as many as Gorgas could find, since the Federal horsemen were superior in sharpshooters.[16] The general expressed his wants in a letter to Seddon, who passed it on to Gorgas:

> HEADQUARTERS ARMY OF NORTHERN
> VIRGINIA
> December 5, 1862.

Hon. Secretary of War, Richmond:

SIR:

During the past campaign I have felt, in every battle, the advantages that the enemy possessed over us in their artillery. This arose in part from

---

[15] Gonzales to Gorgas, Charleston, December 29, 1862, *ibid.*, p. 745. On January 6, 1863, Gorgas told Gonzales that Atlanta Arsenal was so fully occupied in supplying the Army of Tennessee that it could do nothing else, but that he had "directed Macon and Columbus, Ga., to send each 50,000 cartridges (caliber .58) to you as soon as possible." He went on to say that "it would be well to consider the question of a supply of rifle projectiles before going too far with the rifling and banding of 32-pounders. The want of proper iron for casting these shells is very serious. Send me a full statement of all you want and cannot get at Charleston, limiting your requisition to, say, 150 rounds per gun. I will do all in my power to supply you." Gorgas to Gonzales, Richmond, *ibid.*, pp. 746–47. See also C. H. Lee to Gen. H. W. Mercer, Richmond, January 16, *ibid.*, pp. 750–51; Gonzales to [Gorgas?], Charleston, January 23, *ibid.*, p. 754.

[16] Col. A. L. Long to Gorgas, Headquarters, Army of Northern Virginia, November 10, 1862, *ibid.*, XIX, Pt. II, 712.

their possessing more experienced artillerists and better prepared ammunition, but consisted chiefly in better guns. These advantages, I am happy to state, are gradually diminishing. Our artillerists are greatly improving, our ammunition is more carefully prepared, and the efficiency of our batteries increased by guns captured from the enemy. I am greatly in need of longer range smooth-bore guns, and propose that, if metal cannot otherwise be procured, a portion, if not all, of our 6-pounder smooth-bores (bronze), and, if necessary, a part of our 12-pounder howitzers, be recast into 12-pounder Napoleons. The best guns for field service, in my opinion, are the 12-pounder Napoleons, the 10-pounder Parrotts, and the approved 3-inch rifles. Batteries composed of such guns would simplify our ammunition, give us less metal to transport, and longer and more accurate range of fire. I urgently recommend to the Department the consideration of this subject, and that measures be immediately taken to improve our field artillery. The contest between our 6-pounder smooth-bores and the 12-pounder Napoleons of the enemy is very unequal, and, in addition, is discouraging to our artillerists. . . .

I have the honor to be, with great respect, your obedient servant,

R. E. Lee,

General[17]

Lee's wants did not catch the Ordnance Bureau by surprise. Gorgas had already issued a circular to all arsenals anticipating Lee's possible needs. Joseph R. Anderson & Company had been directed to operate the Tredegar Iron Works night and day to prepare the type of guns Lee favored, and such weapons were sent to his army as soon as they were made.[18]

Still the desperate need to find more and more sources of supplies, the stock of which became smaller and smaller, continued unabated. Major M. H. Wright at the Atlanta ordnance office confided to Mallet on November 23, 1862, that he did not suppose a gallon of oil could be found anywhere, and he did not know how much zinc and putty were available. He closed on a familiar note: "The whole State has been scoured for Lead."[19]

[17] ORA, Ser. I, Vol. XXI, 1046–47.

[18] The circular regulating artillery manufacture, published by Gorgas' direction, restricted the fabrication, "until further orders" of any guns except bronze light 12-pounder Napoleons, caliber 4.62; iron 10-pounder Parrotts, banded, caliber 2.9, for field batteries of maneuver; iron 20-pounder Parrotts, caliber 3.67, on 12-pounder carriages, for field batteries of reserve; iron 30-pounder Parrotts, caliber 4.2, on 18-pounder siege carriages, for siege guns. See Ordnance Circular, Richmond, November 13, 1862, *ibid.*

[19] Wright to Mallet, Atlanta, CROB, V, 89.

Transportation, too, was a perennial headache. W. H. McMain, in charge of Dalton Ordnance Depot, reported to Gorgas on December 19 that he had received no stores from anywhere since December 3, and consequently was nearly out of everything. Atlanta Arsenal had not replied to inquiries at to what it could supply, and chaotic transportation from Knoxville almost cut that city off from Dalton. A shipment of stores left Dalton on November 11 and another on November 20— neither of which had reached Knoxville by December 19.[20] McMain's complaints about transportation may have influenced Gorgas in securing from the Secretary of War orders placing the transportation of all ordnance items in the complete charge of the Quartermaster Department.[21]

A significant letter had been written to Gorgas on November 26 by Rains, who said that a substitute had been found for the woolen cloth used in making cartridges for field and heavy artillery. Cotton cloth, or paper "soaked in a saturated solution of Alum or sulphate of ammonia, and then in a heated mixture of Beaswax [sic] and tallow not only assumes the condition of woolen material in not holding fire but is *water proof.*" Adequate quantities of the substitute were available.[22] Rains had made an important discovery; but more than that, he had proved that the Ordnance Bureau could encounter and surmount critical shortages—it could still survive.

[20] McMain to Gorgas, Dalton, December 19, 1862, CROB, XXV, 125–26. McMain wanted a clearer definition of his position. He received his only orders direct from Gorgas and thought he was under Ordnance Bureau authority, but since Bragg had assigned him to his station, he wanted the line of command made definite.

[21] General Orders Number 112, Adj. & Insp. Gen.'s Off., Richmond, December 30, 1862, ORA, Ser. IV, Vol. II, 266.

[22] Rains to Gorgas, Richmond [?], CROB, V, 99.

XIII

The Logistics of a Waiting Game

THE LAST DAYS OF 1862 HAD BEEN REDDENED WITH THE BLOOD spilled in the fierce fighting between Bragg and Rosecrans at Stone's River or Murfreesboro, Tennessee, and between Lee and the Army of the Potomac at Second Manassas, Sharpsburg, and Fredericksburg. Murfreesboro, dragging on through January 2, 1863, settled the question of whether Bragg's advance into Tennessee could continue—he withdrew southward to winter quarters around Tullahoma, thirty-five miles below Murfreesboro. In this position, blocking the way to Chattanooga, the Army of Tennessee was dangerous—dangerous to the Yankees and inconvenient to Gorgas. In one of the many tactical maneuverings made throughout Tennessee during this campaign, the Holston River bridge, essential to keeping open the route between Knoxville and Richmond, had been burned. This unfortunate contingency posed a critical problem for the ordnance officer at Knoxville, who turned to McMain, the efficient officer at Dalton depot, for assistance. Feeling that he should undertake the interim supply of Knoxville until the restoration of communications, McMain informed Gorgas of his increased needs.[1] This added duty would not have materially overtaxed his depot had it not been coupled with emergency requisitions from Bragg's chief ordnance officer. Colonel Hypolite Oladowski telegraphed an order for all the small arms ammunition which McMain had in store, along with a quantity of field ammunition.[2] McMain's source of supply was Atlanta Arsenal, which had distribution responsibility for the Department of West Tennessee. The destruction of the Holston bridge and McMain's consequent expansion of duties threw

---

[1] McMain to Gorgas (telegram), Dalton, January 1, 1863, CROB, XXV, 131; and letter, January 1, *ibid.*

[2] McMain to Gorgas, Dalton, January 10, 1863, *ibid.*, p. 135.

[155]

the supply of the Knoxville Department squarely on Atlanta Arsenal. Despite the wonted energy and ability of Colonel Wright, commanding there, that establishment was simply overtaxed. McMain, who soon recognized this fact, corresponded with Wright, asking specific information about what Atlanta could not supply, and asked him also to inform Gorgas of the deficiencies.

On January 13 McMain confided to the Chief of Ordnance that Dalton depot was entirely out of small-arms ammunition, and that only a limited amount of field ammunition remained. Colonel Oladowski was persistent in his demands for ample supplies of all sorts for field service, and Gorgas read that McMain wanted at least 1,500,000 buck and ball cartridges, 5,000 rounds of field ammunition, and 5,000 sets of infantry accouterments.[3]

If affairs in McMain's area had been all that troubled Gorgas, he would have been well off indeed. But there were, of course, myriad other needs and problems. Organizational policy centered around his earnest desire to centralize the bureau's activities as much as possible. To Colonel Burton he had written in September, 1862, his hope that "the *Armory* will . . . be our great National Work—even superior to that of Rains." His confidence in Burton's administration of Macon was complete, and he said of things there, "I have had no leisure to think over it, and am content to leave it in your hands, with the assurance that it will be well done."[4] But there was one other person whose concern it was to see that Macon Arsenal got into production rapidly. In July, 1862, following the Seven Days Battles, Major General Benjamin Huger had been assigned to duty as Inspector of Artillery and Ordnance. He admitted that he was late entering on his duties, but by October, 1862, was hopeful of devoting his "time entirely to the business." On examining the contracts of the Ordnance Bureau, he found that a large business was being carried on, and that "the Govt. has to do many things, and make itself many supplies we used to get from individuals." He was impressed with the progress made by the bureau and told Burton that "when I see what has been done, and the limited means we have had to work with, I think we have cause of congratulation that we have got on so well."[5]

---

[3] McMain to Gorgas, Dalton, January 13, 1863, *ibid.,* p. 137.
[4] Gorgas to Burton [Richmond], September 29, 1862, *Burton Papers, Winchester*. In the same letter Gorgas tried a diplomatic question, asking Burton if "you even in your thoughts set a date for results?"
[5] Huger to Burton, Richmond, October 7, 1862, *ibid*.

The concern and hopes of Huger, sincere and honest as they were, seem to have irked some of the ordnance officers at Macon. Burton, in particular, voiced his objection to the inspection of his work by this superior officer. Possibly reflecting lingering resentment over past trouble in Mexico, Gorgas told Burton: "Gen. Huger's orders are intended to cover all Ord^n Establishments. He will do no harm, if he can do no good."[6] And this sentence pretty well summed up the prevailing trend to ignore Huger's job. And yet this probably was a mistake which Gorgas ought to have recognized, for Huger had vast experience in ordnance, and had been in general charge of foundry work for the United States Army before the outbreak of war. He possessed a trained and practiced eye in such matters and he had the discrimination to observe that "our Arsenals have sprung up suddenly, & are already capable of turning out much work—Our present great necessity is *Iron*, and tho' the high price must stimulate the manufacture, it takes some time to get such works in operation."[7]

Now faced with the necessity of pushing the rapid expansion of his bureau to meet the heavy demands which would assuredly be made upon it, Gorgas had to tap every possible resource, every avenue of succor. He gave vent to excusable pride when he told Burton, "we have done well in the way of importing & capturing arms. The sum total of our *gain* in five months by captures & importation is 106,000 since May 1st or thereabout."[8] He kept hard at work. Since the principal installations of the bureau were to be situated in Georgia, a major portion of his attention had to center there. No effort to do anything in that state, however, could gain any measure of success without the blessing of difficult Governor Brown, whose hatred of the President was no secret. And on nothing else did Brown (and, incidentally, North Carolina's Zebulon Vance, almost as difficult as Brown) exert more loving supervision than the production and distribution of grain spirits. That there was a sound economic reason for a measure of gubernatorial interest in this matter is beyond argument, but Brown took his interest beyond reasonable limits. Gorgas, who, to meet the needs of his bureau, had to find another source of alcohol than the unpredictable Commissary Department, sought its distillation in Georgia—only to find that Brown exercised licensing power over all alcohol products in the state.

[6] Gorgas to Burton [Richmond], September 20, 1862, *ibid.;* Burton, *Diary,* January 1, 1863.

[7] Huger to [Burton?], Columbia, January 31, 1863, *Burton Papers, Winchester.*

[8] Gorgas to Burton, [Richmond], September 29, 1862, *ibid.*

Application for an Ordnance Bureau license brought word that under no circumstances could the bureau pay more than $2.50 for a gallon of alcohol and $1.50 for a gallon of whiskey. In addition, no distiller working for either the Commissary, Medical, or Ordnance departments would be permitted (and they had taken an oath on it) to use any grain within twenty miles of a railroad or navigable stream.[9] While Brown seemed willing enough to grant a license if his stipulations were observed, he nevertheless proved to be the main obstruction in Mallet's path toward securing alcohol for his laboratories.

Mallet had extended his efforts to secure alcohol all over Georgia and neighboring districts, and had requested assistance from the Medical Purveyor's Office at Savannah. At that place able Dr. W. H. Prioleau stood ready to do whatever he could to further the Confederate cause. But even this energetic man, who told Mallet that he would be glad to lend his laboratories alcohol from time to time, had to confess that he did not know how he could get any for himself. "Governor Brown," he wrote, "positively refuses to allow my Contractors to make it at the prices which I have agreed to pay. I am not greatly in want of Alcohol, myself, and know not where to look for it."[10]

Though Georgia's Chief Executive proved a stumbling block to Mallet's progress at Macon, Gorgas did all he could to compensate for Brown. He informed Mallet that because of the need for early results, as little time as possible should be spent erecting buildings at the laboratories. "It is of course desirable (as we have so few mechanics at command) to do as little work of preparation as possible, . . . it would be better to go on and get results with temporary buildings than to delay in order to erect better ones."[11] There were sound reasons for curtailing Mallet's building program, but the action did represent a confusing change of policy. Shortly after receiving Gorgas' orders reducing his task, Mallet expressed his perplexity to his chief. This new concept, he said, was entirely foreign to all previous instructions. In an order dated August 26, 1862, Gorgas had directed Mallet to "select a suitable location at Macon, Ga. for a *permanent* Laboratory establishment." The same order contained authority to secure ground, make out plans and drawings for the buildings, and let contracts for carrying out the plan. Until this new policy had come in the mail from

[9] N. N. Waters to W. H. Prioleau, Milledgeville, Ga., December 28, 1862, CROB, V, 161; Waters to Mallet, Milledgeville, January 2, 1863, *ibid.*, p. 160.
[10] Prioleau to Mallet, Savannah, January 15, 1863, *ibid.*, p. 184.
[11] Edward B. Smith to Mallet, Richmond, January 14, 1863, *ibid.*, p. 191.

Richmond, Mallet had no hint that anything other than permanent buildings was wanted. For this reason, he protested, his efforts had been entirely directed toward a complete and permanent laboratory. To Gorgas he said that at the time of his original orders he had been unable to see any good reason for adding to the already considerable number of temporary establishments.[12] Having devoted no little time to considering this problem, Gorgas believed that the best he could direct his bureau officers to do was "hire, rather than buy any more" real property. His reasons for this belief were sound: "Details of men cannot be relied on. The matter is referred to the Generals in the field and they usually refuse." Then, too, the need of cutting War Department expenditures as much as possible led him to direct Mallet not to "erect more permanent buildings than are within the scope of 50 to 75,000 Dollars."[13]

On January 22, 1863, two days after he had cautioned Mallet concerning the need for economy, Gorgas again wrote him, giving in some detail reasons for strict adherence to curtailment of efforts at Macon. "Your progress and the energy displayed is satisfactory," he said, "but I must caution you not to extend your plans too much. I fear you will attempt what may delay *results,* which are most important." He said that when they had first discussed their plans, he had understood that Mallet intended only to erect the most important permanent buildings, leaving the rest to a later time. "The funds disposable will not admit of a very large expenditure—say 100 to 125 Thousand dollars for the current year, at the very utmost." Four days later he stressed the need for getting into operation.[14]

The attention paid by the Chief of Ordnance to home manufacturing was in direct line with the tactics which circumstances forced upon him. Recent actions, including Second Manassas, Sharpsburg, Fredericksburg, Murfreesboro, Chickasaw Bluffs, Galveston, and Arkansas Post, while clearly not decisive, all tended to establish the existence of a waiting game—a waiting game that Gorgas wanted to play with great care and with far-sighted logistics. The only feasible course open to him was to do everything possible to prepare his bureau for whatever actions the future might bring. Then, too, a diligent expansion of home production would buttress his bureau against further stringency of the Federal blockade.

---

[12] Mallet to Gorgas, Macon, January 19, 1863, CROB, XXVIII, 192–93.
[13] Gorgas to Mallet, Richmond, January 20, 1863, CROB, X, 212.
[14] Gorgas to Mallet, Richmond, January 22 and 26, 1863, *ibid.,* pp. 214, 230.

Not only was this course the one forced upon Gorgas, but it also came to be regarded by the War Department as a panacea. In a report to Davis on January 3, 1863, James Seddon laid a foundation which the President would build upon when he sent his message to Congress on January 12. Seddon took the optimistic view that the growing efficiency of the blockade was having a good effect on Confederate ingenuity. Since it was becoming increasingly difficult to import supplies, those responsible for their procurement redoubled their efforts to secure them in domestic markets. This, of course, led to the development of home manufacturing, and the Secretary of War told Davis that supplies were at least as abundant (this was the term of the optimist) as at any time in the past. The prospects for the future, he said, were promising, and the recent addition of two large centers of ordnance production in interior towns had relieved the department's anxiety over dependence on one source of supply. Davis was confidently told that the War Department could now furnish more adequate amounts of arms and ammunition than at any previous time and had no dread of a deficiency of munitions. Seddon said that the government was daily becoming less dependent on foreign supplies by encouraging and establishing manufactures in the Confederate States, and looked to the time when it could "dispense altogether with that reliance."[15]

Seddon's rosy picture undoubtedly received a deeper tint from a statement submitted by Gorgas on January 7, 1863, giving the amount of fabrication and issues of ordnance stores to September 1, 1862. This document listed 14,349 small arms fabricated, 294,753 issued, and 9,876 remaining on hand. Of infantry equipments, it listed 137,913 fabricated, 252,415 issued, and 18,579 remaining on hand. Gorgas reported the monthly production of rifles, muskets, and carbines at public armories to be 2,050; at private armories, 1,550. He listed 3,500 sabers made each month and said that the average cost of a rifle or musket was $21.50, a carbine, $42.50, and a saber, $18.00. The Chief of Ordnance said that with other private armories under contract, he

---

[15] Seddon to Davis, Richmond, January 3, 1863, ORA, Ser. IV, Vol. II, 291–92. See Davis' message to Congress dated January 12, delivered on the 14th, in which he said: "Dependence on foreign supplies is to be deplored, and should, as far as practicable, be obviated by the development and employment of internal resources." Dunbar Rowland (ed.) *Jefferson Davis, Constitutionalist: His Letters, Papers and Speeches* (Jackson, Miss., 1923), V, 413; James D. Richardson (comp.), *A Compilation of the Messages and Papers of the Confederacy* (Nashville, 1906), I, 295; *Journal of the Congress of the Confederate States of America,* III, 6, 7.

expected the supply of arms to be increased by 500 per month during 1863, and added that armory capacities would be expanded.[16]

While the hope of ultimate release from dependence on foreign supplies might well prove illusory, it did move the War Department to pay more attention to the wants of the bureau in regard to domestic expansion. At any rate, several factors combined to give Gorgas ample opportunity to secure departmental co-operation for some of his most important plans.

Nothing plagued the various chiefs of Confederate supply agencies more, as has been indicated, than the drastic scarcity of skilled labor. In the ordnance shops, arsenals, armories, depots, and all other points of manufacture, the type of workers most sought after—and once obtained, most coddled—were the skilled craftsmen: mechanics, gunsmiths, puddlers, founders, and the like. The skilled machinist was in demand by all supply bureaus; unless he had specialized he was just as useful in a shoe factory as in an armory. This fact did not contribute to friendly labor relations between different bureaus, nor did it do much to foster the continued efficiency of privately owned government contracting shops. Control exercised by the Confederate government over private industries had already grown to such proportions as to dictate completely the activity of most such plants—excepting, of course, the exasperatingly independent textile factories in North Carolina, protected as they were by Governor Vance. These comprised more than one-third of the whole number of textile mills in the eastern Confederacy.[17]

[16] Gorgas to Seddon, Richmond, ORA, Ser. IV, Vol. II, 299.

[17] Charles W. Ramsdell, "The Control of Manufacturing by the Confederate Government," *Mississippi Valley Historical Review*, VIII (1921–22), 242. The matter of pay scales was of increasing importance. Burton said that his scale was from $5.00 per day for master machinists to $3.00 per day for carpenters. Burton to Gorgas, Macon, February 2, 1863, CROB, XX, 284. Mallet was concerned about wages for Negro labor. He and Gorgas both favored extra money for extra work—this money to be for the Negroes themselves, not for their owners. This would stimulate the slaves to do overtime work. Seddon approved the plan. See Mallet to Gorgas, Richmond, February 12, 1863, *ibid.*, XXVIII, 216–17; Mallet to Gorgas, Macon, February 20, 1863, *ibid.*, pp. 227–28; Gorgas to Mallet, Richmond, February 16, 1863, *ibid.*, V, 262. Realizing the need for some kind of standardization of wages, Gorgas issued two circulars, one on March 14 and the other on March 23, 1863, which said, in essence, that wages paid at arsenals and ordnance establishments on March 31 would be considered fixed and would not be changed without reference to the Chief of Ordnance. See *General Orders, Confederate States Army,* Series of 1863, p. 236, for circular of the 14th; CROB, V, 345, for circular of March 23. The idea behind the wage-scale fixing was sound, but there existed such a wide difference in the pay scales at the various ordnance plants that much dissatisfaction arose.

The Chief of Ordnance, who may well have felt considerable sym pathy for the average private contractor who was earnestly trying to do his job, nevertheless found that he had vast authority over each factory under contract with the Ordnance Bureau. This authority rested, in large measure, upon the conscription laws which held the Confederacy's manpower supply tightly in the hands of the military. Bureau chiefs wielded the power to decide who should and should not receive labor exemptions from the ranks, and who should and should not retain the details which had already been granted, although final decisions rested with enrolling officers. In this power lay a coercive potential strong enough to command co-operation from almost all private industrialists who wished to stay in operation. Gorgas, however, had an even stronger authoritative weapon to use, after passage of the Exemption Act of October 11, 1862. This law had superseded the inadequate Exemption Act of April 21, 1862, and replaced it with a much more detailed list of those who were considered indispensable. It included all those artisans, mechanics, and employees working in government munitions plants and in contract agencies. The law pro- vided that exemptions of ordnance technicians should not be made un- til "the Chief of the Ordnance bureau, or some ordnance officer author- ized by him for the purpose, shall approve of the number of the opera- tives required in such establishments."[18] Then, too, Gorgas had the advantage accruing to supply bureaus of the virtual government con- trol of railroads. This last advantage almost completed the Confederate industrial monoply. After the Quartermaster General had instituted a system of transportation priorities for such army supplies as food and munitions, the rickety railroads were unable to carry anything not specifically contributing to the war effort. This, of course, made every factory dependent on the government for raw materials. "When the raw material must be brought, under military orders, over an army-con- trolled railroad to a factory operating with labor detailed from the army, there was no way for the manufacturer to avoid selling to the government as much of his product as was demanded."[19]

---

[18] *Statutes at Large (Confederate),* 1 Cong., Stat. II, Chap. XLV.
[19] Ramsdell, *Mississippi Valley Historical Review,* VIII, 240. For an example of such operational problems faced by an important Alabama iron company, see Vandiver, "The Shelby Iron Company in the Civil War," *Alabama Review,* I (1948), 117–18. For authority to impress railroads, see Ramsdell (ed.), *Laws and Joint Resolutions of the Last Session of the Confederate Congress, Together With the Secret Acts of Previous Congresses* (Durham, N. C., 1941), pp. 167– 69.

From the point of view of a bureau chief, this dictatorship of production, which made almost every producer a government ward, had its distinct advantages. But it had also its responsibilities. The vast control and power wielded by Gorgas over his bureau's arsenals, shops, armories, and contracting agencies placed a terriffic added strain on him, particularly since he was not a man who craved power.

Regular bureau business continued apace. In January, 1863, Gorgas received from Burton a significant communication touching the labor shortage and another point. One of Burton's prime concerns was the construction of machinery for Macon Armory, and he told Gorgas that though he could use at least seventy skilled machinists at the work, he had only thirty-five such men. The refusal of the Secretary of War to detail artisans from armies facing the enemy (and most Confederate armies were in that category) made it impossible to secure more. He was confident that if machinists could be had, the machinery could be built in Macon, but without them he predicted failure. Burton's solution was to import machinery from abroad. "I know of large machine shops in England," he told Gorgas, "in which I had much of the machinery for the Enfield Armory constructed, and I have no doubt but that contracts could be entered into with the proprietors of these shops for the construction of much of the machinery required for this Armory." Developing this theme further, he added: "I regard it as absolutely necessary to go to England for the large steam engines required for propelling the Armory Machinery as there are no shops now in the Confederacy capable of constructing such as are required except the Tredeger Iron Works at Richmond which are necessarily otherwise employed—the machinery for barrel rolling & welding would also have to be obtained from England as it has never been made in this country." To Burton, the best way to put the plan into practical execution was to send some competent person to England with authority to make contracts for the necessary machinery and building materials. The machine shop at Macon could be kept busy making tilt hammers, power punches, and other machines that could be made locally. As to how the foreign-bought machinery might reach the South, Burton could offer two suggestions: either it could run through the blockade, or it could remain in Europe until the establishment of peace and then be brought in for the permanent works.

It is doubtful whether Burton when he wrote to Gorgas had any other motive than a desire to strengthen the bureau. And Gorgas apparently so interpreted the letter. Then, too, Burton had taken the precaution of talking his ideas over with Colonel Rains, General Huger, and Major Cuyler before he broached the subject to Gorgas. With the approval of such reliable officers to back him up, he could feel fairly confident of a favorable response from a reasonable man.[20] Such a man should be quick to see that there was only one person really qualified to undertake a purchasing mission of the sort proposed: James H. Burton. Irrespective of how it may have looked, this was the truth. Burton had invaluable connections with English industrial firms; he had the advantage of past dealings with many of them and knew just where to look for what he wanted. Whether or not he was a good bargainer only time would tell. Meanwhile, the plan was sound; the principal ordnance men of the Confederacy approved it, and anything was worth trying. Gorgas thought it over. The stumbling block would be money. Seddon would have to agree, and slowly he was cajoled into supporting the scheme.[21]

Ever since the beginning of 1863 Gorgas had been watching, doubtless with eye askance, the growing maldistribution of foodstuffs throughout the Confederacy. As early as February, Mallet had written Gorgas describing the dissatisfaction among his Negro laborers because of the insufficient rations issued them by the Subsistence Department. It had been made the duty of the Chief Commissary of Georgia to supply with food all of the Negroes whom Mallet hired by the month. When first the Subsistence Department took over this duty, the Negroes were issued regular Army rations, which had been severely reduced. This ration proved so inadequate that it increased runaways tremendously and brought Mallet complaints of starvation, which he discovered were well founded. He ordered the rations increased sufficiently to sustain a laboring man. Subsistence Department officials ordered the reduction of Mallet's rations, and he requested Gorgas to secure authority from Commissary General Lucius B. Northrop to maintain it.[22] But in this

[20] Burton to Gorgas, Macon, January 10, 1863, CROB, XX, 343–44.

[21] Rains heartily approved of Burton's trip and felt it would be much more economical to have Burton's machinery built in England. See Rains to Burton, Selma, March 15, 1863, *Burton Papers, Winchester*. This is a long letter on the better workmanship available in England and generally extolling the merits of Burton's scheme. Rains thought that some arrangement might be made "with the assistance of the friends of the Confederacy in Liverpool who might consent to guarantee the payments on a deposit of Government Bonds." Perhaps Rains's financial ideas as here expressed had more to do with subsequent Confederate policy than many other factors, though his views have been overlooked.

[22] Mallet to Gorgas, Macon, February 24, 1863, CROB, XXVIII, 236–37. For Gorgas' comments on Northrop see GCWD, pp. 157, 163, 164, 165, 172.

instance Gorgas was powerless to help. With an undertone of deep concern he replied that the regulations of the Subsistence Department would have to be complied with. He said that the general scarcity of bacon was probably the reason for the Commissary's stringency—though while writing he knew that Northrop was just as much, if not more, concerned about rules and would stick to them even if this hampered the feeding of troops. The railroads, too, were greatly responsible for curtailed rations.

Gorgas was probably willing to concede that Northrop had many vexing deterrents to the efficient execution of his job—he had them, too. He knew perhaps better than most men what superhuman juggling was necessary to secure railroad transportation for army supplies. While the office of the Quartermaster General was doing all it could to maintain a semblance of order in the muddled railroad picture, it was not omniscient. Some supposedly necessary regulations issued from that office did not materially increase the flow of supplies and often hindered other bureaus. One such order, requiring all ordnance stores to be shipped by freight train, proved particularly trying.[23] The Chief of Ordnance had learned how to be tolerant.

He knew that while short rations were causing much discontent, the greatest source of dissatisfaction was the haphazard wage policy of all the supply bureaus. Early manifestations of serious disaffection came from the lower South. Although Gorgas' wage-fixing circulars of March, 1863, had been designed to avoid controversies on this sore subject, they had failed to satisfy the majority of workers and had left the private industries in a state of uncertainty. It was an arbitrary point whether a plant such as the Shelby Iron Company of Alabama was an "ordnance establishment" or not. To all intents and purposes, of course, it was entirely an ordnance installation, but the definition was open to different constructions. And by those who felt keenly the bite of inflation into their fixed wages, an ordnance circular could be regarded as having no authority whatever.

The machinists, smiths, and other workmen at Macon Armory asked Burton in late April for an increase in wages; and Burton, in referring the petition to Gorgas, opined that the wages paid at the armory were the same as those paid at Macon Arsenal and seemed to him to rank

[23] See for instance, Capt. J. T. Trezevant to Gorgas, Charleston Arsenal, March 22, 1863, CRLR, 1863, Doc. TWD 93. In speaking of the difficulties involved in getting government cotton to Wilmington, Trezevant said: "All the cotton . . . has been sent to the R. R. but some maneuvering is also required there or private [freight] will always monopolize the trains."

among the highest allowed in any of the private works in Macon.[24]
This inharmonious note struck in Macon was accompanied by an
equally sour one at Columbiana, Alabama. The Shelby Iron Company
at that place, one of the most important in the whole Confederacy, had
been having its own peculiar problems since the start of the war. But
it also had the perennial personnel problems common to all Confederate industries. There, in May, 1863, twelve company employees
struck[25] for wages equal to those paid in Richmond and for a regular
monthly pay day. The strikers stated their case to the plant superintendent:

Gentlemen of the Shelby Iron Co.
Mr. Giles Edwards, Supt[n]
We the undersigned employees in these works having stop[p]ed work on
account of the low prices paid for our labour and the high prices of provisions and all the nesesaries [*sic*] of life do hereby agree to resume our
several capacities in these conditions. 1st, That you pay us the prices now
paid in the works at Richmond from the time of their advancement. 2nd.
Also that you make a regular pay day (monthly) Hoping this will meet
with your approbation we subscribe ourselves &c.
[Twelve signatures]

Captain B. Sloan, at the Richmond Ordnance Depot, echoed the
feeling of discontent with pay. He told Gorgas that the men in the
depot shops were using every means to get away since they could not
live on the prevailing income. Sloan knew them to be telling the truth
and reported that many had to pay as much as $80 and $90 per month
for food. He asked permission, as a consequence, to raise wages of all
hands, for the present, thirty-five per cent.[26]

From another part of the Confederacy came equally disturbing news.
Lieutenant Colonel J. L. White, commanding the Army's part of the
Selma Ordnance Shops, told Gorgas that wage competition between
the Army and Navy at Selma was serious. He wrote that "under these
circumstances it cannot be expected that the work under my charge can
thrive, or that the workshops of the Arsenal can compete with others
where this condition of affairs does not exist." He said that workmen
naturally sought the highest wages, and while it was true that the services of many might be compelled, their work would not be cheerful
nor good. "It seems but a matter of justice and right that the different

[24] Burton to Gorgas, Macon, May 1, 1863, CROB, XXXI, 24.
[25] Notice of strike cited in Vandiver, *Alabama Review,* I, 115.
[26] Sloan to Gorgas, Richmond, April 7, 1863, CROB, XC, 274.

branches of Government *at the same place* should be upon an equality as to the wages paid to employees." To the hard-pressed Chief of Ordnance this was indeed bad news, especially since similar complaints had come from the commanding officers at Atlanta and Columbus Arsenals. Gorgas sent White's letter to the Secretary of War with the request that it be passed on to Davis. To Seddon, Gorgas remarked that there were but two courses of action open to the services which would solve or ameliorate the wage problem: either the Navy would have to reduce its wage scale or the Ordnance Bureau would have to increase its own an average of about a dollar per day to each workman. The second alternative did not appeal to Gorgas, who felt that an unnecessary and heavy strain would be put on the Treasury. Nor would it aid his efforts to cut down bureau expenditures.[27]

The whole labor problem, particularly the shortage of skilled help, pushed Gorgas into the expedient of trying to import workmen from abroad—at Mallet's suggestion.[28] Huse managed to hire a number of British workers who consented to come to the Confederacy; but only if the inducements substantially outweighed the risks. Huse had to use gold as an infallible persuader. The workers, after all, stood to lose little since their passage was paid by Huse. When they embarked for the South, it is doubtful whether many of them were aware how inflation would affect their wages. Fortune did them proud, for by the time they got to Wilmington, gold had risen to such heights in Confederate currency that their salaries dwarfed those paid to Southerners doing the same work. The natives naturally resented the intruders. Gorgas had foreseen this resentment and tried to prevent it by offering to pay half the wages promised in gold to the workers' families in England if they would accept the rest in Confederate money. But even a British Consul could not persuade them to accept this offer. A greatly disgusted Chief of Ordnance was irritated by the adamant attitude which the workmen assumed and regarded their scrupulous adherence to their bond as branding them among the "most unreasonable" people he had ever seen. He did the only possible thing—paid their passage and shipped

[27] White to Gorgas, Selma, June 20, 1863, and Gorgas' indorsement of the twenty-seventh, CRLR, 1863, Doc. WWD 454.

[28] Mallet to Gorgas, Macon, August 3, 1863, CROB, XXIV, 231–32. It is hard to determine just who did originate the idea of importing foreign workers to the South. Mallet's scheme did not come from him; he heard it from a Mr. Dever, a slate contractor on the Laboratory buildings. Gorgas himself so completely approved of the scheme that it is hard to see how he could have had no hand in formulating the plans.

them home. This venture had cost the South some £2,000 in gold and no little patience.[29]

As the Army of the Potomac began to give indications of its intention to move, Gorgas tightened the reins on bureau operations. It was a matter of increasing difficulty to replace ordnance and ordnance stores wasted by the various armies, to say nothing of replacing the equipment lost in action. If the bureau were to function smoothly, without embarrassing time lags and errors, Gorgas knew that standardization would have to be pushed to the limit. Getting everything reduced to a standard type was all part of the "waiting game." Time was yet working with the Ordnance Bureau—a most important factor. In the over-all picture of Confederate supply activities, the time element played a prominent role. There existed a nebulous, hypothetical time balance which would work for a while in the Confederacy's favor —then against it. To decide just where along the line that point of change lay was an impossible task. And yet some approximation had to be worked out—for all Confederate supply chiefs worked against that imponderable factor. In a supply organization such as the Ordnance Bureau, forced by circumstances to function closely timed and yet loosely-geared, standardization was obviously a prime necessity. Standardization of every item took on a prime importance—nothing was too insignificant to escape. For instance, Mallet, with Gorgas' approval, declared by circular the desirability of having all paper for laboratory uses standardized, and of uniform quality, and distributed a list of bureau-approved types of cartridge and cannon paper.[30]

The race toward inflation, with its resultant increase in the price of everything, and the necessity for bureau expansion to meet the needs of the service, forced the Chief of Ordnance into the role of perennial bookkeeper.[31] He had not only to receive and establish priorities on all the estimates of the bureau's expenditures, but also to decide what the total requests for funds should be. Since nothing about Confederate finances remotely suggested stability, Gorgas had a superhuman task; an estimate of, say $10,000,000 for a quarter, subject to congressional reduction, might have considerably less buying power three months after it was appropriated. Gorgas wrestled with just such a problem in

---

[29] See Gorgas' candid summary of this dismal failure in GOC, pp. 284–85.

[30] Ordnance Circular, Macon, January 21, 1863, AGPF, Mallet. For problems concerning standards of ammunition, see Gorgas to Mallet, Richmond, February 24, 1863, CROB, V, 278.

[31] See, for example, Capt. B. Sloan to Gorgas, Richmond, January 28, February 13, 1863, CROB, XC, 125, 155.

early 1863. His estimate of $15,900,000 needed for the period February 1 to June 30, 1863, based on the best information available to him and approved by Seddon, was allowed by Congress on February 10; but inflation was running rampant,[32] and the real purchasing power of the allotment could not be predicted.

This very fact forced upon the Chief of Ordnance an even stiffer operating economy. He was worried about the rapid spending done by bureau officers and particularly about the money being spent in Macon. Although he desired that city to be the main ordnance center of the South, he wanted this accomplished without wasting the tax-payers' money. Mallet's building program could be a terrible drain on the bureau; he had to watch that business. Then, too, Rains was perturbed about the amount of money that could be thrown away trying to make something out of the foundry at Selma, Alabama, run by Colin McRae, who had lost no time in getting himself appointed iron agent in Alabama.[33]

Rains, whose professional sagacity ranked with the best, a year before had had deep fears about locating a large ordnance establishment at Selma and had reported against it to the bureau. He had not in the least modified his views and felt anything but optimistic about the Selma installations. The Army and Navy jointly purchased the plant from McRae before he left for England early in 1863 on an important financial mission for the Confederate government. He made it a condition to his acceptance of the mission that he be relieved of his works and contract "without pecuniary loss to himself."[34]

Gorgas' attitude toward the Selma plant is the most confusing element in the whole fabric of his ponderings over which plant should be located where. For some time he had looked forward longingly to the day when Macon Armory would be the great national work, and all indications were that he intended a concentration of heavy indus-

---

[32] Seddon Memorandum, no date, ORA, Ser. IV, Vol. II, 294. In this memo Seddon requested $171,707,927 for the Quartermaster Department; $48,656,500 for the Subsistence Department; $3,540,000 for the Medical Department; $3,-000,000 for the Engineer service; $172,638.23 for civil expenditures—a total of $242,977,065.23. In a letter to Davis, January 3, 1863, Seddon said that he did not believe these estimates to be excessive. *Ibid.*, p. 293. See also *Statutes at Large (Confederate)*, 1 Cong., Stat. III, Chap. III.

[33] Gorgas to Mallet, Richmond, February 11, 1863, CROB, V, 249. In this letter Gorgas frankly told Mallet that funds disposable for the rest of the year at the laboratories could not exceed $150,000, "& with this you will be expected to *complete* the work entered upon this season." On McRae and Selma see Vandiver, *Alabama Review*, I, 18–19, 117–18.   [34] GOC, p. 284.

try at that place. But his idea changed, possibly because of the transportation problem and of enemy activity, and he became desirous of having Selma grow into a major ordnance center. This change of view represented involved reasoning. First, declaring the advantages of centralization, he came to understand (and so did all the other ordnance officers) that Confederate transportation was not equal to the task of supporting it and that it would be advisable to switch to decentralization instead. And yet, in the case of McRae's Selma works, he could take the view that they could become the "Pittsburgh of the South."[35] Gorgas might believe this, but apparently a sizeable block of opinion among his officers failed to support him on this point. Rains probably stated the views of the opposition with greatest candor. In a letter to Burton, written from Selma on March 15, he expressed "regret that the Army assisted in the purchase of the Foundry works at this place" and added that he "would like to see the Navy in full possession."[36]

From the outset, operations at Selma were not particularly encouraging. Thinking himself optimistic, Rains told Burton in his letter of March 15 that "several weeks will yet elapse before even the first gun can be cast." But as far in the future as November, 1863, Commander John M. Brooke, the extremely able and energetic officer in charge of the Navy's Office of Ordnance and Hydrography, would be writing the Secretary of the Navy describing efforts still made to get Selma into production.[37] Brooke's letter to Stephen R. Mallory qualified Rains as a seer to a certain degree. Rains had confided to Burton that not only was the physical disposition of Selma Gun Foundry inappropriate for an Army installation, but its location was logistically absurd.

The Works are entirely too far to the Southwest for army supplies in general for three fourths of all the castings would be required east of the Main Georgia line of communication and this is some 300 miles off connected by a river and two separate grades of roads at West Point [Georgia,] requiring reshipment . . . should the Army retain it, farewell to all ideas of a *National Foundry* (I would not apply that name to these works) for

[35] *Ibid.;* and Gorgas to Burton, Richmond, September 29, 1862, *Burton Papers, Winchester.*

[36] Rains to Burton, Selma, *ibid.* Rains favored the Navy's control of the works because they were "well situated for that branch of the service having a Rail Road already graded immediately connecting this place with Pensacola Navy Yard of which these works would form an offshoot." He thought the physical layout of the plant inadequate for an Army foundry.

[37] Rains to Burton, March 15, 1863, *ibid.;* Brooke to Mallory, Richmond, November 25, 1863, ORN, Ser. II, Vol. II, 549.

its cost has been too great to put it aside, and like the old man of Sinbad's it will continue to cling tenaciously around the neck of the Ordnance Department notwithstanding all its unavailing struggles.[38]

After Gorgas, doubtless influenced by Rains's views, had unloaded the Selma plant on the Navy, it fulfilled Rains's prognostication as to its leech-like proclivities; he erred only in assuming that the Army might retain the works.[39]

In the meantime, Gorgas had certain other important moves afoot.

[38] Rains to Burton, March 15, 1863, *Burton Papers, Winchester.*
[39] See Brooke's report of the condition of the foundry on November 25, 1863, Brooke to Mallory, Richmond, November 25, 1863, ORN, Ser. II, Vol. II, 548–49.

XIV

Months of Hard Work

ON FEBRUARY 2, 1863, GORGAS WROTE BURTON THAT HIS SUGGES-
tion to procure machinery abroad would probably be acted on. How
much money would Burton need to place his orders? It seemed scarcely
necessary to tell the Superintendent of Armories that the exchange
problem was "somewhat difficult of solution," or to add that payments
should be delayed as much as possible.[1] The trip itself was assured by
the War Department's espousal of the plan. With an estimate of proposed expenses[2] already drawn up, Burton wrote Gorgas that at least
$287,013 would be required. In Gorgas' initial concern about how the
purchases might be financed, he hit upon a scheme which was obvious,
yet simple and practical—and sounded like Rains's idea. It seemed possible to work out credit arrangements with Fraser, Trenholm and Company of Liverpool, whose financial reputation would permit advance
buying in European markets. The fact that Congress had passed the
Bureau's appropriation with no cut[3] meant nothing in foreign banking
circles. But the Chief of Ordnance realized that the Confederacy possessed a commodity as valuable as specie—cotton. This had been proved
in blockade-running operations, and shipment of cotton directly to
Fraser, Trenholm and Company in payment for Burton's goods might
solve the problem. At length he told Burton, "the question of finance
need probably not detain you. You may therefore prepare all your plans,

[1] Gorgas to Burton, Richmond, February 2, 1863, Burton.
[2] Burton, "List, & Estimated Cost of Machinery for the C. S. Armory, Macon, Ga. proposed to be procured in England . . ." Macon, January 30, 1863,
ibid.
[3] See Gorgas to Burton, Richmond, February 12, 1863, *ibid.; Statutes at
Large (Confederate),* 1 Cong., Stat. III, Chap. III. The bill, a general appropriation law "for the support of the Government," passed February 10, gave
Gorgas his required $15,900,000.

to submit here for approval & action coming on here for that purpose."[4] The idea of shipping out cotton as a basis of credit strongly appealed to Burton "as affording the best and cheapest means of providing the necessary funds abroad."[5]

He arrived in the capital on April 11 and went at once to the Ordnance Office, where Gorgas received him about one in the afternoon. A long talk ensued which Gorgas wanted to continue in the evening. Burton returned at half past six, bringing his plans and drawings. Gorgas, who already knew of Burton's doings, approved of all these without any modification whatever and offered no objection to the estimated cost of $287,013 at current prices. The next day, Sunday the twelfth, Gorgas formally presented Burton's plans to Seddon, who approved them *in toto*. Burton accepted an invitation to take tea and spend the evening with the Gorgas family, and it was probably then that Gorgas gave him his letter of instructions concerning the trip.

In this letter Gorgas gave a concise description of what he expected Burton to do. Contracts for Burton's machinery would be made, and the funds for these purchases would be administered by Major Huse, who was advised of Burton's voyage. The manner in which contracts were to be made was left to the discretion of Huse and Commissioner James M. Mason, and Burton was obliged to defer to their dictates. Gorgas thought "that it will be advisable to operate through a resident of the Country and have the shipments made in good faith to Bermuda as his property, there to change ownership." He added some judicious advice when he said, "keep steadily in view that the machinery is to be of good workmanship and to be delivered at the earliest possible moment." The Chief of Ordnance did not lose sight of the need for haste in directing Burton's movements. "It will be worthy of your consideration whether the machinery may not be furnished and forwarded in sets so that the Armory may be set in operation without waiting for the completion of the entire lot." He intrusted to Burton's "knowledge of the wants of the service," anything concerning the purchase of material for the Macon laboratories, and promised to instruct Huse to pay for as much of this as was possible.

With charming offhandedness Gorgas said that "it is presumed that your presence in London will not be needed longer than is necessary to consumate the Contracts and purchases and to see the former under satisfactory progress." Then, in an equally candid manner:

[4] Gorgas to Burton, Richmond, February 12, 1863, Burton.
[5] Burton to Gorgas, Macon, March 10, 1863, *ibid*.

The forwarding and payments will be made by Major Huse. As he is general financial agent of the War Dept., all your contracts must necessarily be subordinate to his views of our resources abroad; these it is hoped will be sufficient for the purpose contemplated. The War Department has great confidence in the judgment and devotedness of Major Huse and expects you to act in full consultation with him.

Though Gorgas was keeping a loose but tangible rein on the impetuous Colonel Burton, he finished the letter of instructions on a note of strong personal regard: "Confiding in your knowledge of the resources of England and France in reference to the purposes intended, the Dept. relies on your ability and energy to bring your mission to an early and satisfactory close."[6]

On the thirteenth Gorgas affixed his signature to the Macon plans, removing all possibility of disapproval. He saw Burton the next day and took up again the question of the trip, and an interview between the two men during the evening settled the final details.[7]

It was during these conversations that Gorgas learned what personal compensation Burton wanted. Burton thought that he should receive either mileage or actual traveling expenses and $150 commutation for fuel and quarters per month. He did not want to lose "from an already insufficient salary on account of this mission."[8] Gorgas agreed.

Burton had hoped to leave for England about May 9 but was delayed and did not manage to sail from Wilmington until May 13, 1863. He presented himself at the Confederate Commission in London on June 10 and reported to Mason.[9] His meeting with Huse, postponed

[6] Gorgas to Burton, Richmond, April 12, 1863, ibid. There is some doubt about the date of this letter, but it follows so closely ideas propounded in a letter from Burton to Gorgas on April 12, 1863, ibid., that that date is followed. For general background on Burton's mission and preparation therefor, see Capt. Edward B. Smith to Burton, Richmond, February 24, 1863; Gorgas to Burton, Richmond, April 11, 1863; Seddon to Burton, Richmond, April 15, 1863; Rains to Burton, Augusta, April 19, 1863, ibid.

[7] For the details of Burton's Richmond visit, see Burton, Diary, April 11–14, 1863.

[8] Burton to Gorgas, Macon [Richmond], April 13, 1863, Burton. Gorgas was successful in requesting higher pay for Burton. In a letter dated April 15, Seddon fixed Burton's commutation for fuel and quarters at $150 per month, paid in London. As Seddon explained: "Your absence it is presumed will not exceed 3 or 4 months. This high rate of commutation is allowed to you in consideration of the extraordinary expenses you will be subjected to in connexion with the duties to which you are assigned." Ibid.

[9] Some uncertainty exists about the date of Burton's departure from the Confederacy. It is known that he expected to leave Wilmington about May 9, but that as late as the 13th he had not got away. Burton to Gorgas (telegram),

because of the latter's absence in Paris, took place there on June 11, when he presented a copy of his letter of instructions from Gorgas. No funds were on hand to pay for Burton's machinery, but Huse suggested he return to England, proceed to Leeds, and get estimates from the firm of Greenwood and Batley on how much his orders would cost. Meanwhile, Huse promised to press his efforts to secure funds.

The Confederacy's new financial agent abroad, Colin McRae, showed every indication of co-operating with Huse but found that debts amounting to £592,000 had already been contracted. Punctual payment alone would maintain the South's foreign credit, and Huse seemed to think outstanding bills could be paid from proceeds of the Erlanger Loan. In fact, his faith in this scheme went so far that he suggested that McRae set aside a given amount for the immediate use of the War Department. Since Fraser, Trenholm and Company had undertaken to act as credit bankers for the Confederate States, Huse had advised Gorgas to turn the part of the loan earmarked for the War Department over to that company. As the loan stood in June of 1863, no one could appropriate any of it for any purpose whatever, and Huse had been forced to desperate measures. On June 12 he wrote Gorgas that the loan was not the success which the Chief of Ordnance had anticipated, and added that he had had to hypothecate cotton expected to be shipped from the South on Gorgas' order, by giving cotton warrants as security for the payment of the account due to Saul Isaac, Campbell and Company, and as a stopgap means of maintaining purchasing power. This arrangement had all but tied Huse's hands, anxious though he was to help Burton.[10]

In the meantime, Burton returned to England, discovered that Greenwood and Batley were in a position to undertake a large order of the sort he wished to place and, working closely with them, so perfected details of his business that he was able to leave for London on July 3, armed with specifications, estimates, and contracts. Upon meeting Huse there, he discovered that financial arrangements were not yet complete, but Huse hoped to have them worked out in a week at most. Embarrassed, Burton determined to carry on nevertheless. Gorgas had

Macon, May 5, 1863, CROB, XXXI, 31; Cuyler to Burton, Macon, May 18, 1863, *Burton Papers, Winchester.* For his arrival in London on June 10, see ORN, Ser. II, Vol. III, 805. Burton reached Liverpool on June 8. See Burton to Gorgas, Leeds, July 11, 1863, Burton. Cuyler was left in charge of the Macon Armory in Burton's absence.

[10] Huse to Gorgas, Paris, ORA, Ser. IV, Vol. II, 645–47.

not been wrong in thinking that Burton's intimate acquaintance with English munitions firms would prove invaluable. Because they knew him, Greenwood and Batley were willing to go on preparing drawings according to Burton's directions, and the red brick Albion Foundry had even completed some of the simpler machines.

After much agitation Huse finally fell back on Fraser, Trenholm and Company for help and on July 28 concluded an agreement between that firm and Greenwood and Batley for Burton's needs. The agreement stipulated that Greenwood and Batley were to furnish certain items for the manufacture of a rifle-musket, for which they would receive £54,400, or $272,000, from Fraser, Trenholm and Company. The speed exhibited by the Liverpool concern in concluding the negotiations pleased Burton greatly, and he urged that cotton be sent to repay them for their timely attention.[11]

Certain other items which Burton needed for Mallet's laboratories, Rains's powder works, and his own armory, Huse could not immediately pay for, and recommended that Burton leave the specifications with him for purchase later. Unsatisfactory as this solution was, it was the best available. Burton sent Huse estimates of the gun-carriage machinery and told him he hoped that arrangements could be made to buy this along with the laboratory machinery.[12] Unable to wait until Huse could fill his exchequer, Burton departed, sailing from Liverpool for the Confederacy on September 5, 1863.[13] That financial troubles should hold up Burton's building supplies saddened Huse, the more so because "all the really productive efforts to get money to Europe appear to have been made by the Ord: Bureau."[14]

But Burton's mission had not helped alleviate the critical shortage of materials in the Confederacy; it seemed that remedies could not be

[11] Vandiver, "A Sketch of Efforts Abroad to Equip the Confederate Armory at Macon," *Georgia Historical Quarterly*, XXVIII (1944), 36–37. Fraser, Trenholm and Company had not received a single bale of cotton on Burton's account as late as August, 1864. *Ibid.*, p. 37; Burton to Huse, July 20, 1863, Burton.

[12] Huse to Burton, August 19, 1863; Burton to Huse, September 3, 4, 1863, all in Burton. Several long lists of the machinery made by Greenwood and Batley for the laboratories and Burton are in the writer's possession.

[13] Burton to Huse, September 9, 1863; Greenwood and Batley to Burton, January 8, 1864, Burton. For some of the background of Huse's efforts to finance his operations, see Burton to Greenwood and Batley, Leeds, June 20, 1863; Burton to Huse, Leeds, July 14; Burton [to Huse], Paris, July 17, 18; Huse to Burton, Paris [undated, but Burton noted the date as July 18, 1863], *ibid.*

[14] Huse to Burton, date not indicated, but the envelope carries a postmark of August 19, 1863, *ibid.*

found for the deficiency of lead. Nothing could have brought this fact home to the Chief of Ordnance more forcefully than Mallet's frightened plea for lead in March. The need was so urgent that he actually doubted the ability of the arsenals in the Deep South to meet any sudden demand for ammunition. Threatening moves of the enemy along the South Carolina and Georgia coastlines prompted him to tell Gorgas, who already was well aware of the fact, that if the Federals did launch an attack in these sectors, it would find the more southern arsenals in a very poor condition to meet the onslaught. As an added alarm he reminded the Chief of Ordnance that even while he was writing, a period of relative inactivity, requisitions for small arms ammution were constantly coming in, and left to his imagination what the flood of requisitions occasioned by a sudden Yankee advance would do to the Ordnance Bureau's practice of robbing Peter to pay Paul.

But Mallet was not an alarmist without a remedy. He had two suggestions to make concerning the expansion of lead resources. First, he advocated requiring blockade-runners to bring a fixed amount of lead into the Confederacy on every incoming run—to be paid for at a set price. Second, he advocated the manufacture of sporting percussion caps to exchange for lead. Sporting caps were even more in demand by the people than powder and shot, as an earlier experiment by Gorgas had proved. This barter might not yield much, but even a little seemed very important. With an overtone of quiet desperation, he wrote: "The question of the lead supply is nearly if not altogether as vital as that of niter, and such a demand upon the owners of vessels 'running the blockade' would seem no illegitimate exercise of authority at such a crisis as this."[15] Gorgas, who may well have resented the imputation that he slept while the southern arsenals gradually expired, did not allow Mallet to labor long in the illusion that nothing was being done. He replied that several weeks before, he had anticipated Mallet's suggestion to stockpile lead at Nassau and then systematically to run it to Charleston. Probably with the specter of yellow fever in mind, however, he had decided to concentrate the supply at Bermuda, and had ordered 500 tons of lead there from London. John Fraser and Company of Charleston had undertaken to bring some of this in at their own risk. And, said Gorgas, the Nitre Bureau had ordered sporting caps to various points to be exchanged for lead.[16]

[15] Mallet to Gorgas, Macon, March 10, 1863, CROB, XXVIII, 265–66.
[16] Edward B. Smith to Mallet, Richmond, March 16, 1863, CROB, V, 330.

Gorgas and Mallet were joined in their worries over lead by the man who knew better than anyone else the emergency of the situation: Major St. John, of the Nitre and Mining Bureau. Agreeing in principle with Mallet's ideas about the necessity of more import control, St. John had practical knowledge of what was needed to improve the transportation of lead. The main objection posed by most blockade-running captains was its absolute dead weight—and that was considerable. This factor caused weak-kneed officers to jettison lead pigs as soon as they were pursued, a practice which had cut into the over-all possible supply and proportionately reduced the gross import figure. This condition, of course, threw added stress on the development of domestic mineral resources and fitted into the "waiting game" philosophy. But the period of waiting seemed about over; to meet the Federal juggernaut (whose possible size staggered some of Richmond's citizens)[17] every domestic fiber would have to be stretched, particularly those propping up the lead supply. Many hindrances worked against St. John's efforts to nurse along his faltering supplies of this sorely needed commodity; the weather, for instance, fought Gorgas, St. John, Myers, and Northrop with paralyzing effect, and succeeded in practically eliminating the trickle of lead coming from Wytheville and other mines. The month of March boasted as bad weather as any winter month, with snow still falling in Richmond on the 19th.[18] Snow was a prime retarder of transportation, and railroads, in turn, were an even more important reason why the lead supply moved so slowly. Yet the supreme cause of the deficiency was coldly summarized by St. John. "You are aware," he wrote Mallet on March 10, "that the serious controlling want in these operations is competent mining labor—foremen and workmen. Details are now declined altogether—and I have to complain of a recent effort to remove good miners, in the mistaken zeal of a Genl. commanding an important district." St. John echoed the necessity of stimulating the home supply of lead.[19]

Shortages of critical items, feeble and deteriorating railroads, Federal muscle-flexing, and Confederate efforts toward troop concentrations for the coming campaigns—all of these dictated a basic change in Gorgas' logistics. He was not slow to see nor slow to make the

[17] Jones, *Rebel War Clerk's Diary,* I, 268. See Bill, *Beleaguered City,* p. 163, for optimism felt by some.   [18] Bill, *Beleaguered City,* p. 164.
[19] St. John to Mallet, Richmond, CROB, V, 331. The shortage of lead was probably an underlying factor in preventing the early fabrication of ammunition at the Central Laboratory, which still was not producing cartridges in March, 1863. See Mallet to McMain, Macon, March 25, AGPF, Mallet.

change. From his field officers he solicited information on what portion of shot and shell should be packed in Napoleon gun caissons—he wanted the benefit of field experience in making any necessary alterations.[20] And on the same day, March 31, that he told Mallet of his desire to alter artillery ammunition packages, Gorgas ordered into effect a new system of supply distribution. A general circular, over his signature, approved by Seddon, recognized conditions and directed that "requisitions for ordnance stores will be made on the arsenals and depots nearest to the troops requiring them." Strict adherence to the chain of command was directed, with orders that requisitions must be forwarded through the chief ordnance officers of armies and departments, excepting in cases of urgency, which had to be certified by commanding generals.[21] This circular was the general authority under which more specific and detailed instructions were issued. On the same day particularized orders went to army and department ordnance officers, giving the arsenals upon which they could make requisitions. Troops in Alabama were to be supplied by Selma and Montgomery Arsenals; troops in Mississippi and West Tennessee, North Georgia, and North Alabama, by Atlanta; troops west of the Mississippi, as far as possible by Jackson.[22]

Railroad transportation was, of course, a prime economic reason for Gorgas' decision to decentralize distribution. He confessed as much by the use of the words "arsenals and depots nearest to the troops" when directing requisition points in his circular. The grand strategy of logistics had to give way before bare necessity in the face of enfeebled rail lines and demoralized railroad policies. River and canal transportation lines were of importance to the Ordnance Bureau, particularly in Virginia, but rails were the bureau's main arteries—and the arteries were hardening.

Gorgas made a variety of other changes. He decentralized at the operational level and centralized command functions. Apparently feeling that his over-all grip on affairs might slip, he put on the brakes. No purchases or contracts amounting to more than $10,000 could be made after April 7, 1863, without previous clearance through the Ord-

[20] Gorgas to Mallet, Richmond, March 31, 1863, CROB, V, 370. Gorgas told Mallet that "rifle guns are now supplied here, with about 15 shell, 33 case and 12 canisters. I have directed the canisters to be reduced to 6 in 60—making about 18 shell, 36 case and 6 canisters."

[21] Ordnance Circular, Richmond, March 31, 1863, *General Orders, Confederate States Army,* Series of 1863, p. 237.

[22] Ordnance Circular, Richmond, March 31, 1863, *Mississippi State Department of Archives and History Manuscripts Collection,* Ser. L, Vol. CXI.

nance Office.[23] Chief officers of corps and departments were directed to submit, on the last day of each month, a report of small arms, artillery, and rounds of ammunition.[24]

Events closer to home forcefully wrenched the attention of Gorgas to matters more sanguinary. Friday, March 13, was a day to confirm the superstitious in their convictions and to convert many who had been unbelievers before. The Ordnance Laboratory on Brown's Island —part of Richmond Laboratory—exploded that day, killing four workers outright, though the final toll reached sixty-nine killed and wounded, with Gorgas estimating that the dead alone would ultimately reach fifty. He recorded that

the accident was caused by the ignition of a friction primer in the hands of a grown girl by the name of Mary Ryan. She lived three or four days and gave a clear account of the circumstances. The primer stuck in the varnishing board and she struck the board three times very hard on the table to drive out the primer. She says she was immediately blown up to the ceiling and on coming down was again blown up. Cartridges were being broken up temporarily in the same room, where many operators were sent temporarily on account of repairs in the shop they usually worked in. The deaths are due chiefly to the burning of their clothes.

Amelia was "untiring in aiding, visiting and relieving these poor sufferers and has fatigued herself very much. She has done an infinite deal of good to these poor people."[25]

Richmond took news of the explosion in stunned shock. Diarist J. B. Jones, in the War Office, devoted his entry for March 13 entirely to it, and spoke the compassion felt by many when he said: "To-day a great calamity occurred in this city. In a large room of one of the government laboratories an explosion took place, killing instantly five or six persons, and wounding, it is feared fatally, some thirty others. Most of them were little indigent girls!"[26]

Sick with the thought that perhaps this fearful accident might have been prevented,[27] Gorgas on the twenty-first ordered an official investi-

[23] Ordnance Circular, Richmond, April 7, 1863, General Orders, Confederate States Army, Series of 1863, p. 238. Buildings and building materials were excluded from this regulation. In May, 1863, Gorgas directed that no improvement requiring an outlay of more than $1,000 should be undertaken without his prior approval. Ordnance Circular, Richmond, May 14, 1863, ibid.

[24] Ordnance Circular, Richmond, March 24, 1863, ibid., p. 237.

[25] GCWD, March 21, 1863, pp. 25, 26. See also the Daily Richmond Examiner, March 14, 1863.   [26] Rebel War Clerk's Diary, I, 273.

[27] GCWD, March 21, 1863, p. 25. Gorgas remarked: "It is terrible to think of—that so much suffering should arise from causes possibly within our control."

gation which, obviously thorough, finally placed the blame on "the careless handling of Fri[ction] primers by the late Mary Ryan."[28] Mallet's safety measures now assumed even greater importance.

President Davis declared March 27 as a day of fasting and prayer—Jones wryly remarked that it was "fasting in the midst of famine!"[29]—and Gorgas went to church and then to work.[30] Too much was piling up to permit time off. But only a few days would pass before the grave import of the food shortage would forcibly strike the public. On the morning of April 2 a group of women and a few exempts assembled in Capitol Square and, in an orderly fashion, proceeded at about nine o'clock down Ninth Street, past the War Department, and spread into Main and Cary streets. Demanding bread, they went along, growing more violent, smashing windows, pillaging stores, and loading their plunder on commandeered carts and drays. In actuality they took little food but concentrated mostly on shoes, clothing, and jewelry. At length the Governor had the Mayor read them the riot act and threatened to fire on them if they did not disperse in five minutes. The timely arrival of the President and his calm words, spoken from an improvised dray-platform, scattered the crowd. Threatening gatherings the following few days were summarily dispersed by the City Battalion and the regulars.[31] But the augury was sad—and frightening. Gorgas, incensed by the riot, recorded that the ostensible cause for the move was bread, "but their motive really was license. Few of them have really felt want."[32] He recognized that there was definite scarcity but denied actual starvation.

From dinner table conversations Gorgas began to get a more depressing picture. General Francis A. Shoup, who had been fighting under Hindman in Arkansas, talked with Gorgas on the evening of April 1 about affairs in the West. It was, to Gorgas, a lamentable story of mismanagement and failure and did little to cheer the other dinner guests—Ethelbert Barksdale, congressman from Mississippi, Major St.

[28] Report of Board of Survey to Maj. W. V. Taylor, Richmond, March 25, 1863, CROB, attached to Vol. XCIX. The Board's report leaves the distinct impression that some officer had not maintained the strictest safety measures. Mary Ryan, perhaps a conveniently defunct scapegoat, was permitted to fill friction primers in a building with a coal stove in operation, and where cartridges were also being broken up.

[29] *Rebel War Clerk's Diary*, I, 280.   [30] GCWD, March 28, 1863, p. 27.

[31] The account of this "bread riot" in Jones, *Rebel War Clerk's Diary*, I, 284–86, is excellent and the reconstruction in Bill, *Beleaguered City*, pp. 165–66, is most helpful. The city newspapers warily played down this affair.

[32] GCWD, April 3, 1863, pp. 28–29.

John, and Lieutenant John Ellicott of the Nitre Bureau. Western affairs
were a serious concern to the Chief of Ordnance. He had several con-
ferences with the President on the question of shipping arms west, and
also about establishing some furnaces and a foundry on the Trinity
River in Texas.[33] The tabulation of materiel losses sustained by the
Confederate forces under Hindman at Prairie Grove, Arkansas, on
December 7, 1862, and at Arkansas Post on January 11, 1863, came
to Gorgas in May—the news was appalling. Hindman, who should
never have fought Prairie Grove in the first place, had suffered a staggering defeat and been forced to retreat to Little Rock with scanty
transport and widespread desertion. Sherman's capture of Fort Hindman at Arkansas Post (an effort to save face after the debacle of
Chickasaw Bluffs) had been equally destructive. Lumped together,
the losses of ordnance items in these two actions amounted to 5,000
muskets, Enfield rifles, and shotguns; 300,000 cartridges, 4,000 canteens, 4,000 haversacks, 4,000 sets of accouterments, along with considerable artillery and artillery ammunition.[34] Gorgas had to do something to replace the losses.

For personal as well as official reasons, the coming spring and summer campaigns were of vast importance to the Chief of Ordnance. As
both sides "squared away" for the onslaught, the preliminary operations went badly for the Confederacy. General Harvey Hill retreated
from his lines around Washington, North Carolina; Longstreet was
unable to take Suffolk and lost some artillery; Federal gunboats were
passing the Vicksburg batteries and augmenting Farragut's squadron;
General Richard Taylor, after a fine campaign with ludicrously inferior numbers, was retiring from Opelousas, Louisiana. But Gorgas
hoped that affairs in the Southwest would improve under the experienced generalship of Kirby Smith, sent to command the far western
theater. Lee's army, ensconced along the Rappahannock, was assuming a pugnacious air, and in early May seemed on the point of fighting
Hooker, especially with Longstreet's corps (sans Hood's and Pickett's
divisions) ordered to join the main body. Gorgas, whose figures were
based on the usually accurate returns of arms, estimated that Lee had
about 60,000 men, and with Longstreet's two absent divisions, could
count 80,000 effective troops. Bragg, with reinforcements from Mobile,
was thought to have nearly 70,000 men.[35]

[33] GCWD, April 2, March 23, and April 3, 1863, pp. 28, 26, 29.
[34] Maj. Thomas G. Rhett to Gorgas, Little Rock, April 30, 1863, ORA, Ser.
I, Vol. LIII, 866–67.   [35] GCWD, April 26, 30, 1863, pp. 33–35.

While the field forces of the Confederacy were making strategic shifts and stirrings in preparation for what was to come, Gorgas made some tactical and logistical moves of his own, all designed to make ready. From Dalton Depot he transferred W. H. McMain to Mallet's Central Laboratory as an assistant to the chemist, whose experiments with substitutes and whose standardization rules were now the mainstays of the bureau.[36] Mallet certainly needed an assistant, for his duties were crowding in on him. Obviously stimulated by the recent fighting, Gorgas urged him on May 2 to inspect personally friction-primer manufacturing at Charleston, Augusta, Atlanta, and Selma laboratories. Mallet later reported that small-arms ammunition production at Richmond, Augusta, Lynchburg, Fayetteville, Charleston, and Selma showed wide deviations from the norm.[37] He had few words of encouragement.

As a means of further preparation, Gorgas, on April 10, dispatched trusted agents through the Federal lines for the purpose of procuring ordnance and other items in the North.[38] But the human element could not, of course, be taken out of the picture. For instance, Gorgas could not escape the personality of Governor Brown of Georgia, even in a time of dire need. Mallet, who was recognized by Brown as the only ordnance alcohol agent in his state, was plagued with requests for licenses by agents of the Navy and Ordnance Bureau. He wanted to help the Navy and requested authority from Gorgas to do so, adding that "the distinction between the Ordnance Departments of the Army and Navy does not seem to be understood at Milledgeville."[39]

On May 4, 1863, Richmond rang with alarms of a Federal cavalry raid directed against the city, and even President Davis's mid-April statement that the armies of the Confederacy were more numerous and better equipped than ever[40] offered little comfort. The Federal column,

[36] McMain to Gorgas, Macon, April 9, 1863, CROB, XXV, 202. For evidence of Mallet's vigilance in matters of standardization, see his letter to Gorgas, May 18, 1863, ibid., XXIV, 84–85, concerning understrength powder; and for evidence of his abiding interest in experimentation, see his letter of May 30, ibid., p. 107, about experiments he wished to conduct with Whitworth Sharpshooter rifles, recently arrived at Charleston.

[37] Gorgas to Mallet, Richmond, CROB, V, 443; Mallet to Gorgas, May 7, 1863, ibid., XXIV, 49–50; Mallet to Gorgas, Macon, May 18, ibid., p. 85.

[38] W. S. Downer to Gorgas, Richmond, April 10, 1863, CROB, XC, 284. Downer requested a general pass for Vincent Camalier and his agent, J. W. Sands. Downer asserted that Camalier had been working with the bureau for some time and had brought many valuable supplies through the Union lines.

[39] Mallet to Gorgas, Macon, April 10, 1863, ibid., XXVIII, 310–11. Gorgas approved the request. Gorgas to Mallet, Richmond, April 14, ibid., V, 414.

[40] Bill, Beleaguered City, p. 169.

after cutting the Central Railroad at Louisa Court House, proceeded down toward Richmond, striking the Fredericksburg road at Ashland, capturing a train of sick and wounded, burning cars and depot buildings, and tearing up some of the track. The force continued down the Brooke Turnpike almost to within sight of the city (Gorgas estimated it was about four miles away).

Richmond was in no condition to withstand an attack. Most of the regular troops had been sent forward to Lee, who was even then rumored to be fighting a great battle. When the tocsin sounded on the morning of the fourth, citizens turned out with all sorts of arms and mustered on the public square. Senators and cabinet members fell into the ranks with butchers and cobblers and were marshaled to the defensive batteries under direction of General George Randolph. Government workers from the arsenal as well as old men and boys had been pressed into service by General Arnold Elzey, commanding Richmond, who had declared, when he heard of the raid, that "we were ruined." But the enemy came no farther; the dispatch of Wise's brigade (all the regular troops to be found in the city) in pursuit of them calmed the people rapidly; and excitement subsided by ten o'clock. Alarm gave way to jubilation—over glorious news from Chancellorsville. A dispatch came in the morning from General Lee, who recorded a great victory over General Joe Hooker. The severe wounding of Stonewall Jackson, who had lost his left arm in action, marred the public joy; but he was reported to be doing well.[41]

Even in the midst of celebration over Hooker's repulse, Gorgas could make a sound and all too prophetic observation: "We have not the genius to achieve decisive victories, it appears; and it is probably a problem not often solved, except with the concurrence of fortunate incidents, that a large army is defeated and routed by a very inferior one."[42]

---

[41] For several accounts of the raid on Richmond, see GCWD, May 3, 4, 5, 1863, pp. 35–36; Bill, *Beleaguered City*, p. 172; Jones, *Rebel War Clerk's Diary*, I, 306–8.   [42] GCWD, May 6, 1863, p. 37.

XV

A Sense of Responsibility

STILL DISSATISFIED OVER HOOKER'S INCONCLUSIVE DEFEAT, COLONEL
Gorgas kept speculating on the deplorable fact that "all our sacrifices
of life and all our successes lead to no decisive result." He asked himself
why. "Is this owing to our inferior numbers, or to want of solidarity in
the commands, or, finally, to want of genius in our commanders?"[1]
It was a legitimate question, and the streams of wounded coming to
Richmond from Chancellorsville echoed it forcefully. Amelia, who
could never resist her desire to aid the sick, had gone to a hospital on
the evening of May 8 to do what she could for the sufferers, and Gorgas
wished she could spare more time from her household duties to help
the wounded, "as she is a very apt nurse."[2]

For a few days after the battle—Gorgas tells us they were cool, delightful days—Richmond took time out to care for the maimed and
recuperate from the strain of raids and rumors. Gorgas allowed himself to consider the general trend of the war and became angered anew
at the Yankees. He noted in his diary on May 10:

It is said that Lincoln has ordered another draft of 500,000 men. No
doubt that the war will go on until at least the close of his administration.
How many more lives must be sacrificed to the vindictiveness of a few
unprincipled men! for there is no doubt that with the division of sentiment existing at the North the administration could shape its policy
either for peace or for war.[3]

Conditions on the various battlefronts gave rise to uneasiness, for
there was little news—Gorgas notes particularly the absence of news
from Vicksburg. But by evening of Sunday, May 10, word of one

[1] GCWD, May 8, 1863, p. 37.   [2] GCWD, May 9, 1863, pp. 37–38.
[3] GCWD, p. 38.

of the Confederacy's greatest losses crept around the capital. At about three o'clock that afternoon Stonewall Jackson, who had been wounded at Chancellorsville, died. That his wounded arm had been amputated was a matter of common knowledge, but there was no expectation of any complication serious enough to cause his death. The General, however, had aggravated his condition "by causing himself to be bathed about the chest with cold water."

On the eleventh all the government and business offices closed and flags flew at half mast. Crowds lined Richmond's streets, silently weeping, awaiting the arrival of Jackson's body, which reached the city at five o'clock that afternoon. On the twelfth it was carried in solemn procession from the Governor's house to the Capitol, where, after the funeral ceremonies, it lay in state during the day. In the words of one who was present, the

funeral was very solemn and imposing, because the mourning was sincere and heartfelt. There was no vain ostentation. The pall bearers were generals. The President followed near the hearse in a carriage, looking thin and frail in health. The heads of departments, two and two, followed on foot—Benjamin and Seddon first—at the head of the column of young clerks (who ought to be in the field), the State authorities, municipal authorities, and thousands of soldiers and citizens. The war-horse was led by the general's servant, and flags and black feathers abounded.[4]

Following the funeral service, and the transfer of Jackson's body to the Capitol, in that greatest and one of the last of Richmond's dismal pageants honoring her beloved dead, twenty thousand stricken people filed past the guard of honor to view the face of their fallen champion.[5] Among these thousands were Amelia, Josiah, and Willie. Gorgas particularly wanted Willie to see Jackson's face, despite the fact that both he and his son were nearly crushed by the crowd. Amelia "had to be satisfied with a peep at the door where the coffin lay."[6] Gorgas' reaction to the death of Jackson was profound. Not only had Jackson been a fine and good man, but his loss "would more than counterbalance a victory ten times as decisive" as Chancellorsville.[7]

While the Gorgases and the Confederacy were mourning their dead leader, two Federal generals were making important moves in Mississippi. Grant, whose forces had successfully passed the Vicksburg bat-

---

[4] Jones, *Rebel War Clerk's Diary,* I, 321.
[5] Bill, *Beleaguered City,* pp. 173–74. This is a most readable, touching account of Jackson's funeral, embracing most available contemporary reports.
[6] GCWD, May 13, 1863, p. 38.   [7] GCWD, May 14, 1863, p. 39.

teries, was marching with Sherman on the city of Jackson, where General Joseph E. Johnston was too weak to withstand an attack. Without undue delay, he evacuated the city, and Grant occupied it on May 14, 1863. These operations, of course, deeply concerned the Chief of Ordnance, since he had works of some importance in Mississippi's capital city.

In addition to concern about Jackson Arsenal, Gorgas had to give careful attention to the ordnance wants of General John C. Pemberton, who was trying to prevent a siege of Vicksburg. If a siege did develop, however, reserve ammunition and other supplies were of vital importance. Efforts to rush percussion caps to the West succeeded in placing 2,507,100 at Selma by June 6, plus an unspecified number designated particularly for Johnston's army.[8] Even so, Gorgas was still disturbed about Vicksburg. He understood the city had provisions sufficient for at least two months and was comforted at the news, but feared there were not enough munitions for a long fight. With characteristic candor, he admitted that "it has not been possible to give . . . [Vicksburg's defenders] over perhaps 150 rounds per man. However, they have the means of making cartridges for themselves."[9]

All of Pemberton's efforts notwithstanding, Grant invested Vicksburg. True, it had not been easy; Pemberton had fought him at Champion Hill, and again while retreating across the Big Black River, but Grant kept pushing on. Federal artillery opened the siege on May 18, 1863, and thereupon permanently changed the pattern of Confederate strategy and logistics.

In the meantime, Gorgas had not been entirely preoccupied with western affairs. The question of his bureau's finances was absorbing, and a modicum of social life helped to take his mind off his troubles. Gorgas' estimate of the funds needed by his bureau from February 1 to June 30, 1863, had been $15,900,000, which Congress, it will be recalled, appropriated.[10] Increasing operating costs and probably the strain of severe losses of artillery in Mississippi made it impossible to continue operations without additional funds, and consequently Gorgas sought and received an additional appropriation in May, which gave him $5,000,000 for the period to end on June 30, and $17,500,000 for the period July 1 to December 31.[11]

[8] Bayne to Capt. L. R. Evans, Richmond, June 15, 1863, *Mississippi MSS.*, Ser. L, Vol. CXI. Bayne said that "orders have been issued to bundle cartridges with caps in *all* cases, viz.: 15 caps with every 10 cartridges. This being done but few extra caps will be required for troops in the field."
[9] GCWD, May 23, 1863, p. 40.   [10] ORA, Ser. IV, Vol. II, 294.
[11] *Statutes at Large (Confederate),* 1 Cong., Stat. III, Chap. LXVI.

But nothing could hide from Gorgas' notice the intense preparations for military operations going on in northern Virginia. Whatever these, coupled with the siege of Vicksburg, might lead to, they would require diligent attention. Accordingly, Gorgas issued a series of circulars and bureau orders designed to anticipate requirements for the summer campaign. One of the most important items to consider in this connection was a possible shortage of cartridges, for the Confederacy's lead supply was still meagre.[12] Moving swiftly to conserve cartridges, Gorgas issued to all installations under his control an important circular suspending the practice of issuing to infantrymen on the eve of battle twenty rounds of ammunition above the capacity of their cartridge boxes. He directed that "issues of cartridges, except to cover expenditure in battle, will be limited to three cartridges per man, per month, for the whole effective strength of any army or of the forces serving in any department." Gorgas instructed distributing arsenals to regulate issues according to his new policy.[13] Such other frugal measures as directing the repacking of ammunition chests for artillery[14] only pointed the way toward more stringencies which would develop as the war progressed.

Not only Confederate ammunition supplies, but the question of what to do with stores captured in action, received Gorgas' official attention. Since many Federal bullets varied considerably in caliber from the Confederate brands, severe embarrassment might arise should Johnny Rebs elect to use the bullets they had taken from a fallen foe. Obviously with this danger in mind, Gorgas directed that all captured ammunition should be kept separate and not mixed with that of Confederate manufacture.[15]

Over-all command instructions attended to as well as could be anticipated, Gorgas turned his attention to the specific needs of different areas and forces. To the wants of Braxton Bragg, Gorgas gave some priority. His careful supplying of the artillery needs of the Army of Tennessee drew a warm letter of appreciation from its leader. Of some telescopic rifles he had ordered Bragg wrote: "When received,

[12] For indications of the dire shortage of lead, see Mallet to Gorgas, Charleston, July 5, 1863, CROB, XXIV, 182–83; *Blockade Running,* ed. Vandiver, pp. xxxi, n., 74, 75.

[13] Circular, Adj. & Insp. Gen.'s Off., Richmond, June [?] 22, 1863, *General Orders, Confederate States Army,* Series of 1863, p. 225; ORA, Ser. I, Vol. XXVII, Pt. III, 1091–92.

[14] Ordnance Circular, Richmond, June 5, 1863, *General Orders, Confederate States Army,* Series of 1863, p. 239.

[15] Gorgas directed that no Federal ammunition be mixed with Confederate, whether of the same caliber or not, because the powder was of different quality.

they will be judiciously assigned, and I have no doubt will do excellent service in the hands of some of our old sharpshooters. Please accept my cordial thanks for the prompt and active assistance you so constantly afford me in the armament and supply of this Army. Our artillery is much improved and will no doubt prove itself worthy of the care and labor you have bestowed."[16]

From northern Virginia came one of General Lee's rare complaints. On June 8 he wrote Gorgas that he had reviewed five brigades of Confederate cavalry—Stuart's division. His attention was called to the saddles and carbines manufactured in Richmond, a subject which he had before mentioned to Gorgas. Some of the cavalry officers complained that the saddles ruined their horses' backs and that the carbines were so ineffective as to be demoralizing. With his accustomed moderation, the General-in-Chief went on to say:

I am aware of the difficulties attending the manufacture of arms and equipments, but I suggest that you have the matter inquired into by your ordnance officers, and see if they cannot rectify the evils complained of. It would be better, I think, to make fewer articles, and have them serviceable. The English saddles which you import are said to be good. It is the tree of the Richmond saddle that is complained of.[17]

Upon inquiry Gorgas learned that nothing could be done about the saddle trees, for the present at least. There was a six-months supply of them on hand at Richmond Ordnance Depot, paid for, and already covered with rawhide.[18] Bureau economy would not, of course, permit scrapping so much valuable material, nor would Confederate resources.

Other items issued also showed certain inadequacies. The laboratories at Charleston and Augusta Arsenals were the prime offenders. "A large quantity" of Enfield ammunition sent to Richmond from Augusta had balls too large to fit the muzzle of a .577 caliber arm. Spherical case shells for artillery were sent from Charleston "with wooden fuze plugs which has all to be condemned." In a letter to Mallet on June 7, Gorgas requested him to visit again these laboratories *"and remain at each long enough to see these and other faults corrected."* Then, thinking perhaps of Mallet's devotion to his pet project, Gorgas diplomatically added, "it is scarcely necessary for me to say that the duty of supervising the buildings at Macon must be subordinate to

[16] Bragg to Gorgas, Shelbyville, Tenn., June 4, 1863, GMSS.
[17] Lee to Gorgas, Headquarters, Army of Northern Virginia, ORA, Ser. I, Vol. XXVII, Pt. III, 872–73.
[18] Downer to Gorgas, Richmond, July 23, 1863, CROB, XC, 457.

that of the laboratories. The sense of responsibility in reference to these latter is painful to me."[19] And even after Mallet had reported an inspection of the trouble spots, Gorgas would not relax his worry. On July 7 he wrote Mallet that his frequent and careful visits to the various installations would undoubtedly lead to good results. Augusta still distressed him, and he said to Mallet: "As to the bullets used at Augusta I myself took from a *package* labeled Augusta Arsenal, a cartridge, the ball of which would not enter the muzzle of an Enfield Rifle. This may have been an unfair sample of their production; but such work must not be turned out at all."[20] Irregularities in cartridge sizes were confusing field ordnance men, and Gorgas had directed Mallet's attention to this most vital factor, especially from the standpoint of jamming. In Mallet's opinion:

The question is not how many rounds of ammunition can be fired from a clean musket carefully loaded and fired by a man undistracted and unhurried, with new ammunition, but how many rounds will a soldier probably be able to fire from a gun not previously in the best condition, loaded hastily in the excitement of battle, with ammunition more or less smeared with powder & grease from shaking about in the cartridge box and certain therefore soon to foul the gun to a serious extent. I have been informed by . . . a General officer in the Army of Northern Virginia that the men have repeatedly sought to obtain Miss. rifle ammunition (cal. .54) for their Enfield rifles and rifled muskets (cal. .577 & .58).

Mallet was unable to condemn the workings of the bureau without a few words in explanation. In the same letter he defended the Ordnance Bureau to a degree, and succinctly stated some of his most trying problems:

It should be observed in extenuation of *some* of the faults observable in our ammunition that they arise from the extremely irregular character of our supplies of material, both as to quality and quantity. No sooner have a number of Laboratory hands been trained to habits of work of the proper kind than either the material in use changes in quality or fails altogether—in the latter case compelling the discharge of hands who frequently cannot be had again when fresh supplies . . . have been obtained.[21]

On July 6 Gorgas wrote that the size of the Enfield rifle musket ball would have to be determined at once. He decided that balls made ac-

---

[19] Gorgas to Mallet, Richmond, CROB, XXXVIII, 74. Gorgas' remark concerning his responsibility is one of the best illustrations of his sense of duty.
[20] Gorgas to Mallet, Richmond, *ibid.,* p. 151.
[21] Mallet to Gorgas, Macon, June 9, 1863, CROB, XXIV, 126.

curately to moulds and gauges were "too small for efficient use in arms of precision." He wanted the Superintendent of Laboratories to devise new moulds and gauges.[22]

While Mallet busied himself with these and other matters, Gorgas had resorted to the widest decentralization. As was indicated, the investment of Vicksburg changed the plans of Confederate ordnance. More particularly, it changed administrative procedure in the various branches of the Army as well as of the government. It will be remembered that following the Seven Days Battles Major General Benjamin Huger had been given the somewhat unnecessary position of Inspector of Artillery and Ordnance. Gorgas picked him as the logical man to send west for the task of handling the affairs of the bureau in the Trans-Mississippi Department. This would get him out of the way, and such an assignment would have the added advantage of importance. Accordingly Huger went west as chief of ordnance under General Kirby Smith.[23]

Gorgas was not alone in his concern for that area. In early April President Davis had spent an hour discussing the possibility of establishing furnaces and a foundry on the Trinity River in Texas.[24] Davis' interest in war establishments in the West was constant and constructive. On July 14, 1863, in a letter to Senator Johnson of Arkansas, he reiterated this interest and said that for some time he had "seen the importance of establishing manufactories for all munitions of war in the Trans-Mississippi Department." He maintained that he had directed the dispatch there of skilled workmen and that every possible inducement had been offered to encourage the development of the area's mines. Undecided about the place at which a foundry or arsenal should be located, Davis told Johnson that he had sought Gorgas' advice in relation to manufactories and the supply of munitions in the West.[25]

For some months Gorgas himself had been particularly concerned about supplying arms and ammunition to Texas. San Antonio Arsenal had been nursed along, and other plants in that city were contributing

[22] Gorgas to Mallet, Richmond, CROB, XXXVIII, 147.

[23] Huger to Gorgas, Alexandria, La., July 6, 1863, ORA, Ser. I, Vol. XXII, Pt. II, 907. Huger's arrival apparently deranged some of Smith's own plans for handling the ordnance bureau west of the Mississippi. A month to the day before Huger announced his arrival in Alexandria, Smith had assigned Maj. Thomas G. Rhett as his Chief of Ordnance and Artillery. General Orders Number 17, Headquarters, Trans-Mississippi Department, Shreveport, June 6, 1863, AGPF, Thomas G. Rhett.   [24] GCWD, April 3, 1863, p. 29.

[25] Davis to Johnson, Richmond, ORA, Ser. I, Vol. LIII, 880.

greatly toward maintaining a modest store of munitions for "Kirby Smithdom."[26] But a large establishment of fabrication, backed by adequate and convenient iron resources, had to be provided before any real progress toward filling the critical shortages in the West could be made. The answer, probably fostered by the wisdom of Huger, was the erection of a large armory at Tyler, Texas. Under the able guidance and command of Lieutenant Colonel G. H. Hill, this installation soon became indispensable to the western commanders and overshadowed other ordnance plants in the Trans-Mississippi.[27]

While Tyler Arsenal was taking shape, Gorgas was not neglecting the immediate needs of Smith's troops. Instructions were sent to Huse and other purchasing agents in Europe to arrange for the shipment of a cargo of arms directly to Texas, but this scheme ended in the debacle of the "Ella and Annie," mentioned earlier.[28]

As military events in the Confederacy were shaping toward a tremendous climax in Pennsylvania and at Vicksburg, the sense of values possessed by some of his subordinates was probably a source of mild humor to Gorgas. Mallet, who had contributed the "Polygonal Shell" to Confederate artillery not long before,[29] had, in June, other less mundane things on his mind. From Macon on June 27 he requested Gorgas to inform him of the exact inscription wanted on the stone slab over the door of the main tower entrance at the Central Laboratory.[30] To Mallet this was a vital problem, for, being a man of scientific and serious mind, he regarded each of his projects as of long-term importance. While Gorgas was not unduly perturbed about the laboratory inscription, he was at the same time far too discreet to slight his subordinate's request. Through Tom Bayne he replied that he was much gratified to learn of the fine progress made at Macon and expressed the view that Mallet should suggest a suitable inscription for the building

---

[26] A large Confederate powder mill located in San Antonio exploded on July 4, 1863. At this time it was estimated that 80,000 pounds of reserve powder were stored in the arsenal there.

[27] Letter book of G. H. Hill, CROB, CXLVII. A microfilm copy of this volume is in The University of Texas Archives Collection.

[28] Gorgas to E. Kirby Smith, Richmond, July 22, 1863, ORA, Ser. I, Vol. XXVI, Pt. II, 118–19; Blockade Running, pp. 53, 95.

[29] This shell was a new departure in ordnance. Gorgas had approved its introduction September 6, 1862. Mallet pointed out that its main advantage was its definite "lines of weakness" or "lines of easy fracture," so that it was possible to predetermine the number and size of the pieces into which the shell would burst. The new shells rapidly became popular. See Mallet's "Memorandum in regard to shells with polygonal cavities," January 21, 1863, AGPF, Mallet.

[30] Mallet to Gorgas, Macon, CROB, XXIV, 170.

himself. "Erected according to your own plans and under your immediate supervision," wrote Bayne, "your name should appear in any inscription in the connection with its history."[31]

Suddenly active operations forced an abrupt change in routine at the Ordnance Office. To Gorgas, who had, on June 16, trusted that "we are not to have the Maryland campaign over again," the rumored approach of an enemy column toward Richmond and the lack of accurate news about Lee's army were not encouraging. He spent his forty-fifth birthday in uncertainty about what was going on.[32] He faced, of course, the irritation of having his skilled workers suddenly pulled from their tasks in Richmond's shops and once again thrown into the various city defense units. On July 2, just after he was told that the volunteer companies had been ordered out, he penned an urgent note to the Secretary of War. He indicated that such action at this particular time was extremely dangerous, since it "of course involves the total suspension of supplies of ammunition to the army of General Lee. . . . I venture to suggest that this step should only be taken in the last necessity, especially as to the companies from the arsenal and laboratory on 7th Street under Lt. Col. W. Leroy Broun."[33]

Conditions were such as would irritate the calmest of men, and Gorgas' peculiar position was even more subject to the rattling effects of rumors and counter-rumors. Since news from Lee's army was slow in arriving and then usually unreliable, Gorgas had little idea of the true military picture. His sources of information at such times were the same as those of the everyday citizen—the newspapers. True, he had the advantage of correspondence with his field officers, but they could hardly be expected to write from the battlefield. Conversations with high War Department officials indicated they knew about as much as the Chief of Ordnance. After great actions Gorgas had much more accurate information about what had happened than others, but during a prolonged, arduous campaign, he conducted his bureau business in an atmosphere of uncertainty. Before such campaigns he was usually informed of what would probably be needed, and after supplying the ordnance trains he relied on his old policy of continuous preparation to provide for emergency requisitions. Gorgas suffered as much the effects of the "fog of war" as did the Confederacy's field commanders. In some respects he suffered more than they did, for he

[31] Bayne to Mallet, Richmond, July 4, 1863, CROB, XXXVIII, 144.
[32] GCWD, July 1, 1863, p. 46.
[33] Gorgas to Seddon, Richmond, CRLR, 1863, Doc. GWD 281.

was exposed not only to this uncertainty but to disturbing demands from the rear areas as well. He did not possess the advantage of being able to devote his undivided attention to a particular situation or engagement. His consideration was necessarily given to every Confederate military force, and to the million and one things involved in supplying arms and munitions to these forces. While his personal interest might center on the activities of the Army of Northern Virginia somewhere in Pennsylvania, his official eye watched with equal anxiety the resistance offered by Pemberton's heroic defenders of Vicksburg and the needs of the hastily forming force under Joe Johnston, designed to do what it could to break the stranglehold on the South's vital Mississippi bastion. To provide artillery for this force Gorgas found almost impossible since most of the war material in Mississippi rested inside the Vicksburg lines.[34] But he kept trying.

By July 9 Gorgas and other Richmond residents were becoming alarmed about the possible fate of Lee's army. From Martinsburg, Lee's advanced base, came telegraphic news that Lee had beaten General George G. Meade, new commander of the Army of the Potomac, and captured half his force. News from the flag of truce boat, however, had it that Lee had retreated on Sunday, the fifth, from Gettysburg, where a great battle had been fought on July 1, 2, and 3. The only certain tidings were that the Confederates had held their positions up to the morning of the third—Friday. But worse yet was the news which was received on the seventh, as yet unconfirmed, that Vicksburg had capitulated on the fourth of July. To Gorgas this calamity was "incredible," and he recorded it with obvious reserve, along with the news that Vice-President Stephens had failed, as Gorgas had thought he would, in his mission to Newport News for the alleged purpose of settling certain points of disagreement in the exchange cartel.[35]

On July 10 the Vicksburg news was confirmed, as most had feared it would be, and Gorgas saw the loss in its true perspective. "It is indeed a terrible blow to our cause," he wrote; "it apparently sets us back indefinitely. It will enable the Yankees to again recruit their armies, and will greatly depress our credit abroad. It is believed that over twenty thousand men were surrendered, and of these nearly seventeen thousand have been fit for duty. Why an effort was not made

[34] See the fine account of Johnston's pitiful shortage of equipment in Henry, *Story of the Confederacy*, p. 262.
[35] GCWD, July 9, 1863, p. 48. See also the entry of July 5, p. 47.

to cut thro' is not yet known."[36] In recording these sentiments, Gorgas apparently forgot that on June 3 he had written that if Johnston "allows Vicksburg to fall his reputation will be gone past all redemption." Later on, in September, he would say that both Johnston and Pemberton had "lost the public confidence."[37]

Reports about Gettysburg were true—Lee had retreated to Hagerstown. On July 10 Gorgas expressed the feelings of many when he said that "on the whole our affairs look gloomier now than ever."[38] By the thirteenth, authentic news from Lee himself reached the anxious War Office—the fighting of July first had been punishing to the enemy, that of the second indecisive, and that of the third had resulted in Lee's repulse. But—and here was a straw to clutch desperately—Lee appeared to have taken about 10,000 prisoners. News of the terrible Confederate losses was slow to arrive, but on the thirteenth the trains of wounded began to roll into Richmond, dreadfully remindful of the Seven Days, Second Manassas, Chancellorsville.

On the sixteenth Gorgas received a letter from Colonel Briscoe Baldwin, Lee's chief ordnance officer, which described Pickett's charge on July 3 as a disaster, and Gorgas felt that "as such I fear we must accept it," though he firmly believed that "General Lee will make an attempt to retrieve it by some signal blow at the enemy."[39]

The South's measure of bad news was not yet full. On the fourteenth came word that Port Hudson, Louisiana, had also been surrendered by its heroic commander, General Frank Gardner, after a siege every bit as desperate as that of Vicksburg, if not more so.[40] And from Charleston: the Federals had launched an assault on Morris Island which threatened Fort Wagner. If that work should fall, Fort Sumter stood in jeopardy.[41]

As the stunning impact of the Confederacy's reverses hit Gorgas, his confidence was shaken. "Can we believe in the justice of Providence," he asked himself, "or must we conclude that we are after all wrong? Such visitations give me to great bitterness of heart and repining at His decrees. It is apparent that we are not yet sufficiently tried."[42]

[36] *Ibid.*, July 10, 1863, p. 49. Grant reported that 31,600 prisoners were taken at Vicksburg. *Memoirs*, I, 572.

[37] GCWD, June 3, July 10, September 8, 1863, pp. 43, 49, 61.

[38] GCWD, p. 49.

[39] GCWD, July 16, 1863, p. 50. Gorgas did not name the officer from whom he received the letter concerning Gettysburg, but he referred to him as "writing from General Lee's headquarters." It is reasonably certain, therefore, that the writer was Baldwin.   [40] Jones, *Rebel War Clerk's Diary*, I, 378.

[41] GCWD, July 16, 1863, p. 50.   [42] GCWD, July 17, 1863, pp. 50–51.

XVI

". . . But the Flesh Is Weak"

IN THE FIRST WEEK OF JULY THE CONFEDERACY HAD LOST A GREAT
deal more than the city of Vicksburg and the battle of Gettysburg. As
the terrible shock began to subside, Gorgas was able to get a rational
idea of what had happened, so far as his department was concerned.
The initial reports were far from encouraging; and as later news filtered
in, the picture grew worse.

Grant reported that he had captured 60,000 muskets, 172 cannon,
and "a large amount of ammunition" at Vicksburg. Banks had taken
at Port Hudson "20 pieces of heavy artillery, 5 complete batteries,
numbering 31 pieces of field artillery, a good supply of projectiles for
light and heavy guns, 44,000 pounds of cannon powder, 5,000 stand
of small-arms, 150,000 rounds of small-arms ammunition, besides a
small amount of stores of various kinds."[1] With a heavy heart Gorgas
asked for a statement of the losses at both these points so as to map
out his immediate plans.[2] He had to know, too, what Lee had left behind at Gettysburg and along his line of retreat. When early tabula-
tions of these losses had been turned in, Gorgas found that actually
45,000 small arms had been surrendered by Pemberton and Gardner,
and that Lee had lost some 25,000 arms—70,000 altogether.[3] The Ordnance Bureau was face to face with an appalling task.

Three days after the surrender of Vicksburg, ordnance officers began to notice a shortage of lead in the arsenals farther south. Gorgas,
who learned of it almost immediately, quickly gave instructions to
Stansbury in Bermuda, and other transshipment agents, "to send in lead

[1] Grant, *Personal Memoirs*, I, 572; Banks to Gen. H. W. Halleck, Port Hudson, July 10, 1863, ORA, Ser. I, Vol. XXVI, Pt. I, 55.
[2] Gorgas to Capt. Evans, Richmond, July 18, 1863, *Mississippi MSS.*, Ser. L,
Vol. CXI.   [3] GCWD, July 28, 1863, p. 55.

by each of the Government steamers," and offered inducements to private parties to bring in as much as possible.[4] On July 7 Gorgas told Mallet that because of Huse's diligent activities a large amount of lead from Bermuda would be sent to Augusta for distribution. The Richmond laboratory, which made most of Lee's ammunition, could be supplied from the Wytheville mines, but since that source did not average a hundred thousand pounds per month, very little would be left over for shipment to other places.[5] Mallet was glad to get Gorgas' news concerning importation; in acknowledging this information he felt obliged to reiterate the need felt at the southern arsenals.[6]

A bureau circular, dated June 22, 1863, which restricted cartridge issues to three per man per month had been a direct result of this shortage, which was reflected in a letter, of July 18, from Gorgas to Hypolite Oladowski, chief of ordnance of the Army of Tennessee. In this letter Gorgas remarked that if it became impossible to keep up the supply of bullets to one hundred forty rounds per man in action, the failure would be due to lack of lead.[7] His specific orders about curtailing ammunition production were probably equally traceable to the dwindling stock of that precious metal. Importations during the month of July were not encouraging,[8] and the available amounts could sustain no unusual expenditure, despite Gorgas' hope that recent receipts

[4] Gorgas to Mallet, Richmond, July 7, 1863, CROB, XXXVIII, 150.

[5] Gorgas to Mallet, Richmond, July 7, 9, 1863, *ibid.*, pp. 149, 156.

[6] Mallet to Gorgas, Macon, July 14, 1863, CROB, XXIV, 202. On July 5 Mallet had reported nearly all the arsenals except Richmond as "altogther without lead." *Ibid.*, pp. 182–83.

[7] Oladowski to Brig. Gen. W. W. Mackall, Chattanooga, July 23, 1863, ORA, Ser. I, Vol. XXIII, Pt. II, 927. Oladowski wanted an order issued directing the careful conservation of ammunition.

[8] See Gorgas to Mallet, Richmond, August 8, 1863, CROB, XXXVIII, 235. In this letter Gorgas listed the following shipments of lead as having reached the Confederacy in July:

July 16, from "Emma,"	Ordered to Selma,	80 pigs
July 17, " "Cornubia,"	" " " ,	208 "
July 17, " "Eugenie,"	" " Augusta,	85 "
July 17, " "Atalanta,"	" " Atlanta,	85 "
July 31, " "R. E. Lee,"	" " Augusta,	250 "

Since each pig of lead weighed approximately 72 pounds, a little over 25 tons is accounted for in this table. But Gorgas indicated that Maj. Trezevant at Charleston had probably received an additional 25 tons, while 15 tons had reached Wilmington. See also *Blockade Running*, p. 114. From the cargo lists there printed, it appears that the 208 pigs of lead mentioned as carried on the "Lady Davis" were the same as those Gorgas indicated were carried on the "Cornubia."

would prevent a serious calamity.[9] Either he was misinformed, or he deliberately deceived himself about recent arrivals. Mallet, whose duties kept him well posted, complained on September 7 that conditions were still bad. He reminded Gorgas that current arrivals, based on orders given to Huse in December, 1862, could not approximate the present needs of the bureau. Not only were Huse's cargoes based on the idea of a six-months supply, but "the difficulty of obtaining almost all these stores from the internal resources of the Confederacy has increased *enormously* since the list was made out." He went on to say: *"Lead we must import, and largely as no Arsenal—except Richmond—can otherwise be depended on for small arm's ammunition."*[10] Four days later, September 11, he disabused Gorgas of any hopes the latter might have retained. Admitting that some 200,000 pounds of lead had reached Augusta from abroad, he pointed out that of this large amount, only 69,604 pounds still remained on hand. Forty thousand pounds had been used at Augusta, the rest issued to different arsenals. What proved most alarming was the short time it had taken to expend this amount—two months and seven days (July 1 to September 7). From this information Mallet concluded that only 100 of the 1,100 tons ordered from Huse had reached the Confederacy, though he thought that 500 to 600 tons were awaiting transport from Bermuda. The situation had become so acute and so dangerous, wrote Mallet, that "the supplies to the four Arsenals (Atlanta, Selma, Macon, and Columbus) will scarcely suffice for one month's active work, and the amount still on hand at Augusta . . . is estimated as sufficient for but two month's work there."[11] On October 9 he penned another warning of impending crisis. The southern laboratories still lacked adequate resources of the metal, he said. The first installments of Huse's shipments had arrived just in time to prevent "a general suspension of work on small-arm's cartridges, but this stock is rapidly becoming exhausted, and I cannot learn that any further amounts are on the way to Augusta or this place." Because Gorgas' views of the importance of securing scrap lead were

[9] Gorgas to Mallet, Richmond, August 26, 1863, CROB, XXXVIII, 292. Gorgas reported that Selma had a two-month's supply of lead, while Rains had sent some to Atlanta, Columbus, and Macon.

[10] Mallet to Gorgas, Macon, September 7, 1863, CROB, XXIV, 305.

[11] Mallet to Gorgas, Macon, September 11, 1863, *ibid.*, pp. 319–20. Mallet appears to have suspected that some favoritism was accorded to arsenals and other ordnance installations in Virginia. Witness his hope, expressed in this letter, that "a liberal share [of imported lead] may be allotted to each of the more Southern Arsenals."

well known to Mallet, he pointed out reasons why no faith could be placed on this source of supply. "It is to be remembered," he said, "that scrap lead is not now to be bought except in quantities so small as to be insignificant, and that consequently Augusta, Charleston, Atlanta, Macon, Columbus and Selma Arsenals are dependent upon foreign importations for the means of continuing the manufacture of small-arm's cartridges."[12]

Like many shortages, the shortage of lead involved a number of factors. Foremost, of course, was cartridge production. According to Gorgas' estimate of bullet output for the year September, 1862, to September, 1863, monthly production must have averaged over 3,000,000. He himself estimated that daily output totalled 150,000 throughout the Confederacy. The irregular sources to which the Nitre and Mining Bureau had found recourse for lead were so unpredictable as to be an important factor in the uncertainty of the supply. Writing after the war, Gorgas remarked that he had to rely on window weights from Charleston and unused water mains from Mobile for one third of the total amount.[13]

The Trans-Mississippi Department had done its bit to boost lead resources early in the war by furnishing no less than 400,000 pounds, and 140,000 pounds had been captured with the southern arsenals. Gleanings from battlefields and scraps collected throughout the country accounted for 5,300,000 pounds during the course of the war, while importations provided not over 2,000,000 pounds.[14] The Wytheville mines remained the principal, and most reliable, source of lead. Gorgas calculated their yield at 60,000 pounds per month; but at times they did much better.[15]

[12] Mallet to Gorgas, Macon, *ibid.,* p. 379. In June Gorgas had instructed his field officers to increase prices for scrap iron, but the pickings were lean. For example, see Capt. Henry Myers to Mallet, Mobile, June 11, 1863, CROB, XXXVIII, 80.

[13] See Gorgas to Seddon, Richmond, November 15, 1863, ORA, Ser. IV, Vol. II, 955–59. Gorgas stated that during the year upon which he was reporting 36,531,466 cartridges were fabricated in Confederate shops and 81,750 were purchased, 940,440 were repaired, and 44,933,907 were issued to the armies. His estimate of the daily production is in GOC, p. 287.

[14] This is Gorgas' calculation of the amount of importation (GOC, p. 287), but it is probably based on memory and is erroneous. Seddon, in a report to Davis, December 10, 1864, said that 1,507,000 pounds of lead reached the South from abroad between November 1, 1863, and December 8, 1864, ORA, Ser. IV, Vol. III, 930.

[15] GOC, p. 287. Maj. Richard Morton of the Nitre and Mining Bureau reported to Gorgas in July, 1863, that the Wythe mines had produced 85,561 pounds in May and 85,453 in June. All of this lead had gone to Richmond, ex-

Summer passed with Gorgas, as usual, occupied with preparations. Military operations in Virginia remained fairly static, but in September General Bragg, reinforced by Longstreet's corps from Lee's army, administered a stunning defeat at Chickamauga to the Union army under General William S. Rosecrans. Even so, few of the common people could manage to overlook a glaring evil. Confederate armies were holding their own in gallant fashion, but the country's economy was not keeping pace. Even as early as the beginning of 1863 it had become clear that government attempts to stabilize the currency were coming to naught. State paper commanded more buying power than Confederate notes, and prices were an intelligible index of the financial abyss into which the South was plunging at breakneck speed.

This economic disintegration affected the people behind the lines much more tangibly than it did the men in the ranks. As the Gorgas family well knew (and they were better off than most) cloth was almost impossible to get, as were shoes and salt. The people also found that the war took out of circulation the little things of everyday comfort. If a family did not directly feel the heavy hand of war by having someone in the armed forces, it could not escape the pinch of the necessities of life. Truly, by the summer of 1863 the Confederacy had become a fortress undergoing a siege of attrition from which it could scarcely hope to achieve lasting relief.[16]

And if prices served as a good indication of the economic trends, so did affairs in the Ordnance Bureau. General Cooper's admonition to Beauregard concerning the growing scarcity of resources[17] was only the chorus to the refrain heard daily in Gorgas' office. For months before the battle of Chickamauga, this other barometer had been steadily falling. A severe scarcity of leather, manifested clearly in July, 1863, merely emphasized the general shortages indicated by the information reaching the Chief of Ordnance. Under pressure from the fierce

cepting 47,091 pounds, which were sent south. Morton complained of the poor quality of the ore at that time. He also noted that the Nitre and Mining Bureau had begun some mining operations at Wytheville on government account.

Some credence may be lent to Mallet's suspicion of favoritism toward Virginia plants by the fact that almost three-fourths of Wythe's two-months' production went to Richmond. Morton to Gorgas, Richmond, July 8, 1863, AGPF, Morton.

[16] For an excellent discussion of the economic disintegration of the Confederacy see Charles W. Ramsdell, *Behind the Lines in the Southern Confederacy* (Baton Rouge, 1944), Chap. II, and *passim*.

[17] Samuel Cooper to Beauregard, Richmond, September 1, 1863, ORA, Ser. I, Vol. XXVIII, Pt. II, 329.

inflation, Gorgas had to scale upward the prices which officers should pay for building materials in the field and had to give his sanction to a moss saddle blanket for the cavalry, a shabby compromise with pride.[18]

Another note of impending trouble came in late August from Colonel St. John, who wrote Seddon that "the supply of Ordnance, of projectiles, and of ammunition depends upon our ability to hold those parts of the country where the mines of iron, lead, copper and niter are situated. The question is a vital one." Seddon "noted" the urgent letter. And then, following the colossal ineptitude displayed by Bragg in Tennessee, the Ducktown mines were lost and Wytheville, with its incalculably valuable lead mines, was endangered. St. John feared, as did Gorgas, that if some means of adequate protection were not found for the furnaces, saltpeter works, and mines of his bureau, "the present system must give place to one even more unreliable."[19] This was clearly understatement. Temporary relief from Federal destruction of important works in southeast Tennessee and western Virginia had been obtained as a consequence of Longstreet's East Tennessee campaign; but the operation soon disclosed its own futility, and all but the northeastern corner of Tennessee passed permanently to the Union.

The loss of the Ducktown copper mines had a more far-reaching effect on the Confederate Ordnance Bureau than has generally been recognized.[20] From them had come fully ninety per cent of the South's copper, according to an officer in the Nitre and Mining Bureau;[21] and when they no longer produced, Gorgas could see clearly that unless a new avenue for copper was opened, his department was approaching the end. Like almost all commodities in everyday use, copper did not

[18] Downer to Gorgas, Richmond, July 21 and August 11, 1863, CROB, XC, 452–53, 492; Gorgas to Mallet, Richmond, August 14, *ibid.*, XXXVIII, 258.

[19] St. John to Seddon, Richmond, August 27, 1863, CRLR, 1863, Doc. SWD 561.

[20] Surprisingly, there seems to be no exact record of the date at which these important mines finally passed from Confederate control. Most of the available accounts suggest that the mines fell to the Federals after the battles around Chattanooga, which seems reasonable. See for instance, *Southern Historical Society Papers*, XVI (1888), 287; XXVI (1898), 368; XXXVII (1909), 10–11. Apparently by mistake the date of the fall of the mines is put at the end of 1864 by William Diamond in "Imports of the Confederate Government from Europe and Mexico," *Journal of Southern History*, VI (1940), 482. In a letter to the writer, September 20, 1951, Mr. Richard Fields, of Milan, Tennessee, said: "Went through Ducktown this summer. . . . They never surrendered, however the shipment of copper by wagon was stopped when Cleveland, Tenn., was captured in '64, I believe."

[21] Report of Lt. Col. Richard Morton, January 1, 1863, to January 1, 1865, ORA, Ser. IV, Vol. III, 990.

seem important until it was on the verge of being no longer available. Mallet appears to have been alone in fearing the possible extinction of the Ducktown supply. Gorgas in a serious miscalculation, had come to depend on Ducktown entirely, and, in fact, was so sure of its safety that in August he had directed the discontinuance of the manufacture of all but copper friction tubes.[22] Mallet's anxiety was proved justified by subsequent events. He told Gorgas on October 9 that the copper question, like that of lead, had become acute. He could not find out how much damage the Federals had done to the Ducktown mines and to the rolling mill at Cleveland, Tennessee. Indeed, he was not sure they were still in Confederate hands. With the rapid approach of real scarcity, Mallet could now urge the introduction of paper friction-primer making on a small scale in the laboratories, as a means of ac-quainting workers with methods used in fabrication.[23] Confidence in the relative security of Ducktown and in the abundance of its output had relegated the question of copper importation to a minor role through 1862, and by February, 1863, only 10,000 pounds had been sent through the blockade by Huse. Increased demand naturally accel-erated importation, but despite efforts to speed up, the Nitre and Min-ing Bureau succeeded in obtaining only 31,208 pounds through the blockade during the two years ending January 1, 1865. This amount represented less than four per cent of the total Confederate supply dur-ing that period. To make up the deficiency the bureau impressed tur-pentine and apple-brandy stills in North Carolina and got enough copper coils for the last two years of the war.[24]

Now, as always, money was the all-important factor. Gorgas himself entertained little fear of the Confederacy's ability to protract the war ("we have war material sufficient—men, guns, powder," he wrote on October 29, 1863), but felt great concern for the ability of Southern financing to furnish the necessary backing. Bankruptcy seemed im-minent to him, and he viewed this evil as possibly the lesser of several. "Perhaps it is better that this paper of six or seven hundred million should come to naught," he punned unintentionally, "and so relieve posterity of a debt too heavy to be borne." His personal and official experience with inflation pointed all too clearly to the contingency he

[22] Gorgas to Mallet, Richmond, August 28, 1863, CROB, XXXVIII, 293. In this letter Gorgas expressed the belief that paper friction tubes could not be made serviceable and was surprised that Mallet had voiced an interest in them.
[23] Mallet to Gorgas, Macon, CROB, XXIV, 379.
[24] Diamond, *Journal of Southern History,* VI, 482.

foresaw. His own family, their friends and neighbors, in fact everyone, found the prices of commodities all but prohibitive. On October 29 Gorgas recorded that beef could be had at $1.25 per pound, butter at $4.00, eggs at $3.00 a dozen. Clothing had already passed from the reach of most people, calico selling for $8.00 and $10.00 a yard. Coffee was disappearing from Richmond's tables since it cost $8.00 a pound. The soaring of the cost of shoes to $50.00 and $60.00 a pair inspired Gorgas to wonder "where all this will stop."[25] He discovered as well that the Quartermaster General's estimate of funds needed came to $54,000,000 a month alone, and this exceeded the congressional limit on issuance of paper currency by $4,000,000.

Inflation at home only confounded the already chaotic condition of Confederate finances abroad. By October 1, 1863, Seddon knew how much of the Erlanger Loan could be used. Colin McRae, the European financial agent, had instructions to apportion that part of the loan applicable to War Department needs on the basis of £85,000 for the Quartermaster Department, £40,000 for the Commissary Department, £55,500 for the Ordnance Department, £30,000 for the Medical Department, £40,000 for the Nitre and Mining Bureau, and £12,000 for the Engineer Department. Requisitions were to come from department and bureau heads, and the Treasury Department would then send a draft for the sum required to McRae.[26] But even with this increment in sterling Gorgas faced monetary difficulties. The policy of his bureau dictated that funds abroad "must be husbanded to the utmost."[27]

Military events seemed to be following the depressing pattern set by the Confederacy's economic ills. Between November 23 and 25, 1863, Bragg's army sustained a series of defeats around Chattanooga— Lookout Mountain, Orchard Knob, and Missionary Ridge—which hurled it back to winter quarters at Dalton, Georgia, with a loss, according to Gorgas' estimates, of some forty pieces of artillery.[28] Following that debacle, Gorgas could certainly test the validity of his

[25] GCWD, p. 68.
[26] Seddon to McRae, Richmond, October 1, 1863, AGPF, Bayne.
[27] Bayne to Mallet, Richmond, October 8, 1863, CROB, XXXVIII, 434.
[28] For a graphic account of the various actions, see Henry, *Story of the Confederacy*, Chap. XXV. For Gorgas' tabulation of guns lost at Missionary Ridge, see GCWD, December 6, 1863, p. 70. His estimate proved correct. Col. Oladowski reported on December 3 that a total of forty guns had been lost, though the ordnance stores at the Chickamauga depot had been saved and sent to Calhoun, Ga. Oladowski to Gorgas, Calhoun, December 3, 1863, ORA, Ser. I, Vol. XXXI, Pt. II, 683.

boast, made a scant ten days before, that "the condition of the department and its ability to meet demands upon it is better than it was a year
ago." He had counted heavily on the productive capacity of the arsenals
and workshops for field and siege artillery, and on the Tredegar Iron
Works for seacoast guns. A total of 113 guns had been fabricated
within the Confederacy between September 30, 1862, and September
30, 1863, while 239 had been purchased. At the time Gorgas made his
yearly report to the Secretary of War for 1863 (on November 15),
he remarked that "the army is now adequately supplied on this side of
the Mississippi River with artillery quite equal to that possessed by the
enemy." His bureau had placed 677 guns in the field since the first
of October, 1862, with an appropriate supply of ammunition. Even
with the terrific losses at Vicksburg, Port Hudson, and Gettysburg,
Gorgas recorded a steady upswing in the supply of small arms. "The
armories at Richmond, Fayetteville and Ashville have produced an ag-
gregate of about 28,000 small arms within the year. Those produced
at private establishments will swell this number to full 35,000 (it may
be fairly assumed that this number will be increased to 50,000 during
the year ending September 30, 1864)." He waxed almost as optimistic
in the matter of powder, saying that the Government powder mills
had produced a supply adequate to the wants of the Army, in spite of
the fabrication of 36,531,466 cartridges during the year, as well as
298,305 rounds of artillery ammunition.[29]

But the stunning shock of Missionary Ridge, combined with the
painfully obvious lack of success which Lee had had in the abortive
Mine Run affair in late November, and the steadily rising prices lowered the pitch of Gorgas' enthusiasm. He still saw that currency remained one of the worst thorns in the Confederacy's side, and in his
diary viewed with alarm the fact that flour sold in December for as
high as $125.00 a barrel; potatoes, $15.00 to $20.00 a bushel; eggs,
$3.00 a dozen; butter, $5.00 a pound; sugar, $4.50 to $6.00; "coffee
any price, $20.00 on."[30] Gold had risen sharply in value and a pair
of shoes which Gorgas got from Baltimore cost him $87.50.

Even though he maintained close touch with bureau affairs and
displayed uncanny judgment about probable troop movements, Gorgas
still fell victim to Richmond's particularly virulent variety of rumors.
He allowed himself to rationalize that the defeat at Missionary Ridge
had been overemphasized; for, after all, Bragg had saved his army.

---

[29] Gorgas to Seddon, Richmond, November 15, 1863, ORA, Ser. IV, Vol. II,
955–59.   [30] GCWD, December 6, 1863, pp. 70–72.

Musing on the Confederacy's general military situation on the evening of December 7, Gorgas entered in his diary:

It is singular to reflect that had Longstreet remained with Bragg the left of our army where he commanded would have repulsed the enemy, as did the right, and Missionary Ridge, instead of a shameful defeat would have been a bloody repetition of Fredericksburgh; if on the other hand the movement on Knoxville had been carried as begun a few days after the battle of Chickamauga Burnside would have been captured, and Rosecrans's Army forced out of Chattanooga. If, again, Longstreet had been with Lee, or even two of his divisions, Meade would have been "ground to powder" as one of General Lee's chief staff officers expresses it, before he could have recrossed the Rapidan, during the last days of November. For the late advance of Knoxville the President is perhaps responsible, as he was with the Army of General B. when the movement began. It was an unfortunate move then, as the result proved. As Longstreet's Chief of Artillery said then, it was undertaken too late, and in inadequate forces. It was early in November, six weeks after the battle of Chickamauga, before Longstreet marched![31]

Gorgas remained upset over the condition of the Army of Tennessee. He felt that Johnston would probably assume command of that force, as he did, and "unless Bragg remains as his Chief of Staff, I do not hope good from the change." He felt that with the reinforcements sent to Johnston, his army ought to be stronger than it was prior to Missionary Ridge. This hope, perhaps, served as an antidote to concern about Amelia's health—she was still bedridden, as she had been since late November—and about the weather, which had turned rainy and would probably make the roads impassable for troops.[32]

Christmas and the New Year were passed in the customary gloom of war holidays for the Gorgases. General William W. Averell of the United States Cavalry helped usher in the new year by visiting Salem, Virginia, toward the end of his southwestern Virginia raid. This, the sorry affair of the capture and recapture of the "Chesapeake," and Amelia's continued illness all contributed to dampening Gorgas' Christmas spirit: "Christmas was not a merry one to me, and I passed it very quietly, almost sadly, at home."[33]

Yuletide was not any happier for the whole Confederacy. It signaled the ending of the year which had brought with it Vicksburg, Gettysburg, and Missionary Ridge. What would 1864 hold in store?

[31] *Ibid.*, December 7, 1863, p. 72.   [32] *Ibid.*, December 18, 20, 1863, pp. 73–74.
[33] *Ibid.*, December 28, 1863, p. 74.

XVII

Growing Confusion

FROM AN ACTIVE MILITARY STANDPOINT 1864 BEGAN INAUSPICIOUSLY enough, but it was a false start. In so far as the Ordnance Bureau was concerned, General Lee had already set the pattern for the new year's activities. With characteristic foresight he had expressed to Davis in September, 1863, his belief that "Colonel Gorgas should commence at once to enlarge his manufacturing arsenals, &c., in the interior, so that if Richmond should fall we would not be destitute. These are only recommended as prudential measures, and such as, should the necessity for them ever arise, we will then wish had been taken."[1]

Gorgas had long before anticipated Lee's ideas, and it will be recalled that one of his main efforts had been to decentralize geographically so as to afford more even distribution and adequate reserve installations. Decentralization, as has been pointed out, had its inconvenient side. Gorgas would have infinitely preferred to locate almost all his manufacturing centers in a single fairly safe place, from which supplies could be shipped to the various armies, but of course the Confederacy's railroads precluded such a policy. As it was, the necessity of decentralizing multiplied the tasks of the bureau a hundredfold. No other phase of the history of the bureau so clearly illustrates Gorgas' quality as an administrator than does the supervision and management of his many subordinates and the arsenals, depots, and shops over which they presided. He gave careful attention to the selection of assistants and managed them with wisdom. Mostly men of great ability, they came to regard him as a sort of father-confessor to whom they could take every problem, no matter how trivial, for solution or ex-

---

[1] Lee to Davis, Camp Near Orange Court House, September 11, 1863, ORA, Ser. I, Vol. XXIX, Pt. II, 711.

planation. They trusted Gorgas to give them the backing and the where-
withal to create supplies, and he never betrayed their confidence. At
times, naturally, he could not give them all they needed, but he never
blamed them for failing when he himself had been unable to provide
the basic requisites for production. He ministered to their wants, listened
to complaints, supplied their funds, and praised their successes; he
furnished food for their crews, tried to get them skilled workers from
the armed services, and saw that they supplied the Confederate armies
with munitions as promptly and as competently as possible. He had said
to Seddon, in his report for 1863, that the Ordnance Bureau was at
last able to "respond to all calls made upon it."[2] Now that the year
1864 had begun, under the shadow of Missionary Ridge, he would
have to make good that rash promise.

From the time-consuming and urgent task of furnishing materiel to
the troops, Gorgas at last was able to turn his attention toward bol-
stering the internal organization of his bureau, something he had long
regarded as necessary. Its extra-legal condition having always disturbed
him, he continued pressing for status as a separate entity, detached from
the Corps of Artillery. He was continually pleased with the success
of Briscoe Baldwin and Hypolite Oladowski in bringing some kind
of order out of the chaos existing in their respective armies. Gorgas believed that the "loose organization of the Department" had materially
contributed to this confusion, and had also inspired "loose notions of
responsibility to superiors."[3] Congress, he thought, should pass legislation looking toward a separate and distinct governmental department
with the usual amount of autonomy. Ample evidence could have
been presented to show that some congressional assistance ought to
have been given to his plan. From different parts of the Confederacy
came calls for additional officers, now appointed from the list of
passed examinees. In reply to these requests Gorgas had to say that
"the number of officers at present is inadequate to the wants of the
service."[4] This same scarcity had affected Lee's army as early as November, 1863. Colonel Baldwin had been forced to use ordnance sergeants
in some tasks normally performed by commissioned personnel.[5] To be
sure, all the staff bureaus were made painfully aware of the manpower

[2] ORA, Ser. IV, Vol. II, 955–59.   [3] Ibid.
[4] Gorgas to Lt. Col. J. M. Kennard, Richmond, January 4, 1864, Mississippi
MSS., Ser. L, Vol. CXI.
[5] Baldwin to Capt. Eugene Carrington, Ordnance Office, Army of Northern
Virginia, November 25, 1863, AGPF, Baldwin.

problem by September, 1863, when the Surgeon General issued a circular directing that men adjudged unfit for field service, but able to do limited duty, be assigned to one or the other of the staff departments to replace men able to go to the field. The circular had particular reference to men employed in the Ordnance Bureau.[6] The shortage of officers forced Gorgas still further into the policy of robbing Peter to pay Paul. He found it difficult to avoid collecting officers at depots, and finally determined to ask the arsenals to give up supernumerary men for field duty. Later in 1863 one man apiece was directed to be sent from Macon, Augusta, and Atlanta arsenals to Colonel Oladowski.[7] But the very fact that the chiefs of the staff departments had authority to make these shifts and changes in personnel created an impression of confusion and duplication in the minds of many. An officer in the Adjutant General's Department reported to the Secretary of War on November 11, 1863, that chiefs of the Quartermaster, Medical, Commissary, and Ordnance bureaus "communicate directly, and transact business personally with officers of their respective departments in the field, holding them to strict responsibility, and interfering in some measure to direct and control their discharge of duties."[8] The essential fact overlooked by this inspector was that although some confusion did arise from the control exerted from Richmond, much more confusion would have existed without it. Gorgas, particularly, kept his finger on the pulse of his organization and never stopped trying to quicken the beat.

In the case of Colonel Oladowski, he had other worries. Not only did that officer allow his grip on the ordnance service of the Army of Tennessee to grow slack; becoming disturbed at the thought that perhaps Atlanta Arsenal would not respond to his orders quickly enough, he also asked Gorgas if he could, in such an event, call on other arsenals for emergency requisitions. The Chief of Ordnance frowned on this scheme and did not hesitate to tell Oladowski so:

The mode of supply has been instituted & approved by the Secretary of War himself; and beside calling for a violation of the order of the War Dept., the method proposed would not hasten the reception of the stores desired; and for the simple reason that there being but one route, the

    [6] Mallet to Dr. S. P. Moore, Macon, September 18, 1863, CROB, XXIV, 344.
    [7] Bayne to Oladowski, Richmond, November 14, 1863, *Mississippi MSS.*, Ser. L, Vol. CXI.
    [8] Maj. Samuel W. Melton to Seddon, Richmond, November 11, 1863, ORA, Ser. IV, Vol. II, 945.

supplies must necessarily pass through Atlanta. Were Colonel Wright a careless & inattentive officer, delay might result from want of promptness, in calling for and forwarding supplies; but his attention and energy are too well known, to warrant the indulgence of such a suspicion; it is therefore deemed best that no change should be attempted.[9]

Control of personnel did not devolve on any one particular agency or person. While the Chief of Ordnance exercised vast authority over field installations and officers, there still remained many undefined areas of personnel action. Generals of forces in the field could, of course, requisition labor and men from plants, and even the chief ordnance officers of armies facing the enemy could direct that workers in arsenals be put on some special duty, such as repair of arms, in order to meet a sudden deficiency occasioned by conflict.[10] Other factors were equally involved in the personnel picture.

While, under normal conditions, food and clothing for the ordnance workers would have been provided either by themselves, or in the case of enlisted or noncommissioned workmen detailed from the army, by the Quartermaster and Commissary departments, this solution now became impossible. Inflation rendered civilian workers unable to support themselves and their families on the wages in government plants and shops. Several plans were tried to relieve these workers of the unequal financial position in which they were inadvertently placed. One of these schemes was to have the Commissary supply food to civilian employees. For a time this plan worked; its ultimate failure was due to many factors, among which, of course, was the unique personality of Commissary General Lucius B. Northrop, who spent more time in explaining why the army was hungry than in trying to feed it.

While not entirely despairing of help from this collateral branch of the services of supply, Gorgas lost no time in directing that the Ordnance Bureau would make its own arrangements to feed, clothe, and house its skilled and unskilled workers, including Negro laborers. This policy led to a practice of obtaining food from the Commissariat whenever possible, and then adding to it whatever could be had elsewhere.[11] Gorgas hit upon the idea of establishing at installations under his direction a government store where employees could purchase simple

[9] Julius A. de Lagnel to Oladowski, Richmond, March 15, 1864, AGPF, de Lagnel.
[10] Burton to Gorgas, Macon, July 26, 1864, CROB, XXXI, 511.
[11] Bayne to Lt. Col. Broun, Richmond, November 16, 1863, AGPF, Bayne.

necessities at greatly reduced prices.[12] This, of course, did not relieve the condition of the colored laborers hired by the department. Negro laborers always stood as a prime problem to Gorgas. They were indispensable in performing the menial tasks around the plants, jobs that would take too much time to be done by the skilled artisans employed in barrel turning and stockmaking. The former were of vital importance in Mallet's and Burton's building enterprises in Macon, and did real yeoman service there. Gorgas and his subordinates did not overlook the contribution which these loyal workers made and spared no effort to better their lot. Unfortunately, in the matter of rations little could be done for them beyond what was being done for Confederate soldiers. As a consequence there were constant grumblings, both by the Negroes and by their owners, about the amount of food provided. Colonel Northrop saw that he could evade responsibility and promptly availed himself of the opportunity. This blow fell with particular force on Macon and threw the whole financial burden of feeding the laborers on the Ordnance Bureau.[13] Hence the value of co-operative buying missions, in use at Macon, became obvious.

But food alone did not comprise all that Gorgas had to provide for the colored workers he employed. By the terms of the contracts under which slave-owners hired chattels to his bureau, clothing and, usually, medical care, too, were to be provided. The clothing of so many individuals placed a real strain on the ingenuity of ordnance officers. Gorgas determined that the custom of the country must be followed in the matter of clothing slaves taken for government work. Complaints from slave-owners caused him to instruct Mallet that

the same am't of clothing allowed by others must be allowed by the Government. With reference to food it seems to me the rations provided ought to suffice, nevertheless as soon as supplies admit you will I hope be able to procure and issue say a pint or more per man per month of

[12] Mallet to Gorgas, Macon, November 21, 1863, CROB, XXIV, 495, suggesting co-operative buying missions for the combined ordnance plants in Macon; memorandum of the General Supply Store, Richmond, April 1, 1864, *ibid.*, XCIV, 21, stating that detailed operatives in the ordnance department in Richmond who draw a per diem of $3.00 or less will be allowed to buy in that store in lieu of other compensation, with rations at cost price from the first to the seventh of each month. Employees of the Ordnance Depot under Capt. James Dinwiddie would also be served from that store.

[13] Mallet to Gorgas, Macon, April 2, 1864, CROB, XXIV, 766. Mallet reported that the post commissary of Macon was "ordered to cease furnishing provisions to negro laborers at the Ordnance establishments."

sorghum in addition. I suppose that some provision has been made to supply . . . vegetables.[14]

Included in the combined procurement efforts for laborers at Macon was the problem of shoes.[15] The Quartermaster Department co-operated with Mallet in his efforts to get a supply of them, and its local representative in Macon agreed to exchange good footgear for bad at the ordnance establishments in the city.[16] Gorgas' concern about this matter had been so acute that he condoned the use of precious space on blockade-runners to bring in shoes for the workers.[17] Colonel Cuyler, of Macon Arsenal, had general charge of co-ordinating the feeding and clothing of government Negroes in that city.[18]

Although Gorgas and his field men made these sincere efforts to guarantee the relative well-being of the slaves who were impressed or hired, conditions were so unstable that their owners could never fully trust government or private plants working on military contracts. While Gorgas and most of his contractors tried honestly to treat slaves as well as the situation would permit, there were instances of laxity and misconduct. In March, 1863, for instance, the Shelby Iron Company had to mollify an irate slave-owner who was angered at the death of one of his hands working for the firm. He had lost faith in the Company's promises of good treatment, and wrote that, according to reports,

negroes are made to work in rain and snow and are under a "hard driver." . . . I have a perfect *horror* of a "hard driver." . . . I have learned that a "hard driver" is but another name for a *reckless—heartless—cruel wretch.* . . . I do not write in a querulous or fault-finding spirit but in the desire to [show] a sense of duty toward those who are dependent alone on me for their *condition* in *this* life.[19]

All things considered, however, the lot of the slave was probably better than that of the average white laborer in a government plant—

[14] Gorgas to Mallet, Richmond, July 22, 1864, CROB, XXXVII, 41. See also Mallet to Capt. McMain, Columbus, Ga., April 16, 1864, AGPF, Mallet; and Capt. James Ker to Burton, Macon, February 12, 1864, AGPF, Ker, for information on the purchase of shoes for Negro laborers.

[15] Mallet to Gorgas, Macon, January 11, 1864, CROB, XXIV, 588.

[16] Mallet to Capt. McMain, Columbus, Ga., April 16, 1864, AGPF, Mallet.

[17] Ker to Burton, Macon, February 12, 1864, AGPF, Ker; Mallet to Gorgas, Macon, January 11, 1864, CROB, XXIV, 588.

[18] CROB, XXIV, 588. Apparently the only serious objection to the shoes obtained for the colored workers was their hardness.

[19] George H. Harris to Andrew T. Jones, Columbus, Miss., March 3, 1863, quoted in Vandiver, "The Shelby Iron Company in the Civil War," *Alabama Review,* I (1948), 120.

and in some cases better than that of skilled workers. The slaves could look to the Army to provide them with some of the necessities of life, but the white workers could expect nothing more than fixed amounts of constantly depreciating currency. And there were different levels of inequality within the white worker group. On May 1, 1863, the Confederate Congress had declared that:

non-commissioned officers, musicians or privates, when employed on detached or detail service by a departmental or other commander of a district, or under the direction of any of the military bureaux, instead of the compensation now allowed, may be allowed the sum of not more than three dollars per day, in lieu of rations and all other allowances, upon the recommendation of the officer immediately in charge of such men, with the approval of the commander or chief of bureau, as the case may be, and the sanction of the Secretary of War.[20]

The fact that this law did not mention the Navy made for a great deal of trouble between the land and water branches of the service. This trouble had arisen earlier, but it continued to intensify. From the cities in which were located both Army and Navy establishments, Gorgas received indications of the growing antipathy. Actually there was little competition—the Army had nothing with which it could fight back. The Navy, untrammeled by blundering legislation, offered unlimited civilian wages to men detailed from either branch of the service to its field manufactories, and the officers in the Army installations watched in helpless rage. Complaints of this injustice came from Atlanta, Columbus, and Selma. In the last city, Colonel J. L. White, at the arsenal, stated the problem candidly and forcefully when he told Gorgas on October 12, 1863, that the congressional act was the more galling because "the men who did not wait to be conscripted, but volunteered for service in the Army, and who were detailed afterward for service *at the Arsenals*, were reduced to *three dollars* per day, as wages, while those employees at the Naval Foundries, Yards, &C are allowed unlimited wages." He observed that some of his men had asked to be transferred to the Navy, but he had steadfastly refused since to grant such requests would open the dikes to a mass job migration. On the other hand, some applied for return to their regiments, and these requests he could not deny, though he felt morally certain that some of

[20] "An Act to provide for the compensation of certain persons therein named," *Statutes at Large (Confederate)*, 1 Cong., Stat. III, Chap. LXXII.

the men obtained details to naval installations shortly after their return to the field.[21]

This complaint did not fall on deaf or untuned ears. Having considered this question for some time, Gorgas had already decided upon, and now broached to Seddon in a conference, the best course to pursue in obtaining a measure of relief. As far as he could see the only solution, at best only a partial one, would be for the Secretaries of War and Navy to issue a joint order requiring "consultation between the officers of their respective Depts. commanding establishments at the same post, before any advance in wages of the employees of either is made, and forbidding such advance except on mutual agreement between them."[22] Concurring in this view, Seddon applied for the approval of Mallory; but Gorgas had, as he feared, solved only a portion of his problem. Still another type of inequality existed—between the wages paid non-detail workers in the different plants doing the same tasks. The result, naturally, was a tendency on the part of those so discriminated against to wander to the greener pasture or to work in sullen silence.[23] Macon seemed to be the center around which general wage policies in the lower South revolved. Although certain scales might be established at other installations, Macon served as the testing ground. If these policies caused dissatisfaction there, then the chances were good that a similar reaction would be forthcoming from other places below Richmond. Consequently, when Burton wrote to Gorgas in March that mechanics and other workers were "generally . . . so much dissatisfied with the wages allowed them that it is impossible to get them to apply themselves to their work in anything like a satisfactory manner," the words carried the sting of reality.[24] Burton's letter had been preceded by another from him dated January 12, 1864, recalling a conversation with Gorgas in Richmond, during the course of which the Chief of Ordnance had promised that detailed mechanics would be put on an equal wage footing with civilians. That nothing was done to alleviate their hard lot, however, reacted unfavorably not only on Burton's armory but also on Mallet's laboratory. In February Mallet wrote that he had received a letter, signed by almost all the foremen and workmen in his employ, which set forth the difficulty

[21] White to Gorgas, Selma, October 12, 1863, CRLR, 1863, Doc. WWD 557. White asked for equality in all matters of wages and classes of employee compensation.   [22] Gorgas to Seddon, October 19, 1863, indorsement, *ibid.*
[23] Gorgas to Seddon, January 5, 1864, CRLR, 1864, Doc. GWD 82.
[24] Burton to Gorgas, Macon, March 8, 1864, CROB, XXXI, 287.

of living at the existing rate of pay. Noting that rising costs made this argument all the more valid, Mallet agreed they needed more money. Gorgas' permission to employ an agent to purchase food and fuel for them had produced little material return, and the new currency bill[25] appeared designed to reduce their income further. Mallet now wanted permission to raise wages substantially to tide the men over this crucial period. Burton, too, wanted authority to match the wages paid at Columbus and Augusta, and desired to raise the standard to a maximum of $7.00 per day for machinists, smiths, patternmakers, and moulders, and $6.00 per day for carpenters and brickmasons until the cost of living decreased.[26]

By May, 1864, the situation had deteriorated to such an extent that Burton expected trouble to break out among the workers at any moment. "At the present time," he wrote Gorgas, "much discontent prevails among them, and much time is being lost by them. If you can do anything to remove the difficulty I respectfully urge you to take action at once."[27]

Wrestling with the important task of finding adequate reservoirs of Negro labor, Gorgas came to the conclusion that he must decentralize authority to his field representatives to the extent of allowing them to secure this requisite themselves. But in the case of Macon, where so many important ordnance works were closely grouped, he directed a concerted effort. Maintaining that such had always been his policy on all important questions, Burton promised continued support and reported that he and Mallet were most in need of Negroes, since Cuyler had managed to supply himself rather well. "From present indications," Burton wrote Gorgas on April 2, "I am of the opinion that impressment will have to be resorted to" inasmuch as advertisements for slaves in the public press had failed.[28] Ten days later Mallet joined Burton in a plea to resort to impressment as the only means of securing labor. The two declared that they had made every reasonable effort

[25] This was "An Act to reduce the currency and to authorize a new issue of notes and bonds," approved February 17, 1864, *Statutes at Large (Confederate)*, 1 Cong., Stat. IV, Chap. LXIII. This law called for the funding of all treasury notes above the denomination of five dollars on or before April 1, 1864, in the Cis-Mississippi, and July 1 in the Trans-Mississippi areas. See also Ordnance Circular, Richmond, February 29, 1864, *Mississippi MSS.*, Ser. L, Vol. CXI.

[26] Mallet to Gorgas, Macon, February 18, 1864, CROB, XXIV, 712–13; Burton to Gorgas, Macon, March 8, 1864, *ibid.*, XXXI, 287.

[27] Burton to Gorgas, Macon, May 13, 1864, *ibid.*, p. 398.

[28] Burton to Gorgas, Macon, April 2, 1864, *ibid.*, p. 331.

to hire slaves, offering $25.00 per month, with rations, clothing, quarters, and medical attention, but had met with no success. Obviously disliking this expedient, they nevertheless felt compelled to request authority to requisition Negroes.[29]

Gorgas understood that he would have received no such request unless the situation absolutely demanded it, and he acted accordingly. On May 27 Special Orders Number 51 authorized Mallet and Burton to impress laborers for their establishments. Gorgas expected that Confederate military commanders in Georgia would help them find the men, but in this hope he was disappointed. Major General Samuel Jones, to whom they applied for aid, asserted that with the power of their orders Mallet and Burton were just as able to secure workers as he.[30] Not to be dismayed, Mallet tried to obtain the services of free Negroes subject to conscription in Augusta and Savannah, but with indifferent results.[31]

The growing seriousness of Joe Johnston's military situation also added to Mallet's and Burton's troubles. The Army of Tennessee had retreated from the lines around Dalton to positions at Smyrna Station, and on July 5 had been flanked out of these and had taken up the defense lines surrounding Atlanta. Negroes were urgently needed for duty on the entrenchments, and post commanders ruthlessly carried out instructions to impress a third of the number working in the armories and laboratories. Gorgas undoubtedly paled at Burton's news that the orders for the impressment of the Macon slaves came from post commander Colonel D. Wyatt Aiken, Gorgas' brother-in-law. Under these instructions, Burton wrote,

an armed guard in charge of a commissioned officer, visited this Armory and took away by force twenty three (23) negroes in the regular employ of the Armory—laborers and mechanics—This was done *without my knowledge or authority.—After the seizure had been made* the officer making it called upon me and exhibited his instructions . . . and they instructed the officer to seize one third of the negroes employed at this Armory, and at the C. S. Central Laboratories in Macon, regardless of the remonstrances of myself and the Comdg. officer of the Laboratories.

Aiken, who had orders not to impress government Negroes, but to take only those in private employ, disregarded his instructions and took them

[29] Burton and Mallet to Gorgas, Macon, April 12, 1864, CROB, XXIV, 799.
[30] Burton to Gorgas, Macon, June 24, 1864, CROB, XXXI, 460; Burton to Gen. Sam Jones, Macon, June 16, 1864, *ibid.*, p. 444.
[31] Mallet to McMain, Dalton, Ga., May 6, 1864, AGPF, Mallet.

anyway. But his ultimate purpose was foiled, for Burton and Mallet, able to report serious interruption of work at their plants, secured authority from General Marcus J. Wright, commanding the Post of Atlanta, to have the slaves returned on July 2.[32] Still, Gorgas could not escape the import of such actions to the efficiency of his bureau.

As the military situation at Atlanta grew more critical, conditions in the ordnance establishments in the Deep South grew proportionately more confused. Overworked, and continually charged with supplying the Army of Tennessee (since July 18 under John B. Hood's command), these plants sustained a shock of such magnitude as to beggar imagination. In the chaos attending Hood's retreat from Atlanta in the first days of September, a train of reserve ammunition of the Army of Tennessee had to be burned.[33] The Ordnance Bureau had made supreme efforts to provide this train in the first place, and now to have to replace it strained Augusta and Macon Arsenals to the limit—particularly so since Atlanta Arsenal was no more. But under the able and calm guidance of Rains, women toiled doggedly at Augusta Arsenal and at Summerville to make 75,000 cartridges a day for Hood. The heroic work of these Georgia ladies had, perhaps, more immediate effect in steadying the resistance of Hood's army than any other single factor.[34]

Mallet, whose responsibility it was to see that usable ammunition got to the armies in quantity and on time, grew panicky at the loss of this ammunition. He telegraphed Gorgas: "Gen. Hood has blown up his reserve ordnance train. Can any cartridges of calibre fifty-four and fifty-eight or rifle shell—three inch, ten pounder Parrott, and two and a half inch Blakely be had from North of Augusta?"[35] Gorgas, who knew the over-all situation, injected a less hysterical note into the correspondence when he telegraphed Colonel James M. Kennard, now chief ordnance officer of the Army of Tennessee, that he would send supplies to Selma as desired by General Hood, if Kennard would say just what was needed.[36] Gorgas took other quick and sure measures to meet the Army's wants. He directed Kennard to call on the Georgia state reserves, who could be resupplied by Macon Arsenal and elsewhere. He reported that

[32] Burton to Gorgas, Macon, July 1, 4, 1864, CROB, XXXI, 471, 476.
[33] GCWD, September 12, 1864, p. 140; Stanley F. Horn, *The Army of Tennessee* (Indianapolis, 1941), p. 366.
[34] Rains, *Confederate Powder Works*, p. 29.
[35] Mallet to Gorgas, Macon, September 5, 1864, AGPF, Mallet; also in CROB, XXIX, 36–37. There are slight textual differences in the two versions.
[36] Gorgas to Kennard, Richmond, September 26, 1864, *Mississippi MSS.*, Ser. E, Vol. LXIV.

saddles were on the way from Mount Vernon Arsenal as well as from Richmond.[37] Colonel Oladowski, now at the arsenal in Columbus, Georgia, reported that he had no arms which could be issued to Kennard at once, but that Gorgas could authorize the issuance of 600 rifles in Columbia and that Captain W. D. Humphries had 2,000 arms to send. He would send accouterments as soon as possible.[38]

General Rains, at the Augusta Powder Works, carried the major load of replenishing Hood's ordnance stores; and he executed his task in spite of adverse conditions and external irritations. To Kennard, a man to whom he obviously could speak freely, he explained that he had shipped ordnance stores to Selma on September 26, as requested—4,000 rounds of fixed ammunition, mainly for 12-pounder Napoleons, and 500,000 rounds of small-arms cartridges of .57 and .54 caliber. This consumed all of his present stock, "the ammunition as fast as made having been shipped to Macon for some time past." He estimated that 350,000 small-arms bullets and 1,200 rounds of fixed ammunition could be made at Augusta per week, and he thought that if coal and iron could be procured in sufficient quantities, the quota of fixed ammunition could be doubled. If it became absolutely necessary, he said, the amount of small-arms cartridges produced could be raised to 400,000 per week, contingent on the steady work of his employees. This point was the thorn in Rains's side. He wrote Kennard principally to call his attention to the manner in which laborers were being taken from the Augusta works. "A little while since," Rains said, "all the works here were stopped for some days, the employees having been ordered off to reinforce Gen. Hardee at the fight at Jonesboro; nearly or quite one third of the working time at the different works is consumed in details for local guard duty; such as guarding prisoners, supplying escorts for do.; guarding public property at different points and drills." On September 27 Rains noted:

A considerable number of my bullet moulders were taken off suddenly without my knowledge by the Enrolling Officer, thus suddenly reducing the amount of small arm cartridges made to about one half; these men were sent to the Camp of Instruction. Col. Brown in charge of Conscription, who knew nothing of the matter, has ordered them to be sent back, but this does not prevent the loss of time experienced. My principal agent attending to the transportation of wood for the Steam Engine &c for the powder works, has been taken from the works to do duty with a local

---

[37] Gorgas to Kennard (telegram), Richmond, September 22, 23, 1864, *ibid.*
[38] Oladowski to Kennard (telegram), Columbus, September 22, 1864, *ibid.*

company here, so that these works are liable to be stopped for want of wood on any day, and as the supply for all the Arsenals depends on the powder daily made at the works, such interruptions are likely to be disastrous. I write you these facts in order that General Hood may see to what interruptions I am liable to continually in preparing supplies, and hence cannot certainly say as to the amount of stores I can send him but presume it will be as above stated. I think it would be well for the General to give directions that the employees of the *Small Arm Cartridge Laboratory* (but few able bodied men are employed in the Powder Works at this place) should be exempted from the local duties, or in other words that they should remain under my control at all times. I think this very important for the public interests.[39]

Kennard must have been perturbed at the thought that Rains was irritated and uncertain that he could carry out his assignment, for the output of all the Augusta plants, excepting the Powder Works, would go to the Army of Tennessee.

Rains, of course, did not suffer alone. Burton and Mallet were sharing equally in the loss of workers. General Hood, whose appreciation of the need for a staff behind the lines left something to be desired, on August 3 ordered that Burton "send at once all the negroes you may have employed in any capacity upon public buildings to the front."[40] After Burton had complied with this order, he had to report to Gorgas that as a result brickmaking had been stopped completely. He added, with understandable ire, that the loss of the Negroes hurt the more because he had had such trouble collecting them.[41]

In doing all he could to see that Hood got sufficient supplies, Gorgas hoped to get swift and effective co-operation from every arsenal in the South. Richmond Arsenal and other ordnance plants in that vicinity could not be expected to extend very substantial aid to any force other than Lee's army. Gorgas, who hated to refuse any requisition coming to his office, on September 2 had to inform General Samuel Jones, commanding at Charleston, that

the demand upon the arsenals in this vicinity caused by the presence of the army, precludes almost the possibility of being able to supply calls from

[39] Rains to Kennard, Augusta, September 27, 1864, *ibid.*, Ser. L, Vol. CXI.
[40] In Burton to Gorgas, Macon, August 3, 1864, CROB, XXXI, 520.
[41] *Ibid.* As one means of circumventing this trouble with Negroes, Burton suggested the employment of day laborers. Burton to Gorgas, Macon, August 24, 1864, *ibid.*, p. 540. Mallet and Cuyler had been ordered on August 1 to send their Negroes to John B. Hood. Hood claimed his authority emanated from General Bragg. Hood to Cuyler and Mallet (telegram), Atlanta, August 1, 1864, ORA, Ser. I, Vol. XXXVIII, Pt. V, 939.

Charleston for material needed. The arsenals in the Department of South Carolina, Georgia, and Florida must be relied upon for the supplies required, and to this end calls should be made upon the different establishments south. After supplying the wants of the army here assistance will be rendered to the extent possible.[42]

Pressure from Lee's army on the Richmond installations only intensified Gorgas' policy of decentralization. This situation proved the wisdom of his circular of March 31, 1863, directing that each army should call upon the ordnance plants closest to it for supplies. Now military conditions were such as to preclude the possibility of operation under any other plan, particularly since Sherman had taken Atlanta.

Hood, a dashing fighter with grandiose ideas, by mid-September had definitely committed himself and his army to attacking Sherman's line of communications. His position at Palmetto, Georgia, placed him in range of supplies from all parts of the lower South, and these he proceeded to demand. The railroad from Montgomery through Opelika, LaGrange, and Palmetto, connecting with Columbus, and tortuously with Macon, gave him promise of adequate stores. The Selma Arsenal was not in direct railroad contact with his force, there being no track between Selma and Montgomery. But Selma's location on the Meridian to Blue Mountain road made it strategically valuable. If Hood continued his campaign along Sherman's line of march from Chattanooga and Dalton, material from Selma would be needed badly and could be transported from Blue Mountain by wagon trains.

While refitting and resting his troops at Palmetto, Hood determined to secure all the arms and ammunition he could collect before starting his expedition. Having already directed that Hood could take the arms of the Georgia state reserves, Gorgas felt that these were the most readily available source of supply,[43] but he found that this opinion was mistaken. Colonel Cuyler, at Macon, had to telegraph Colonel Kennard

[42] De Lagnel to Capt. Feilden, Richmond, ORA, Ser. I, Vol. XXXV, Pt. II, 620. On August 31 Gorgas had asked Maj. N. R. Chambliss, at Charleston Arsenal, to aid Hood as much as possible. See *Mississippi MSS.,* Ser. L, Vol. CXI.

[43] On September 21, 1864, de Lagnel wrote Kennard that his suggestion regarding arms of the Georgia reserves was approved, and he was authorized to "see General Hood & impress upon him the necessity of securing some of the Enfield and other first class arms—from the Georgia reserves; & arming the returning soldiers. The reserves when called again can be supplied from the arms being now cleaned. Every exertion will be made to assist you, but the drain is simultaneous and difficult to meet." *Mississippi MSS.,* Ser. L, Vol. CXI. Cuyler first asked Governor Brown for the arms on the 27th. Cuyler to Brown (telegram), Macon, September 27, 1864, CROB, CI, 363.

on September 28, that Georgia's Governor Brown, pursuing his usual selfish policy, refused to part with any of the arms. Kennard, who did not appreciate the delicate nature of Confederate relations with Georgia, urged that Cuyler seize the guns peremptorily. Cuyler hastily declined to do so, realizing that such an act might well precipitate disaster.[44] Not wishing to appear as though he were doing nothing at all to help Hood, Cuyler on the twenty-eighth decided to query Brown again on the subject of the militia arms. Again he met with rebuff. Brown simply would not be persuaded that these arms were of vital importance to the defense of Georgia.[45] He clung tenaciously to his defense of state rights, despite the emergency. Disgruntled at Davis' administration, he could see no reason for co-operation.

Cuyler appealed to Gorgas for orders and informed the Chief of Ordnance that the arms were stored in Macon Arsenal for safekeeping.[46] Confederate authorities who wanted to impress the arms met with stony refusal by Georgia officials, and finally the matter reached the courts. By October 1, the day the case came up, Hood was preparing to move into line of battle a few miles west of Marietta, Georgia, and by the fourth Stewart's Corps had captured the Federal garrison at Acworth and Big Shanty. In the face of battle and orders from Hood, General Howell Cobb, commanding the Georgia reserves, contrived a deal with the Governor whereby the arms would be given to Kennard if, and only if, they would be returned when the militia was again called to duty.[47]

The altercation with Governor Brown had been going on in the midst of hurried efforts to provide Hood with ammunition and other material. This huge effort was not devoid of fortuitous circumstances. On September 28 General R. C. Tyler, at West Point, Georgia, reported to Hood that he had just discovered 400,000 percussion caps and would hold them for Kennard.[48]

---

[44] See Cuyler to Kennard (telegram), Macon, September 28, 1864, *Mississippi MSS.*, Ser. E, Vol. LXIV. Cuyler said: "Gov. Brown will not give up the Arms—I cannot undertake to take them as you request." On the same day Cuyler wrote Kennard, attempting to explain: "Your telegram recd. Gov. Brown has refused to give up the Arms. I must have high authority before I conflict with him. If Col. Gorgas, my immediate superior or the President order me I will take them. Have telegraphed Col. Gorgas." *Ibid.* Cuyler's copies of these dispatches are in CROB, Vol. CI.

[45] Cuyler to Brown (telegram), Macon, September 28, 1864, CROB, CI, 368.

[46] Cuyler to Gorgas (telegram), Macon, September 28, 1864, *ibid.*, p. 367.

[47] *Ibid.;* also Cuyler to Gorgas (telegram), Macon, October 3, 1864, *ibid.*, p. 369.

[48] Tyler to Hood (telegram), West Point, September 28, 1864, *Mississippi MSS.*, Ser. E, Vol. LXIV.

On the other hand, the situation was not without its moments of agonizing conflict of authority and activity. Hood's supply officers were all desperately trying to get their respective needs moved up as quickly as possible, and, as usual, the Commissary Department seemed to get the first chance at railroad cars. Ordnance officers at Macon and Columbus had to delay sending urgent freight until the Commissary officials released some transportation.[49] Only one carload of ammunition could leave Columbus for Hood's army on September 28, and Captain W. D. Humphries, ordnance officer at Hood's intermediate base, West Point, confessed that he had no ammunition to send, though he could forward arms and accouterments.[50] Humphries probably counted on the arrival of 1,000 Enfield rifles and 1,500 accouterments from Columbia to make good his promise. On September 28 Major J. T. Trezevant, commanding Columbia Arsenal, had been directed by Gorgas to ship supplies to Humphries.[51]

Probably unaware of the hard work being done by Gorgas' organization to anticipate his wants, Hood must, nevertheless, have realized that a miracle had been performed. Keeping track of the supply of small arms and ammunition for Hood, Mallet on August 26 had frantically called for percussion caps.[52] His plea brought the immediate dispatch of 1,000,000 caps from Richmond and of another 1,000,000 from Danville.[53] These, combined with the extra 400,000 discovered by General Tyler, provided a comforting number with which to start a campaign.

When one considers the general chaos prevailing throughout the supply organization, the job done in keeping Hood supplied is seen to rank as an accomplishment worthy of Carnot. The opposition of citizens in North Carolina hampered the commanding officer of the Salisbury laboratory in getting walnut for gunstocks, since the main source of this timber lay in an area populated by disaffected persons; as a consequence, millowners were loath to undertake government work[54]—

---

[49] Cuyler to Capt. W. D. Humphries (telegram), Macon, September 28, 1864, ibid.   [50] Humphries to Kennard, West Point, September 28, 1864, ibid.

[51] Trezevant to Kennard (telegram), Columbia, September 28, 1864, ibid.

[52] Mallet to Gorgas (telegram), Macon, CROB, LII, 20. Mallet had almost completed a cap factory at Macon.

[53] Broun to Mallet (telegram), Richmond, August 26, 1864, CROB, XXXVII, 97.

[54] Burton to Gorgas, Macon, August 12, 1864, CROB, XXXI, 528. Salisbury laboratory and the foundry and blacksmith shops there were designated "Salisbury Arsenal" on August 29, 1864. See General Orders Number 70, Adj. & Insp. Gen.'s Off., Richmond, August 29, 1864, ORA, Ser. IV, Vol. III, 609.

another example of the myriad problems which had to be faced. Shortages of lead and copper also were embarrassing, and on September 12,
1864, Mallet had to telegraph Gorgas that Rains had only five weeks'
supply of lead for himself—yet all the southern arsenals depended upon
him for that commodity.[55] On the fifteenth Mallet wrote that the supply of sheet copper for the cap factory had dwindled sharply and would
soon be exhausted. He wanted the Chief of Ordnance to order some
from Bermuda or Nassau at once, "or, if new sheet copper cannot be
had . . . [request] you will direct some of the material procured from
turpentine stills taken down this summer in N. Carolina to be sent to
me. It would save transportation to cut the stills up before shipping."[56]

The failure of the government to meet some of its financial obliga-
tions also contributed to making Gorgas' task superhuman. During July
and August, 1864, nothing had been paid for work done by the Cook
& Brothers Armory in Athens, Georgia. As a consequence, this model
private armory had to cease operations. Thomas W. Cook, one of the
proprietors, had become worried about its position and wanted the government to buy the whole installation. He claimed that the firm was
indebted to the Confederacy in the amount of $250,000, but that the
machinery and buildings were worth much more than that. Favorably
impressed with the plant on an inspection tour in April, 1864, Burton
recommended its purchase. He greatly regretted that the Cooks had
had to give up their enterprise.[57] The closing down of Cook & Brothers constituted a loss that the Ordnance Bureau could ill afford but
could not prevent.

The manpower problem had also continued to grow worse, with increasingly stringent detail regulations appearing. This problem kept
pace with the equally serious one of food. Gorgas had to establish a
strict rationing system for arsenals to husband what little food became
available,[58] and Burton began to speculate on the possibility of using

[55] Mallet to Gorgas, Macon, September 12, 1864, CROB, LII, 23.

[56] Mallet to Gorgas, Macon, September 15, 1864, AGPF, Mallet. Gorgas referred this letter to Broun for his attention on the twenty-second. That same
day Broun reported it back with the indorsement: "We have no copper to send
to Macon. I bought in N. Carolina about 130,000 lbs. old stills &c—of which
27,500 lbs. have been received here—am now making efforts to have the rest
transported—Col. Mallet can purchase stills in Southern portion of N. C. @
$2.50 pr lb." Gorgas promised Mallet that he would order sheet copper, but
called his attention to Broun's remark about purchasing. *Ibid.*

[57] Burton to Gorgas, Macon, September 27, 1864, CROB, XXIX, 69.

[58] Ordnance Circular Number 71, September 28, 1864, CROB, XXXVII, 233,
directed that all men not *"indispensably necessary"* in ordnance plants be turned

Federal deserters in his plant. "There may be some mechanics," he wrote Colonel Wright, the post commander of Macon, "among the Federal deserters in your charge, and who would be glad of employment. I have no objection to employing such of them as are *foreigners,* and if you will send me by bearer the necessary order in writing, I will send my Master Carpenter to the camp to make a selection."[59]

All of these makeshifts managed, somehow, to do the job for which they were devised, albeit with something less than efficiency. But nevertheless, the job was done so well that Colonel Cuyler could tell Kennard on October 7 that although frightened by the size of Kennard's needs, "I can help you very considerably." He could supply large quantities of .57 and .58 caliber small-arms cartridges; haversacks; canteens; artillery harness; 10-pounder Parrott, 3-inch rifle, and 12-pounder Napoleon shells; artillery implements and equipments. He could furnish, but not quite so abundantly, cartridges for Colt Army and Navy pistols; horseshoes and nails (the supply of iron was running low); cavalry equipments (it was hard to get saddle trees quickly); and infantry accouterments (the proper sort of leather was short).[60]

The presence of Sherman in Georgia created additional difficulties for Gorgas and his field administrators. They had not only to attend to the needs of Hood, Charleston, Savannah, Mobile, and the local units in the Deep South, but now also to safeguard the plants against possible enemy raids. Concerned about the safety of the stock machinery at Macon, Burton had several large flatboats constructed, sixty feet long and fourteen feet wide, to transport the machines down the Ocmulgee River to some safer place. After building the barges, he asked Gorgas' approval of the plan, which he did not get. Gorgas thought it better to move the machinery to Columbia, South Carolina, and Burton hastily accepted this scheme in place of his own—even rationalizing that Columbia offered advantages. An engine already there, he reasoned, would give sufficient power to operate the machinery, in addition to that already emplaced, and that location would be much more

over to enrolling officers; Burton to Gorgas, Macon, October 5, 1864, *ibid.,* XXIX, 81, stated that the above circular had been received and that all of his men were essential. For rationing, see Ordnance Circular Number 74, October 13, 1864, *ibid.,* XLVII, 309.

[59] Burton to Wright, Macon, September 30, 1864, *ibid.,* XXIX, 75.

[60] Cuyler to Kennard, Macon, October 7, 1864, *Mississippi MSS.,* Ser. L, Vol. CXI.

economical in transportation costs. It seemed all the better, too, since rough-hewn stocks could be procured in the vicinity.[61]

Conditions were so confused, following Hood's withdrawal from Atlanta, that the ordnance officers in Macon and environs were unaware of exactly what was happening. Burton, who had seen a telegram from Gorgas to Cuyler concerning the removal of surplus stores, had wanted to send the stock machinery first to Savannah, along with the pistol machinery. Although later dissuaded by Gorgas, he had prepared everything for this move and was awaiting word from Cuyler, who had gone to see Hood about the prospect for the immediate future.[62] Such a state of disorganization prevailed that a conflict of instructions resulted. Although Gorgas expressly directed that the stock machinery should go not to Savannah but to Columbia, he did order "all surplus, spare machinery & tools not required for immediate use" at Macon Armory to be sent to Savannah.[63] Gorgas simply did not trust the ultimate safety of Savannah enough to send the vital stock machinery there. Then, too, he knew it could be set up and used at Columbia, but not at Savannah.[64] He did not want to interfere with the operation of the pistol factory at Macon, which had but recently resumed work,[65] unless it became necessary for the safety of the plant. On the other hand, he did want to

secure those parts and pieces of machinery which have been constructed with reference to future wants of the Macon Armory, and to this end direct . . . that you box, & prepare it for instant shipment—to Columbia,

[61] Burton to Gorgas, Macon, August 29, September 10, 1864, CROB, XXIX, 27, 41.   [62] Burton to Gorgas, Macon, September 5, 1864, *ibid.*, pp. 36–37.
[63] Burton to Gorgas, Macon, October 6, 1864, *ibid.*, p. 88; de Lagnel to Mallet, Richmond, September 27, 1864, *ibid.*, XXXVII, 226.
[64] Because of a scarcity of transportation Burton had not been able to ship anything to Savannah as late as October 20. Burton to Gorgas, Macon, October 20, 1864, *ibid.*, XXIX, 110.
[65] On October 5 Burton telegraphed Gorgas that Col. Cuyler had no more arms for the armory hands to repair and asked if he ought to unpack the pistol machinery and put it into production in order to give the men something to do. Burton to Gorgas, Macon, October 5, 1864, *ibid.*, p. 85. The same day Gorgas replied by telegraph: "Put your pistol factory in operation & push the works." AGPF, Burton. On October 13 Burton reported the factory back in operation. Burton to Gorgas, Macon, CROB, XXIX, 101. On September 7 Burton had replied to a query of Gorgas' about the cost of pistol manufacture to the effect that the total cost of making a revolver at Macon Armory was $62.21. This included $8.00 interest on capital invested, $200,000 at 8 per cent. The material cost was $19.59 and the labor and supervision was $34.62. Burton to Gorgas, Macon, *ibid.*, p. 38.

S. C., whenever the emergency demanding it arises. Should you receive peremptory orders to remove, obey the order and report at once by telegraph. If the order is only advisory, then communicate promptly, with this office, by telegraph.[66]

The emergency of the situation changed the prevailing policy toward the machinery for Macon Armory which had begun to arrive from abroad. Louis Heyliger at Nassau announced on August 22 that the "first lot of machinery" for Burton had been shipped on board the "Hope." On September 13, Lieutenant John M. Payne at Wilmington, wrote Burton that Gorgas' assistant, Colonel Julius A. de Lagnel, had instructed him to "send the 25 cases machinery marked *BURTON,* lately arrived by the 'Hope' to *Columbia* for storage."[67] Things were now so unpredictable that Colonel Mallet urged the cancellation of Huse's arrangements with Greenwood and Batley for supplying laboratory machinery. Gorgas approved, and on September 28 de Lagnel wrote Mallet: "By direction of Colonel Gorgas—I have already written to Major Caleb Huse—directing him, if possible, to procure a release from his engagement with Messrs Greenwood and Batley;—and as an alternative to dispose of the engines. The Colonel does not contemplate, for the present at least, purchasing the engine abroad."[68]

The incredibly heavy load put upon the Ordnance Bureau by events in the Deep South had proved that Gorgas, working alone, could not cope with everything coming to his office. He had to reorganize his staff in such a way as to shift a portion of the burden, as he had done in the cases of blockade-running and niter and mining. In late August he issued a circular directing that thereafter de Lagnel be "specially charged with the conduct of the Arsenals, Armories and Depots with supplies of Ordnance & Ordnance Stores to troops in the field, with the details of enrolled and enlisted men in the Ordnance Dept. and with the general supervision of the business of this Office." Two other trusted assistants, Major E. B. Smith and Captain R. H. Glenn, Gorgas "charged with the revision of estimates from Ord Officers, the application of the appropriations of the Ordnance Bureau, the examination of all contracts—the disbursements connected with the office, the examination of property & cash accounts & of all stated returns."[69]

[66] De Lagnel to Burton, Richmond, September 30, 1864, AGPF, Burton.
[67] Payne to Burton, Wilmington, Burton.
[68] De Lagnel to Mallet, Richmond, CROB, XXXVII, 231.
[69] Circular Number 60, no date, 1864, *ibid.*, 219. Circular Number 59 is dated August 15, 1864.

Gorgas trimmed his own task down to that of general supervisor over everything dealing with ordnance in the Confederacy. He made further shifts in his field personnel, delegating wide authority to Colonel M. H. Wright, who on August 4 was given temporary charge of all the government establishments in Macon, apparently to the discomfiture of Cuyler.[70]

In field administration of ordnance affairs in the Trans-Mississippi Department Gorgas had little knowledge and less authority, having delegated all of his rights and privileges to General Huger in 1863. This, of course, did not preclude his continued active interest in matters there but did relieve him of strain.

Conditions had so changed by late 1864 that Lee's admonition to Davis about enlarging interior arsenals had lost its significance. Now the safest arsenals and ordnance plants in the Confederacy were those in the vicinity of Richmond, protected by Lee's army. These, and not those in the interior, had become the mainstays of the Ordnance Bureau.

[70] See Capt. Ker to Capt. Richard Lambert, Richmond, August 22, 1864, AGPF, Ker. Ker wrote: "How does the Col. [Cuyler] like Wright's commanding all the government establishments? Not much I guess." Wright left on August 19 to command Columbus, Ga., Arsenal. Gorgas had assigned him to Macon to handle efforts to supply Hood. See CROB, CI, 309.

XVIII

Success Beyond Expectation

FIELD ADMINISTRATION, HOWEVER, WAS FAR FROM BEING THE ONLY thing that had occupied Gorgas' attention during the year 1864. Military possibilities had seemed brighter when the year opened, and Gorgas estimated that while Lee's army counted only 30,000 muskets in January, the number could be swelled to 80,000 by the troops under Longstreet, General Sam Jones in West Virginia, and the troops in and around Petersburg. Still the social life in Richmond continued gay. The craze for charades continued, and Gorgas attended some parties with his customary reluctance and lack of appreciation. His social contacts, moreover, were spoiled for him by Amelia's confining illness. She had not been able to leave her bedroom during the holidays but seemed somewhat improved in January.[1]

Colonel Gorgas took more than casual interest in the proceedings of Congress and earnestly hoped it would push through some sort of currency bill which would reduce the inflation eating at the vitals of the Confederacy's economic structure. He seemed apprehensive of a tendency toward a swing of the pendulum, and a growing "disposition to sacrifice everything to putting men in the field at the expense of the industrial interests."[2] He observed this tendency to a marked degree in the Senate, where probably under Seddon's influence there was an increasing propensity to

drive the enginery of war under too great pressure. A Bill has passed it to place in the Military Service, for details, all men between 45 and 55. This is unnecessary. In such a war as this—a war for national existence—the whole mass of the nation must be engaged. It must be divided into

---

[1] GCWD, January 10, 1864, p. 75.
[2] GCWD, January 17, 21, 1864, pp. 76, 77.

those who go to the field and fight, and those who stay at home to support the fighting portion—supplying all the food, and material of war. Between the age of eighteen and forty-five has been fixed on for the fighting population—the rest must be devoted to agriculture, arts, mines, and manufactures. It is simply absurd to call on all to fight. Some must labor or all will starve. There is much crude legislation going on, but we shall work thro' this revolution with some blunders.[3]

This, indeed, was a broad-minded view for a professional soldier.

Finances, of course, remained one of the prime concerns of the Chief of Ordnance. From all parts of the Confederacy came new estimates for funds needed during the first quarter of 1864. Macon set the pace by requesting $204,000, an increase of $13,500 over the last quarter.[4] More funds were needed everywhere. The Tredegar Iron Works felt that an additional allowance of 16.36 per cent on contracts should be made to them in order to keep them in line with prices paid to other contractors. Gorgas disagreed, holding that recent nation-wide increases in prices paid for products more than compensated them.[5] But they were only one voice among a multitude. The scarcity of money gave rise to a grotesque situation in one of the Richmond ordnance shops. The Old Dominion Iron and Nail Works, located on Belle Isle, fell victim to a practice which could have developed only in the face of depreciated currency. Placed on the island, along with the Iron Works, was a Federal prisoner of war depot which had first been established there after the battle of Chancellorsville. The management of the Iron Works had all along feared that the presence of Federal prisoners on the island would impair the efficiency of work done in the plant, but the War Department had answered these protests with platitudes. After trying unsuccessfully to cope with the situation, the agent of the iron works, R. E. Blankenship, penned a letter to Seddon on January 13, 1864, explaining why it had been virtually impossible to get any work done on the island for some time.

---

[3] GCWD, January 31, 1864, pp. 77–78. The bill to which Gorgas referred was "an Act to organize forces to serve during the war," and directed the enrollment of men between the ages of 17 and 18 and 45 and 50 for reserve forces. The President was given authority to detail men to the various bureaus. *Statutes at Large (Confederate)*, 1 Cong., Stat. IV, Chap. LXV.

[4] Burton to Gorgas, Macon, October 5, 1863, January 13, 1864, CROB, XXXI, 105, 188.

[5] J. R. Anderson and Company to the Secretaries of War and Navy, Richmond, October 13, 1863, CRLR, 1863, Doc. AWD 347.

As soon as it became known that the Yankees were on the Island, the employees in the Iron & Nail works immediately neglected their labour and began a system of trading with the prisoners for whiskey, tobacco, Bread &c &c in exchange for their clothing & Greenbacks by which several of our hands have amassed several thousand dollars apiece and all of them money enough to make manual labor irksome. . . . This mania for trading is not confined to a few but is engaged in by every man, woman & child on the Island with the solitary exception of the Superintendent of the Works. And it is also true that the guard from the City Battalion, which is brot from Richmond every day, are the great promoters and abettors of the traffic between workmen and prisoners. Only last week two of our hands and one of the guard were arrested in the act of furnishing whiskey to the Camp and all sent to Castle Thunder, and the operation of two puddling furnaces, out of six, stopped thusly.

The Iron Works on Belle Isle have been diligently working for the various departments of Government since the breaking out of the War, and they contributed as much to the success of our Armies as any in the Country. All of the Nails, Sheet Iron for Sword cases, Hospital uses and other purposes, Shovel plates, Tacks, and nearly all the Boiler plates are made there and it is a plain question . . . whether this establishment with all its various resources is of more value to you than the simple occupation of the Island as a prison post? If in your judgment it is proper to remove the prisoners the evil will be eradicated at once, but if you can not do this, the construction of a high fence around the Camp so as to make communication difficult . . . will in some degree mitigate it and force the Hands to Work in order to support themselves and families.[6]

The Secretary of War sent this communication to the heads of bureaus for their reaction. St. John, who confessed that his bureau relied on the Old Dominion plant for rolled iron for entrenching tools, sword scabbards, and horseshoe iron, recommended that prompt action be taken to correct the evils about which Blankenship complained. On the same day, January 14, Quartermaster General Alexander R. Lawton indorsed the letter, saying, "the scarcity of nails & horse shoes is becoming an alarming feature in our condition; and too much importance cannot be attached to the preservation of the few mills & shops that remain to us." Next, Gorgas, who also indorsed on the 14th, wrote, "the representation of this necessary establishment is respectfully commended to the attention of Secy of War." The Engineer Bureau indorsed in stronger terms and added that "Col. St. John informs . . . that we will

[6] Blankenship to Seddon, and indorsements, Richmond, *ibid.*, Doc. BWD 94.

have to rely upon the Old Dominion . . . Works for the necessary supply
of iron plates. This communication is therefore earnestly commended to
Hon. Sec. of War." The Navy's Engineer-in-Chief also heartily con-
curred in these views and recommended in his indorsement that the
Works "should be rendered as efficient as possible, by any means within
the control of the Govt." Seddon's own indorsement was succinct, to
the point, and so like him: *"File."* He might do something later.

Faced with dwindling funds and lack of most everyday needs,[7]
Gorgas changed his plan of operations. Keeping in mind the factor of
security, he decided to try making various ordnance plants into specialized centers of manufacture. He told Rains that he wanted to "establish specialities in some things for the diff[eren]t posts . . . hoping by this
means to improve the quality, & economize the cost." He wanted to
make Richmond and Atlanta centers for the manufacture of percussion
caps, Richmond and Charleston centers for the fabrication of friction
primers, Richmond and Macon centers for field fuses.[8] In adopting this
point of view, he accepted the long-held ideas of Mallet, who had long
been pushing the need for uniformity in manufacture. As early as
October, 1863, Mallet had urged that some sort of standard be established among the arsenals, and said that he constantly endeavored
"to promote such uniformity—its want, as I have said . . . *is the great
evil* of our Ordnance work." With this in mind, Mallet proposed the
interchange of samples of laboratory products between arsenals, thinking that he was carrying out Gorgas' oft-expressed maxim that "the
true way is to hold up *one method* to all and get them to conform to
it."[9] He was right, of course, but Gorgas had to veto the plan inasmuch
as conditions in different portions of the Confederacy were so disparate
at to render such a policy useless. Nevertheless, Gorgas continued to

[7] Many letters could be cited to illustrate this point. See, for example, Mallet
to Gorgas, Macon, February 6, 1864, CROB, XXIV, 655, saying that little gum
arabic was on hand, but proposing the substitution of flour paste in its stead.
"If we should need gum arabic at any time we can easily prepare *dextrine* from
starch—the universal substitute for gum on the large scale in Europe. We do
however much need isinglass or fine white glue for the cases of fuzes, and I respectfully request that an order be sent out for 200 or 300 lbs. of it as soon as
possible."

[8] Gorgas to Rains, Richmond, February 28 [1864], photostatic copy in *Ramsdell Note Files*. It seems reasonable to assume that Gorgas accepted the necessity of having at least two centers for the manufacture of ordnance stores in
view of the condition of transportation and of the demanding needs of the Army
of Northern Virginia.

[9] Mallet to Gorgas, Macon, October 31, December 5, 1863, CROB, XXIV,
427, 517.

push his plans for specialized installations. Mallet saw the dangers inherent in the scheme: it would be necessary to have the new centers of production in operation before any of the "work of other establishments is curtailed." Then, too, "there is of course the risk . . . of the loss of places thus designated for special work by the progress of the enemy's invasion." On the credit side of the ledger, Mallet agreed wholeheartedly with Gorgas that "the policy of such an arrangement is unquestionable so far as efficiency and economy are concerned."[10] Under the watchful eye of Mallet, Gorgas went ahead with his plan and especially directed the stabilization of ammunition manufacture. He ordered that once the process of ammunition fabrication was established, it was not to be changed without his authority, which would be transmitted through Mallet. He hoped this new departure would eliminate ammunition requiring constant inspection and would promote the making of regulation calibers.[11]

Production figures on iron made east of the Mississippi River for the first quarter of 1864 were not encouraging. The combined production of Virginia, North Carolina, Tennessee, Alabama, and Mississippi for that period amounted to 1,771 tons of pig iron; 142 tons of blooms, and 61 tons of hammered iron. This indicated a decline in output from the last quarter of 1863, when the respective amounts had been, 3,702, 165, and 38.[12] The outlook seemed anything but bright.

This appeared all the more true as it became clearer that several installations, which had been operating as private enterprises, were on the verge of giving up the struggle and selling out to the Ordnance Bureau. Accordingly, the pistol factory operated by Messrs. Spiller & Burr in Atlanta was purchased in January, 1864, and its machinery transferred to Macon Armory, along with the operatives detailed from the Army of Tennessee.[13] The factory of Haiman Brothers & Company, in Columbus, Georgia, which was designed to make pistols, also came under Burton's scrutiny, with a view toward purchase. On January 22, 1864, Burton recommended buying the machinery in the plant for $80,000 and the continued operation of the works by the Ordnance Bureau.[14] The Red Mountain Iron and Coal Company in Montgomery

[10] Mallet to Gorgas, Macon, February 5, 1864, *ibid.*, pp. 648–49.

[11] Ordnance Circular Number 59, Richmond, August 15, 1864, CROB, XXXVII, 84.

[12] "Report of Iron Made East of Mississippi River during the year 1863, and 1st Quarter of 1864, arranged by States," *Nitre and Mining Bureau File Box.*

[13] See Burton to Gorgas, Macon, January 6, 1864, CROB, XXXI, 180; Burton, *Diary,* January 17, 1864.   [14] Burton, *Diary,* January 19, 22, 1864.

inquired if the government would bail them out. They had found it impossible to run their works, which they represented as of the first class. Evincing some interest, Gorgas asked Burton to run down to Montgomery and have a look at the physical plant. The company offered to sell "provided the amount of an outstanding bond (for $250,000, with interest) be reimbursed to the State of Alabama in rifles at $35 each." Burton reported the plant as unsatisfactory, incomplete, and thoroughly inferior. Since it was patently impossible to make anything worth-while out of the place, he refused to recommend its acquisition.[15]

On the other hand, he waxed enthusiastic about the prospects of buying Cook & Brothers Armory in Athens, Georgia. Here, he discovered, was a plant operated by a private concern which knew exactly what to do with the machinery on hand. He remarked in his diary that he "found the best fitted up and regulated private armory I have yet inspected in the C. States." In a letter to Gorgas on April 15, the day of his inspection, Burton said that "the establishment of the works reflects much credit upon the senior partner, and he has exhibited a much better appreciation of the requirements of an Armory than any other person who has attempted a like enterprise in the Confederacy." Burton unhesitatingly recommended its purchase. It will be recalled that Thomas Cook also wanted to sell out.[16]

As the time drew close for the resumption of active military movements, Gorgas again took up his policy of making ready for any contingency. In February he asked Seddon for authority to impress "all stores and materials used in the various Ordnance establishments."[17] The reasons for this request were manifest, and the growing scarcity of operating supplies sharply pointed up Gorgas' communication. One of the most clearly defined areas of shortage was that of leather. In late 1863 it had become obvious that this item would probably remain on the critical list throughout the rest of the war. By orders of the War Department all hides belonging to the Army were turned over to the Quartermaster Department, and Ordnance officers could get their

[15] Gorgas to Burton, Richmond, March 10, 1864, AGPF, Burton; Burton, Diary, March 27, 1864.

[16] Burton, Diary, April 13, 15, 1864; Burton to Gorgas, Athens, Ga., CROB, XXXI, 353. Burton estimated the monthly capacity of the Cook Armory at 600 rifles and carbines.

[17] Gorgas to Seddon, Richmond, February 25, 1864, CRLR, 1864, Doc. GWD 114.

share only through that Bureau.[18] Gorgas carefully explained to Seddon the urgent need of leather in his bureau. The supply was so scant that he had found it impossible to meet all requisitions.

Colonel Kennard supported this plea, saying that Colonel White, commanding Selma Arsenal, had applied to him for a portion of beef hides of the army under Johnston. Kennard could not help White without express authorization from Gorgas or an order from the War Department. On November 1, Gorgas urged Seddon to permit at least one-fourth of the hides of Johnston's cattle to be assigned to the bureau, adding pointedly: "It will be impossible to keep up the supply of cartridge boxes & artillery harness, unless this is done." The Quartermaster General, to whom this plea was forwarded, replied on January 21, 1864, that careful consideration would not permit diversion of hides to any other bureau, since the Quartermaster Department supplied harness for 60,000 transportation animals and shoes for the troops. Even with the advantage of having all army hides sent to his department, he confessed that his officers had to draw from the country at large to make up deficiencies. His suggestion for relieving the shortage was blockade-running, and he pointed out that the Ordnance Bureau was much better prepared to undertake this operation than any other agency. So Gorgas did not get his leather from Lawton.[19]

The attitude of Lawton did not prevent Gorgas from applying directly to Johnston for assistance in this extremity. On October 28, 1863, he explained to the general that if some of the hides belonging to his army were turned over to the Ordnance Bureau, quick repairs could be made on all accouterments then on hand and equipment captured at Chickamauga could also be made serviceable. It was, simply, a "matter of necessity."[20]

But Lawton's attitude did have a distinctly negative effect—it sowed the seeds of deep and bitter interdepartmental distrust.

As the situation grew more acute, Gorgas took strong measures to secure some leather somehow. On December 29, 1863, he issued a circular to all installations of his bureau, directing that if it became impossible to obtain leather by purchase at fair rates, "you are hereby authorized to resort to impressment. . . . Impressment should only

---

[18] Gorgas to Chief Ordnance Officer, Army of Tennessee, General Hardee's Headquarters, Richmond, December 19, 1863, *Mississippi MSS.,* Ser. L, Vol. CXI.

[19] Kennard to Gorgas, Meridian, Miss., October 26, 1863, and indorsements; Gorgas to Seddon, Richmond, December 28, and indorsements, CRLR, 1863, Doc. GWD 58.

[20] Gorgas to Johnston, Richmond, ORA, Ser. I, Vol. XXXI, Pt. III, 603.

be resorted to when the articles cannot be procured, at reasonable rates, and then in strict accordance with law."[21] And on the thirty-first he took even stronger action. He requested the Secretary of War to grant authority to stop the transportation of any hides or leather from Richmond. He asked for power to pay liberally for hides, as well as permission to impress those on railroad cars and canal boats in Richmond, to prevent their being taken from the city.[22] His efforts seem to have succeeded, for in March, 1864, when it was learned that Lee's army needed carbine slings, Gorgas reported that he could furnish "*4000* gunslings made of good leather."[23]

Lawton's recalcitrance in this matter led Gorgas to assume an attitude of extreme selfishness where his own supplies were concerned. He directed his officers in the field to pay strict attention to the provisions of general orders directing that there be no interference by officers and agents of the Quartermaster Department in purchases of leather by the Ordnance Bureau. If any such interference should be encountered, Gorgas ordered his men to prefer charges against the offending quartermaster.[24] Carrying this policy further Gorgas asked his men not to give out any information concerning the amount of stores on hand to heads of other supply bureaus without first referring the matter to his office. "If the Chf. of another Dept. addresses a requisition to this Dept, let it be sent to me, take no notice of any other. Officers of other Dept's who are liberal toward you, may be met, however, in a corresponding spirit, without reference to me. It does not follow, because we have stores *to spare* here, that they can be spared by the Dept. as they may be much needed elsewhere."[25]

Gorgas' troubles with other bureaus had to take a back seat in early March, 1864. During the first week of that month some of the cavalry from Meade's army made a feint in the direction of Richmond. Colonel Ulrich Dahlgren, son of the Federal admiral, had come within the inner defenses of Richmond, accompanied by three hundred picked troopers, on the avowed mission of liberating the Union prisoners on Belle Isle and in Libby.

[21] Ordnance Circular, Richmond, CRLR, 1864, Doc. GWD 71.
[22] Capt. B. Sloan to Gorgas, Richmond, December 31, 1863, and indorsement, CROB, XC, 746.
[23] Baldwin to Gorgas, Ordnance Office, Army of Northern Virginia, March 22, 1864, and indorsements, AGPF, Baldwin.
[24] Gorgas to Kennard, Richmond, February 10, 1864, *Mississippi MSS.*, Ser. L, Vol. CXI.
[25] Quoted in Col. Broun to Capt. Dinwiddie, Richmond, May 28, 1864, CROB, XCIV, 130.

His raid, ending in his ambush and death, had reached the vicinity of Richmond on March 3, two days after a pervious alarm had galvanized Richmond's home defense units into action. In these skirmishes along the entrenchments the local battalions had distinguished themselves by their presence of mind and gallantry. They had actually beaten off the raiders, aided by a provisional brigade made up of officers and men on leave and furlough in the city. But the cost to Lee's army and to the Ordnance Bureau was high. The battalion made up of workers from the carbine factory and armory had lost one man, John Jones, in action. This seemed relatively small on the face of it, but the loss of this expert barrel straightener proved far more disastrous than appearances indicated. Without his sure eye and steady hand, the armory production dropped at least 360 rifles per month. It would take several months to train another man to fill his place, and the master-armorer, S. Adams, hoped that someone might be detailed from the Army who already had some idea of the sort of work in store for him.

The loss of Jones did not encompass all the bad effects of the fighting on the personnel of the armory. Adams reported that a general apathy seemed to be growing in the minds of the workers, who took no joy in the thought that they would have to leave their jobs for the trenches at every alarm. Dahlgren had taken about sixty armory men prisoner, and only because he was unaware of their skills were they paroled. Adams observed that "the late fight has produced disastrous results in this armory, and it will be a long time before we shall recover if we ever do." Angry about the whole affair, Gorgas wrote Seddon that

it is entirely within bounds to say as a result of the policy pursued the product of the Armory will have diminished four hundred arms per month, and that of the Carbine factory, one hundred per month for the year ending July 1, 1864, making a loss of Six Thousand arms for the year —the expenditures remaining the same. At one half the rates of exchange now prevailing the arms are worth to us $300.00 each making a loss in Confederate money of $1,800,000 in the year. The Dept. is aware that I have strenuously objected to the employment of these valuable operatives as a military force. I now renew my request that orders be issued that the carbine and armory forces . . . be held in reserve—not to be called out except on Special Orders given to the Commander of the battalion through me.[26]

[26] Gorgas to Seddon, Richmond, March 9, 1864, and enclosed letter from Adams to Maj. F. F. Jones, March 8, 1864, CRLR, 1864, Doc. O 87; GCWD, March 3, 1864, p. 85.

General Custis Lee, who had been commanding the local troops, replied that as long as he held that post, the orders concerning the local units would have to go through him; otherwise Gorgas should take over the job. He maintained that the losses sustained by the armory and carbine units were caused by the ignorance of the commanding officer of the battalion, who had managed to get his men outside the intermediate defenses, ahead of the Confederate line of battle, and had precipitated an engagement. Obviously wanting no trouble with Custis Lee, Gorgas gracefully withdrew his request that orders pass through him, and confined his request to the plea that drill periods for the ordnance workers be reduced to a bare minimum.[27]

Recent military operations around Richmond had interrupted a pleasant interlude of social activity for the Gorgas family. The man soon to be charged with directing the "military operations of the armies of the Confederacy" as chief of staff to the President, General Bragg, spent several evenings at the Gorgas home playing whist with Josiah, and other good friends took up other evenings. Family life had gone on about the same, with continuously scanty rations and continued high prices. Flour sold for $1.50 per pound, potatoes for $50.00 per bushel, and tea $30.00 a pound. Gorgas thought that there was real suffering in many families and had a momentary pang of conscience at the realization that "*we* should be so well off." The good results anticipated by the funding of the currency had failed to materialize, and Gorgas remarked that the problem was indeed curious, inasmuch as the Confederacy had stricken out of existence some $500,000,000 and still prices were high. "It is evident that parties holding food and supplies mean, for the present, to hold on to them. . . . Until the farmers are forced by taxation to sell their produce it is possible these prices will continue." Gold remained the best medium of exchange, when it could be had at all, of course. Eggs cost $6.00 in currency, but only twelve and one-half cents in gold. Currency had become of such little worth that Gorgas, by April, had ceased to draw his pay and determined "to live on the sale of such things as I can spare."[28]

His interest in the general military condition of the Confederacy had lost none of its keenness. Sharing the popular lack of information on Sherman's intentions, he noted with delight the defeat of the Federal

[27] Gorgas to Seddon, Richmond, March 9, 1864, indorsement by Gorgas, April 26, 1864, CRLR, 1864, Doc. O 87.

[28] GCWD, February 21, March 4, 1864, pp. 84, 86; April 7, p. 90; and April 26, p. 94.

expedition into Florida at Olustee on February 20, 1864. Forrest's success at Okolona, Mississippi, also contributed to his good spirits. He classed as brilliant the capture of Plymouth, North Carolina, on April 19, and praised the excellent work of the Confederate ironclad "Albemarle," which had played a prominent role in the capture of the town.[29] But General Robert F. Hoke, commanding the attack on Plymouth, had had as his prime objective the recapture of New Bern. In this being unsuccessful, he abandoned the project; but the victory-starved Confederacy forgave him his transgressions and rejoiced in his partial triumph.

One relatively minor domestic altercation intervened to change briefly the pattern of Gorgas' home life. Tom Bayne and his wife Maria, who had not been getting on very well in the same house with Amelia, Josiah, nurse Anne, and the children, in late March finally decided to move into rooms on Main Street. Gorgas entered the fact in his journal with the observation that "two families can rarely get along without some discontents in one house, and it is well that we have quietly broken in two—pleasantly. Bayne is the most amiable and best man to get along with I have ever known. Maria is a little more difficult to please, and is too fond of having her own way, to get along perfectly well with others." Things had been complicated by the fact that Amelia had not been well.[30]

On April 4, the day that a severe faceache put Amelia in bed, Gorgas recorded in his journal that Grant, who had joined Meade's army, on March 9 had been made commander of all Union armies with the rank of lieutenant general, and it seemed that serious work lay ahead for Lee's troops.[31] And as these operations gradually took shape, Gorgas' preparations for action went along apace. The President's query about too much artillery in the armies had been the result of a letter which Gorgas had sent Bragg in early April. Gorgas estimated that the number of guns in Lee's army was 197, not including a battalion of the Washington Artillery at Petersburg, of which about one-half were rifles. Longstreet's Corps had 27 guns, of which 14 were rifles. General Joseph E. Johnston's army had 123 guns, of which about one-fifth were rifles; and Polk's Corps had 24 guns, three of which were rifles. Gorgas suggested

that a maximum be fixed for the artillery, not to exceed five pieces for each brigade of infantry. Three pieces for every 1,000 men, for a full

[29] GCWD, April 24, 1864, p. 92.
[30] GCWD, April 1 and 4, 1864, pp. 88–89.   [31] GCWD, pp. 89–90.

organization, is the largest allowance of modern equipment. It is possible, however, that as the organizations recede from their maximum strength it no longer becomes a safe rule to apportion the artillery exactly by the strength present. I propose, therefore, to apportion it by brigades or by regiments, and as our brigades are generally composed of five regiments and scarcely exceed 2,500 men now, and are more probably reduced to 1,500, five guns to a brigade would be an ample allowance. Of these one might be reserve. The equipment of so much artillery overtaxes our means and necessarily renders the equipment of the whole less complete than it would be if reduced to moderate limits.

Gorgas thought that, by allowing 20 pieces to a division of cavalry (quite too much in his opinion), Lee's artillery would be reduced to about 170 guns, including the guns at Petersburg, instead of 213.[32]

Bragg sent copies of this letter to both Lee and Johnston for their information and comment. In forwarding it to Johnston, Bragg pointed out another cardinal difficulty inherent in supplying the artillery for the armies. "The supply of horses on the present extended scale cannot possibly be kept up, and were the supply sufficient they cannot be foraged without endangering the subsistence of the troops."[33]

Lee's reaction to the letter was not altogether favorable. He remarked that he had never found the proportion of artillery with his army too large in battle, particularly since it had usually been opposed by at least 300 pieces of larger caliber and longer range, equipped with better ammunition. "If, however, its equipment overtaxes the means of the Ordnance Department, or, as you suggest, its supply of horses cannot be kept up, that decides the question, and no argument is necessary." By the European standard of three guns to every 1,000 men, the Army of Northern Virginia fell far short on guns. Lee agreed with Gorgas in thinking it better not to adhere to that standard "when the organizations recede from their maximum strength." Lee estimated that his army would require 230 in view of Gorgas' proposed standard; he already had 240 and observed that the excess certainly did not appear large, especially since under European usage he should have 395 cannon. Lee did not agree with Gorgas in believing 20 guns too many for the cavalry; on the contrary, he considered the number far too small.[34]

[32] Gorgas to Bragg, Richmond [April 5 or 6?], 1864, ORA, Ser. IV, Vol. III, 293–94.

[33] Bragg to Johnston, Richmond, April 13, 1864, *ibid.*, p. 293.

[34] Lee to Bragg, Headquarters, April 16, 1864, ORA, Ser. I, Vol. XXXIII, 1285–86.

Concern about excess artillery was only one manifestation of Gorgas' growing worry about maintaining adequate supplies. This worry had prompted him to set a limit on the number of rounds of ammunition which would be issued to each soldier in the various armies. On April 4, 1864, Julius A. de Lagnel, writing for Gorgas, informed Colonel Oladowski that every effort would be made to supply the Army of Tennessee with ammunition but cautioned that "the resources of the Dept. will not permit, at present, a greater allowance of ammunition than 120 rounds per man; this is all that the other armies have." Gorgas had discovered that there existed an unequal distribution of cartridges between the different corps of the army: Hardee's Corps had only 78 rounds per man of .577 and .58 calibers, while Hood's Corps had 209 rounds per man of the same bullets. The average, 143 rounds, should be achieved by a division among the different corps.[35] De Lagnel wrote to Colonel Wright, commanding Atlanta Arsenal (charged with supplying the Army of Tennessee), advising him of Gorgas' decision to keep Johnston's troops supplied. De Lagnel estimated that Wright had ample quantities of caliber .69 cartridges on hand, but would need calibers .57, .58, and .54. In order to assist Wright, de Lagnel told him that 30,000 pounds of lead had been ordered to him that day, April 4, and with that reserve he should push the manufacture of .54 caliber bullets. Large quantities of horseshoes, nails, Napoleon shells, and case shot had been ordered to Wright from Salisbury, North Carolina, "and thus you are in great measure provided for. For what else you can not furnish, call on the adjacent arsenals to aid you in providing."[36]

[35] De Lagnel to Oladowski, Richmond, *Mississippi MSS.*, Ser. L, Vol. CXI.

[36] De Lagnel to Wright ("Confidential"), Richmond, April 4, 1864, AGPF, de Lagnel. In this letter de Lagnel included a table giving his estimate of the ammunition distribution in the Army of Tennessee:

Arms	"on hand"				
Cal.		.54			9,590
"		.57 & .58			19,408
"		.69			6,730
"		.70			274

Rounds in Boxes & Wagons

Cal.	.54	85 ⎤	76 ⎤	Avg.	80 rds.
"	.57 & .58	78 ⎟ Hardee's	209 ⎟ Hood's	"	143 "
"	.69	88 ⎟	94 ⎟	"	91 "
"	.70	[?] ⎦	74 ⎦	"	74 "

Needed to reach 120 rds. per man.

Cal.	.54	383,600 rounds
"	.57 & .58	None "
"	.69	262,864 "
"	.70	9,864 "

The movements of Grant's army soon indicated that Gorgas' concern about supplies was well founded. On May 4, 1864, the Federal juggernaut opposing Lee in the Wilderness of Virginia began to move, and from the fifth to the seventh the two armies joined battle in the woodland. By the eighth Grant had moved on Lee's right flank and met him again at Spotsylvania, where a bitter engagement followed, including the affair of the "Bloody Angle." Grant kept moving by Lee's right flank, at length paying a ghastly butcher's bill at Cold Harbor during the first three days of June. This series of events doubtless occasioned surprise and disappointment to Gorgas, who in April had expected that Lee would take the offensive.[37]

As a matter of fact, in the days immediately preceding Grant's move, which he made in conjunction with Sherman's march toward Atlanta, beginning on May 5, Gorgas had remained optimistic and calm, apparently not anticipating the staggering blows which were about to fall. He had taken comfort in the news that Bank's Red River expedition had met with disaster at Mansfield, Louisiana, on April 8, 1864, and had exhibited his usual interest about conditions in Richmond. He noticed with apprehension the growing scarcity of food in the capital, and observed that the government seemed to be continuing to send employees to the south as a means of alleviating the shortage, a solution he deprecated. And on April 8, the third anniversary of his assuming charge of the Ordnance Bureau, he took time enough to indulge in legitimate self-satisfaction. He noted in his diary:

It is three years ago today since I took charge of the Ordnance Department of the Confederate States, at Montgomery—three years of constant work and application. I have succeeded beyond my utmost expectations. From being the worst supplied of the Bureaus of the War Department it is now the best. Large arsenals have been organized at Richmond, Fayetteville, Augusta, Charleston, Columbus, Macon, Atlanta and Selma, and smaller ones at Danville, Lynchburgh, and Montgomery, besides other establishments. A superb powder mill has been built at Augusta, the credit of which is due to Col. G. W. Rains. Lead smelting works were established by me at Petersburgh, and turned over to the Nitre and Mining Bureau, when that Bureau was at my request separated from mine. A cannon foundry established at Macon for heavy guns, and bronze foundries at Macon, Columbus, Ga., and Augusta; a foundry for shot and shell at Salisbury, N. C.; a large shop for leather work at Clarksville, Va.; besides the Armories here and at Fayetteville, a manufactory of carbines

[37] GCWD, April 26, 1864, p. 94.

has been built up here; a rifle factory at Ashville (transferred to Columbia, S. C.) ; a new and very large armory at Macon, including a pistol factory, built up under contract here and sent to Atlanta, and thence transferred under purchase to Macon; a second pistol factory at Columbus, Ga.;—All of these have required incessant toil and attention, but have borne such fruit as relieves the country from fear of want in these respects. Where three years ago we were not making a gun, a pistol nor a sabre, no shot nor shell (except at the Tredegar Works)—a pound of powder—we now make all these in quantities to meet the demands of our large armies. In looking over all this I feel that my three years of labor have not been passed in vain.[38]

As he sat at his desk that night, writing in his journal, he may have been thinking of what lay ahead for the bureau he had made so strong. Would that strength continue to sustain the heavy burdens the bureau must surely bear? Amelia (who was again ill) and the children had no doubt about it, but were they right? And yet his own estimate of the job done was an understatement. The outlook seemed good. Scholarly Colonel John Mallet, with his chemical genius; handsome, gifted Colonel Burton, with his experience; quite, erudite Colonel Rains, and the galaxy of others in his bureau surely would not let him down. But was the loyalty and determination of these men enough?

Pressure accumulated from all sides. Grant kept coming closer to Richmond, and Sherman pushed Johnston inexorably back toward Atlanta. Gorgas stayed at his office night and day; the government had doubts about keeping up the food supply, and Gorgas had lost faith for a time in Bragg, whom he now thought "a *little cracked*."[39] Gorgas could give very little attention to his family, and the children would miss being taken out of church during the Sunday sermon for a walk in Capital Square.[40]

General Beauregard had been called to Petersburg to take charge of rallying some sort of defense. Gorgas had to scrape together some ordnance for his troops, and, at the same time, had to do all the office work alone. His staff had been summoned to local defense on May 10 and 11. A visit to Seddon's office at five o'clock in the morning of May 11 found the Secretary up and convinced that Richmond's last hours were

[38] GCWD, April 29, May 2, 1864, pp. 95, 96; April 26, p. 94; April 8, pp. 90–91.
[39] GCWD, April 29, 1864, p. 95. Special Orders Number 111, Adj. & Insp. Gen.'s Off., Richmond, May 12, 1864, directed heads of bureaus to keep their offices open day and night until further orders. ORA, Ser. I, Vol. XXXVI, Pt. II, 993. [40] GCWD, April 25, 1864, p. 93.

near; he believed that the entire cavalry force of Meade's army was descending in a body on the capital, with Stuart trailing them at a distance. Gorgas wore himself out trudging about the streets, trying to do all the myriad things that had to be done to keep the Ordnance Bureau running. With the rumors and counterrumors flying about Richmond in the pattern peculiar to the capital, Gorgas did not lose confidence in the men under Lee. "If supplies do not fail I have no doubt of Lee's ability to maintain himself." Supplies were indeed the unknown quantity. A Federal cavalry raid on the important railroad center of Beaver Dam Station on May 10 destroyed three trains of commissary stores, including 200,000 pounds of bacon. Such losses, at this time, seemed almost the last straw.[41]

As the fighting drew nearer, Gorgas became alarmed about his carbine factory in Richmond and finally decided to move it to a safer clime, along with all its operatives and their families. The site selected was Tallassee, Alabama, a place which Burton had inspected and approved.[42]

The immediate danger to Richmond subsided when Stuart beat off the Federal cavalry at Yellow Tavern on May 11. The retreat of the Yankees via Mechanicsville, however, welcome at it was, seemed a hollow victory when it was learned that "Jeb" had been mortally wounded. The temporary withdrawal of the Federals did not give Gorgas a prolonged sense of security. He expected the enemy to "harass us in every possible way." Yet the Confederate armies seemed to be holding their own; news from Johnston was that his troops had repulsed two Yankee assaults on May 14. A dark spot in the picture was that on the fifteenth Lee had lost 20 guns in the Wilderness. Gorgas thought that "if Johnston had the happy inspiration that Desaix had at Marengo, he would send here one of his corps, without waiting for orders; as the enemy is evidently not to attack him and he must have 65,000 men idly waiting there, while the roar of battle thunders over a dozen fields in Virginia and the fate of the nation is being decided here."[43] Then news of Sherman's attacks came in. Gorgas forgot his idea and probably apologized to Johnston in silence.

The rapidity with which things happened in these days gave the Chief of Ordnance a better chance to keep himself well informed. He had occasion to call frequently on the Secretary of War and President

[41] GCWD, May 11, 1864, p. 101; May 10, p. 100.
[42] Burton, *Diary*, May 26, 27, 28, 29, 1864; GCWD, May 8, p. 99.
[43] GCWD, May 13, 14, 1864, pp. 101, 102; May 15, p. 102; May 15, p. 103.

Davis and in his conversations with them obtained first-hand information on the course of the war. For instance, on May 20 he visited the President and found him in jovial spirits, telling jokes and not at all perturbed by recent events. Nevertheless, Gorgas watched with growing disgust Johnston's retreat down the Western and Atlantic Railroad toward Atlanta and confided to his diary that he hoped "the country will sooner or later find out what sort of a general he is. I don't think he will suit the emergency."[44] Yet, later Gorgas would be glad to see Johnston again commanding the Army of Tennessee.

As Lee's line formed at Cold Harbor on June 1, Gorgas, ill, was dubious about Beauregard's ability to hold off Butler at Bermuda Hundred. By the third Gorgas had recovered enough to ride out to the battlefield at Cold Harbor, where he saw a field "covered with dead Yankees." In company with Major Merlin, of his bureau, Gorgas was subjected to sharpshooter fire, and retired from the front with alacrity. On the way to the rear he and his companion met General Ambrose P. Hill, who said that he was on the point of "arranging for a little expedition to drive the enemy from a position." Shortly thereafter sharp firing indicated that he had carried out his design. Gorgas was impressed with the elaborate system of breastworks thrown up along the Confederate lines and observed that the troops had

acquired quite a respect for this sort of entrenchment, and work like beavers when they take up a new position. They began the war with a contempt for the spade, but now thoroughly believe in it. They use bayonets, tin pans, and even, I am told, split their tin canteens to get a utensil that will throw up earth.

On his excursion to the battle lines, Gorgas had a chance meeting with General Lee and the President. "The General kindly stopped and beckoned me to him, cautioning me not to go near the lines as I might be shot, with my blue cape, by either side; would rather, he added in a half jocular way, that I would return and send him ammunition."[45]

As the fighting came to a halt along the Cold Harbor line, Gorgas shared the general suspicion that Grant's army was crossing south of the Chickahominy, but could not see what such a maneuver would accomplish, since it would take the Federals farther away from Richmond. But the uncertainty had its effect on everyone. In an interview with Gorgas on June 7 the President displayed a pettiness about official

[44] GCWD, May 20, 1864, pp. 105–06; May 21, p. 107.
[45] GCWD, June 4, 1864, pp. 111–12.

prerogative in minor affairs that struck the Chief of Ordnance as unbecoming. Gorgas, too, found the tension wearing. Things looked more and more critical to him. He wrote on June 9:

I cannot see where farther reinforcements are to come from—Lee is waiting and Grant is gathering strength here. The same appears to be the condition of things at Atlanta. Johnston is waiting while Sherman is receiving reinforcements. What the issue will be is in God's hands—nothing but an unforeseen event can, it seems to me, save us from the gradually rising strength of our opponents; or rather from the defeats our waning strength must entail. Our losses here all told are about 25,000 men, killed, wounded and captured, in Lee's Army alone, and perhaps five thousand on the South side. Where can we supply such a waste of men? We can hold out in all else.[46]

The fighting in western Virginia seemed to bear out Gorgas' prediction that attrition would prevent the Confederacy from gaining any more victories. Federal General David Hunter had entered New Hope and Staunton, where many Confederate sick and wounded had been collected. General Sam Jones had reportedly been killed trying to rally the 60th Virginia in the defense of New Hope. As Quartermaster General Lawton, his wife, Mrs. Mary Jones (Amelia's close friend), Dr. Richardson, and General Arnold Elzey drank tea with the Gorgases on the evening of June 15, the conversation probably included talk of the death of Bishop-General Leonidas Polk, who had been killed at Pine Mountain, Georgia, the day before.[47] Too many of the Confederacy's good soldiers were disappearing from the rolls. Who could adequately fill their places?

Gorgas continued to be disappointed at Johnston's actions around Atlanta and had no confidence in his intention of holding the city. This fact probably colored his conversations with Mallet, who spent a few days with the family in late June, before leaving for Georgia on the 29th. If Johnston did abandon Atlanta, this would necessitate certain changes in the functioning of the Bureau in the Deep South. Gorgas' lack of faith in Johnston was equalled by his dissatisfaction with Christopher G. Memminger, the hapless Secretary of the Treasury, who finally resigned on June 15, 1864. Gorgas, whose dealings with that official had been numerous, felt that Memminger treated people with a narrow-minded rudeness unbecoming to his portfolio. "*His* time, and

[46] GCWD, June 6, 7, 1864, p. 113; June 7, 9, 1864, pp. 113–14.
[47] GCWD, June 15, 1864, pp. 115–16.

his method," observed Gorgas in April, "are more important than any subject can possibly be! Whenever I leave Mr. M. after an interview, I feel somehow as tho' I had been trying to do something very much out of the way, so injured and *put upon* does he represent himself. He always assumes a bristling defensive, and makes you appear to be on the aggressive toward him. Mr. Seddon compares him to a dog who, when a new dog enters his domain, runs alongside of him erecting his bristles and curving his back!"[48]

On the other hand, Gorgas's respect for Davis grew as the war progressed. In October, when he heard from one of Lee's staff officers that the General had said "if we can't get the men, all that is left for us is to make peace on the best terms we can," he observed that "our brave President never wavers thus, in act or thought." But certain personal considerations probably influenced Gorgas' growing admiration for the Chief Executive. In a conversation with Davis on June 29 Gorgas had the pleasure of hearing the President say, "Colonel, I find my conversations with you have more reason and less politics than any others."[49] The effect of that compliment was lasting.

On July 19 Gorgas heard with relief that Hood had succeeded Johnston in command of the Army of Tennessee. That meant only one thing; the Army of Tennessee would fight soon; and Hood would fight well enough. He did attack Sherman twice in two great waves—and then abandoned Atlanta on September 2, 1864. But Gorgas could not foresee this. He still rejoiced in the change of leaders, and thought it a pity that Davis had not acted sooner.[50]

Other news brought smiles. Although some of the Columbus ordnance machinery had been moved in an effort to avoid capture, Gorgas noted that one of Sherman's schemes to wreck part of the Ordnance Bureau had failed. Burton's Armory had had to suspend operations from July 29 until the morning of August 2 because of an attack against that place by General George Stoneman with over 2,000 Union cavalry. But a staunch defense by the small Confederate force, consisting of a fragment of a Tennessee battalion, some Georgia troops, the Ordnance unit from the combined works in Macon, and a rumor of the approach of Rebel cavalry, drove him off on the thirtieth and saved the city. On his retreat Stoneman clashed with General Alfred Iverson and sustained a serious defeat, being himself captured. Imprisoned in

[48] GCWD, June 30, 1864, p. 122; April 11, July 1, pp. 92, 122.
[49] GCWD, October 11, 1864, p. 146; July 1, p. 123.
[50] GCWD, July 22, 1864, p. 127.

Macon Armory, he must have considered the poetic justice of his situation—incarcerated in the very place he had attempted to take. He had done some damage, however; the Georgia Central Railroad would be out of service for two or three weeks, interrupting communication between Augusta and Macon.[51]

But this little victory did not counteract the dearth of good news, nor the drouth which was ruining the badly needed crops about Richmond. The weather continued so warm and dry that Gorgas and Willie resorted to swimming in the river as a means of cooling themselves.[52] On the other hand, the weather helped General Grant. On July 30 he exploded the famous "Crater" mine under Elliott's salient in the Petersburg trenches and attempted to break Lee's line with Negro troops, who sang as they marched to certain death:

> We looks like men a-marching on,
> We looks like men er war.[53]

Thwarted in this attempt by the timely counterattack of William Mahone's men, Grant nevertheless had frightened Richmond and killed some irreplaceable men.

The mass Federal moves throughout the South imposed an incredible strain on all the Confederate supply bureaus. Although Colonel Baldwin, Lee's chief ordnance officer, estimated that the arms collected in the first few days' fighting in the Wilderness had totaled 10,000 rifles and large quantities of cartridge boxes and accouterments,[54] these could constitute no appreciable reserve in the face of the siege of Richmond and Petersburg. From different parts of the country came requisitions, not only for items of standard issue, but for extraordinary weapons as well. And Gorgas generally could supply these oddities and improvements, though the resources of his bureau had been seriously curtailed. General William N. Pendleton, commanding Lee's reserve artillery, queried Colonel Baldwin in June about the possibility of using stink bombs in 12-pounders. His idea, prompted by a newspaper article, embraced the principles of chemical warfare when he questioned whether "the explosion can be combined with the suffocating effect of certain offensive gases, or whether apart from explosion such gases may

[51] GCWD, August 3, 1864, p. 131; Mallet, pp. 17–18; Burton to Gorgas, Macon, August 2, 1864, CROB, XXXI, 517.
[52] GCWD, August 10, 1864, p. 133.
[53] Quoted in Bill, *Beleaguered City*, p. 224.
[54] Baldwin to Gorgas, Ordnance Office, Army of Northern Virginia, May 7, 1864, CRLR, 1864, Doc. BWD 394.

not be emitted from a continuously burning composition as to render the vicinity of each falling shell intolerable." Pendleton coupled his request for stink bombs with one for hand grenades. This requisition was turned over to Colonel Broun at Richmond Arsenal, who replied that he could supply the hand grenades, "very superior, explode always," and would make the "stink balls."[55] Unfortunately records do not indicate the effectiveness of these weapons.

As the pressure from the Union armies increased, Gorgas found it necessary to decentralize even further his command authority. He delegated it in huge lots. Kennard received permission to use cotton and tobacco in obtaining indispensable supplies for his army.[56] Burton on June 9, received an assignment as general inspector of all armories in the Confederate States, and in the emergency created by Hood's defense of Atlanta, Colonel Wright, as has been indicated, on August 4, took temporary charge of all the Ordnance establishments in Macon.[57] Gorgas did not neglect Mallet in passing out discretionary powers. On June 21 he gave him detailed permission to contract for alcohol; to increase the pay of his clerical force as he deemed proper; to supply draft animals of the laboratory with corn and fodder; to proceed with the erection of such laboratory buildings as he thought necessary; to buy twelve acres of land; to increase contract prices for laying a brick wall, and to sell Burton 100 pounds of white lead for private use at cost.[58]

In this emergency Gorgas looked abroad for assistance, but discovered that yellow fever had practically eliminated Bermuda, as well as Nassau, as *entrepots*.[59]

Depressed about Hood's retreat from Atlanta, Gorgas hoped that Beauregard would take over his command. The disaster which had befallen Atlanta seemed paralleled, though fortunately on a small scale, by the series of defeats General Jubal Early had sustained in western Virginia. Still, Gorgas hoped for some kind of success somewhere

[55] Pendleton to Baldwin, Headquarters, Artillery Corps, Army of Northern Virginia, and indorsement, June 10, 1864, ORA, Ser. I, Vol. XXXVI, Pt. III, 888–89.

[56] Gorgas to Kennard, Richmond, April 28, 1864, *Mississippi MSS.,* Ser. L, Vol. CXI.

[57] Burton to Gorgas, Macon, June 9, 1864, CROB, XXXI, 435; Wright to de Lagnel (telegram), Macon, August 4, 1864, *ibid.,* CI, 309; General Order Number 1, Government Works, Macon, August 4, 1864, *ibid.,* XXXVII, 60; ORA, Ser. I, Vol. XXXVIII, Pt. V, 946.

[58] Special Orders Number 56, Ordnance Bureau, Richmond, June 21, 1864, AGPF, Mallet.   [59] GCWD, August 24, 1864, p. 137.

and looked to Hood's new plan of attacking Sherman's line of communications to provide it. The Chief of Ordnance devoutly wished for
a Confederate victory. "God grant it! We need a victory to close this
bloody year." By now, though, he did not believe Lee could put 30,000
infantry into the lines, and observed that "the time is coming now when
it will be necessary to put our Slaves into the field and let them fight
for their freedom, in other words give up a part of *the institution* to
save the country, *or the whole* if necessary to win independence."[60]

Life in Richmond was becoming one long series of alarms and exciting rumors. On September 29 the Federals made a strong attack on
Lee's line, succeeded in taking Fort Harrison, and then repulsed two
Confederate attempts at recapture. Though Gorgas believed Confederate losses to be only half those of the Yankees, he noted that "even
this disparity will ultimately ruin us." The thought again brought
him to the conclusion that the use of slaves seemed the only answer
to the manpower problem.[61] The Conscript Bureau, which had done
a notoriously wretched job, again tightened the regulations for details,
and Gorgas had to do his best to hang on to the few mechanics left in
his plants.[62]

And he did not forget the loyal troops who stayed in the siege lines:

Our poor harrowed and overworked soldiers are getting worn out with
the campaign. They see nothing before them but certain death, and have,
I fear, fallen into a sort of hopelessness, and are dispirited. Certain it is
that they do not fight as they fought at the Wilderness and Spotsylvania.
The cure for this is I think to *limit the term of service.* They are now in
for the War, and as there appears no end to it, at present, they begin to
look upon themselves as doomed men. A term of service for five years
would perhaps correct this without imperiling the existence of the Army.
Under such a term the men would begin to go home in the middle of

[60] GCWD, September 25, 1864, p. 142.
[61] GCWD, October 2, 1864, p. 144.
[62] Circular, Conscription Bureau, Richmond, April 6, 1864, CROB, XXXVII,
1; memorandum, Mallet to Gorgas, Macon, April 4, 1864, AGPF, Mallet.
Under terms of General Orders Number 82, Adj. & Insp. Gen.'s Off., Richmond, October 20, 1864 (ORA, Ser. IV, Vol. III, 741), Gorgas had to put one
fifth "of all the men employed in his department" in the field. He complied by
issuing to all installations Circular 75, October 20 (CROB, XXXVII, 303),
directing that each post turn over one fifth of its men to enrolling officers, keeping the best. These orders reduced the number of men between the ages of 18
and 45 working for the Ordnance Bureau from 3,433 to 2,691. Gorgas to Seddon, report, Richmond, February 2, 1865, ORA, Ser. IV, Vol. III, 1054–55.

1866, but most of them in '67, and there would be constantly veterans enough to keep up the quality of the Army.[63]

News of Lincoln's re-election seemed to insure the continued prosecution of the war; and word that Sherman, instead of following Hood northward, had abandoned Atlanta and was marching to the sea, gave fresh fuel to Gorgas' depression.[64] The news about Sherman meant consternation in the southern ordnance plants.

There was one thing, at least, about which Gorgas did not have to worry so much at present—money. Congress on June 13 appropriated $25,000,000 for his bureau for the period July 1 to December 31, 1864,[65] and that seemed enough. Still, when compared with the money given to the other bureaus, the Ordnance share seemed small—Quartermaster got $74,249,951, and Commissary got $100,000,000. Gorgas' bureau had done the best job on the least money, and that certainly should have meant something. It did mean a great deal to Francis S. Lyon, Representative from Alabama, a good friend of the Gorgases, who had long thought that Gorgas' rank was not commensurate with his position or his ability. On November 9, 1864, Lyon wrote Davis from the House of Representatives:

I have known Col. Gorgas . . . for a number of years, and regarding him as a most valuable and efficient officer, and a very worthy & reliable man would in common with many of his other friends be gratified to see him promoted to the rank of Brigadier General. I need not remind you of his valuable & efficient services as an officer—but as Col Gorgas was for a long time a resident of Alabama and is connected and identified with the state in such manner as to authorize us to claim him as a citizen I have ventured to call his case to your attention under a hope that you will concur in opinion with his many friends that he has earned a higher rank than that of Col. of Ordnance.

This letter presented a problem to Davis. Legally he could not promote Gorgas, since there existed no statutory provision for a general in the Ordnance Bureau, which still was technically a branch of the Artillery Corps. But Davis wanted to make the promotion. He indorsed the letter over to Seddon on the 10th, saying, "if the organization will permit the promotion might be made of Col. Gorgas as one of the

[63] GCWD, October 6, 1864, p. 145.
[64] GCWD, November 20, 1864, p. 150.
[65] *Statutes at Large (Confederate),* 2 Cong., Stat. I, Chap. XXXIX.

twenty additional generals." Seddon inquired of the Adjutant and
Inspector General if Gorgas might be promoted, and received word
on the eleventh that vacancies existed under the Act of October 13,
1862, granting the President the right to appoint twenty general officers
in the Provisional Army, and to assign them to such duty as he deemed
expedient. On the same day Seddon indorsed the letter back to Cooper:
"Nominate as Brig. General, in accordance with the President's endorsement and your report."[66]

After his nomination had gone into the senatorial mill, Gorgas discovered that he had important influences working for his promotion
outside of the government. On November 14 the *Daily Richmond
Examiner* published a long editorial in praise of his bureau's activities,
speaking of him in glowing terms—so glowing that with his natural
modesty he probably turned red as he scanned the article. The last
paragraph seemed most significant just at this time:

In point of numbers the Chief of Ordnance commands more men than
any division in the army. In point of scientific attainments his duties require more knowledge than any branch of the service—and yet his rank
is only that of Colonel, while the Chiefs of the Conscript Bureau and the
Quartermaster's Department have been promoted to the rank of Brigadier
General. We hope it may be the pleasure of Congress to examine into the
Ordnance Department, and where investigations to hunt out fraud and
speculation are so numer[o]us, one may be instituted to promote and
commend the skill, energy, zeal and faithfulness of the Chief of Ordnance
and his subordinate officers.

This tribute certainly helped. Combined with the President's own
recommendation, it achieved confirmation of Gorgas' nomination as
brigadier general on November 19, 1864.[67] This, in a way, was the
President's reward to Gorgas for success beyond expectation.[68]

With Hood fairly launched on his way to Nashville, with Grant
hammering at the Petersburg siege lines, and Sherman ravaging the
industrial heart of the shrinking Confederacy, Gorgas had done all
he could to make his bureau able to weather the hurricane. He thought
he had succeeded, and he was almost right.

[66] Lyon to Davis, November 9, 1864, and indorsements, AGPF, Gorgas; *Statutes at Large (Confederate)*, 1 Cong. Stat. II, Chap. LXIV.

[67] *Daily Richmond Examiner*, November 14, 21, 1864. Another, much more
detailed, editorial praising the Ordnance Bureau appeared in the Richmond *Enquirer*, November 24.

[68] Gorgas attributed his promotion directly to the President. See GCWD,
November 24, 1864, p. 152.

XIX

"Where Is General Gorgas?"

THE MILITARY SITUATION AS IT APPEARED TO THE NEW BRIGADIER WAS anything but comforting. Sherman seemed well on his way to Savannah, with Bragg, who had gone south, apparently unable to stem his advance or seriously slow him down. General Gorgas could not quite see Sherman's reasons for abandoning Atlanta and striking for the sea; he feared that the Federals might, rather, turn and establish themselves somewhere on the Chattahoochie, after destroying Macon and Columbus. Sherman, Gorgas devoutly hoped, did not see his way clearly. There continued the usual sort of activity along the Richmond-Petersburg lines, with local actions. Gorgas noted hopefully on December 11 that the returns of arms in the hands of Lee's troops indicated 61,-700 infantry, artillery, and cavalry present for duty.[1]

From the Army of Tennessee came conflicting reports—first a victory at Franklin, Tennessee—costly, to be sure—then defeat at Nashville—total, abject rout—on December 15 and 16, 1864.[2]

But it was Sherman's movements which captured the public eye; he was much closer to home and was doing damage all could understand. Gorgas had urgent reason to watch his movements anxiously. Burton had already moved some of the Macon machinery but had not been able to move all of it before the enemy cut the Central Railroad. He had managed to send most of the machinery for pistol manufacture, along with the foreign rifle-making equipment, to Columbia. But only about half of the latter had gotten away. He encountered trouble in keeping what was left protected from the weather since it had been stored in boxes at the behest of General Howell Cobb.[3] Gorgas di-

---

[1] GCWD, November 30, 1864, p. 153; December 11, 1864, p. 154.
[2] GCWD, December 19, 1864, p. 156.
[3] De Lagnel to Burton, Richmond, November 18, 1864, AGPF, Burton; Burton to Gorgas, Macon, December 7, 1864, CROB, XXIX, 165.

rected that Burton either erect or hire a warehouse in which to store tools and equipment until the military situation cleared. Burton had other problems—he needed money desperately, reporting on December 8 that he had not been able to meet a payroll since September 30. He had contrived to make some payments by borrowing $125,000 from the Confederate Depositary in Macon, a personal friend. The last shipment of money he had received arrived September 30, when he got $60,000, of which $20,000 was in certificates of indebtedness which he could not negotiate.[4] Burton was not alone in his want of funds; the Quartermaster General had commented acidly on November 5 that "it is not perceived why there should be any difficulty in the way of the men obtaining their pay, other than the want of Funds. This cause delays payment to troops in the Field."[5]

Mallet, Burton, and Cuyler all needed money to help them in supplying their Negroes with food and clothing, in addition to meeting their payrolls. Their plight caused Gorgas to send a strong plea to Seddon, asking that food, clothing, "and *security from interference,* might be assured them." In the meantime, and until Seddon could act, Burton and the rest were directed to make the best possible efforts to supply their Negroes. Clothing had been sent for, and Gorgas hoped it would arrive in quantities to meet their wants for the coming season. "Every confidence is had in your energy & ability," de Lagnel wrote Burton, "to cope with the difficulties that embarrass you; and it is hoped you will overcome them, in this instance, as you have in others." He could promise that Burton would no longer have his colored help summarily taken from their tasks—past experience had taught the War Department a lesson on this point.[6]

But the removal of other workers from ordnance plants still worried Gorgas. He told Seddon on October 25 that the loss of mechanics had "reduced the number so much, as to render it necessary to take such action as may tend to retain those that yet remain to us. I have frequently called attention to this subject, as one well worthy the solicitude of those in authority, and the present condition of affairs is, permit me to assure you, one deserving your most earnest & serious consideration: it will not do, longer to pass this matter by, in silence." The best

[4] Burton to Gorgas, Macon, CROB, XXIX, 168–69.
[5] Mallet to Gorgas, Macon, October 24, 1864 (indorsement), AGPF, Mallet.
[6] De Lagnel to Burton, Richmond, December 1, 1864, AGPF, Burton. See Burton to Lt. Gen. Richard Taylor, Macon, November 26, 1864, CROB, XXIX, 152, for some of the lengths to which Burton had to go to provision his Negro labor.

interest of the government would surely suffer unless the few mechanics left were retained at their machines. "Already large amounts of machinery are laying idle; in all parts of the country, for want of workmen to operate them; while three years since, the want felt, was of machinery." Gorgas asked that a general order be published assuring the remaining skilled workers in Ordnance employ, and in the shops of contractors, that they would be left at their various jobs and that they were definitely not subject to military duty. Gorgas even recommended the passage of a law (a draft of which he sent to Seddon) embracing these points.[7]

Gorgas had a friend on the *Daily Richmond Enquirer,* or else he had acquired an unofficial public relations officer, for there appeared in that paper on November 24 another long editorial in praise of the Ordnance Bureau which contained his exact views on the retention of skilled workers. After a well-informed resumé of some of the Bureau's early troubles, the article said:

It is not too much to assume that with a proper application of the labor still at our disposal—should it become necessary by the closing of our ports, to rely wholly upon ourselves—the armies of the Confederacy could be supplied with all the arms needed for an efficient prosecution of the war. But to this end it would be necessary to retain our skilled mechanics; and it is a question well worthy of consideration, whether steps should not be taken at once to secure to us the skilled labor, still remaining after the havoc of a sanguinary war, by attaching it permanently to these branches of labor *now,* instead of waiting until compelled by necessity to do what may then be too late to do successfully. We think, and have always thought, that our best interests require us to husband our skilled labor, and place it in the workshops of the Government, rather than risk its loss on the battlefield, and by disease. Legislation to this effect would be wise forecasts.

As the year 1864 drew toward a close, Gorgas found that Sherman's presence in the South had pushed him into many changes of operational procedure. Though he had not wanted to expand the Salisbury, North Carolina, laboratory into an armory of manufacture, this had been "the result of circumstances not entirely within the control of the Bureau."[8] He did not want Burton to stop work on the Macon Armory buildings, yet while not directing him to halt operations entirely, had to curtail his activities drastically, relying on Burton's "energy and resources, for a final triumph over all obstacles."[9]

[7] Gorgas to Seddon, Richmond, CRLR, 1865, Doc. GWD 27.
[8] De Lagnel to Mallet, Richmond, November 7, 1864, CROB, XXXVII, 337.
[9] Gorgas to Burton, Richmond, November 5, 1864, AGPF, Burton.

Mallet was in much the same predicament as Burton. General Howell Cobb had advised him to move all the laboratory stores and machinery, and he followed Gorgas' advice in the removal—sending most of the stores to Savannah and the percussion cap factory with employees to Selma.[10] But Savannah turned out to be the worst possible place for that purpose. The city was evacuated by Confederate troops on December 21, and Gorgas' officer there reported that all the ordnance and stores had fallen into enemy possession. He made a futile attempt to save the furnishings of his office.[11] Gorgas was despondent on receipt of this news, observing that it was a sad "denouement to such laborious preparations." The loss of Savannah, of course, made it imperative that all ordnance men husband the supplies they had on hand. They had already been instructed to collect private arms in the vicinity, as well as accouterments—the duty was considered so important that men might be employed on regular monthly salaries to go into the field and collect these items.[12] But as the fall of Savannah became a certainty, Gorgas told his officers that "the most rigid economy is enjoined in the use of imported Stores, of all kinds, as the supplies, now on hand, may not, soon be replenished.—The following articles are named, as, especially, requiring economical use; Steel, Tin, (Sheet and Ingot), Ingot-copper, Zinc, Flannel, Files, and Ordnance tools of all sorts; Also stationery of all kinds."[13]

In the confusion prevailing in the area surrounding Sherman's army, the first real failure of the bureau was encountered. Colonel G. W. Brent, at Montgomery, who had been trying to repulse a Federal raid at Pollard on December 16, complained with anger to General Beauregard that he had managed to collect troops for the operation but not guns.

Columbus, Ga., and Selma were both called on, and the replies of Colonels Wright and Moore was [sic] that they had no guns and ammunition. This is an important matter and deserves attention. Arms and ammunition are becoming a desideratum. The arsenal at Columbus is closed; the one here is idle. Should our communications continue to be interrupted, serious difficulties might occur for want of arms and ammunition here.

[10] Mallet to Gorgas, Macon, two telegrams, November 17, 1864, and letter, November 21, 1864, CROB, LII, 30, 31.
[11] Capt. S. J. Smith to Gorgas, Pocotaligo, S. C., December 26, 1864, CRLR, 1865, Doc. SWD 4.
[12] Ordnance Circular Number 83, Richmond, November 26, 1864, CROB, XXXVII, 384.
[13] Ordnance Circular Number 89, Richmond, December 20, 1864, ibid., p. 435.

He actually believed that he was giving Beauregard information that he did not already possess and paid the Ordnance Bureau an unconscious compliment by feeling so irritated that it had failed him.[14]

Even so, the Army of Tennessee was not overlooked. The combined arsenals would supply ammunition of all types to Kennard, excepting that for pistols, and would make pistol ammunition until Hood was supplied, despite the fact that they were low on lead.[15]

Christmas was not a happy day for the Gorgases. Josiah noted bitterly that the citizens contrived to eat heartily, while the soldiers had not had meat for several days. "The Commissary General has signally failed in his duties," he observed; "while there is plenty of food in Georgia there is none here. There is no sufficient excuse for this. The food must be brought here, and the means to do so provided and organized." Gorgas hoped that this affair would end in the removal of Northrop, who, he felt, "is not the man for the place which requires plain practical sense, just the sort of sense that Northrop has not."[16]

On December 27 Gorgas noted the deep feeling in Congress that Lee ought to be made generalissimo of all Confederate armies—an idea that appealed to Gorgas, since his faith in Davis' military sagacity had been badly shaken by Hood's Tennessee campaign.[17]

Richmond lay in the grip of the worst depression it had yet experienced during the war—prices had gone to unbelievable heights and there was no money in the hospital funds for extras to give the wounded men on Christmas. But one committee of citizens determined that Lee's gallant skeletons should not go unremembered on New Year's Day. A gigantic dinner was in preparation for his soldiers, and it was hoped that a regular New Year's meal, complete with all the trimmings, could go to each man in the lines. Although turkeys sold for as much as a hundred dollars,[18] General Gorgas presented the dinner committee with twelve birds for the troops—the troops he never forgot.[19]

The new year was ushered in for Gorgas by seeing his crews marched out to the lines. There certainly seemed desperate need for them—the

[14] Brent to Beauregard, Montgomery, December 18, 1864, ORA, Ser. I, Vol. XLV, Pt. II, 704. Gorgas said, in his indorsement on this letter, that on the day Brent mentions there were 320 rifles in store in Columbus, and 831 caliber .69 muskets at Mobile, with over 1,600,000 rounds of small-arms ammunition at the latter place.
[15] Capt. Humphries to Kennard, Columbus, December 23, 1864, *Mississippi MSS.*, Ser. E, Vol. LXIV; Mallet to Gorgas (telegram), Macon, October 10, 1864, CROB, LII, 26: "Want of lead is fast becoming serious at all Southern Arsenals." [16] GCWD, December 26, 1864, p. 157; January 4, 1865, p. 163.
[17] GCWD, p. 158. [18] Bill, *Beleaguered City,* p. 246.
[19] *Daily Richmond Examiner,* December 28, 1864.

Federals had 15,000 Negro troops north of the James, opposed only by a thin curtain of vedettes. Lee preferred not to call the armory and ordnance men to duty at all because each time they were put in the trenches large portions deserted—as Gorgas had said they would.[20]

And, ominously enough, the Secretary of War reported to the new Secretary of the Treasury, George A. Trenholm, on December 29, 1864, that the Ordnance Bureau had closed out the year $5,640,388 in arrears.[21]

New Year's Day passed, as had Josiah's and Amelia's anniversary, in depression and sobriety. Still, Richmond had its gay social whirl—many marriages and dances in the midst of the siege, perhaps because of it. Congress could not satisfy itself of the reasons for the food shortage in Lee's army, and Northrop tried to fasten the blame on the Secretary of War—an impossible task. Indications were that Charleston, too, would fall to Sherman. "No money in the Treasury—no food to feed Gen. Lee's army—no troops to oppose Gen. Sherman—what does it all mean. . . . Is the cause really hopeless? Is it to be abandoned and lost in this way? I fear as I have feared for two years past, there is no master hand at our helm."[22]

Events during January only tended to confirm this suspicion. On the twelfth, after a fire had burned 22,000 sacks of corn at the Charlotte station and heavy rains had washed away a portion of the Piedmont Railroad, it was discovered that Lee's army had only two day's provisions and a call was issued to the citizens of Richmond for a part of their supplies.

In this dark hour of our struggle there is of course strong feeling against the administration for having mismanaged our affairs. This must be expected in adversity. I have cherished and long ago expressed my conviction that the President is not endowed with military genius, but who would have done better? It is impossible to get anyone to say who, and it is probable that as much has been done with our armies as ought to be expected. The odds against us have been very great. But our finances have been badly conducted. For this the President can scarcely be held responsible. It is not a province he is expected to control. The hostility to the administration will however force some change in the cabinet no doubt. Benjamin, Mallory and Seddon are obnoxious, especially the latter. The Commissary Gen'l too, who has failed wretchedly, will be replaced I have no doubt. He has hitherto been supposed to be very partial to the

---

[20] Bill, *Beleaguered City*, pp. 247, 249.   [21] ORA, Ser. IV, Vol. III, 975.
[22] GCWD, January 6, 1865, p. 164.

President, and the President to him on account of old friendship at West Point, but this appears to have ceased, and those about Northrop abuse the President grossly, from which I infer that their principal has changed his tone.[23]

By January 18 everything seemed blacker than ever. Fort Fisher, guarding the entrance to Wilmington, had fallen on the 15th, thereby closing the last port open to blockade-runners on the eastern seaboard. Congress, the Gorgases learned from a friend, showed tendencies to make peace with the enemy, "feeling that we cannot carry on the war any longer with hope of success." Josiah and Amelia sat around the living room fire, discussing the possibility of going to Mexico "to live out there the remnant of our days." But a week later Gorgas had gotten over his hopelessness; he felt his courage come back when he thought of "the brave army in front of us, sixty thousand strong. As long as Lee's army remains intact there is no cause for despondency. As long as it holds true we need not fear. . . . We must sustain and strengthen this army, that is the business before us."[24]

His concern for the Army of Northern Virginia did not, of course, mean that he had forgotten the Army of Tennessee. On January 4, 1865, he had informed Colonel Kennard that 60,000 Sharps and 5,000 Whitworth rifle cartridges were ordered to him.[25] And in the excitement Gorgas took time to think about Charleston. He suggested to General Lee a plan whereby he felt the city might be held long enough to permit a Confederate troop concentration in the vicinity. Briefly, this plan, as approved by Lee and forwarded to Beauregard, was to have the Navy hold the forts and the citizens the lines. Beauregard, who really did not think the plan feasible, nevertheless recommended it to Lafayette McLaws, in charge of Charleston, on February 18, 1865,[26] a day after the city had been evacuated by Confederate forces.

In the meantime, Gorgas had directed that Mallet should not be too precipitate in moving all his laboratory machinery. If, at the end of January, no hostile force appeared to be threatening Atlanta, he could

[23] GCWD, January 15, 1865, p. 165.

[24] GCWD, January 18 and 25, 1865, p. 166.

[25] Gorgas to Kennard, Richmond, January 4, 1865, *Mississippi MSS.*, Ser. E, Vol. LXIV.

[26] Beauregard to McLaws, Ridgeway, S. C., ORA, Ser. I, Vol. XLVII, Pt. II, 1217; Beauregard to Lee (telegram), Ridgeway, February 17, 1865, *ibid.*, p. 1208: "I believe the suggestion of General Gorgas impractical, but will recommend it to General McLaws."

return his stores to Macon, since the Confederate railroad connections through Atlanta should be reopened by then.[27]

The demand for small arms, especially for the cavalry, pushed Gorgas to redoubled efforts in that direction. Lee had already appealed to the people to turn in any cavalry arms in private possession and asked Gorgas to direct the importation of these weapons from abroad.[28] The need was urgent, and Gorgas invited Burton on January 26 to come up to Richmond for a consultation on the subject.[29]

Burton, too, had been having his troubles. Afraid that the pistol factory at Columbus, Georgia, might be forced to move, he did not know just where to advise Gorgas to put it. Nor could he make immediate answer to a query from the Chief of Ordnance as to how many pistols could be made without fail by the first of May. Gorgas had said that the need of pistols would be great and had directed that the total output at Macon would go to Richmond; also, he had stopped the sale of cavalry pistols fit for service.[30] But conditions were so uncertain that no accurate prediction could be ventured.

Burton arrived in Richmond on February 7 and went down to the armory to stay with the Gorgases during his sojourn in the capital.[31] He and Gorgas went at once to work, and after a few days' close study of the general outlook, on February 11 Burton submitted a plan which he thought might provide means for supplying small arms. He advocated the erection of an armory in England, equipped with the machinery which had been purchased from Greenwood and Batley, most of which had reached Bermuda and Nassau. If this proved impossible in the Confederacy's present circumstances, he suggested as a "dernier resort" that the machinery be sold abroad and the proceeds used in purchasing arms. He declared himself ready and willing to go abroad as agent in the event either suggestion was approved.[32]

Although Gorgas did not seem to think this plan feasible, he did decide to give Burton a special assignment. On February 21 he issued instructions, approved by John A. Campbell, Assistant Secretary of

[27] Gorgas to Mallet, Richmond, January 4, 1865, CROB, XXXVII, 482; Burton to Gorgas, Macon, March 28, 1865, CROB, XXIX, 233.

[28] Lee to Gen. Wade Hampton, Headquarters, January 9, 1865, ORA, Ser. I, Vol. XXXVI, Pt. II, 1028.

[29] Gorgas to Burton (telegram), Richmond, January 26, 1865, AGPF, Burton.

[30] Gorgas to Burton, Richmond, January 5, 1865, AGPF, Burton; Maj. E. B. Smith to Burton, Richmond, January 24, 1865, ibid.; Ordnance Circular Number 4, Richmond, January 1, 1865, CROB, XXXVII, 513.

[31] Burton, Diary, February 7, 1865.

[32] Burton to Gorgas, Richmond, February 11, 1865, GMSS.

War, giving Burton the duty of directing the operations of the Macon, Athens, Columbus, and Tallassee Armories. His orders concerning them would be considered as those of the Ordnance Bureau, "when not in conflict with previously received instructions therefrom." The reasons for this assignment were, first, to insure maximum production in the armories and, second, to give better and closer supervision since Gorgas could not be sure of reliable communications.[33] At the same time Burton received authority to sell or exchange any unneeded armory products for provisions for his operatives. Gorgas also gave him verbal permission to raise funds by loans from private individuals, pledging government property as security.[34]

In the midst of Richmond's excitement about the visit of Francis Blair, ostensibly in connection with peace negotiations, Gorgas continued his struggle to keep ordnance going to the troops. On January 16 he had telegraphed Mallet to return the cap factory, with all its appendages, to Macon, and on the eighteenth Mallet replied that he had done so.[35] The problem now was to get the machinery running. Mallet had to have funds to buy stills since he had no copper with which to begin operations. The supply of sulphuric acid, needed in making fulminate of mercury for caps, also was exhausted, and Mallet wondered whether the government lead chambers at Charlotte would be able to furnish enough. Colonel St. John thought so.[36]

A serious shortage of arms and ammunition appeared so imminent, particularly if Columbia should fall, that Gorgas on January 18 directed subordinates at each of his installations to select someone to go out in the country and collect rifles and carbines, percussion muskets, Colt army and navy revolvers, bayonets, infantry accouterments and cavalry equipment. If money was not available Gorgas directed that such iron castings or other stores as could be spared be given in exchange. "All Ordnance Officers are urged to use their best discretion in carrying out these directions so as to secure all arms in the vicinity of their commands, not in the hands of troops."[37] The ammunition

[33] Gorgas to Burton, Richmond, Burton.
[34] Gorgas to Burton, Richmond, February 14, 1865, AGPF, Burton; Burton, *Diary*, February 23, 1865.
[35] Gorgas to Mallet, Richmond, CROB, XXXVII, 492; Mallet to Gorgas, Macon, CROB, LII, 35.
[36] Mallet to Gorgas, Macon, January 11, 1865, AGPF, Mallet; Mallet to Lt. Col. William R. Hunt (telegram), Macon, January 23, CROB, LII, 36; Mallet to Gorgas (telegram), Columbia, S. C., February 2, *ibid.*, pp. 38–39.
[37] Ordnance Circular Number 7, Richmond, CROB, XXXVII, 514.

question loomed so large that Gorgas directed on January 27 that "one-third of small arm ammunition of each sort made between the 1st of Febry and the 1st of May, will be placed in permanent reserve for the coming campaign."[38] He still held to his plan of preparation.

But the fabrication of ammunition presented additional problems. On February 2 Mallet telegraphed from Columbia that "Augusta, Macon, Columbus, & Selma Arsenals still want lead. It is extremely desirable that authority be given to send some at once. I have tried all means to collect scrap lead in Charleston & here."[39] He had not entirely given up hope yet, however, for on February 11 he wired Colonel William R. Hunt, Nitre and Mining Officer at Selma, that efforts should be made to collect lead water pipes from houses and streets in Mobile.[40] On the fourteenth he reported to Gorgas that he had been in touch with Major Henry Myers at Mobile, with a view to getting water pipes, but "Genl. Maury thinks it inexpedient. Whence is lead to come for all South Western Arsenals and troops?"[41] As the need became more urgent, Gorgas took an interest in Mobile's pipes, and on March 4 Major Myers wired Mallet that Maury had placed 3 tons of scrap lead at his disposal, plus about 50 tons from the water works. He had discovered 50 additional tons which could be obtained from water mains and had taken steps to secure them. On March 28 Mallet told Gorgas that, barring enemy interference, he expected to get 100 or 150 tons of lead from the same source.[42] And although some lead arrived through the blockade in time to forestall the removal of the mains, Mallet urged that the work not be stopped. He had already received some lead from Mobile, and on March 30 reported that he still was in great need of it.[43]

Having watched with growing anxiety the approach of Sherman toward Columbia Gorgas had convinced General John C. Breckin-ridge, the new Secretary of War, that its loss would be well-nigh dis-astrous. On February 16 Breckinridge advised Beauregard, who was then reportedly at Columbia: "If there be danger at Columbia take the promptest and most efficient measures to save the machinery at the

[38] Ordnance Circular Number 10, Richmond, *ibid.*, p. 524.
[39] Mallet to Gorgas, CROB, LII, 38.
[40] Mallet to Hunt, Macon, *ibid.*, p. 41.
[41] Mallet to Gorgas (telegram), Macon, *ibid.*
[42] Mallet to Gorgas (telegram), Macon, *ibid.*, p. 49.
[43] Gorgas to Mallet (telegram), Richmond, March 29, 1865, CROB, XXXVII, 649; Mallet to Gorgas (telegram), Macon, CROB, LII, 50.

armory."[44] But Columbia fell the next day, and all the equipment was lost. Gorgas entered in his diary on the night of the nineteenth: "Charleston has been evacuated (17th) and Columbia occupied by the enemy. My losses in valuable machinery and I fear stores, have been very great, greater than ever before—perhaps than the sum of all my former losses. Why it was necessary to evacuate so hastily is not yet known."[45] Visiting General Joseph E. Johnston (now again to Gorgas' satisfaction,[46] assigned to command the remnant of the Army of Tennessee), at Charlotte on March 1 Burton heard from the general that no equipment remaining in Columbia was in working condition.[47]

Following the fall of Columbia, the affairs of the Ordnance Bureau deteriorated at a frightening pace. Gorgas himself had received temporary rejuvenation by the fact that on February 6 Lee had been made Commander-in-Chief of the Confederate Armies and that on the 16th Seddon had been replaced by Breckinridge. Perhaps the best news, however, was that Northrop had been supplanted by Brigadier General I. M. St. John, the erstwhile head of the Nitre and Mining Bureau—a man whom Gorgas had selected as possessing the highest administrative talent. St. John started his new job in a manner which thoroughly pleased the Chief of Ordnance. On the night of February 18 "we held a meeting (or rather he did) at his office. . . . He invited a dozen of the principal citizens to advise him and assist with suggestions. It was a good inauguration. With Gen. Lee in command and a good Commissary Gen. we need now only vigorous measures in the dept. of finance."[48]

By February 23 there hung an agonizing and incredible dread throughout the city that Richmond would be evacuated. Amelia spoke anxiously to Josiah about family plans in such event. "She is most inclined to stay, with her six little children, within the enemy's lines, and perhaps it is better than to fly one does not know whither." But on the twenty-seventh all department heads were notified to prepare to move, and all cotton and tobacco ordered out of the warehouses preparatory to being burned.[49]

[44] Breckinridge to Beauregard (telegram), Richmond, ORA, Ser. I, Vol. XLVII, Pt. II, 1201.   [45] GCWD, p. 170.

[46] GCWD, February 3, March 2, 1865, pp. 168, 173.

[47] Burton, *Diary,* March 1, 1865.

[48] GCWD, February 19, 1865, p. 170. He noted on the 16th that on the 15th General Lee had received him somewhat sternly and looked "very much troubled."   [49] GCWD, February 23, 1865, p. 171; February 27, p. 171.

People are almost in a state of desperation, and but too ready to give up the cause. . . . It must be confessed that we are badly off for leaders both in the council and in the field. Lee is about all we have and what public confidence is left rallies around him, and he it seems to me fights without much heart in the cause. I do him wrong perhaps but I doubt if he believes we will or can succeed in this struggle.[50]

On March 6th Gorgas concluded that "the crisis of our fate is rapidly approaching," and he was right. He observed little groups of people standing on street corners, whispering, shaking their heads—are things this bad?—should we go away or stay?—can General Lee hold out? And then on March 19 came news that Hugh Aiken had been killed in action at Cheraw, South Carolina. This, coupled with the recapture of Dick Gayle, with the blockade-runner "Stag" on January 20, filled the family's cup of bitterness to the full.[51]

Concerned about the ability of the various supply bureaus to keep themselves going, the War Department queried Gorgas for his ideas on the subject. He frankly told Assistant Secretary Campbell that he had only 25,000 arms on hand as of March 5, 1865; up until that time he had been dependent on importation for about one-half of the supply. That avenue no longer remained open; workshops had in large measure been destroyed, and those remaining were badly impaired by lack of workmen, who had to be detailed from the Army. The chances were that "the most important of the manufactories of arms will be destroyed in a short time, and we have to contemplate a deficiency of arms and ammunition." Considering this report, Campbell recommended strongly to Breckinridge that some consideration be given to ending the war.[52] Gorgas would have been shocked had he known that his report was used as evidence that the Confederacy should give up.

[50] GCWD, March 2, 1865, p. 172.
[51] GCWD, February 3, March 6, 9, 1865, pp. 168, 174, 175; also Vandiver (ed.), "The Capture of a Confederate Blockade Runner: Extracts from the Journal of a Confederate Naval Officer," *North Carolina Historical Review*, XXI (1944), 136–38. By a strange coincidence Gen. Sherman had talked with Mary Aiken just a little while before Hugh was killed, and had agreed with her surmise that Hugh would have to "submit or get killed." Sherman recorded the conversation in a letter to Gen. O. O. Howard, March 3, 1865: "I met at Winnsborough Mrs. Aiken, wife of the very Colonel Aiken you report as killed in the fight with Duncan. She was Miss Gayler [sic], of Mobile, sister of Mrs. General Gorgas, of the rebel Ordnance Department. . . . I hardly thought so soon to be a prophet." ORA, Ser. I, Vol. XLVII, Pt. II, 661–62.
[52] Campbell to Breckinridge, Richmond, March 5, 1865, ORA, Ser. I, Vol. LI, Pt. II, 1066.

Fayetteville Arsenal and Armory fell to Sherman on March 10, its commanding officer wailing to Gorgas that the government seemed oblivious to the value of the place—"eight cotton factories here, machinery of navy ordnance works, coal and iron of Deep River country, besides what we have."[53] There was no need to tell Gorgas; he knew.

Everything seemed to be coming apart at the seams. Time no longer favored the South. The Clarksville Harness Shops had to cease functioning because no transportation or supplies could be obtained, and Captain Dinwiddie, who was trying to keep on manufacturing, asked authority to impress supplies and wagons.[54] On March 14 Gorgas felt compelled to tell Burton that "Selma and Montgomery should not be considered places of safety, during the spring & summer." He had received this advice from the headquarters of the Army, and if true, it meant that Tallassee Armory would be endangered. Burton's attention was called to the possible propriety of moving the works to Athens, Georgia. Gorgas gave him permission to do as he thought best.[55] And there was more bad news to come. Colonel Richard Morton, St. John's successor in charge of the Nitre and Mining Bureau, on March 24 reported to Breckinridge, and four days later to Lee, that his detailed men in North Carolina and southwest Virginia had been ordered into the ranks, with the consequent stoppage of lead-mining operations. Unless some corrective action were taken, there would be no more lead.[56]

Despondency seemed to permeate the whole country. Even effervescent Colonel Mallet felt it; on March 25th he inquired of Gorgas if he should suspend all work on permanent buildings at the laboratories, in view of the want of money and pressure on the bureau.[57] But Gorgas was not yet ready to quit. He replied on the twenty-seventh that Mallet should keep working on the buildings, but make that work secondary. He promised to send money at once.[58]

With the growing chaos following Sherman's destruction of the railroads, Gorgas knew he could not hope to retain close control of his

[53] Lt. Col. F. L. Childs to Gorgas, Fayetteville, February 23, 1865, ORA, Ser. I, Vol. XLVII, Pt. II, 1264.

[54] Dinwiddie to Gorgas, Richmond, March 15, 1865, CROB, XCII, 36. He secured permission to impress his needs. Dinwiddie to Capt. John Kane, Richmond, March 15, *ibid.*, p. 37.

[55] De Lagnel to Burton, Richmond, March 14, 1865, AGPF, de Lagnel.

[56] Morton to Breckinridge, Richmond, ORA, Ser. IV, Vol. III, 1164–65; Morton to Lee, Richmond, March 28, *ibid.*, pp. 1175–76.

[57] Mallet to Gorgas (telegram), Macon, CROB, LII, 47.

[58] Gorgas to Mallet (telegram), Richmond, CROB, XXXVII, 636.

arsenals, armories, and shops. So he did the next best thing. He gave virtually plenary powers to General Rains, who took charge of the arsenals and ordnance depots in Augusta, Macon, Columbus, Montgomery, Selma, and Demopolis on March 14, 1865. Rains was to receive the reports usually sent to the Chief of Ordnance and exercise the authority of that officer until further orders. No sooner did Rains take over his job than he cautioned his commanders that since there were few arsenals north of the Savannah River (and these in a precarious condition), "the main, if not entire ordnance supplies of our Armies, may at any time fall upon the [southern] arsenals. . . . The earnest and hearty co-operation of the officers in immediate charge, bringing to bear all their resources and exertions will manifestly be required to meet the anticipated demands."[59]

As the evidence of the coming evacuation of Richmond grew more imminent, the managers of the Tredegar Iron Works became worried about the fate of their plant. They could not see why it should be destroyed, since it could not give the enemy anything he did not already possess. The Secretary of the Navy, who shared a contract with the Army for the output of the works, advocated destruction, with the aid of the company. But Gorgas gave a contrary opinion, taking the view that such a procedure would be wasteful in the extreme.

The resources of the enemy are so great in machinery and manufactures that no addition the Confederacy can make will increase their power to do us harm or to do harm to others; and any unnecessary or objectless destruction of private property, or even public, ought to be avoided. I see no adequate result in the case from the destruction of the establishment.[60]

Thus the company owed the continued existence of its business to the foresight of Gorgas.

News of military operations around the Confederacy continued dire. Sheridan seemed to be running wild, and on March 15 rumor placed him fifteen miles from Richmond with 8,000 men. Troop concentrations above Raleigh indicated where Johnston might give battle, but Gorgas felt that the Confederate forces would retreat behind the Roanoke. The spirit of the people, on the other hand, seemed to be rising, and that of the Army remained good. Gorgas and Tom Bayne still were undecided about where they would go in case Richmond fell. But on

[59] Circular Number 1 (Rains), Augusta, March 14, 1865, *ibid.*, p. 618.
[60] Joseph R. Anderson & Co. to Breckinridge, Richmond ("Confidential"), March 7, 1865, and indorsements, ORA, Ser. I, Vol. XLVI, Pt. II, 1287–89.

the nineteenth news of Johnston's victory at Bentonville, North Carolina, turned people's minds from the fall of Richmond. Here at last was a Confederate victory, not decisive, of course, but a victory nonetheless. Gorgas wanted Lee to detach 10,000 men to Johnston's army.[61] The Chief of Ordnance must not have known how few and ill-prepared were the men between his quarters and Grant's bluecoats. But Lee tried.

On March 25 Lee attempted to take Fort Stedman, a work close to the south bank of the Appomattox, and to slip a picked force to the aid of Johnston; he failed miserably and with ghastly losses. Gorgas reported that Colonel Baldwin, Lee's ordnance officer, considered the affair a *"bad failure."* The Gorgases prepared their baggage for transportation to Danville, though they were not yet sure where they might go. Amelia grieved at the prospect of leaving their comfortable and cherished home, but there seemed little else to be done.[62] Gorgas had firsthand knowledge of the serious nature of things when, on March 29, he received a note on small stationery, marked *"Private."*

29 March 1865

Genl' Gorgas—
My dear sir
Will you do me the favor to have some cartridges prepared for a small Colt pistol, of which I send the moulds, and the form which contained a set of the cartridges furnished with the piece—The ammunition is desired as promptly as it can be supplied—

Very truly yr's—
JEFFN DAVIS—[63]

And on April 1 Grant's army made a terriffic attack against Pickett's semidetached force at Five Forks, almost eliminating two divisions as factors in the war. Pickett had attacked Sheridan on March 31 with some success, but then had stopped and entrenched. Gorgas again had firsthand information about these events. Baldwin on March 31 had penned a letter from the field in which he gave his first and unprejudiced impressions of the battle as a spectator and limited participant.

In our Department the expenditure of ammunition has been very great— entirely disprotionate [*sic*] to the magnitude of the engagement. In fact in all our recent fights I notice an apparent nervousness on the part of our

[61] GCWD, March 19, 21, 1865, pp. 177, 178.
[62] GCWD, March 26 and 29, 1865, p. 178.
[63] This note is in GMSS. Gorgas sent it to Col. Broun, asking that he make fifty cartridges and send both the note and the bullets to the Ordnance Office.

men and of the enemy causing an unusual rapidity of fire either at random
or at ranges too great to be effective. The expenditure of Artillery ammunition especially of Napoleon[s] has been very great. Owing to our deficiency of men, a good many portions of our lines were held by skirmishers
and Artillery and a heavy artillery fire was maintained against the skirmish lines of the enemy.

As Baldwin was writing, Pickett was engaged at Five Forks, but Baldwin did not know the extent of the action, though "from the urgent appeal for ammunition I presume the fight was sharp."[64]

April 1 passed quietly enough, with Richmond's attention bemused
by a rumor that the Confederacy had signed a treaty with Emperor
Maximilian of Mexico. And the weather, as Sunday, April 2, dawned,
left nothing to be desired. But the tocsin sounded at daybreak, and
"locals" went to the lines north of the James to replace part of Longstreet's men, who had gone to Petersburg. An ugly rumor had it that
Pickett's men had been roughly handled the day before, but Richmond
followed its usual Sunday routine with little show of concern. The
churches were crowded, with a great many of the worshippers wearing
mourning. The Gorgases were at St. Paul's, where Josiah had been
baptized and confirmed, and were sitting one pew behind the President (Mrs. Davis had already gone south). During the service, and
before the Reverend Mr. Minnegerode had begun his sermon for the
day, the sexton, a man well known to Richmond's churchgoers, stepped
quietly down the aisle to the President's pew, touched him on the
shoulder, bent over, and whispered in his ear. The President arose and
calmly walked out. In a moment the sexton returned, tapped General
Gorgas on the shoulder, and told him he was wanted outside. A
messenger waiting at the door told him that General Lee's line had
been broken and Richmond would have to be given up.

The rest of the day seemed to move too fast. Gorgas got in touch with
General Jeremy Gilmer, the Chief of Engineers, and induced him to
join in an appeal to the War Department for the issuance of orders preventing the destruction of tobacco and other property by fire. Gorgas
thought that turpentine spilled on the bales would destroy the tobacco
effectively with much less danger. The suggestion was approved, but
in the confusion attending the government's withdrawal, part of the
tobacco in the warehouse on Shockoe Slip was burned, ultimately contributing to a general conflagration.

[64] Baldwin to Gorgas, Ordnance Office, Army of Northern Virginia ("Private
and Confidential"), March 31, 1865, 11 o'clock P. M., AGPF, Baldwin.

Gorgas heard by one o'clock in the afternoon that Lee expected the government to be gone from Richmond by eight that evening. He and Amelia had been planning to move the children and their effects to Danville on Monday, but now Amelia decided to remain in Richmond. She and Josiah moved their things up to Maria Bayne's house, where she and the children were to stay. During the afternoon Gorgas issued instructions that nothing under his charge should be burned, lest a general fire start and innocent people suffer. He stayed with his family as long as he could, then, in company with Bayne, bade them good-bye and set out about midnight for the Danville Depot. As the two wended their way down Cary Street, they passed one of the arsenal gates, and Gorgas saw that a sentinel was posted there as usual. The rumble of the artillery caissons retreating across the James bridges was distinctly audible, but everything gave promise of an orderly evacuation. Shortly after one on Monday morning, the train on which Bayne and Gorgas had secured space left the Richmond yards, but it did not clear the vicinity of Manchester before three. Fortunately their train had gotten too far away for them to hear the explosion of the arsenal. It would have sickened Gorgas.[65]

Before he took leave of his family (Willie was able to sleep, even during the height of the excitement), Gorgas gave Amelia a note to a friend of his in the Federal Army, who would have charge of affairs in Richmond, General E. O. C. Ord. This note, dated at Richmond, April 4, read: "I am obliged to leave my wife and children and Mrs. Jones. They occupy a house on Cary St. between 4th and 5th. I beg you will extend to them such guard and protection as may be needed."[66]

One of Gorgas' last orders before leaving Richmond was to Colonel Broun, whom he instructed to use the Lynchburg Canal to move stores from the arsenal to Lynchburg. Broun complied with the order in so far as he could, dispatching the boats by midnight, but they never reached their destination.[67] Broun received instructions to report to Gorgas at Danville—an order he did not carry out for fifteen years.

Having arrived at Danville, Gorgas and Bayne did what they could to hold their bureaus together. They had no idea what was going on in the rest of the Confederacy, nor did their field officers know the where-

---

[65] I have drawn heavily on the excellent account of the events of April 2 in Bill, *Beleaguered City*, pp. 266–71, and on Jones, *Rebel War Clerk's Diary*, II, 465–67. GCWD, April 30, 1865, p. 179, gives a good resumé of Gorgas' activities after about one o'clock in the afternoon of the second. For the story of Gorgas' being called from St. Paul's I relied on Broun, p. 375.

[66] Gorgas to Ord, GMSS.   [67] Broun, pp. 375–76.

abouts of their chiefs. One of the greatest testimonials to the efficient manner in which Gorgas had organized the bureau is the performance of his field officers during the last hectic days before the surrender of the Army of Tennessee. The main reason why the bureau managed to go on functioning was that Gorgas had given so much authority to the lower echelons. Rains shouldered responsibility with ease, and Mallet continued his usual operations with no hesitation.

Mallet knew by April 5 that Selma had fallen and as a consequence determined to press the manufacture of friction primers at Columbus.[68] He also continued to make percussion caps at Macon, obtaining a supply of nitric acid from sulphuric. He wanted Rains to advise him whether or not to keep the suphuric acid for telegraph batteries, using only chlorate of potash for caps.[69] By April 14 Mallet had a slightly clearer idea of what was happening. He advised Rains that the stores at Columbus had been moved and that Macon seemed about to be taken. He thought of moving the cap factory but delayed because of the time it would take to get it going again in a new location. This factory was the only source of caps left to the Confederate armies, but Mallet confessed himself at a loss about where to move it. Colonel Wright had told him that 100,000 pounds of lead and a little niter were safely in store at Eufaula and that some would be sent to Augusta. A little bacon, flour, and coffee had been obtained and was stored on the St. Mary's River.[70] By the fifteenth the post commander of Macon told Mallet that the question of moving the cap factory would have to be decided at once since the Federals were approaching Columbus. In a frenzy Mallet telegraphed Rains: "Where is General Gorgas?"[71] But Rains did not know. By the seventeenth the post commander had peremptorily ordered everything moved from Macon, and Mallet assured Rains that he would "try to move all ammunition and finished stores for field service first. Columbus has been taken."[72] Mallet himself stuck to his laboratories and so fell into Federal hands when Macon was occupied on April 20.[73]

[68] Mallet to Wright (telegram), Macon, April 5, 1865, CROB, LII, 52.
[69] Mallet to Rains (telegram), Macon, April 8, 1865, ibid., p. 53.
[70] Mallet to Rains (telegram), Macon, April 14, 1865, ibid., p. 54.
[71] Mallet to Rains, Macon, ibid.
[72] Mallet to Rains (telegram), Macon, ibid., p. 55.
[73] Statement of Public Property in Macon Armory, Burton; Mallet to Rains (telegram), Macon, April 26, 1865, AGPF, Mallet. In this telegram Mallet protested the legality of the manner of his capture.

While his officers tried to keep things going, Gorgas himself was having some exciting times. He and Bayne remained in Danville until April 10, when the news of Lee's surrender at Appomattox the day before came to them. "I saw the President the same evening, and he was preparing to leave Danville. He was evidently overwhelmed by this astounding misfortune. He had sent for Gen. Cooper, myself and Col. Morton, the only Chiefs of Bureaus present. But he had no instructions to give me, and I told him I would probably receive some from the Secr. of War, who would be in the following day."[74]

Gorgas and Bayne, in company with some friends, left Danville in ambulances about one o'clock in the afternoon of the eleventh—the President having gone the night before to Greensboro by train. They finally arrived at Charlotte on the nineteenth, their wagon having broken down; they saw more food on the trip than they had dreamed of in years.[75]

In Charlotte Gorgas performed his last official act as a general in the Confederate army when he examined a young aspirant for a lieutenant's commission. On April 25 he had received formal notice that he, General Lawton, and General Gilmer of the Engineers, constituted a Board of Examiners to examine this cadet.

We met a little before sundown in the ample upper story of a warehouse, in Charlotte, N. C., and by the waning light of the last day of the Confederate government we went through all the stages of an examination of an expectant lieutenant of the Confederate Armies. Lawson [Lawton] I think took him on Geography and History, Gilmer on the Mathematics, while I probably tested his English Grammar. He passed the ordeal in triumph and got his commission, which I dare say he prizes very highly as he ought to do, considering the august body that signed the certificate which pronounced him qualified for it.[76]

On the 26th, the day that Joseph E. Johnston surrendered the Army of Tennessee, Gorgas and Bayne, Captain William Aubrey, and

[74] GCWD, April 30, 1865, p. 180. Gorgas did not hear for some time that Gen. Lee had remembered him gratefully during the heart-breaking time of the surrender of the Army of Northern Virginia. Lee told Col. Baldwin to give Gorgas a message for him when he had the opportunity: "Tell Gorgas if other Depts had been conducted as was the Ord. I would not have been in such a strait as this." Quoted in Amelia Gorgas to Thomas L. Bayne, Tuscaloosa, August 9, 1883, GMSS. Bayne mentioned this remark in his "Sketch of the Life of Josiah Gorgas," *Southern Historical Society Papers*, XIII (1885), 222–23.   [75] GCWD, April 30, 1865, pp. 180–81.   [76] GOC, p. 287.

Joseph Denegre started for Winnsboro, South Carolina, which they reached by April 30. Once there, Gorgas found time to write again to Amelia—he had written hurriedly from Danville on the tenth[77]—this time telling her in some detail about the condition of things, saying that the President was on his way south with a strong escort of cavalry, and would probably get to the Trans-Mississippi Department, where he might follow. His main concern, however, was his family and how he would take care of them. He considered it possible that the United States authorities might banish him but thought it unlikely.

You & I with our little flock must retire to some sequestered village where we can live at little expense, for the present, & have schools for our children. I have no fears that I shall not be able to take care of you; but for a year or two to come I should be glad to get a little home in some place in northern Ga. or Ala. where the climate is bracing & where there is some society. Indeed so far as I am personally concerned I am not at all alarmed or intimidated at being compelled to change my profession. I am not yet old, & the world is open to me.[78]

The full shock of what had happened did not hit Gorgas for some time. He wrote on May 4 that "the calamity which has fallen upon us in the total destruction of our government is of a character so overwhelming that I am as yet unable to comprehend it. I am as one walking in a dream, and expecting to awake." He admitted that he was drifting until he could get hold of himself and decide what to do.[79]

He and Bayne were trying to get to Alabama but were afraid they could not make it without being paroled. On May 11 they heard that Davis had apparently given up all hope of reaching the Trans-Mississippi, and this caused them to alter their plans as well. They now felt they might as well give their paroles and keep moving quietly toward Alabama.[80] Relatives at Winnsboro had supplied them with ample clothing for the trip, and Gorgas was enjoying the exercise.

Feeling that an unkind Providence had abandoned them to their enemies, on May 12 they left the Aiken home at Stony Point and drove to Abbeville, where they spent the night. On the thirteenth they had a leisurely ride, stopping for the night at the home of a Widow Gary,

[77] Gorgas to Amelia, Danville, GMSS.
[78] Gorgas to Amelia, Winnsboro, S. C., May 4, 1865, GMSS.
[79] GCWD, pp. 183–84.
[80] GCWD, May 11, 1865, p. 185; Gorgas to Amelia, Coronacco, May 11, 1865, GMSS.

who entertained them well. "It would be a nice place," Gorgas wrote, "to spend a summer month or two."[81] On the fourteenth hearing that the enemy was in the vicinity of Elberton in force, they crossed the Broad River at Barker's Ferry, taking the Washington-Centerville road. "Met a squad of 6 Yankees whom we mistook for our own people. Bayne asked them whether there were any 'Yankees' at Washington. They seemed to be quite as willing to pass us as we were to pass them." Bayne and Gorgas went on to Washington, and the wagons to Centerville. "We got paroles for ourselves, and the two others."[82] But they did not attempt to get pardons.

The war was over.

[81] GCWD, May 12, 1865, p. 186.   [82] GCWD, May 14, 1865, p. 186.

XX

In Business, Failure

MAKING HIS WAY SOUTH AT THE CLOSE OF THE WAR, GORGAS REAL-
ized it would not be easy to readjust himself to the comparative inactivity of private life. A large portion of his personal fortune had been
invested in Confederate securities; and since these were now valueless,
he had very little money with which to make a new start. While the
war was still going on, he had been unwilling to decide what course he
would follow if the South were defeated. But after Lee's surrender he
had been forced to face the issue. Despite his boast to Amelia to the contrary, for a man of forty-six he saw nothing but a bleak future.

Long before Gorgas and Tom Bayne reached Montgomery, May 26,
1865, the ravaged, chaotic condition of Alabama had become obvious.
There was extremely little food in that part of the country, and only in
cities where the Freedmen's Bureau and Federal troops were located
did the people appear to eat with any regularity. Gorgas was worried
about the possibility of arrest, but an old friend from his service in the
United States Army, General A. J. Smith, told him in Montgomery
that there were no orders to arrest Confederate officers. Unmolested,
Gorgas and Bayne continued their journey by river steamer to Selma.
Bayne disembarked at that place, and Gorgas went on alone, finally
reaching Greensboro, Alabama, on May 29.[1]

For some time after he arrived in Greensboro, he could not fully
grasp the disaster that had befallen the Confederate States. While he
allowed himself time to readjust gradually, making no serious efforts
to obtain a job, he observed the pathetic conditions about him. Alabama, as well as most of the other former Confederate States, had
sustained almost incredible material losses, and the standard of living

[1] GMSD, May 29, 1865.

had sagged alarmingly. Everywhere was firsthand evidence of economic paralysis. Property losses, including the value of slaves, were estimated as high as $500,000,000. Widespread confiscation of livestock by both armies had reduced the number of animals far below that of the prosperous prewar days. The total value of farm property, which in 1860 had amounted to over $250,000,000, was now estimated at only $97,716,055. All banking capital, of course, was gone, and assets of the state had greatly depreciated.[2] The transportation network was bankrupt. Alabama had boasted some 800 miles of track in 1860, but during the war few or no additions were made. The continued use of rolling stock in the face of governmental inability or refusal to repair it had brought ruin to the roads. At the close of the fighting the Tennessee & Alabama Railroad had no more than three serviceable cars. Rails were unsafe, locomotives out of order, and depots, bridges, and trestles destroyed. The Mobile & Ohio had lost $5,288,562.23 in Confederate currency; 37 miles of track were worn out, 21 miles had been burned, and 184 miles were devoid of bridges, trestles, and stations. In addition, the Federal Army had destroyed shops and other repairing facilities. The Alabama & Tennessee Rivers Railroad alone had lost at least a million dollars in Confederate money, "its shops, tools, and machinery at Selma, 6 bridges, its trestle, some track and many depots, its locomotives and cars."[3]

Perhaps the general apathy of the people in the South immediately following the war may be partially attributed to this economic stagnation in the wake of widespread destruction. But to a man in Gorgas' position lethargy was a luxury he could ill afford. His family, which had by now moved from Richmond to Maryland, looked to him for money. He had had good luck in obtaining a small sum through the sale of some cotton rescued from the war, and additional funds came to him as a result of a blockade-running enterprise, but his stock of capital was still quite limited. He now needed a means of permanent support, and he needed it quickly.

There were some possibilities: the Red Mountain Iron Company, not far from Elyton, Alabama (now Birmingham), appeared to offer an opportunity in a business with which he was moderately familiar. Then, too, several railroad companies, in need of an executive officer, were to be considered.[4] Gorgas wrote to Robert Jemison, Jr., a former

[2] Walter L. Fleming, *Civil War and Reconstruction in Alabama* (New York, 1905), p. 254.

[3] *Ibid.*, pp. 259–60.   [4] GMSD, June 12, 16, 19, 1865.

Confederate senator and would-be industrialist, about the possibility of resuming work on the North East & South West Railroad (which might serve Elyton), confiding that he thought seriously of "applying myself to the development of the mineral resources of the region of country which that road will penetrate. . . . One can hardly go wrong in that region so fertile in the elements of future wealth. The mining interest and the Rail Road interest must go hand in hand—that latter must lead the former & must then be sustained by it—"[5] Jemison seemed a likely person to query about this problem, since he belonged to that class of men whom Gorgas recognized as anxious to forget the war as soon as possible and return to their former pursuits.[6] But in this case Jemison could offer the former General nothing.

Gorgas by no means abandoned hope. On July 1 he wrote in his diary: "I am now at the age of 47, beginning life anew so far as my provision for my family is concerned. If the country were in a prosperous or even settled condition, it would be easy enough to earn one's bread and something more, but prospects are gloomy enough and it may be some time before I get at settled work."[7]

The necessity of earning a living had evidently caused a significant change in Gorgas' personal attitude toward Andrew Johnson's Proclamation of Amnesty. Bitter at the thought of taking an amnesty oath when he first heard of it, Gorgas had so modified his views by August, 1865, that he wrote Amelia: "I have not yet taken the oath of amnesty, tho' I am entirely ready to do so, whenever I get a good chance." True, he cited reasons why it would be unnecessary for him to take the oath: "I dont want to vote and have no property which is confiscable . . . no object in being in a hurry,"—but this admission was a large concession to existing conditions.[8] Like many others, he had decided to make the best of a bad situation.

By August another idea had crystallized in his mind. Although he heard that he might obtain the superintendency of the Selma & Meridian Railroad and thought that this would be a better job, he made up his mind to try the iron business. As he told Amelia, all of his training fitted him much more adequately for that sort of work than for the

[5] Gorgas to Robert Jemison, Jr., Greensboro, Ala., no date, *Jemison Collection.*   [6] See Gorgas to Amelia [Greensboro, Ala.], July 1, 1865, GMSS.
[7] GMSD, July 1, 1865.
[8] Gorgas to Amelia, Greensboro, August 21, 1865, GMSS. Gorgas took the oath of amnesty on August 22. See GMSD.

management of a railroad. It was also a "business which I have more *heart* for than any other I have tho't of." There was one drawback: Amelia hated the sort of isolated existence which the administration of an iron factory would necessitate. But Josiah had decided, and he maintained that the thing to do was to adjust their lives to the isolation.[9]

After this decision, the remaining questions were where to find suitable iron works and the money necessary to buy them. He believed that without too much trouble he could obtain the presidency of the Shelby Iron Company. These works were well known to him, since they had supplied much vital iron to the Confederate Ordnance Bureau, and this enterprise seemed to be ideally suited to him.[10] Though bitterly lonely and longing to go to Cambridge, Maryland, to see his family, he persevered in trying to find a permanent home for them in Alabama. Throughout the month of September and early October, therefore, he tried to work out an arrangement with Shelby which would give him gainful employment. But the company, itself badly in need of money, could offer little encouragement.[11]

After trying for several weeks to locate some fairly promising sites for an iron establishment, Gorgas had his attention called to the furnaces and plant at Brierfield, near Ashby, Alabama. This company had been established in 1860 under the management of Caswell C. Huckabee and Jonathan N. Smith, who had sold out to the Confederate government during the war. Consequently the plant now belonged to the Federal government as the successor to the defunct Confederacy. It would require special permission to buy the company, and Gorgas felt he would have to go to Washington to secure it. Here, too, he was probably rationalizing, since he was on personally friendly terms with General Wager Swayne, Assistant Commissioner of the Freedmen's Bureau in Alabama, who probably could have obtained the property for him easily. But a trip to Washington for the ostensible purpose of purchasing land would also offer opportunity to see his family in Maryland. His departure for the North hinged on the uncertainty of obtaining special authority to make such a trip.

A request for aid from his brother-in-law, Tom Bayne, who now lived in New Orleans, brought prompt response in the form of approval

[9] Gorgas to Amelia, Greensboro, August 21, 1865, GMSS.
[10] Gorgas to Amelia, Greensboro, September 11–12, 1865. See also Vandiver, "The Shelby Iron Company in the Civil War," *Alabama Review,* I (1948), 13–26, 111–27, 203–17.   [11] GMSD, October 14, 1865.

by General Philip Sheridan.[12] Consequently, armed with official sanction, he started for Maryland October 26 or 27 and arrived there November 2.[13]

After spending about a week with his family on Chesapeake Bay, Gorgas went to Washington to inquire at the Treasury Department about the possibility of purchasing the Brierfield plant. He hoped to form a company to help him finance it. After a considerable delay he obtained a letter from General O. O. Howard to General Swayne authorizing the sale of the property, if it was not needed for the Freedmen's Bureau.[14] Elated, Gorgas returned to Alabama and set about finding money. His efforts were successful. Francis Lyon, his close friend, brought several others into the project with him, and soon the company boasted some eleven stockholders, commanding a combined capital of $95,000, with $5,000 in reserve.[15] General Swayne consented to the disposal of the property as authorized by Howard, and the "Canebrake Company" purchased the plant at auction in January, 1866, for $45,000.[16]

The iron works, as they had existed during the war, had not been operated on an imposing scale, nor was the physical plant large or especially well equipped. The Federal Army, moreover, during the great cavalry raids directed against Alabama's iron regions, had considerably damaged it. Nevertheless, Gorgas observed that a good train connected the mills and furnaces and that two stacks, with one arranged for hot blast, were serviceable—and of course there was the land, 4,000 acres of it.[17] The iron ore was scattered, but sufficient, and Gorgas had no real doubt about the success of the enterprise, of which he was to act as manager. He planned to utilize $30,000 of the re-

[12] Gorgas to Amelia, Greensboro, August 14, September 29, 1865. Sheridan's approval was further strengthened during a trip to New Orleans in late September, when Gorgas and Bayne both visited Gen. E. R. S. Canby, Federal department commander. He told Gorgas, whom he had known when they were both in the "old army," that he did not foresee any trouble arising over Gorgas' trip to Maryland. By the middle of October Gorgas had abandoned hope of obtaining title to the Brierfield property without a trip to Washington.

[13] GMSD, October 15, 21, November 4, 1865. The equivocation about the date of departure is Gorgas' own.

[14] GMSD, December 17, 1865.   [15] GMSD, January 20, 1866.

[16] Ethel M. Armes, *The Story of Coal and Iron in Alabama* (Birmingham, 1910), p. 204. The Alabama legislature incorporated the company on January 28, 1867. See "An Act to incorporate the Brierfield Iron Works Company of the county of Bibb," *Acts of the Session of 1866-7 of the General Assembly of Alabama* . . . (Montgomery, 1867), pp. 229–30.

[17] GMSD, October 15, 1865.

maining capital to repair the plant and put in new machinery. This would leave $25,000 with which to begin operations. The company had no fears about being able to increase the number of stockholders and looked forward to larger capitalization.[18]

The Gorgases' outstanding objection to Brierfield was the primitive surroundings and the isolation. Although Amelia and the children had been exposed to living of this kind when Gorgas was in the United States Ordnance Department, they had grown to dislike it intensely. Gorgas did not wish to impose it upon his family, but there was nothing else to do. As it turned out, the family discovered certain compensations when they began to consider Brierfield carefully. Many of Gorgas' Confederate comrades were living fairly close at hand, and General William J. Hardee, whose plantation was within a day's trip, was a frequent visitor to the works.[19] Then, too, the people who lived in the vicinity established a neighborliness which it would have been impossible to achieve in a city. "Storms," as some parties were called, were organized and eagerly attended. Society, while lacking much in fashion, lacked little in energy and enthusiasm. The Gorgases were somewhat better off than others might have been in similar circumstances, since they had many family connections and old friends throughout Alabama.

Gorgas had made plans to receive his family in January, 1866, but delay in arranging a place for them to stay had made it impractical to have them come from Maryland until April. By then he had succeeded in having a house made ready for occupancy. Amelia and the children reached Brierfield on April 12, and moved into the home which all of them hoped might be permanent.

The house itself was not pretentious, since pretention had given way to necessity in the South of that era. It needed paint and was situated distressingly close to the railroad, but it had several advantages. It had been built atop a small rise in the hilly ground near the rolling mill, and on one side the lawn sloped gently down toward a small creek that gave the garden added lushness. The house had been located high enough to catch whatever breeze might blow during the hot summer days, and the general effect was that of easy-going comfort.[20]

Gorgas had gained his family's acquiescence to country life by promising that during the winter months the family might visit New

[18] GMSD, January 20, 1866.
[19] GMSD, July 12, 1865; Gorgas to Amelia, Greensboro, August 21, 1865, GMSS.
[20] This description is based in part on observation of the site of the Gorgas house.

Orleans. Amelia could take comfort, too, from the guests that frequented the house, including such notables as Generals Hardee and Joseph E. Johnston.[21] Railroad connection with Selma provided mail service for the family and brought them newspapers which prevented complete stagnation.[22] Food came by the same medium. On the whole, Brierfield was a fairly pleasant place to live.

As the days went by, Gorgas' outlook became progressively darker, not because of living conditions, but because of the troubles he continually encountered in getting and keeping the works in operation. His own bitterness and growing disillusionment added to the problems of the family. His depression, partly a carry-over from the last hectic months of the war, was heightened by the election of Alabama's Reconstruction Convention. "What an end to our great hopes!" he wrote in his diary. "Is it possible that we were wrong? Is it possible after all that one set of men can force their opinions on another set? It seems so, and that self government is a mockery before the Almighty. . . . Let us bow in submission and learn to curb our bitter thoughts."[23] Since the failure of the Confederacy, he confessed, his life had been "bitter and barren."[24] As a matter of fact, his despondency grew so marked that the material needs of his family on several occasions were the only things that carried him through, though a continuing interest in current events helped considerably.[25]

There appeared in his depression an essentially new symptom, one that seemed so unlike him as to indicate the possible existence of illness. He became frightened at the thought of the responsibility that the management of the company entailed and admitted in his diary that "I am in constant terror lest our funds may fail before I can get any returns from them. The load of responsibility is even greater than that of Chief of Ordnance in the Confederacy." He could not throw off the dread of failure at Brierfield, and this possibility preyed constantly on his mind. His anxiety grew so acute that he recognized its abnormality and sought to attribute it to dyspepsia or to some other organic ill. The lowest point in his outlook came in January, 1867, when he

---

[21] Johnston to Gorgas, Selma, January 19, 1867, GMSS; GMSD, January 7, 1867. It is interesting to note that among the cherished relics of the Gorgas family is a bed seven and one-half feet long, affectionately called "the Hardee bed," which Gorgas had built especially to accommodate the long frame of his friend.

[22] Gorgas to Col. J. L. White, Brierfield, January 23, 1867, *Brierfield Iron Works Collection, Letter Book*, p. 61.   [23] GMSD, August 3, 1865.

[24] GMSD, July 1, 1866.   [25] GMSD, August 6, 21, September 16, 1866.

wrote in his diary: "For no imaginable recompense would I live this life over again. I can now see how these poor doomed, destroyed wretches whose life destruction we daily see chronicled, are forced to their doom. Nothing is so terrible as despair."[26]

By April, 1867, however, something of his old determination had returned; and although reasonably convinced that the works would fail, he vowed his intention to "persevere to the last."[27] Certainty of failure came fully upon him in June and made the Fourth of July hardly a day for celebration. The political sham of the Carpetbag regime, although not actually in full swing as yet, doubtless contributed to his feeling of disgust; and he almost reached the point of readiness to take up arms against the Union again had it not seemed so futile. In September, after alternate hope and gloom, Gorgas received the news that President Johnson's latest Amnesty Proclamation included everyone except Jefferson Davis and members of the Confederate Cabinet, governors of states, and officers above the rank of brigadier general. This news meant little to him, and he did not look with pleasure upon the necessity of taking the oath of allegiance.[28] Christmas of 1867 did not pass happily at the Gorgas home, and Amelia observed that "our misfortunes seem to come towards Christmas . . . it is never a season of rejoicing with us." The children, fortunately, were more than content with the little gifts they received and seemed oblivious to the fact that their father was so downcast that he took a long, lonesome walk by himself.[29]

In January, 1866, when Gorgas had begun his work at the Brierfield Iron Works, he had planned to build the firm along the same lines he had used in developing the Confederate Ordnance Bureau. First, he wanted able men as his subordinates, and it was natural that he should seek the services of those who had served him well during the war. As his first assistant he employed W. H. McMain, who had been in charge of the Dalton Ordnance Depot, and later, as chemist, his friend and former Superintendent of Confederate Laboratories, John W. Mallet, who was also a stockholder.[30]

From the outset Gorgas realized that the task of getting the plant into operation was not to be easy. Expenses were overwhelming— over $200 per day for labor alone—and the purchases of material,

[26] GMSD, September 16, 1866; September 30 (a typical entry); October 15; January 7, 1867. [27] GMSD, April 3, 1867.

[28] GMSD, September 15, 1867. [29] GMSD, December 14, 25, 1867.

[30] GMSD, May 3, July 1, 1866.

machinery, and food continued heavy. He estimated that it required $10,000 per month to cover the plant's outlay. The only salvation he could imagine in July, 1866, was to get the furnace in blast by August,[31] and at best this was an uncertain prospect. The labor supply was an indeterminable factor. Negroes proved particularly unreliable, and those who did work well were not entirely satisfactory, chiefly because of the activities of the Ku Klux Klan, which, on at least two occasions, frightened them away from their work.[32] In addition, the Freedmen's Bureau did not function with efficiency, at least not in that section of Alabama, and this left Brierfield at times in possession of "workers" who would not work.[33] As early as March, 1867, the lack of money had forced Gorgas to refuse to hire additional labor. The number of his skilled workers could not be increased, nor could those he already had be relied upon to any great extent.[34] All things considered, labor was almost a liability.

Another major problem in the initial operation of the plant was the purchase of needed equipment. One example will suffice to show the sort of trouble encountered in securing machinery for the rolling mill. On September 11, 1866, Gorgas ordered some small rolls from a manufacturer in Pittsburgh, Pennsylvania. They failed to arrive for several weeks and Gorgas wrote a series of letters to the factory between November 16 and February 8. Finally, he learned that shipment had been delayed by ice and that the rolls would ultimately arrive. But in the interim he had been forced to put off prospective orders, much to the detriment of the company's trade.[35]

Underlying all other problems was that of money, just as it had been in the management of the Confederate Ordnance Bureau. Banks in the South had been wiped out because of the worthlessness of Confederate currency, and by 1867 they had not been able to recuperate.

[31] GMSD, July 1, 1866.

[32] Gorgas to Francis S. Lyon, February 22, 1867, *Brierfield Collection, Letter Book,* p. 104.

[33] Gorgas to Lt. George Shakley, April 1, 1867, *ibid.,* p. 152. In this letter to an officer of the Freedmen's Bureau, Gorgas wrote: "An aged Freedman named *Brutus* is here in a very destitute & helpless condition. He was brought here from Georgia during the war & can look to no one here for care in his old age. This company has supplied him with food & shelter for a year past for which he has been unable to render much return. It is a case you will find calling for immediate relief & I beg your *earliest* attention to it."

[34] Gorgas to William T. Quimby, March 3, 1867; Fowler, Hessee & Co. (Mobile), June 18, 1867, *Brierfield Collection, Letter Book,* pp. 121, 268.

[35] Gorgas to Messrs. A. Garrison & Co., November 16, 30, December 5, 1866, February 7, 1867; *ibid.,* pp. 3, 12, 22, 84.

Of course, Gorgas had begun his work with the confident hope that the company would make money. But in this he was sorely mistaken—by late 1866 he had to scrimp even to secure enough cash to buy corn. He requested some of the company creditors to extend their loans or bills and urged upon stockholders the necessity of a loan of $25,000.[36] As president of the company, a position the stockholders voted upon him in February, 1867, Gorgas had more authority to make financial arrangements than before. He left no stone unturned.

Among the expedients to which he resorted were liens against future production, sight drafts, and sales of the company's foodstocks. As credit became tighter (it finally became impossible to deal on credit at Selma), Gorgas grew almost desperate. "We are heavily in debt and with the present condition of our country—the South—it is impossible to sell stock or to borrow money," he wrote Colonel J. L. White. In view of these conditions he feared that Brierfield might be forced to sacrifice its property. "We could make money and work ourselves out of debt could we but find a market for our products at any rate which we had a right to calculate on."[37]

As the firm's financial condition grew worse, Gorgas resorted to frantic measures to keep going. On June 20, 1867, he mortgaged the iron works to his wife for the sum of $5,244.74, and on October 1, he borrowed from her the amount of $1,354.[38] Decreasing returns from sales of its products and the stringency of the currency forced the company into a practice of barter not unlike that practiced in war days, which it should have avoided at all costs. The large quantities of food needed at the Works cost more than the receipts would cover, and Gorgas sought to exchange iron for food. He tried the same scheme to obtain coke and other supplies.[39]

The sale of iron, which should have been the source of greatest revenue, did not bring anything like the expected profit. The reasons were several. Cost of production of foundry pig iron ran more than

[36] Gorgas to Col. White, December 16, 26, 1866; Dr. J. W. Watkins, January 1, 1867; D. F. Prout, January 23; *ibid.*, pp. 27–28, 36; 39; 62–63.

[37] See Gorgas to White, May 16, 1867; Guyol, Gayle & Co. (New Orleans), June 11; Col. James Crawford, June 17; *ibid.*, pp. 202; 251; 264; and GMSD, June 30.

[38] See Mortgage, June 20, 1867, and note, signed by Gorgas as president of the Brierfield Works, October 1, 1867, GMSS.

[39] Gorgas to J. E. Prestridge, November 15, 1866; L. F. Mellen, February 7, 1867; Messrs. G. & C. Place, February 12; Harville Steren, Superintendent, Central Mining and Manufacturing Company of Alabama (Montevallo), February 18; *Brierfield Collection, Letter Book,* pp. 1; 83–84; 88; 95.

$32 per short ton. The company made other, "fancier" types of iron and sold its best charcoal iron for $60 to $70 per short ton. New York offered a better, more lucrative market than the South, but Gorgas recognized several drawbacks to making New York profitable as an outlet. These included charges for drayage, breakage, and weighing, plus the cost of transfer from railroad to steamboat at Selma, Alabama.[40] On the other hand, prices for iron in nearby markets, such as Mobile, scarcely paid the cost of production. A firm in Mobile sold some Brierfield iron for $43 per ton. Better prices could have been obtained, except for competition from Selma, where "number one" iron was offered for $35 and "number two" for $34 per ton. In view of this, Gorgas thought it might be well to raise the price of his product in the local market. The low prices brought by all types of iron in the South had pushed Brierfield's down so low that the company was probably taking a loss in much of its production. In one letter, dated May 9, 1867, Gorgas stated that he would deliver pig iron "on the cars" at Brierfield for $32 per short ton, while in another letter, dated June 15, he said that production costs were more than $32.50 per ton.[41]

Another factor in the decreasing returns on production was an error in management, almost as costly as operating expenses. In the frenzy attending the efforts to sell its output, the company made a tactical blunder in permitting too many concerns to market its products, both in the North and South. This mistake was accentuated because of the practice of varying the price according to the wishes of the agencies. By April, 1867, Gorgas, in a letter to General Zachariah Deas, his New York agent, admitted this error and confessed that "it is undoubtedly unfortunate that all of our iron was not placed with you or some other one party but as we had to sell *here* we could not control it."[42]

The ultimate result of this policy, of course, was that the company, through its selling agents, competed with itself for a market, in addition

---

[40] Gorgas to Messrs. J. C. Graham & Co. (Selma), December 3, 1866; Zachariah C. Deas, December 4, 1866, April 13, 1867; *ibid.*, pp. 15; 21; 156–57.

[41] Gorgas to J. M. Parkman, April 1, 1867; McMain to Messrs. Gilkerson & Sloss (St. Louis), May 9; Gorgas to Deas, June 15; *ibid.*, pp. 171–72; 189; 261–62. Gorgas had quoted the price of $35.00 per short ton in Selma and added that "these prices are much too low & must soon go up we think." Gorgas to B. H. Micou, February 21, 1867, *ibid.*, pp. 103–04.

[42] Gorgas to Deas, April 13, 1867; J. C. Graham & Co., December 3, 1866; N. M. Robinson, January 15, 1867; Messrs. Ware & Davis (Montgomery), February 12; D. F. Prout, April 9; J. M. Parkman, April 16; *ibid.*, pp. 156–57; 15; 50; 88; 160; 171–72; McMain to Messrs. Gilkerson & Sloss, May 9, *ibid.*, p. 189; Gorgas to Charles M. Williams, May 31, *ibid.*, pp. 230–31.

to competing with other iron manufacturers. As each of the many official outlets for Brierfield iron put their stock on the market, the price came down in proportion, and some of the Northern agents advised Gorgas "how much our iron has suffered by being forced on the market thro' various hands."[43] This practice created a "bull market" condition, which the company could ill afford, and badly affected future production.

Most of the raw materials were secured from the near vicinity of Brierfield. Coal and coke came from the Cahaba Coal Mines, with offices in Selma, and most of the ore came from Brierfield's own fields.[44] But the transportation of the raw materials posed a problem intimately connected with the reasons for the eventual failure of the Brierfield Iron Company.

If money was the prime factor in keeping the plant running, Gorgas discovered that railroad transportation troubles were largely responsible for the gradual collapse of the company's venture. High freight rates on the Alabama & Tennessee Rivers Railroad made shipping to Selma ruinously expensive, since the rate stood at $3.25 per short ton in November, 1866, and was raised to $3.92 by January, 1867.[45] Gorgas complained persistently to officials of the road but got only unsatisfactory responses. He carried the campaign to his friend, General Hardee, president of the Selma & Mobile: "The rates over your road are sufficiently moderate & if we can get the same rates over this road, we may be able to compete in the market of St. Louis, as our iron is of such a nature as to command an advanced price. . . . Perhaps you can assist me in this matter."[46]

These efforts resulted only in still higher rates. The freight charge per mile in 1866 had amounted to six and one-half cents, but it climbed steadily until in June, 1867, Gorgas had to pay twelve cents per ton per mile for wrought iron to Selma. By that time he had become convinced that the railroad did not want to aid the Works—"I fear it is not the design of this company to accomodate us"—and he did not like the necessity of having to beg for a reduction to 6½ cents again. But

[43] Gorgas to Deas, June 15, 1867, *ibid.,* pp. 261–62.
[44] Gorgas to L. F. Mellen, January 4, 1867; Col. R. M. Moore, January 18, February 19, April 12, 1867; *ibid.,* pp. 41; 53–54, 99, 166–67.
[45] Gorgas to Hardee, November 23, 1866; E. G. Barney, Superintendent, Alabama & Tennessee Rivers Railroad, November 23; Messrs. A. J. Moses & Co. (Mobile), January 5, 1867; *ibid.,* pp. 6; 7–8; and 43.
[46] Gorgas to Hardee, November 23, 1866, *ibid.,* p. 6.

without a return to something like that rate, "it seems impossible to struggle on against such very high freight."[47]

The railroad proved unco-operative in many other ways than high costs. The Iron Works depended on the line for the importation of coal and coke from the Cahaba company, and if the service did not remain efficient, the daily production of iron suffered accordingly. The railroad apparently made no consistent effort to see that freight trains stopped to pick up cars loaded with iron at Brierfield. As a result some cars waited several days for movement to Selma. Then, too, the road made no great effort to move coal from the Cahaba and Montevallo mines to Brierfield in adequate quantity and on time. This resulted in the partial suspension of activity in April, 1867.[48]

In other ways the railroad managed to hamper Gorgas' operations. Maintenance of track and switch connections, a vital function of the road, was never looked after adequately, and damaged sidetracks in the Brierfield yards frequently held up shipments. The poor condition of the switch connecting these yards with the main line of Alabama & Tennessee Rivers track had the same effect. In addition, the railroad overlooked numerous little courtesies which would have improved the Iron Works. No agent was designated for Brierfield, and consequently no one could sign for freight. Brierfield was not made an approved stopping point but was kept on the list of flag stations. Mail addressed to the plant was frequently put off the trains at Ashby Station, some distance from the works. While these little irritations were not disastrous in themselves, they were the added straws that finally broke the back of the company.[49]

There were other adverse factors hampering Gorgas' endeavors. He protested in March, 1867, to tax collector William Berney against tax for castings "made for our own works & used in putting up the machinery for making the products covered by our license. I cannot think this correct. . . . We are taxed for example for castings used in building our blast furnace the products of which *namely;* pig iron are exempt from taxation."[50]

[47] Gorgas to Barney, November 23, 1866; White, June 25, 1867; Barney, June 25; *ibid.*, pp. 7–8; 242; 280–81.
[48] Gorgas to Cahaba (Alabama) Coal Company, June 9, 1867; M. Stanton, January 8, 9, April 10; Mellen, January 7; C. B. Barnes, April 9; *ibid.*, pp. 48; 45, 46, 165; 43; 164; McMain to C. B. Andrews, May 4, *ibid.*, p. 187.
[49] Gorgas to Stanton, January 5, March 12, April 1, 1867; Andrews, April 12, 1867; E. G. Barney, June 25, 1867; *ibid.*, pp. 41–42, 135, 150–51; 151; 280–81.
[50] Gorgas to William Berney (Selma), March 15, 1867, *ibid.*, p. 139.

It would be unfair, however, to give the impression that Gorgas and his assistants failed to make any progress whatever in the face of these obstacles. On the contrary, they did very well for a time and were particularly successful in perfecting the physical condition of the plant. An officer of the United States Army Engineer Corps, writing about the condition of these works in 1868, described them as follows:

All of the structures are of the most substantial kind. First, within one hundred yards of the railroad is the large rolling mill; within this there are three engines at work, one driving the "muck train," and intended also to drive the "nail plate train," a second which makes bar iron, and a third, which pumps water, cuts off iron, and a machine for making buckles for cotton ties. Here are eight puddling furnaces, two heating furnaces, and four boilers supplying steam to the engines. The boilers are placed by the heating furnace, and the steam is made by the waste heat from those furnaces. The machinery all appears to work well, is placed on stone foundation, and is well disposed for work. The puddling furnaces will convert sixteen gross tons of pig iron into muck bar in twenty-four hours, and these are daily converted into twenty thousand pounds of bar iron, and one hundred kegs of cut nails—the machinery for which is all on the spot, though not yet put up.

The engineer then described the cupola crane, machine shop, pattern shop, small brass factory, blacksmith shop, school, and the building intended for the nailery, all of which he considered to be of the first order. He described the hot blast furnace and the ore beds feeding the works in complimentary terms and thought that the plant showed great promise—and this was as late as 1868.[51]

In spite of the progress made, however, the passage of time pointed clearly to Brierfield's ultimate failure. The periodic stoppage of work for a variety of reasons was a clear indication of this eventuality.[52] Gorgas managed, somehow, to keep the plant in sporadic operation throughout 1867, but by June, 1868, he had become so convinced that it would be fruitless to hang on that he began to think of other employment. His idea was shared by Colonel Mallet, who himself quit the Works on August 31, 1868, and went to teach at the University of Virginia.[53]

[51] Quoted in Armes, *Coal and Iron in Alabama,* pp. 204–07.
[52] These factors included bad weather, needed repairs, lack of an adequate market, and breakdowns. See, for example, Gorgas to J. C. Graham & Co., March 1, May 31, 1867; Messrs. Prestridge & Knox (Selma), April 10; Guyol, Gayle & Co., May 28, 1867; *Brierfield Collection, Letter Book,* pp. 142, 229–30; 166; 225. [53] GMSD, August 31, 1868.

By mid-July Gorgas heard about a movement to get him appointed to the University of the South at Sewanee, Tennessee. This neophyte institution needed a headmaster for its Junior Department and seemed to offer a fine opportunity to indulge the propensities for teaching which Gorgas had always felt. After several trips to Sewanee, he secured the position and made definite plans to move there as soon as possible.

Since his appointment was not to become effective until 1869,[54] he had time to arrange for the transfer of Brierfield to other hands. He did not succeed for a year, however, when he finally leased the works to Captain Thomas S. Alvis, who had been familiar with them during the war.[55] Meanwhile, he had been forced to dismantle the furnace and install a new hearth. By July, 1869, the supply of ore had run out entirely, putting the final touch on Gorgas' ill-fated administration of the Brierfield Iron Works.

On July 1, 1869, his birthday, Gorgas moved to Sewanee and took formal charge of the Junior Department of the University of the South.[56] The family, for a time, at least, had to remain at Brierfield, since living conditions at Sewanee were still primitive.

---

[54] GMSD, June 7, July 10, August 9, September 23, 1868.
[55] Articles of Agreement, signed by Gorgas and Thomas S. Alvis, August 2, 1869, *Fitch Papers.*   [56] GMSD, November 5, 1869.

XXI

Experiment in Education

WHEN GENERAL GORGAS WENT TO SEWANEE, HE MAY HAVE BEEN smarting under the sting of self-criticism not unmixed with self-pity, but the new Headmaster of the Junior Department had many friends who had not lost faith in him. A number of his Confederate comrades had recommended him for the new position. His old brother-in-arms during Mexican War days, General W. S. Walker, had informed the Right Reverend William Greene that Gorgas, in his opinion, made an ideal choice for the job.[1] General John B. Gordon, the redoubtable division commander of Lee's army, wrote that "you could probably have found no man more eminently qualified for the position in the whole country."[2] On the same day that Gordon penned this letter, July 24, Jefferson Davis, in Quebec, had written:

I have received yours of the 15th inst when about to embark for Liverpool. It gives me pleasure to say that I have known Genl J. Gorgas intimately— and have the highest estimation of his moral qualities, his intellectual endowment & scientific acquirement. As Chief of Ordinance [*sic*] of the Confederacy his success, considering the means at his command were in my judgment extraordinary. Always diligent, discreet, and conscientious in the discharge of every trust in which I saw him tried, I feel no hesitation in commending him to you unreservedly for the position in which you inform me he is proposed, and feeling a very deep interest in the success of the "University of the South" I shall feel highly gratified if he should be appointed as head of the Junior Department of that Institution.[3]

On July 25, at Warm Springs, Virginia, the man whose recommendation counted most wrote his evaluation of the former Chief of

---

[1] Walker to Greene, Atlanta, July 17, 1868, *University of the South Archives*.
[2] Gordon to Greene, Atlanta, July 24, 1868, *University of the South Archives,* "Fairbanks-Gorgas University Letters, Miscellaneous."
[3] Davis to Bishop Alexander Gregg, Quebec, *ibid.*

Ordnance for Alexander Gregg, Bishop of Texas. General Lee said: "I am very glad to learn by your letter of the 15th Inst: that Gen J. Gorgas has been appointed Head of the Junior Dept: of the University of the South. From my association with him for many years & my knowledge of his character & acquirements, I believe him eminently qualified for the position."[4]

In August, Stephen R. Mallory, former Confederate Secretary of the Navy, added his commendation to the others,[5] and on the twenty-sixth Gorgas' trusted friend, General Hardee, wrote that "his education, habits, and personal qualities eminently qualify him to fill the position with honor to himself, and advantage to the pupils committed to his charge."[6]

The Trustees of the University of the South had certain rules which governed the administration of the University, and these Gorgas had to learn and obey. As Headmaster of the Junior Department, his duties were different from those of the Vice-Chancellor, but it would be well to know the rules governing that official as well, since Gorgas would have to serve during the absences of Vice-Chancellor C. T. Quintard.[7] At first the Executive Committee, functioning in the temporary absence of a superior governing board, appointed Gorgas and Professor Robert Dabney a committee to report a plan of organization of the grammar school or primary department. Possessing definite ideas on this subject, Gorgas and Dabney advised that the junior division should be a separate branch of the University, with the Headmaster in entire command of its operation. They recommended that in matters of curriculum and books, the master of the Junior Department should be obliged to consult with members of the faculty of the University, since the avowed purpose of the grammar school was preparation for entrance to the upper classes. In all other matters pertaining to the junior branch of the school, however, the master was to be autonomous. This plan was approved by the Executive Committee and became part of the body of rules governing the operation of the college. The arrangement had been proposed a year before Gorgas took complete charge of the lower grades, and until his arrival Professor Dabney served as acting master.[8]

[4] Lee to Gregg, Warm Springs, *ibid.*
[5] Mallory to E. [G.] R. Fairbanks, Pensacola, Fla., August 11, 1868, *ibid.*
[6] Hardee to Greene, Selma, *ibid.*
[7] Quintard to Gorgas, Cowan, Tenn., February 13, 1869, *ibid.*
[8] George R. Fairbanks, *History of the University of the South, at Sewanee, Tennessee* (Jacksonville, Fla., 1905), pp. 101–02, 100.

Gorgas had certain ideas on the curriculum and on the management of the University. He had been impressed with the tendency of the country toward pragmatism, and he wrote Dabney from Alabama that "we must try to satisfy in some degree the tendency to the *practical* which is now so general—It is possible we may have too many Latin & Greek authors on our list—This will correct itself as the course unfolds. —I am more solicitous to do a little well, than a good deal not so well." In the matter of discipline he had even more pronounced ideas, which ultimately would result in discontent. Dabney was enjoined to enforce

some degree of order in the boys rooms until their furniture arrives, & they can be regularly installed, & the rules of police fully enforced—I think the formation of *habits of order* of great use. . . . I want them especially to be taught that the study hours are hours of *work*—& that we will insist on their applying that part of the day to their books. Those who will not work in their rooms must do so at the chapel under the eye of the master.[9]

All this concern about habits and courses of study was a trifle premature since the physical plant of the University in 1869 was far from complete.

Thirteen years before, in 1856, bishops of nine Southern states had issued an able address from Philadelphia urging their congregations to support a university sponsored by the Episcopal Church.[10] Two years later, after considerable bickering and faultfinding, Sewanee had been chosen as the site for the University. The officials responsible for the selection of the location had been so badgered that they felt compelled to publish a defense of their judgment, *Address of the Board of Trustees of the University of the South, to the Southern Dioceses, in Reference to Its Choice of the Site for the University.*[11] Unless friends of the proposed school kept in mind the objectives which the Southern dioceses had in view when they undertook to establish a college, they pointed out, "it might not be easy to prove it was the fittest locality." As a line of departure the memorial stated that the University was "not the feeble effort of a single Diocese, but the concentration of the patronage

[9] Gorgas to Dabney, Brierfield, September 28, 1868, *University of the South Archives.*

[10] *An Address to the Members and Friends of the Protestant Episcopal Church in the Southern and South-Western States.* The concern of all these officials had been aroused in July, 1856, by a pamphlet written by the Bishop of Louisiana, Leonidas Polk. David G. Haskins, *A Brief Account of the University of the South* (New York, 1877), p. 28.   [11] Savannah, Ga., 1858.

of ten Dioceses extending from the Southern line of Kentucky and Virginia to the Western limits of Texas and Arkansas." A satisfactory location would have to be centrally situated, with a westward leaning, "since that is the only direction in which this confederation of Dioceses can ever extend itself." This consideration sharply restricted the Board of Trustees in point of geography, but it also established other restrictions. The site must needs give "undoubted healthfulness upon a soil furnishing abundant supplies of freestone water, which should afford easy communication with all parts of the confederation, and which should be surrounded by a farming country providing the necessaries of life in any quantity and at a moderate expense."

With these definite limits constantly in view, the Board decided on still other qualifications. These had to do with social conditions in the South. As the Board explained:

Our citizens have, for the most part, made the summer months their period of travelling, either for pleasure or business. During these hot months their plantations and even their city homes are deserted and they are scattered all the world over, from our own local Springs to Saratoga, Newport, Paris, Rome and Naples. At this season it is inconvenient for them to have their sons returned upon their hands. They do not wish to introduce them, at that immature period of life, to the dissipated society of watering places, and when they return, during vacations, from College, they desire to have them at home. For the South, the proper vacation of an University is the winter; that season when our planters and merchants and professional men are surrounded by their families upon their homesteads; when the cheerful Christmas fire is burning on the hearth, and mothers and sisters and servants can receive the returning student to his home, and revive within him that holy domestic feeling which may have decayed amid the scholastic isolation of a College; when he can engage in the sports which make him a true Southern man, hunting, shooting, riding; when he can mingle freely with the slaves who are in the future to be placed under his management and control. That a literary institution may give the student these precious months, it must be placed where the climate will permit him to apply himself during the hot months of summer, where intellectual labor will not be a burden, where cool nights and mornings will restore the energies which have flagged under close application.[12]

The site chosen admirably filled the need for a balmy climate in summer. Sewanee is perched on a plateau atop the Cumberland Ridge,

[12] *Ibid.*, pp. 6–7.

abundantly forested, and rich in building stone. Sewanee's elevation of 1,900 feet placed it, of course, "above the level of all intermittent disease," and gave it an uncommonly pure water supply.

But the Board had not neglected to consider an equally if not more important question in its deliberations over the site for the University: the problem of social life for faculty and student body alike. Socially, Sewanee had all the advantages of the Klondike or the interior of Africa. The Board, apparently a little disconcerted at its own selection, engaged in overzealous rationalization to justify Sewanee's admirable social potentialities. The mountain on which the University would be located was practically unpopulated. Still, the Board managed to find for its action a reason worthy of quotation:

Could we have found within these limits a city of from fifty to one hundred thousand inhabitants, combining with the refinement of large towns the facilities which cities afford for the conduct of life, and offering the University undoubted healthfulness, the Board would probably not have hesitated in selecting that as the best location for the University. But no such city offered itself, and the question was left to be decided between the neighborhood of a small town or the creation of a social atmosphere of its own around the University. When it was reduced to this alternative there was but little hesitation about the decision, and the Board almost unanimously agreed that it would be preferable to create a society around the University which should receive its tone from the University, and be in a measure dependent upon the University.[13]

The Board carefully pointed out that a railroad (equipped even in 1858 with T rails) connected Sewanee with the outside world, and the citizens of Franklin County, Tennessee, "which lies at the base of the lands upon which the University is to stand," had guaranteed the building of a turnpike from the Chattanooga and Nashville Railroad to the site of the University.[14] Sewanee, boasted the Board, was within forty-eight hours travel time of any of the ten dioceses save Texas, and was connected with all parts of the country by means of the "Electric Telegraph."

In fine, Sewanee, located on a plateau that apparently was

formed by God for the benefit and blessing of the valley of the Mississippi and the cotton growing regions of the Southern States . . . easy of access

---

[13] *Ibid.*, p. 7.

[14] The railroad of the Sewanee Mining Company served the University lands and linked with the Chattanooga and Nashville at Cowan, Tenn.

at many points . . . must become the summer resort of those wealthy planters, who desire to recruit their families during the summer months, and
are yet unwilling to be far separated from their planting interests. . . . This
will be the place of meeting of the South and West, and Wilmington,
Charleston and Savannah will here shake hands with Mobile, New
Orleans, Nashville and Memphis, and cement the strong bond of mutual
interest with the yet stronger ones of friendship and love.[15]

In the face of such rhetorical eloquence the Church bowed, convinced.

On October 10, 1860, the cornerstone of the University was laid
at Sewanee near the wooden building, two hundred feet long, already
constructed for University offices. The Civil War reduced the University on the mountain almost to rubble, and the Trustees had to begin
over again following the close of the struggle.

When Josiah Gorgas took charge of the Junior Department, there
was little in the way of a physical plant. Only the barest essentials were
present, no official residences had been provided for the staff, and the
facilities for classes were extremely crude. With his usual vigor, Gorgas
threw himself into the matter of erecting dormitories, class halls, and
residences. In his report to the Trustees for the year 1869, he frowned
on the idea of having the students board with staff members. This
scheme had been hatched as a means of avoiding, perhaps, the necessity
of building dormitories, but Gorgas felt that it would lead to a relaxation of "that constant supervision which is essential to a boy's
education."[16]

High on the list of things to do Gorgas placed the erection of a
house for himself and his family. He was provisionally lodged in a
four-room dormitory on the campus in company with Dr. F. A. Shoup,
with poor prospects of moving soon into more suitable quarters. The
Church had very little money for the erection of houses for the faculty,
of course, and Gorgas had to reduce his plans to "a small inexpensive
house."[17] Amelia, still in Alabama, longed for the day when the whole
family could again be together under one roof.

Gorgas was convinced that it would be advisable to erect "little
frame cabins" for the boys, since the attendance had, by 1870, climbed
to 170 young gentlemen.[18] Upon his return from vacation in February,

---

[15] *Address to the Southern Dioceses,* pp. 10–11. ·
[16] Fairbanks, *University of the South,* pp. 112–13.
[17] GMSD, May 3, 1870.
[18] GMSD, May 21, 1870; Haskins, *University of the South,* p. 8.

1870, he was struck with the need for more living space for the students. Everything appeared in great disorder when he arrived; the halls were still uncleaned, and nothing was in readiness to receive pupils. Space was at a premium. To make matters worse, the highly vaunted climate had been unbecomingly volatile, and the snow yet remaining on the ground alternately melted and froze, making the roads leading to the campus somewhat unhandy,[19] not to say dangerous.

The ideas of the Headmaster about building needs received the sympathetic attention of George R. Fairbanks, the University's Commissioner of Lands and Buildings, who managed to have a house built for Gorgas during the fall of 1870. It was ideally situated inasmuch as it put the General within easy walking distance of his offices. The Church spent $4,000 for its erection; but in July, 1871, Gorgas agreed to pay the $1,900 still due contractors and to refund the whole amount spent, so that it would ultimately become his property.[20]

In spite of these activities time hung heavily upon General Gorgas. With Amelia and the children away, he busied himself with work, having been appointed to the faculty of the University in addition to his duties as Headmaster of the Junior Department. But even the duties of a professor in the school of civil engineering, construction, architecture, and drawing did not take up all of his time. In his leisure moments he gave serious thought to the possibility of writing a history of the Confederate Ordnance Bureau. He corresponded with General Braxton Bragg on the subject and in June heard from his old friend, who was delighted at the prospect of such an undertaking. Bragg, prominently connected with the Southern Historical Society, wanted Gorgas to contribute an article on the Ordnance Bureau to the *Southern Historical Society Papers.* "I trust you will do so at an early day—It is due to the cause but especially to yourself. And it will establish with military men, the only competent critics, what I have always asserted, 'that you organized the only successful military bureau during our national existence.' And this is the more surprising, as you had less foundation to go on than any of them."[21]

With June came the family. On the twenty-seventh Amelia and some of the children (part of the family was off to school), descended on

[19] GMSD, May 3, 1870.
[20] Annual Report of the Commissioner of Lands and Buildings, *Proceedings of the Board of Trustees* (Sewanee, 1871), pp. 24–25.
[21] Fairbanks, *University of the South,* p. 119; Bragg to Gorgas, New Orleans, June 22, 1870, GMSS.

Sewanee bag and baggage. Although Amelia appeared much fatigued from the strenuous trip, Josiah was amazed at her capacity to recover her usual fine composure. At last it looked as though the Gorgas clan had settled down permanently—at least Josiah hoped so.[22]

The Headmaster had reason to be proud of his neophyte educational institution when, in January, 1871, he observed that it had prospered beyond the expectations of the Church officials. During the year 1870 the total enrollment reached 187; the University received $16,000 in tuition and other revenue, while expenditures had consumed only $13,500. Again General Gorgas' administrative ability was doing the most with the least. He felt he should have more time to devote to organization, but teaching allowed little time for anything else now. He considered relinquishing his teaching duties, but the small sum of $225 per term, offered for the work, proved too much of an inducement, and he continued instruction to meet expenses.[23]

Fortunately for Amelia there was no lack of society at Sewanee. Often old Confederate friends of Josiah's would stop by to see them, the whole month of July, 1871, being taken up by such visits. Then, too, the fact that Willie had at last turned serious attention to studying (certainly an innovation), and had attained the topmost rank of Sewanee scholars gave the family much satisfaction. In the words of his father: "His mother and sisters are very *proud of it and of him,* to say nothing of my feelings on the subject." Willie was not the only one of the young Gorgases who had been studying. The girls, as well, had been making progress under their father's kind and learned guidance. Not only that, but they had attained the age at which it was desirable for them to go away to some girls' academy. Gorgas could barely afford the expense of sending them to boarding school, but he thought this such an important part of their upbringing that he managed it. In September, 1871, he took Jessie and Mamie (Mary Gayle) to their first boarding school, at Columbia, Tennessee. "The poor girls were very homesick when I left them to return home."[24]

Things went along smoothly for the family until the Trustees' meeting on July 10, 1872. Then Gorgas' troubles with the University began. At that meeting Bishop Quintard expressed his conviction that the University should have a resident head, and Gorgas was recommended

[22] GMSD, January 17, 1871.   [23] *Ibid.*
[24] GMSD, August 20, November 14, 1871. Later the girls went to Fairmont, "a great improvement on Columbia." It was much closer to Sewanee, and they could visit every few weeks.

for the position of Vice-Chancellor. He was unanimously elected, with a salary of $2,500 as the bait.[25] He accepted the office with apparent reluctance. In his letter of acceptance Gorgas voiced a warning. If his words of caution had been heeded at the time, the difficulties that later developed between him and the Trustees might have been avoided.

I am not fully informed of the action taken by the board on matters of finance, but unless income and expenditures have been so proportioned as to insure the success of the former, all the efforts of a vice-chancellor cannot avert embarrassment and inefficiency. I can only hope that the board has fully considered resources, and appreciated our expenditures; and that they have not left this vital point in doubt. Expenditures estimated for are always certain to occur, resources confidently relied on are seldom fully attained. The experience of the past years warns us against an overestimate of our receipts.[26]

His election to the vice-chancellorship proved a source of pleasure to the Hebdomedal Board, the faculty committee which, with the Vice-Chancellor, governed the University in routine administrative matters. At the Board's next meeting a resolution was passed to the effect that the election was an action which afforded the group great satisfaction, "and feeling confidence in the conscientiousness and ability which he will bring to the discharge of his high and responsible duties, it hereby assures him of its hearty sympathy and support."[27]

The new chief of administration had severe problems from the outset. He explained to the Trustees on July 13 that the reduction of the teaching staff, necessitated by a shortage of funds, made it imperative that the Vice-Chancellor should have authority to assign professors to duties other than those for which they were paid. Certain faculty members had signified their willingness to co-operate in such a manner without added compensation, in the interests of the ultimate objectives of the University. The board, disposed to grant the new official almost everything he wanted, readily consented. In fact, the statutes governing the University seemed to provide the Vice-Chancellor with sufficient power for most contingencies. In actuality, however, Gorgas found himself severely handicapped. In his annual report to the Trustees for the year 1872 he urged that some recognizable definition

---

[25] Fairbanks, *University of the South,* pp. 142, 145.
[26] *Ibid.,* pp. 147–48.
[27] *The University Record* (Sewanee), September, 1872, p. 6.

of his authority be made, and if the Vice-Chancellor's powers were restricted, there certainly ought to be some resident board, possessing
powers of almost plenary nature, which could act in time of emergency.
This seemed all the more necessary since the Executive Committee had
been abolished on July 10, 1872, and no comparable body was created
in its stead. The Hebdomedal Board had no authority in matters of
policy: its jurisdiction was limited to matters affecting the curriculum
and other academic affairs.[28]

Gorgas appeared optimistic. In 1872 the Board of Trustees had
authorized a loan which had been successfully secured in November
of that year. Although the interest rate was higher than expected, it was
as low as could be had at the time. Gorgas, who loathed the thought
of debt, suggested in his report of 1873 that the houses, dormitories
(excepting Otey Hall), and the depot buildings be sold at fair rates and
the proceeds used to pay off the loan. "I feel sure that a proper hus-
bandry of our resources, and a rigorous supervision of our expenditures,
will place the finances of the University on a basis entirely satisfactory."[29]

After a year at the head of the institution, Gorgas told the Board that
he had too much work to do. In addition to the grueling task as Vice-
Chancellor, he taught engineering and physics, a load beyond his
capacity. He requested that instruction in physics be transferred to the
professor of pure mathematics, and recommended the appointment of
an assistant in that subject as soon as funds would permit.[30]

Another suggestion, concerning the reason why students went to
the University of the South, appeared in his summary of the University's condition. With his characteristic dry phraseology (often a cloak
for shrewd and biting comment) he pointed out the need for granting
degrees at the University, backed by schools competent to offer them.
Without this goal to work toward, he observed, a student's school life
was purposeless. His early advocacy of such an aim did much to raise
Sewanee above the status of a glorified high school.[31] As another

[28] Gorgas to Alexander Gregg, Sewanee, July 13, 1872, *Proceedings of the
Board of Trustees* (Sewanee, 1872), p. 40; *ibid.*, (1873), pp. 10–11; Fairbanks,
University of the South, pp. 143–44, 149. For the rules of the University, see
*Charter, Constitution and Statutes of the University of the South, with the
Rules of Order of the Board of Trustees*. Many of the provisions of these rules
were, of course, inoperative during the period of money shortage experienced in
the school's nascent writhings. Witness the fact that Gorgas received only $2,500,
when the statutes called for $6,000 as the minimum salary of the Vice-Chancel-
lor. [29] *Proceedings of the Board of Trustees* (Sewanee, 1873), p. 10.
[30] *Ibid.* [31] See Gorgas' report for 1873, *ibid.*

method of infusing spirit in the students, Gorgas obtained permission in July, 1873, to recognize the more advanced classes by means of some appropriate badge attached to their gowns. This led to the division of the University into juniors and gownsmen. Although the general regulation about the wearing of gowns was not enforced until 1875, the so-called gownsmen were exempt from a great deal of discipline and were put on honor for their own government.[32]

As the University continued its struggle for recognition under Gorgas' watchful eye, the South began to become aware of the school's attainments. The Sewanee *University Record* copied in its August, 1873, issue, an article from the May number of the *Rural Carolinian*, which praised the admirable curriculum at the University of the South:

The chief executive and administrative officer of the University is the Vice-Chancellor, who fills the chair of [engineering] . . . in which are taught location and construction of roads, railways and canals, masonry, forming bridges, instruction in and investigation of mechanics, electricity, astronomy, &c. Those who remember how faultless was the Ordnance Department of the Confederate Government—that, however scant became the rations of food and clothing, there never was a scarcity of ball and powder—need only to be told that the same efficient officer and accomplished scholar who was chief of our Ordnance Department, is now Vice-Chancellor of the University of the South. His presence is an assurance that the discipline of the University and the teaching of the students will be all that the most doting parent could desire.[33]

There was yet other evidence that Gorgas was, in effect, Sewanee's reputation. Amelia, who was staying for a time with the Baynes in New Orleans, wrote her husband with obvious pride: "I am amused to discover how entirely most persons consider the school as *yours* & how many boys are sent only because we are there—Mr. Seixas[34] says he cares nothing of course for the church but he wants to send his son just as soon as he is old enough to *Gen. Gorgas*."[35]

Routine, which Gorgas had always despised, made it necessary for the Vice-Chancellor to contrive diversions. A six-weeks' visit of the Baynes and friend Jefferson Davis in September and October, 1872, broke the monotony, but Gorgas engaged in other methods of amusing

[32] Fairbanks, *University of the South*, pp. 157, 158, 159.
[33] *The University Record*, August, 1873, p. 32.
[34] Seixas will be remembered as the Confederate War Department agent at Wilmington, N. C., who had general charge of government cotton exportation.
[35] Amelia to Gorgas, New Orleans, Sunday Morning, no date, GMSS.

not only himself but the whole mountain community. In March, 1870, he and a group of his friends founded a literary and social group which Gorgas named the "E. Q. B." *(Ecce Quam Bonum)* club. The society grew in size and in the pleasure it afforded. Male faculty residents of the mountain were members, and all "genteel" strangers who visited the campus were invited to meetings, which rotated among the houses of the membership.[36] The club had the thoroughly healthy rule that no university business would be discussed during its sessions. While Gorgas might inspire "quietness and respectfulness" on the campus or in the classroom when he "lifted his eye glass to view the source of some incipient disorder," he presented quite a different picture when safely ensconced in an easy chair at the home of one of the members. Reticent in public, and loath to speak to a large gathering, "General Gorgas in his chair and at his ease was one of the most companionable and lovable of men." It was in such circumstances that his natural hospitality and wit appeared to best advantage.[37]

These activities and writing his article on the Ordnance Bureau,[38] kept Gorgas from being utterly lonely and depressed, and this fact is reflected by his correspondence and diary entries, which are much brighter than when at Brierfield.

The financial structure of the University had been somewhat strengthened by the collecting trips of Bishop Quintard, who was trying to secure for Sewanee an endowment. The financial situation had improved enough by the middle of 1874 for Gorgas to think of beautifying the grounds and roads of the campus. This was, of course, a manifestation of his love of flowers and beautiful lawns, which he had displayed so strongly in the United States' service. He levied a small tax on the property of Sewanee residents for road improvement in and around the village and through the Church domain.[39]

The peculiar location of Sewanee, high hopes of the founding bishops notwithstanding, made the price of commodities go up because of the difficulty of transportation to the mountaintop. In view of the climb in

---

[36] See *The University Record,* June 22, 1872, p. 2; September 1872, p. 7. There was more to the selection of the name for the club than meets the eye. Gorgas, it is recorded, suggested this because these "were the initials of the motto attached by Bishop Lay to the pamphlet containing the proceedings of the board of trustees at Lookout Mountain, 'Ecce Quam Bonum,' being the title words of the 133d Psalm in the Prayer Book." Fairbanks, *University of the South,* p. 129 and n.   [37] *Cap and Gown* (Sewanee), June, 1883, p. 36.

[38] Gorgas to Jefferson Davis, Sewanee, January 23, [1873?], *Heartmann Collection.*   [39] *Proceedings of the Board of Trustees* (Sewanee, 1874), p. 14.

the cost of living, Gorgas, in his 1874 report, recommended a modest salary increase for the teaching staff, along with a $100 bonus to each professor for every three years of service to Sewanee.[40]

The meeting of the Trustees in August, 1874, was, on the whole, displeasing to Gorgas, and he devoutly wished they had done more to help him meet the growing problems facing the University. They were parsimonious, stubborn, and prone to take their own counsel to the exclusion of the suggestions of everyone else. The only person who appeared to be getting any money for the University was the indefatigable Bishop Quintard, whose trip to England in quest of funds had secured $10,000 in donations and a $25,000 endowment from Mrs. Mary M. Manigault, then of Brighton, for the erection of St. Luke's Theological Hall. She also endowed a theological scholarship in the amount of $5,000. Later she gave several thousand dollars for the completion of St. Luke's and endowed a second scholarship in the same amount.[41]

The year 1875 brought a dread recurrence of the painful faceache and head neuralgia which Gorgas had suffered before. True, the attacks had never really ceased, but now they were serious enough to interrupt his concentration. He wrote Major Fairbanks, Sewanee's Commissioner of Lands and Buildings, who was on vacation in Florida, that he would like to exchange climates with him. "I think it would subdue this neuralgia—a terrible visitation, which has spoiled my vacation."[42] In April the first real effect of these symptoms had manifested itself. The pain, which settled in Gorgas's left arm,

was pronounced atrophy, or wasting of the muscle of the arm, by Drs. Brown and Breckell of N. O. whither I visited early in March. They say the pain will cease with the disappearance of the substance of the muscle. I have slept but three nights since the middle of Dec except under the effects of medicine; I get up and warm my arm several times during the night. The paroxisms of pain recur about every two hours at night and are very severe. In the day time I am less troubled. The cold weather is unfavorable.[43]

Either General Gorgas' physicians did not wish to frighten him, or they were unaware of the critical nature of his affliction.

[40] *Ibid.*, pp. 12–13.
[41] Fairbanks, *University of the South,* pp. 162–63; GMSD, October 19, 1874.
[42] Gorgas to Fairbanks, Sewanee, February 14, 1875, *University of the South Archives.*   [43] GMSD, April 17, 1875.

But despite the distraction of incessant pain, Gorgas continued to manage the affairs of Sewanee, and in August, 1875, he was re-elected to a five-year term as Vice-Chancellor. Though his salary was reduced $500 to help defray the cost of his house, he was given back his dual posts of professor of physics and engineering. Gorgas seemed somewhat put out by the action of the Board. There was considerable agitation about the size of the University's $18,000 debt and some suspicion that it might be traced to faulty administration. The committee of ways and means, however, squelched that rumor and attributed the large expenditure of money to needed building. Nevertheless, Gorgas could not have felt satisfied about the Board's trust in his work.[44] Perhaps the pain held a clue to the cause of this gradually widening rift between the Vice-Chancellor and the Trustees.

Gorgas had certain family worries to add to those of illness and the University. William, now convinced, despite his father's strenuous objections, that he wanted to be a soldier, was trying hard to get an appointment to West Point. Gorgas was helping all he could, but things moved slowly. The young man had to establish residence in some state where he stood a chance of getting an appointment, and in November, 1875, he found himself in East Tennessee. There, it seemed, he might establish social contact with the family of a congressman, and this thought gave his father hope. He told Willie that "Women move the world you know," cautioned him to watch his spelling ("don't spell 'remarcable' with a c!") and advised him to keep lighthearted. "Don't let the future worry you. It will work out in spite of us." At this time Willie's wanderings in search of a place to reside did not cause Gorgas any financial embarrassment. He had entered the sum of $600 in his family budget to finance Willie's study of engineering; but if he wanted to work toward getting into West Point, well and good. "You have used hardly one half of this, so don't feel you are burdening me for the small sums you may require."[45]

In September, 1875, in writing to the energetic Quintard, still in England on his treasure hunt, Gorgas confessed that he had delayed answering a letter from the bishop because of the pain in his arm. "I find I am apt to defer my correspondence until I am myself surprised

---

[44] Manuscript section from report of the Treasurer, 1875, *University of the South Archives.*

[45] Gorgas to William Gorgas, Sewanee, November 5, 1875, February 10, 1876, GMSS.

at my negligence." He reported on the August session of the Board of Trustees, and observed that

the more I see of our Trustees—the men to whom the heart of the undertaking is confided—the more doubts I have of the foundation of the idea. . . . As usual the Board left us in a most unhappy state of mind. In cutting down expenses—dismissing Snyder, Du Bose & all the acting Tutors they left us helpless, & we have been obliged to retain these gentlemen . . . & pay them by outside contributions—a pretty commentary on the action of the Trustees! If they had consulted with me or with the Hebdomadel Board, *and followed their advice,* the curtailment could have been effected without serious embarrassment.[46]

The correspondence with Quintard was resumed in November, and Gorgas wrote him that the success of the trip to England "is our only hope of prolonging the existence of this work. Our good fathers in the church are evidently holding their hands & saying 'God's will be done.' " Gorgas had no fears of being unable to establish the University on a thoroughly sound basis, if it could be held together for eight or ten years. Granted that phenomenon, he felt that such an endowment could be obtained "as will secure us against *death* provided we don't commit suicide."[47]

The recent activities of the Board certainly looked as though it was pursuing a swift course to self-eradication. It had so materially cut the teaching staff that the quality of instruction suffered markedly; discipline was lax, and the general condition of the University was such that Gorgas feared a drop in attendance. In the face of this worry he again told Quintard that his illness was severe. "My terrible malady still continues with perhaps a slight improvement—at least I try to think that there is an improvement—I suppose I shall have to go South as soon as the School closes. I will try to make my absence useful to its interests."[48]

The problem of what Willie would do also bothered Gorgas. In January, 1876, he did something that must have required a great deal of courage and no little humility. He addressed an application for a presidential appointment to West Point to President U. S. Grant. This application was backed by several strong letters of recommenda-

---

[46] Gorgas to Quintard, Sewanee, September 8, 1875, in the possession of Miss Charlotte Gailor, Sewanee, Tenn.

[47] Gorgas to Quintard, Sewanee, November 14, 1875, *ibid.*   [48] *Ibid.*

tion, one from General Hood. But Gorgas had little hope of success, and his fears were justified, for Grant had used his appointments far in advance.[49] Failure to make West Point at length decided Willie on another course. A medical career might insure his admission to the Army Medical Corps. General Gorgas was opposed to the idea. The practice of medicine would be fine, but not the Army Medical Corps—Gorgas had been all too familiar with that branch of the service and had lost whatever respect he ever had entertained for it.[50] But Willie was determined, and in September entered Bellevue Medical College in New York.[51] His father undertook to finance Willie's medical education but had to limit his stipend to barely enough for food—sometimes not quite enough for that.[52]

The year 1876 dragged by with the pain and the Trustees giving running irritation. The passing months indicated that the Board and General Gorgas were no longer able to get along together. He confided to Willie in a letter written on August 8, 1877, that the session of the Board just ended "was quite stormy and disagreeable as usual."[53] Apparently the Board did not wish to make a liberal arrangement with their exchequer. The floating debt of the University almost overbore the best efforts to keep going, and Gorgas resorted to publicity in an attempt to maintain enrollment. He solicited the aid of the professor-elect of ecclesiastical history, Reverend David G. Haskins, who wrote a short history of the University for distribution to the public.[54]

The internal administration of the University continued good; discipline once more was excellent, students seemed to be making satisfactory progress in their studies, and military drill was better executed.[55] But at the August, 1877, meeting of the Trustees one of the prime causes of contention between that body and Gorgas came into the open. The meeting, "stormy" as Gorgas had termed it and unprogressive, produced as one result a document unique in the annals of the University. The Board's committee on organization reported a remarkable preamble and resolutions relating to the vice-chancellorship:

[49] Gorgas to William, New Orleans, January 21, 1876, GMSS (Wrightson).
[50] Marie D. Gorgas and Burton J. Hendrick, *William Crawford Gorgas* (Garden City, 1924), pp. 47–48.
[51] *Ibid.*, and GMSD, October 29, 1876.
[52] See, for instance, Gorgas to William, Sewanee, March 9, August 8, 1877, GMSS.
[53] Gorgas to William, Sewanee, GMSS.
[54] Haskins, *University of the South.*
[55] Fairbanks, *University of the South,* pp. 176, 177.

Whereas, the University of the South was established by its honored and revered founders, not only to be an Institution of learning, but also of religion and piety; and, whereas, by its Constitution it is most intimately bound up with the Parishes and Dioceses of the South, therefore be it Resolved, 1. That, in the opinion of this Board, its acting and responsible Head and the Officer of its Discipline, the Vice-Chancellor, should be, if practicable, a Clerk in Holy Orders; And be it further Resolved, 2. That for the best interest of the University, in its present stage of development, with its Theological Department about to be established, such a Clerical Head should be secured as soon as may be; and that, to this end, the Vice-Chancellor be informed of this preamble and these resolutions in order that he may have full time to make provision for himself, and in such way as shall least affect the University by any sudden change—and all, if possible, within the twelve months next ensuing.[56]

This document, of course, meant that Gorgas' connection with the University of the South would be automatically terminated at the end of the academic year. He made plans accordingly.

The Board, during its meeting, had added insult to injury by inquiring into the effectiveness of the administration, under the guise of trying to find ways of giving the Vice-Chancellor more power over administrative business. The committee on organization, charged with the duty of investigating this problem, reported that it had no additional suggestions inasmuch as the session of the Board was about to terminate, but phrased its report in terms most damaging to Gorgas. The members of the committee, by innuendo rather than direct accusation, gave the impression that more than enough authority already reposed in the office of Vice-Chancellor to insure firm administration, but that for some reason or other the University was not getting the right type of management.[57] The committee overlooked the haphazard and half-hearted co-operation the Board had been giving the Vice-Chancellor, which had done as much to produce the chaotic situation as any other factor. The reduction in the teaching staff was nothing but false economy and made it necessary to increase the number of professors later. Meanwhile, although enrollment had slightly increased, the quality of teaching had sunk to a new low.[58]

The whole situation had become so unsatisfactory that Gorgas gave up hope of success. In correspondence with Jefferson Davis he in-

---

[56] *Proceedings of the Board of Trustees* (Sewanee, 1877), p. 28.
[57] *Proceedings of the Board of Trustees* (Sewanee, 1877), pp. 34–35.
[58] Fairbanks, *University of the South*, pp. 166, 170–71.

dicated he was looking for another job, although he was now almost 60 years old.[59] In January, 1878, he told Davis something of the background of the trouble at Sewanee. Personalities had, of course, done much to make matters worse, and he had been surprised, he said, that of the very few Trustees actually opposed to him, Jacob Thompson was one of the worst.[60] Bishop Quintard, with whom Gorgas had before been intimate, had now lost all of his respect and, according to Gorgas, the respect of everyone on the mountain. "All believe him unworthy of trust, who have had dealings with him. He is a bad man in my estimation unworthy of the robes he wears, & does his holy calling great wrong in exercising it."[61] Davis, always quick to help, agreed that conditions at Sewanee were impossible and suggested that Gorgas obtain a position at the University of Georgia.

By late 1877 Gorgas had already given serious attention to the idea of establishing a military school somewhere around Lookout Mountain. He confessed to Willie on November 29 that he was not really hopeful of success, since he had no capital with which to get things going right. With $10,000 he felt he might try a venture of this sort, since Chattanooga, in his opinion, was one of the most thriving cities in the South.[62]

At the beginning of the new year, Gorgas, who was on vacation, decided to go to Washington, mainly for recreation and, he hoped, relief from the pain; but also to do some research for his history of the Confederate Ordnance Bureau. He reached there on February 7, 1878, and shortly after arrival went to the Senate to hear James G. Blaine on the silver bill. He was kindly received by the Ordnance Office and had several long visits with General Stephen V. Benét, the Federal Chief of Ordnance.

Gorgas did have some slight hope of getting a position for himself in Washington, but shortly after his arrival had realized that this was all but impossible for a Southern man.[63] One incident of the trip, however, should have made it worthwhile. During one of his talks with Benét, the Chief of Ordnance had told him that while touring Watervliet Arsenal shortly after the war he had seen Gorgas' old servants,

---

[59] Gorgas to Davis, Sewanee, September 5, December 24, 1877, *Heartmann Collection*.

[60] Thompson had been one of the Confederates involved in the Canada-Copperhead negotiations during the war.

[61] Gorgas to Davis, Sewanee, January 12, 1878, *Heartmann Collection*.

[62] Gorgas to William, November 29 [1877], GMSS.

[63] Gorgas to Amelia, Washington, February [?], 1878, GMSS; Gorgas to Davis, Washington, February 8, 1878, *Heartmann Collection*.

Ellen and James McContry, "and that James inquired especially after me, & how I was doing. Benét said he supposed like all that had gone I had lost everything & was doing the best I could. 'Well' said James, 'Mr. Gorgas was always mighty good to me, & if a matter of a thousand dollars would do him any good I would not be behindhand in giving it to him.' "[64] Not everyone felt like the Sewanee Trustees, it was good to know. After staying in Washington about three weeks, and renewing acquaintance with some of his relatives in the city, but with no relief from the pain, Gorgas returned to Sewanee.

As the meeting of the Board of Trustees approached in August, 1878, Gorgas became more and more convinced that his connection with the institution was terminated. "They are not likely to make such concession as would induce me to remain," on July 29 he wrote Willie, who still toiled in medical school. "I should do myself an injustice," he added, "in remaining longer, without more control of affairs here than I now have."[65]

Just a few weeks before the assembling of the Trustees for the meeting, Gorgas received some of the most welcome news that had ever come to his household. In July a telegram from an old friend, now a prominent lawyer in Selma, Colonel N. H. R. Dawson, told him: "You are elected President of State University—Am on way to see you."[66] This information transformed the prospects of the meeting. Now he had no fear or trepidation about what the Board might do—he cared less. His delight at the good fortune that had befallen him must have been painfully apparent to the Trustees, who, at the last minute began to show some signs of remorse at what they had done.[67]

Gorgas stole a march on them by sending the Trustees on July 29, the day they assembled, the following letter, written to the Right Reverend William M. Greene, Bishop of Mississippi and Chancellor of the University of the South. The letter, dated the twenty-seventh, read:

I beg to inform the Board of Trustees that I will not be able to meet them again, in consequence of engagements elsewhere requiring my departure on Monday next [the letter was written on Saturday]. In vacating the position which I have held, I beg to express my sincerest wishes for the continued prosperity of the University. I have, under the Statutes, ap-

[64] Gorgas to Amelia, Washington, February [?], 1878, GMSS.
[65] Gorgas to William, Sewanee, July 29, 1878, GMSS.   [66] GMSS.
[67] Amelia to William, Sewanee, July 15 [1878], GMSS. Amelia was happy to see how bright and cheerful the prospect of the change had made Josiah—she thought it a direct act of Providence.

pointed the Senior Professor, Dr. John B. Elliott, Professor of Chemistry, as my substitute, until such time as the wishes of the Board may be made known. I have placed my Annual Report in his hands, with the accompanying papers. Allow me, Reverend Sir, in severing our official relations, to express to you the reverent and affectionate regard I entertain for you personally. With the earnest wish that your useful and noble life may be prolonged,

I remain, your obedient servant.[68]

The Board was shocked; it ordered that a special committee be appointed to talk with General Gorgas "and report *instanter.*" This committee, made up of the Bishop of Tennessee, Reverend Dr. Banister, and Dr. De Rosset, went immediately to see Gorgas. He could see them only for a few minutes since he was about to leave for Alabama. These must certainly have been delicious minutes; at last he could say that his time was limited, that he had other things to do. The Committee said that the Board could not tell whether or not Gorgas' letter constituted a resignation of the vice-chancellorship; obviously the Board hoped it did. Gorgas was not trapped. He quickly denied that he had resigned, but "I have no intention whatever of holding on to the position of Vice-Chancellor," he said—a member of the committee transcribed the conversation—"the Board terminated my connection with the University at the end of the year."[69] He told the Board that he was perfectly willing to negotiate the settlement of the note for his house, but on August 2 Jacob Thompson moved that "in consideration of the past services of Gen. Gorgas, and his long connection with the University of the South as Vice-Chancellor, the Treasurer be directed to return to Gen. Gorgas his note for one thousand dollars, upon receiving from Gen. Gorgas a receipt in full for all claims or demands against this Board of Trustees." Gorgas' "resignation" was accepted by the Board the same day.[70] It sounded better that way.

Gorgas boarded a train on Monday, July 29, 1878, for Alabama, leaving the family temporarily at Sewanee. His hasty departure disappointed a group of warm friends who had planned to give him a tremendous send-off—but he was pleased he had missed them, since a demonstration "would have been disagreeable to me."[71]

[68] Gorgas to Greene, Sewanee, July 27, 1878, *Proceedings of the Board of Trustees* (Sewanee, 1878), pp. 10–11.

[69] Report of the special committee, *ibid.,* pp. 11, 12.

[70] *Ibid.,* p. 37.

[71] Gorgas to Amelia, Blount Springs, Ala., August 30, 1878, GMSS.

When General Gorgas left Sewanee, the University was preparing to give its first Master of Arts degree; the cadet corps had obtained new arms and had perceptibly bettered its drilling, and the various academic schools had vastly improved. What had been nothing more than a few shambling buildings supported by ambition when Gorgas came to the mountain had now grown to a full-fledged college—and the man largely responsible for this transformation had been dismissed.

XXII

Confidence and Respect

THE PRESIDENT-ELECT OF THE UNIVERSITY OF ALABAMA STOPPED
for a month at Blount Springs, Alabama, to rest and get ready for his
new tasks. As he looked forward to taking over his new post, the world
seemed brighter to him than it had for many years.

The University of Alabama had had six presidents before Gorgas
was elected. The campus had been almost thoroughly demolished by
Federal cavalry during the war, and the physical plant still showed
great inadequacy. But there was energy behind this organization;
Gorgas' friend, Colonel Dawson, was one of the more aggressive members of the Board of Trustees, and his presence there seemed to assure
the new president of better treatment than he had received at Sewanee.

The small town of Tuscaloosa, in which the University was situated,
was lazy, gossipy, and very Southern. The harsh effects of Radical Reconstruction had, fortunately, left few visible marks on the serenity of
the people, other than reducing most to genteel poverty. Gorgas was to
find a warm community spirit, into which he entered with customary
vigor. Tuscaloosa was made to order as far as flowers and trees could
make it so. Gorgas was delighted at the pleasant picture which greeted
him.

Shortly after his arrival, probably sometime in September, 1878, he
took a room in town. He went out to the University each morning—
a distance of a mile and a quarter—and enjoyed the walk. He moved
into the President's mansion as soon as the previous occupant had
completely removed his belongings, and took his meals "out."[1]

By the time the term opened, October 4, Gorgas had become
thoroughly familiar with the duties of his position and was ready to

---

[1] Gorgas to William, Tuscaloosa, September 13, 1878, GMSS.

get to work. He and the Trustees were highly encouraged that 80 boys had registered—"far beyond our hopes." It seemed that as many as 150 might be enrolled by Christmas. One great difference was noticeable in the ages of the students here and those Gorgas had seen at Sewanee. The Alabama student body was much older than the Sewanee boys, only one being under sixteen years. The general tone of the student body was somewhat rougher than that of the group with which Gorgas was familiar. For that matter, some of the faculty at Alabama could not be considered paragons of etiquette, but circumstances partially excused them. One professor was observed to eat with his knife, which was, of course, understandable, considering that the University was equipped with unpredictable three-pronged forks. The fastidious Gorgas improved the culinary equipment at once.[2]

The new incumbent had no lack of diversion, of sorts. The honor of his presence was desired at all the social functions, and, of course, he did not decline. He seemed particularly interested in a literary club to which he received several invitations. He thought that it embraced nearly all the literary talent of the town, since it had 71 members. "The ladies go out on the floor in their beautiful trains, & recite, and they read little essays, &c. It is better than the E. Q. B.—but I fear they get very tired unless they are themselves talking, declaiming, reciting &c."[3] Nevertheless, Gorgas was lonely. For a man who loved his family, he had been forced to spend too much time separated from them. On October 6 he wrote Amelia that he wished Richard could come down by November first and begin school with a tutor. "We could get on famously, he & I." Richard was delighted at the prospect, and was on the way to Tuscaloosa three weeks later.[4]

As the term progressed, Gorgas lost his fears about the bad nature of the boys in the university. He did not remember where he had gotten that impression but was glad to have it thoroughly dissipated. He came to have a high regard for the institution, and told his friend Major Fairbanks, at Sewanee, that he could unhesitatingly recommend it to anyone; the drill of the cadet corps was precise and the academic departments appeared to be in excellent condition.[5]

Despite all the good things that were happening to him, General Gorgas felt a dread. A realist, he understood that he might not be able

[2] Gorgas to Amelia, Tuscaloosa, October 4, 1878, GMSS.   [3] *Ibid.*
[4] Gorgas to Amelia [Tuscaloosa], October 6, 21, 24 [1878], GMSS.
[5] Gorgas to Fairbanks, Tuscaloosa, November 25, 1878, *University of the South Archives.*

to retain his job because of his declining health. In a frank letter to
Amelia on October 23, he remarked that he hesitated to get rid of the
Sewanee house because, "unless I improve, I doubt my ability to remain here, & we may have to look for a home elsewhere & support ourselves as best we can, & Sewanee offers as good an Asylum for our old
age as any other place." He would not consider selling the place until
the close of 1879, at the earliest.[6]

In his correspondence with Willie, Gorgas was much more specific
about his ailment. Throughout the exchange of letters is discernable a
warm, close relationship between Josiah and Willie, more than the relationship of elder to junior, rather that of close friend to close friend.
Gorgas had respect for his son's ability and felt him able to assume
responsibility. It might well be up to him to take over the family
someday, so he should know. In August he had written Willie from
Blount Springs that he had no faith in the curative powers of the sulphur water so far as his malady was concerned. He had little hope of
any remedy for his diseased nerves, "and yet I do not *feel* that my nerves
are out of order." He had been told by one doctor that his discomfort
might be caused by his stomach, and he faintly clutched at that straw
for a brief time.[7] By the middle of September pain in his head had begun. He reported it first in a letter to Amelia on the fifteenth: "I
don't feel quite right about the head, in the place where the brain
ought to be. Sudden stooping hurts me, & to-day a decided *sneeze*
hurt my head badly."[8]

Gorgas looked forward almost pathetically to an expected visit
from Willie, who was about to have a vacation. He thoroughly enjoyed
the few days his oldest son stayed with him and Richard and was
greatly interested in Willie's budding enthusiasm for research in yellow
fever. They talked over the attack which Josiah had suffered in Mexico,
and Willie was cautioned to be careful in seeking out the cause of the
disease.[9] The three had a real holiday, and Willie got some serious indications of the tragic illness sapping his father's strength.

Concerned about Willie's future, Gorgas gave him some advice on
the advantage of early rising and moderation in all things. He told
him that he wanted his son to accomplish more in life than he himself

---

[6] Gorgas to Amelia, Tuscaloosa, October 23, 1878, GMSS.

[7] Gorgas to William, Blount Springs, Ala., August 30, 1878, GMSS.

[8] Gorgas to Amelia, September 15, 1878, GMSS. He thought his headache
might be due to biliousness.

[9] Gorgas to Amelia, Tuscaloosa, November 12, 1878, GMSS.

had and did not want him to feel that much of his life had been wasted. Josiah knew that feeling. He wished he could send more money to Willie at Bellevue, but he had to hold his remittances down to very small checks. It would be better if Willie did not choose the Army for a career; but if he was determined, Gorgas was willing to urge the Surgeon General to let him have a year's leave of absence to work at Bellevue—a privilege Willie had won by examination.[10]

In December the family came down from the mountain and established themselves in the President's beautiful, white mansion on the campus. Amelia was ecstatic, and so were the girls. Willie was told by his mother that his father was once again bright and cheerful and "working with all his old time energy & interest." In January, she recorded, a call meeting of the Trustees was held and "it is charming to see with what confidence & respect they treat your Father—the faculty too are in perfect accord & life is altogether different here from what it was at Sewanee—We have been handsomely entertained by every member of the faculty & by Dr. & Mrs. Bryce." Everyone made them "most welcome."[11] Gorgas' success at settling down in Tuscaloosa was not pleasantly surprising to the Gorgases alone. The faculty of the University, though concealing it commendably, had felt a little worried about the General's Sewanee trouble, but "by his firmness in discharging the delicate duties of his office and his sweetness in the manner of discharging them he at once disarmed prejudice and won the good will of everybody."[12]

On February 23, 1879, shortly after the term began, the family had a terrible shock. Amelia sent hurriedly for the doctor—Gorgas seemed paralyzed. By February 27 he was improving, but was still vague and uncertain of things. He could hardly speak, and when he did it was only in short sentences. In Amelia's fright at first seeing him, she thought only that he ought to resign his duties at the University and do nothing but rest. But the doctors seemed to feel he would be able to go back to work, and the faculty, loyal to a man, co-operated in keeping things going.[13]

By April, Gorgas had grown so discouraged at the prospect of resigning that he sank into a sort of apathy. "He never speaks harshly

---

[10] Gorgas to William, Tuscaloosa, December 8, 1878, GMSS.
[11] Amelia to William, Tuscaloosa, January 1 [1879], GMSS.
[12] Annual Report of W. S. Wyman, President Pro Tem., 1879, *University of Alabama Records.*
[13] Amelia to William, Tuscaloosa, February 27 [1879], GMSS.

now, of any one, even making excuses for Bishop Quintard's inconsistencies," said Amelia in writing Willie. Willie himself had become thoroughly alarmed about his father's condition and told his mother that he was afraid Gorgas would never fully recover the clarity of his mind. Amelia was "inexpressably" depressed at this thought and wrote that she had believed recovery certain, though apt to be very slow. The pain in Gorgas' arm had intensified, and his thinking was slightly muddled. She told her son that it was all but impossible to keep back tears when Josiah would say "I shall be all right again, though things look dark enough now." Amelia was convinced that he would have to resign when the Trustees reassembled. If another President was elected who would require the house, she wanted the family to move into a a small residence in town for some six months. After that she thought they might go to Waco, or, if there was no improvement, "we will go to Montgomery or Atlanta & sustain ourselves by taking boarders or opening a school." The sale of the Sewanee house would bring in a little money, and the family certainly could live economically enough after all the experience they had had.[14]

Although Gorgas was ill, the family managed to get along tolerably well; Ritchie did all the driving for his mother and sometimes milked the cow; nurse Anne had full sway in the kitchen, and Minnie, Mamie, and Ria did all the housework. Amelia was an excellent organizer, and after a few months had passed she was to prove it time and again.

Amelia had her way. When the Trustees reassembled on July 1, 1879, Gorgas presented his resignation. The Trustees, instead of accepting it, put him on leave and voted to let the family stay in the mansion. His good friend, Professor W. S. Wyman, acted as president pro tempore. But by September Gorgas had come to the conclusion that since he had moments—increasing in periodicity—when he was not himself and could not think clearly, he ought to give up the responsibilities of president. The Trustees, however, persuaded him to accept the position of librarian of the University. On September 30 they appointed Burwell B. Lewis president and at the same time unanimously appointed Gorgas librarian and Amelia supervisor of the University hospital. They voted also to let the Gorgases occupy the red brick house set aside as an infirmary. This allowed Amelia to indulge her natural ability as a nurse and brought in a small amount of extra

---

[14] Amelia to William, Tuscaloosa, June 20, 1879, GMSS.

money. At the same time the Board put on record its "high appreciation of . . . [Gorgas'] character and services, of the rare tact and ability which characterized his administration until he was stricken by disease."[15]

With more time to rest, and with much less worry in his new capacity, Gorgas was able to take a trip to New Orleans in February, 1880, to see about his condition and to visit Tom Bayne. Mardi Gras being close at hand, he took Richard along, since the boy had never been in a large city or seen such a lavish display.[16] Perhaps Amelia wanted Ritchie to watch Josiah.

Nor did Gorgas lose interest in current events. He took a lively view of politics and told Willie that he had no doubt of the election of Grant. "He is to be our dictator—the panacea for all our ills!" But there were indications in the letters he wrote to Willie that he was not completely himself—"eff[ectionatel]y yr son—J. G."[17]

After his practical retirement to the position of librarian, Gorgas had little to do except watch over the University's modest library. He could not read much, and his moments of lucidity grew fewer and fewer. His kindness never left him, however, despite the pain; and nurse Anne, who suffered from a respiratory disorder, would receive a hot toddy every evening before going to bed, fixed by the General himself.

His pride in Willie knew no bounds and was entirely justified, as was his pride in all his children.[18] Willie got his commission in the Army and was a lieutenant in the Medical Corps, well on the way in his profession. Ritchie was growing up to fine young manhood; the girls were wonderful in the way they helped their mother run the house and in their love for their father.

Tuscaloosa loved Gorgas too. His friends came often to see him and made his days easier, when the pain would lift a little. Among these friends were the Leach family; Gorgas always enjoyed hearing Mrs. Kate Leach play the piano.

[15] Minutes of the Adjourned Meeting of the Trustees, September, 1879, *University of Alabama Records*.

[16] Gorgas to William, Tuscaloosa, February 9, 1880, GMSS.

[17] Gorgas to William, Tuscaloosa, May 10, 1880, GMSS. This signature was the same as he had used to his mother when writing her from Mexico during the Mexican War.

[18] Amelia to William, Tuscaloosa, June 20, 1879, GMSS. GMSD, July 16, 1878: "Our children thanks to a kind providence are all that parents could ask for."

The effect of the tumor upon his brain[19] grew steadily worse as the months passed; finally he became all but helpless,[20] and on May 15, 1883, he died.[21] Willie was unable to get to Tuscaloosa in time, but the rest of the family were there.

Genius is an intangible thing, impossible to define and more difficult to explain. Gorgas had the same peculiar kind of genius displayed by Lazare Carnot during the French Revolution, and if he cannot be called "the organizer of victory," he deserves to be called a wizard of logistics. Gorgas possessed another quality of genius in large measure— a capacity to judge men. This gift enabled him to select a magnificent corps of subordinates in the Ordnance Bureau. His corollary gifts for organization and administration made it possible for him to manage this group of able individuals with rare success. In no small measure the achievements of the Confederate Ordnance Bureau were due to what is perhaps Gorgas' most valued, most human, quality, his capacity to command from his associates a high degree of devotion to himself as leader and as man.

[19] A tumor is one of several possible causes of Gorgas' death; a heart attack might have produced symptoms similar to those Gorgas manifested toward the end of his life. After discussing Gorgas' ailments with several physicians I have decided to leave the text as it is, and to equivocate in a footnote.

[20] According to his surviving daughters.

[21] One story, told in Tuscaloosa, is that Mrs. Kate Leach had come to visit the family on the 15th. Gorgas was in bed, to which he had been confined for some time; he felt better and was anxious to hear Mrs. Leach play. His request was the *Moonlight Sonata,* and as she began playing, he died.

Bibliography

PRIMARY WORKS

Manuscripts

Adjutant General's Office. War Department, National Archives, Washington, D.C.

  a) Letters Received. This collection contains some material on Gorgas, particularly during the years of the Mexican War, 1846–48.

  b) Personal Files [AGPF] (1861–65). These are individual files pertaining to each member of the Union and Confederate armies. They are generally far more informative than might be expected, since many letters appear to have been included merely because a person's name appears in the letter. They are extremely helpful for material on ordnance officers. The files of the following Confederate officers were used extensively: Briscoe G. Baldwin, Thomas L. Bayne, Julius A. de Lagnel, Josiah Gorgas, Benjamin Huger, James Ker, John W. Mallet, Richard Morton, Thomas G. Rhett.

Brierfield Iron Works Collection, University of Alabama Library. This is a collection of one letter book, account books, and daily records (1864–68) of the furnaces at Brierfield. Without this collection chapter XX could not have been written.

  Burton [James H.] Papers (1861–65), in the possession of Mr. Edwin Pugsley, New Haven, Connecticut. These papers contain much valuable information on Burton's efforts to foster small arms production in the Confederacy. The collection consists of several hundred separate manuscripts [Burton] and Burton's *Diary,* a fairly complete document covering the years 1861–65. Microfilm copies are in the University of Texas Archives Collection.

  Burton [James H.] Papers, Winchester (1861–65). This is a small collection of Burton's personal papers in the possession of Miss Genevieve M. Burton of Winchester, Va., a daughter of Colonel Burton.

Confederate Records, Old Records Section, National Archives.

  a) Letters Received by the Confederate Secretary of War (1861–65) [CRLR]. This collection contains many important Gorgas letters.

[315]

b) *Records of the Confederate Ordnance Bureau* (1861–65) [CROB]. In this section of the Confederate Archives, Chapter IV, are 147 volumes, with twelve volumes bearing half-numbers added. Since five volumes are missing, the collection now consists of 154 volumes. This is the most important of the manuscript collections used. An excellent description of these records which includes a checklist of the books is given in Lester J. Cappon, "A Note on the Confederate Ordnance Records," *Journal of the American Military Institute,* IV (1940), 94–102.

Crutchfield [Stapleton] Papers (1862–65), Princeton University Library, Princeton, New Jersey. A small collection of papers concerning the artillery of the second corps of the Army of Northern Virginia.

Dreer Manuscripts Collection, Pennsylvania Historical Society, Philadelphia. One important Gorgas document (1861) was found in this collection.

Fitch Papers, University of Alabama Library. This small collection contains some material concerning Gorgas' administration of the Brierfield Iron Works (1867–69).

Gorgas [Josiah] Manuscripts (1818–83) [GMSS].

I. Manuscript material in the possession of Gorgas' surviving daughters, Miss Maria Bayne Gorgas and Mrs. George Palfrey (Christine Amelia), Tuscaloosa, Alabama:

a) Many important private letters, forming an extensive collection of material on Gorgas' personal and official life. Included here are many letters to his wife.

b) Gorgas' *Manuscript Diary* [GMSD], covering the years 1857–61, 1865–77.

c) *Diary of Josiah Gorgas in the Mexican War.* This document, written some time after the Mexican War, is not thoroughly reliable.

d) *Travel Diary of Josiah Gorgas.* Covering Gorgas' trip to Europe in 1845–46, this deserves publication.

e) Manuscript *Life of Josiah Gorgas,* by Amelia Gorgas.

II. Manuscript material in the possession of Gorgas' granddaughter Mrs. William D. Wrightson, Chevy Chase, Maryland:

f) Five letters written by Gorgas to his mother during the Mexican War.

g) Gorgas family Bible, which contains some important notations.

III. Manuscript material in the Manuscripts Division, New York Public Library:

h) *Copybook of Lieutenant Josiah Gorgas of the Siege Train Sent to Mexico* (1847). This is a scanty and disappointing book, with little significant information on Gorgas in the Mexican War.

Gorgas [Solomon Atkinson] Diary, in the possession of Mrs. Wrightson, contains some material on his brother, Josiah.

Governor of the Bahamas Letters Received from the Colonial Office File, 1823–1863, Government House, Nassau. This collection contains some material on blockade running and much on the maritime history of the Bahamas.

Heartmann Collection, The University of Texas Archives Collection. Several Gorgas letters are to be found in Case IV of the collection, covering the period 1877–79.

Huger [Benjamin] Papers, National Archives. These contain much information on Gorgas' administration of the Vera Cruz Ordnance Depot, 1847–48.

Jemison [Robert] Collection, University of Alabama Library. This collection yielded one letter from Gorgas, written soon after the Civil War.

Milton [John] Letter Book (1861–63), Florida Historical Society, St. Augustine. This is a rather important book of copies of letters sent by the Governor of Florida.

Miscellaneous Military Papers Concerning South Carolina, Library of Congress. These treat South Carolina's efforts to prepare for war, 1860–61. Microfilm copies in The University of Texas Archives Collection.

Mississippi State Department of Archives and History Manuscripts Collection, Jackson, Mississippi. This collection contains some correspondence between Gorgas and ordnance officers stationed in the Deep South.

Nitre and Mining Bureau [Confederate] File Box, National Archives.

Ordnance Records. U. S. War Department, National Archives.

a) *Letters Received by the Chief of Ordnance* [OLR]. These files of correspondence received by the chiefs of ordnance of the United States Army contain many letters from Gorgas in the period 1841–61.

b) *Letters Sent to Ordnance Officers* [OLS]. The letter books, containing letters sent from the United States chiefs of ordnance to their subordinates, are valuable for the period of Gorgas' service in the Ordnance Department, United States Army (1841–61).

Pickens and Bonham Papers, Library of Congress (1860–61). These papers deal with South Carolina's preparations for war during the secession crisis.

Ramsdell [Charles W.] Note Files, Austin, Texas. These papers of the late Professor Ramsdell contain many interesting notes on the Confederate Ordnance Bureau (1861–65).

Shorter [John Gill] Letter Book (Answers to Letters, 1862), State Department of Archives and History, Montgomery, Alabama. This is a letter book of the Governor of Alabama.

State Department [United States] Records, National Archives. The correspondence files of the United States Secretaries of State contain some material on Gorgas in the period 1845–46.

United States Consul's Records of Confederate States Ships at Bermuda, Manuscripts Division, Library of Congress. Highly informative on the spy-activities of the United States Consul in Bermuda. A microfilm copy is in The University of Texas Archives Collection.

United States Military Academy Archives, West Point, N. Y. In the library at the Academy are to be found, of particular value on Gorgas:

　a) *Cadet Battalion Order Books,* 1837–41.

　b) *Post Order Books,* 1833–42.

　c) *Disciplinary Record Books,* 1834———

University of Alabama Records, University Library. These contain, for the years 1879–82, much good material on Gorgas' connection with the University of Alabama. The reports of the President pro tem. to the Board of Trustees, 1879–82, are revealing.

University of the South, Archives, Sewanee, Tennessee. In the library of this institution are to be found some letters to and from Gorgas while he was vice-chancellor of Sewanee (1869–77). The collection is not large and is somewhat scattered in the recesses of the library, but it was worth ferreting out.

War Department [United States] Records (1841–61), Old Records Section, National Archives. These contain scattered material on Gorgas under various classifications.

Periodicals

Bahama Herald (Nassau, New Providence), 1861–65.

Charleston (S. C.) *Daily Courier,* October–December, 1860.

Montgomery (Ala.) *Weekly Post,* April 24, May 8, 11, June 5, 1861.

Raleigh (N. C.) *State Journal,* January 15, 1862.

Daily Richmond (Va.) *Enquirer,* 1861–65.

Daily Richmond Examiner, 1861–65.

San Antonio (Tex.) *Weekly Herald,* 1862.

Cap and Gown, Sewanee, Tenn., June, 1883.

The University Record, Sewanee, Tenn., June, September, 1872, August, 1873.

Other Printed Sources

Acts of the Session of 1866–7 of the General Assembly of Alabama . . . , Montgomery, 1867.

Alexander, Edward P. *Military Memoirs of a Confederate.* New York, 1907.

Anderson, Robert. *An Artillery Officer in the Mexican War, 1846–1847.* New York, 1911.

The American Annual Cyclopaedia and Register of Important Events, for 1861. New York, 1861; reprint, New York, 1868. [*Appletons' Cyclopaedia.*]

Biographical Directory of the American Congress, 1774–1927. Washington, 1928.

Bishops of nine Southern states. *An Address to the Members and Friends of the Protestant Episcopal Church in the Southern and South-Western States.* Philadelphia, 1856.

Broun, W. LeRoy. "The Red Artillery," *Southern Historical Society Papers* (Richmond, 1876——), XXVI (1898), 365–76. [Broun]

Confederate States War Department Reports. Montgomery, Ala., 1861.

General Orders from the Adjutant and Inspector-General's Office, Confederate States Army, from January, 1862, to December, 1863, (Both inclusive). Columbia, S. C., 1864.

Gorgas, Josiah. "Ordnance of the Confederacy, I, II," *Army Ordnance* (Washington, 1920——), XVI (1936), 212–16; 283–88. This article was first printed in the *Southern Historical Society Papers,* XII (1884), 67–94. [GOC]

Gorgas, Josiah, and John Hillhouse. "Epistolary Gossipings of Travel and its Reminiscences," *Russell's Magazine* (Charleston, 1857–60), V (1859), 130–36, 221–28, 308–16, 396–406, 493–507; VI (1860), 109–17, 218–29, 298–307, 394–405, 554–64.

Grant, U. S. *Personal Memoirs.* 2 vols. New York, 1885.

Huse, Caleb. *The Supplies for the Confederate Army, How they were Obtained in Europe and how Paid for. Personal Reminiscences and Unpublished History.* Boston, 1904.

Jones, J. B. *A Rebel War Clerk's Diary at the Confederate States Capital,* ed. Howard Swiggett. 2 vols. New York, 1935.

Journal of the Congress of the Confederate States of America, 1861–1865. 7 vols. Washington, 1904–5.

Journal of the Provisional Congress of the Confederate States of America. Washington, 1904.

Mallet, John W. "Work of the Confederate Ordnance Bureau," *Southern Historical Society Papers,* XXXVII (1909), 1–20. [Mallet]

Official Records of the Union and Confederate Navies in the War of the Rebellion. 30 vols. and index. Washington, 1894–1927. [ORN]

Proceedings of the Board of Trustees [University of the South]. Sewanee, Tenn., 1871–78.

Rains, George W. *History of the Confederate Powder Works.* Newburgh, N. Y., 1882.

Ramsdell, Charles W. (ed.). *Laws and Joint Resolutions of the Last Ses-*

sion of the Confederate Congress, Together with the Secret Acts of Previous Congresses. Durham, N. C., 1941.

Register of the Officers and Cadets of the U. S. Military Academy, West Point, New York. West Point, 1839–41.

Richardson, James D. (comp.). *A Compilation of the Messages and Papers of the Confederacy.* 2 vols. Nashville, Tenn., 1906.

Ripley, Roswell S. *The War with Mexico.* 2 vols. New York, 1849.

Rowland, Dunbar. (ed.). *Jefferson Davis, Constitutionalist: His Letters, Papers and Speeches.* 10 vols. Jackson, Miss., 1923.

Scott, Winfield. *Memoirs of Lieutenant General Winfield Scott.* 2 vols. New York, 1864.

Smith, E. Kirby. *To Mexico with Scott.* Cambridge, 1917.

South Carolina. *Acts of the General Assembly of the State of South Carolina, passed in November and December, 1860, and January, 1861.* Columbia, 1861.

Statutes at Large of the Confederate States of America. ed. James M. Matthews. Richmond, 1862–64.

Statutes at Large of the Provisional Congress of the Confederate States of America. ed. James M. Matthews. Richmond, 1864.

Vandiver, Frank E. (ed.). "The Capture of a Confederate Blockade Runner: Extracts from the Journal of a Confederate Naval Officer," *North Carolina Historical Review* (Raleigh, 1924———), XXI (1944), 136–38.

———. (ed.). *The Civil War Diary of General Josiah Gorgas,* University, Ala., 1947. [GCWD]

———. (ed.). *Confederate Blockade Running through Bermuda, 1861–1865: Letters and Cargo Manifests.* Austin, Tex., 1947.

War of the Rebellion, A Compilation of the Official Records of the Union and Confederate Armies. 70 vols. in 127 and index. Washington, 1880–1901. [ORA]

Secondary Works

Armes, Ethel M. *The Story of Coal and Iron in Alabama.* Birmingham, 1910.

[Bayne, Thomas L.]. "Sketch of the Life of Josiah Gorgas," *Southern Historical Society Papers,* XIII (1885), 216–228.

Bill, Alfred H. *The Beleaguered City.* New York, 1946.

Black, Robert C., III. "The Railroads of Georgia in the Confederate War Effort," *Journal of Southern History* (Baton Rouge, 1935———), XIII (1947), 511–34.

Bruce, Kathleen. *Virginia Iron Manufacture in the Slave Era.* New York, 1931.

Coulter, E. Merton. *The Confederate States of America, 1861–1865. (A History of the South,* Vol. VII.) Baton Rouge, La., 1950.

Cullum, George W. *Biographical Register of the Officers and Graduates of the United States Military Academy.* 3 vols. Cambridge, 1891. A supplemental volume was published in 1901.

Diamond, William. "Imports of the Confederate Government from Europe and Mexico," *Journal of Southern History,* VI (1940), 470–503.

Echols, William H. "John W. Mallet; Scholar, Teacher, Gentleman," *Alumni Bulletin of the University of Virginia,* 3rd series (Charlottesville, 1907——), January, 1913, pp. 4–47.

Elliott, Charles W. *Winfield Scott; the Soldier and the Man.* New York, 1937.

Fairbanks, George R. *History of the University of the South, at Sewanee, Tennessee.* Jacksonville, Fla., 1905.

Fleming, Walter L. *Civil War and Reconstruction in Alabama.* New York, 1905.

Garesché, Louis. *Biography of Lieut. Col. Julius P. Garesché.* Philadelphia, 1887.

Gorgas, Marie D., and Burton J. Hendrick. *William Crawford Gorgas.* Garden City, N. Y., 1924.

A Guide Book to West Point and Vicinity; Containing Descriptions, Historical and Statistical Sketches of the United States Military Academy, and of Other Objects of Interest. New York, 1844.

Haskins, David G. *A Brief Account of the University of the South.* New York, 1877.

Haynsworth, Hugh C. *Haynsworth-Furman and Allied Families.* Sumter, S. C., 1942.

Henry, Robert S. *The Story of the Confederacy.* Indianapolis, 1931.

Hodges, Lt. Col. Leroy. "Guns of the American Civil War." Unpublished manuscript in the possession of Frank E. Vandiver, Austin, Texas.

Horn, Stanley F. *The Army of Tennessee.* Indianapolis, 1941.

James, Joseph B. "Life at West Point One Hundred Years Ago," *Mississippi Valley Historical Review* (Cedar Rapids, 1914——), XXXI (1944–45), 21–40.

Jenkins, John S. *History of the War between the United States and Mexico.* Auburn, Ala., 1851.

Meade, Robert D. *Judah P. Benjamin; Confederate Statesman.* New York, 1943.

Owsley, Frank L. *King Cotton Diplomacy: Foreign Relations of the Confederate States of America.* Chicago, 1931.

Ramsdell, Charles W. *Behind the Lines in the Southern Confederacy.* Baton Rouge, La., 1944.

——. "Texas from the Fall of the Confederacy to the Beginning of

Reconstruction," *Southwestern Historical Quarterly* (Austin, 1897——), XI (1907–8), 199–219.

——. "The Confederate Government and the Railroads," *American Historical Review* (New York, 1895——), XXII (1916–17), 794–810.

——. "The Control of Manufacturing by the Confederate Government," *Mississippi Valley Historical Review*, VIII (1921–22), 231–49.

——. "The Texas State Military Board, 1862–1865," *Southwestern Historical Quarterly*, XXVII (1923–24), 253–75.

Roberts, W. Adolphe. *Semmes of the Alabama.* Indianapolis, 1938.

Smith, Justin H. *The War with Mexico.* 2 vols. New York, 1919.

Thompson, Samuel B. *Confederate Purchasing Operations Abroad.* Chapel Hill, N. C., 1935.

Vandiver, Frank E. "A Sketch of Efforts Abroad to Equip the Confederate Armory at Macon," *Georgia Historical Quarterly* (Savannah, 1917——), XXVIII (1944), 34–40.

——. "The Authorship of Certain Contributions to *Russell's Magazine*," *Georgia Historical Quarterly*, XXXI (1947), 118–20.

——. "The Shelby Iron Company in the Civil War: A Study of a Confederate Industry," *Alabama Review* (University, Ala., 1948——), I (1948), 13–26, 111–27, 203–17.

——. "The South Carolina Ordnance Board, 1860–1861," *Proceedings of the South Carolina Historical Association* (Columbia, 1931——), 1945, pp. 14–22.

Wiley, Bell I. *The Life of Johnny Reb: The Common Soldier of the Confederacy.* Indianapolis, 1943.

Wise, Jennings C. *The Long Arm of Lee; or, The History of the Artillery of the Army of Northern Virginia; With a Brief Account of the Confederate Bureau of Ordnance.* 2 vols. Lynchburg, 1915.

Index

food shortage in, 256; surrendered, 269

Army of the Potomac (U.S.), 124, 155, 168, 194, 234, 237

Army of Tennessee (Confederate), 152 n., 205, 208, 215, 218, 243; ordnance depot of, 121–22; munitions for, 122; supplies for, 137, 148, 255; ordnance examinations, 141 n.; position of, 155; estimated strength of, 182; ordnance needs, 188–89; artillery, 189; defeated around Chattanooga, Tenn., 203; reserve ammunition of, destroyed at Atlanta, 216; commanded by Gen. J. B. Hood, 216, 245; distribution of ammunition in, 239 and n.; defeated at Nashville, Tenn., 251; commanded by Gen. J. E. Johnston, 261; surrendered, 269

Arp, Bill, Confederate humorist, 129

Artillery, 16, 17 and n., 18 and n., 19, 21, 23 n., 24, 25 and n., 29, 31, 59, 139 n., 180; manufacture of, 62, 204; location of, in C. S., 63 and n.; purchase of, 63, 65, 89; loss of, 136, 182, 187, 196, 203 and n., 242; for Trans-Mississippi Dept., 138; defective fuzes for ammunition of, 146 and n.; for Army of Tennessee, 189, 194, 237; with Gen. Leonidas Polk, 237; for Lee's army, 237, 238

Artillery corps (Confederate), 52, 54, 57, 78, 79, 207, 249

Asheville, N. C., rifle factory in, 241

"Atalanta," blockade-runner, 197 n.

Athens, Ga., armory in, 222

Athens, Greece, and blockade, 85

Atlanta Arsenal, 122, 123, 154, 239, 240; and logistics, 148; daily ammunition production, 148 n.; supplies Army of Tennessee, 152, 208; added supply responsibility of, 155, 156; wage discontent in, 167; loss of, 216

Atlanta, Ga., siege of, 216; falls to Sherman, 219; pistol factory in, 241

Aubrey, Capt. William (CSA), 269

Augusta Arsenal, 60, 68, 136, 148, 240; expanded, 65; production capacity of, 82, 148 n.; unable to make artillery ammunition, 152; makes ammunition of irregular quality, 189, 190; lead for, 198; strained to replace Hood's reserve ammunition, 216; supplies Army of Tennessee, 218

Augusta, Ga., 144; powder works in, 76; artificial niter bed in, 107; bronze foundry in, 240

Augusta Powder Works, 218, 240; need niter, 91; better products of, 146

Averell, Gen. William W. (USA), 205

Bacon, scarcity of, 165

Bahama Islands, 84, 85, 86, 90

Baker, Maj. R. S. (USA), 11, 18 n.

Baldwin, Col. Briscoe G. (CSA), 207, 269 n.; needs funds, 83; introduces J. W. Mallet to Gorgas, 113; leaves post, 119; removed, 119, 120; asks for court of inquiry, 120; appointed chief ordnance officer, Army of Northern Virginia, 121; reports on Pickett's charge, 195 and n.; on arms collected on battlefield, 246; reports on attack on Fort Stedman, 265; reports on Battle of Five Forks, 265, 266

Baldwin, John B., 120

Baltimore, Md., 49

Banister, Rev. Dr., 306

Banks, Gen. N. P. (USA), 125, 196, 240

Baring Brothers, bankers, 11

Barksdale, Ethelbert, 181

Barnwell, Robert W., 88

Bartow, F. S., 60

Baton Rouge Arsenal, 20, 21, 23, 60, 61, 65, 67, 74, 82

Bayne, Maria (Mrs. Thomas L.), 237, 267

Bayne, Maj. Thomas L. (CSA), 187 n., 192, 193, 264, 270, 271, 313; on Gorgas, 80; in charge of